The Making of a M

The True Story of Margaret Mitchell's Classic Novel

Gone With The Wind

Sally Tippett Rains

Published by
Global Book Publishers, Beverly Hills, California

Title page Illustration by
Rena Hoyt Hasse

ISBN: 978-0-9818222-2-8

Dedication:

To RRR

Acknowledgments

Thank you to publisher Michael S. Baumohl of Global Book Publishers, for publishing my book; and Ron Kenner (and his associate editor Tom Puckett) at RKedit. Also, thanks to Kirk Thomas of Kirk's Graphics for cover design and typography.

Special Thanks to… Sharon Bedgood for research help and all the fun we had working on it, My parents, Margie and Jack Tippett for their help with deciphering the old scrapbook and for reading the manuscripts and offering insights; my sister, Barb Jochens for her enthusiasm; Voncille Bush for her eager researching; Rhett Turnipseed for all the fun conversations about his interesting great-grandfather. Thanks to Pat Sleade for proofreading help. A special thank you goes to Sheryl Godsy for her valuable help. I really appreciate all the help from Ernie Harwell and appreciate him writing the foreword, enabling me to combine two great American pastimes: baseball and *Gone With The Wind*.

A great deal of thanks goes to Marie Nygren for her kindness and willingness to share the scrapbook and information about her famous cousin, and to Mark Rabwin and Paul Rabwin for getting on board with their memories and tapes saved from their mother, Marcella Rabwin (executive assistant to the Director of *Gone With The Wind*, David O. Selznick). Herb Bridges has been very kind to me. He knows everything about *Gone With The Wind* and I really appreciate his help. Thanks to Gloria Jones for the great idea. I also want to express my appreciation to Dr. Donald Stokes, my agent on this book, Windi Robinson of New Leaf Productions, Dr. Christopher Sullivan and Connie Sutherland.

I appreciate those who took the time to be interviewed or offer insight and help. They are listed in the back of the book. There were so many people who helped me and I will list them in the back of the book also. I really appreciate all of them taking their time with me.

The final thank you is to my wonderful sons, BJ and Mike, who actually showed some interest in this project and had faith in their mother. In the same form that Margaret Mitchell used in *Gone With The Wind*, I dedicate this book to RRR, one half of the really, truly greatest love story ever told.

Table of Contents

Author's Note

When Margaret Mitchell's book was published in 1936 she discussed it freely for a short time and then, for no clear reason, she stopped giving interviews and discontinued public book signings. Looking back now, we begin to understand why. Her larger-than-life novel *Gone With the Wind* may have found a good deal of its essence in real life characters, scenes, and situations and for some reason she felt uncomfortable discussing it in public.

Writers, including Finis Farr, the biographer who worked with Margaret's brother, Stephens Mitchell, noted the Mitchell family's many visits to Rural Home. This was the family homestead in Clayton County where her two aunts who had lived through the Civil War still resided. Books have mentioned the similarities between Scarlett O'Hara and Mitchell's grandmother, Annie.

It was Farr who first observed in print that Mitchell's grandmother, Annie Fitzgerald Stephens, was "strong-willed and fearless" and that Mitchell's great-grandfather Philip Fitzgerald was a Civil War survivor who—just as Gerald O'Hara's family had done in the book—rebuilt his fortune after his slaves were freed and his crops burned. Farr also pointed out that Margaret's grandmother Annie attended the same school, the Fayetteville Female Academy in Georgia, as did her fictional character Scarlett. Other books and writers have pointed to similarities in *Gone With The Wind* and real-life happenings in Clayton County, Georgia.

The suggestion that the novel drew from people or incidents the author was familiar with in no way diminishes the masterpiece that only Margaret Mitchell could have written. Other writers have explored parts of the story, and the Margaret Mitchell House mentions some of this, but The Making of a Masterpiece with three years of research and a scrapbook written by one of Margaret's first cousins (once removed), delves into greater detail about some of the people and events that seemingly inspired *Gone With The Wind.*

Mitchell denied that her characters were based on real people, but even if they were, there's no reason to presume she was lying. She never really said, "None of my characters had any similarities with people I knew." She merely implied that none were exact copies of real people. Throughout the book the author uses vivid descriptions, riveting stories, and compelling dialogues. She wrote a 1,037-page novel with storylines that may have come from stories she had heard or read about in scrapbooks or in the written histories of those who lived through it. Shortly after her novel was published she began having anxiety problems. When she sold the movie rights to David O. Selznick she told him she did not want to be involved. She did not like doing interviews and turned down the opportunity to go to Hollywood to consult on the movie.

By avoiding involvement in the movie the author passed up the first-hand excitement, but was kept informed by her friend Susan Myrick whom she had recommended as a replacement. With the tremendous success of the book, the fame Margaret Mitchell achieved caused havoc on her life. According to a cousin's scrapbook, at least one of her relatives was threatening to sue her when the book first came out. Margaret Mitchell may have wanted to discuss her book and its characters, but, on the advice of her lawyers (father and brother) she said little about them.

Almost seven decades later, when most of the principals have died, one can better take an analytical look at the various possibilities of the people and events that appear to have shaped her book and, in turn, the movie.

I have not come to any great conclusions that will alter history in this book. It does not purport to be a scholarly journal and may disappoint those seeking one. The work is not intended for readers with closed minds, since it includes some new theories that may not yet have been explored in depth. Rather than come to any definite conclusions, possibilities are presented and you, the reader can decide for yourself.

Looking into the real life places and people who may have played an inspiring role in *Gone With The Wind*, I've tried to make this book an interesting collection of facts and research (some of it based on genealogy) mixed with interviews from descendents of people who were there. What is history, if not the stories handed down from generation to generation?

Many in Clayton County have talked about these things for years and some have even written about them. This book also contains first-hand memories from actors and others knowledgeable about the Hollywood production, including Mark and Paul Rabwin, sons of Marcella Rabwin, executive assistant to producer David O. Selznick. I hope this work will be an enjoyable companion to *Gone With The Wind* and the other books written about Margaret Mitchell and her novel. Once you read this you will probably want to read her book and watch the movie again.

In addition to the actors and those connected with the movie, I've had the tremendous opportunity to talk to authors who have addressed the subject, as well as to historians, descendents, collectors, and experts. The journey of writing this book was so pleasant I'd like to thank everyone who helped make it that way. I hope readers will take it in the manner it was written—a fun look at the possibilities that may have inspired parts of Margaret Mitchell's masterpiece, *Gone With The Wind*.

Foreword

By Ernie Harwell

Like millions of Americans and folks from all over the world, I loved Margaret Mitchell's book *Gone With the Wind* and I also enjoyed the movie when it came out some seventy years ago.

One of the reasons I suppose I took an even greater interest in the book and movie was because of the association that existed between my family and Margaret Mitchell.

Our family moved from Washington, Georgia, a small town between Athens and Augusta, to Atlanta when I was a young boy. My father had multiple sclerosis, so he was unable to work much after his 30th birthday, and my mother became the breadwinner for the family, which included me and my two older brothers, Davis and Richard.

My mother was a great cook and her work quickly became known to the well-to-do ladies around Atlanta. Whenever one of the debutantes had a party, the family would contact my mother to bake the cakes and make the sandwiches for the lunch or dinner or some other special occasion. One of these ladies was Margaret Mitchell.

When I was about twelve or thirteen I got a job as a paperboy for the Atlanta Georgian, delivering the papers for $2.50 a week. Two of my subscribers were Margaret Mitchell and her husband John Marsh.

When I was in college, I worked at the newspaper primarily as a copy reader and headline writer, but one special assignment I received was to help cover the movie premiere of *Gone With the Wind* in Atlanta, in December, 1939. That truly was a remarkable and memorable night. Though my journalism career went from the newspaper in Atlanta to the baseball broadcast booth (I broadcast the Detroit Tigers for more than forty years on radio and television), I have fond memories of my time in Atlanta and get down there to visit when I can.

My brother Richard, who is buried in Washington, Georgia, had the greatest relationship with Margaret of anybody in our family. He was a historian and librarian and worked as the editor of the Emory Phoenix, the magazine for Emory University in Atlanta. He wrote a review of the book when it was published, and that began their relationship. In fact since he had an advance copy given to the press he received the first autographed book.

Richard worked with Margaret on another project, Margaret Mitchell's *Gone With The Wind* Letters, 1936-1949, editing her correspondence and letters into a book. He also wrote *Gone With The Wind* as Book and Film and edited Susan Myrick's newspaper articles sent back home to the Macon Telegraph from Hollywood in a book called *White Columns in Hollywood, Reports From the GWTW Sets*, by Susan Myrick. Ironically, he was to meet her for dinner the night she was fatally struck by a speeding car while crossing a street in downtown Atlanta. It was August 11, 1949, and she would die five days later.

Everyone in Atlanta, and the world for that matter knew of Margaret Mitchell. We were fortunate that, through Richard, we got to attend some events where she appeared after the book came out. She was just a normal person who did not like to be treated like the celebrity she had become.

My wife Lulu even got to meet Margaret. We went to the Piedmont Driving Club, where Margaret was making an appearance, and she noticed Lulu's earrings. She said, "I've got a pair just like those. Where did you get them?" Lulu didn't really want to answer her, because she thought they had probably cost less than $5, but Margaret said, 'I bought mine at Rich's for $3!'"

This new book by Sally Tippett Rains brings back a lot of those memories of Margaret Mitchell and the story of *Gone With the Wind*. Through her research and interviews, Rains presents new insight into this classic story, which I found quite compelling. I am sure it will be of interest to every fan of *Gone With the Wind*.

.

Chapter One
A Nightmare Comes True

"My sister's full name is Margaret Munnerlyn Mitchell Marsh," Stephens Mitchell told the *Atlanta Journal* reporter in the lobby of Grady Memorial Hospital. His sister, known to the world as Margaret Mitchell, the best-selling author of *Gone With The Wind* had just died in an upstairs room.

The epic novel of the Civil War and Reconstruction which centered on the unforgettable Scarlett O'Hara, had been published in June, 1936 and in July it was a featured *Book of the Month*. Margaret Mitchell was awarded the Pulitzer Prize in May, 1937 and the book's popularity just kept growing. Eventually the Atlanta History Center would report the novel as having "sold more copies worldwide than any other book except the Bible."

Known to some as Peggy Mitchell and to others as Margaret, or Peggy Marsh, the woman who gave the world Scarlett O'Hara and Rhett Butler would once again be receiving world-wide publicity. This time it wasn't good.

Atlanta, Georgia, August 11, 1949

The wheels of the long, red Chevrolet ambulance screeched as it pulled up to the crowd. The driver pressed on the horn in an attempt to get the people in his way to move. He needed to pull up closer to the victim.

"Someone's been hit by a car!" shouted a man who ran out of his apartment on Peachtree Street near Thirteenth Street to see the small crowd gathering.

"She's on the ground. There's her husband," the man cried out.

The victim's husband, visibly shaken, was both bending over her and waving his hands so as to be seen. He was calling for help, not leaving the side of his beloved wife as she bled on the ground. A few feet away, a distraught Hugh Gravitt, the driver of the car was being restrained by an unidentified man. "Don't you go anywhere, buddy! You're drunk! You hit that lady, you stay here."

Margaret Mitchell's worst nightmare had literally come true. Her crumpled body lay bleeding on the hot pavement and if she could think, she must have been incredulous that in the end it really did occur. After being in two automobile accidents Margaret Mitchell had suffered from recurring nightmares about being involved in another car accident, and now it had happened.

People began running out of buildings to see just what had happened. Screams were heard. Her husband, John Marsh helplessly stayed close to his injured wife.

As he patted his wife's bleeding head with a handkerchief, he said soothing things to her until help arrived. In the distance he heard his name being called. As he looked up, he saw familiar faces in the crowd. The couple was near their apartment, so immediately friends recognized them, but soon the crowd was abuzz when they realized who the woman lying in the street was. There were those who knew her personally, but many knew her as Margaret Mitchell, the author of *Gone With The Wind*. She had a dress and stockings on and the black clunky shoes that she always wore.

Soon the siren wail could be heard over the confusion at the scene. As it arrived, the driver put Ambulance Number One in "Park." He worked for Grady Memorial, the city hospital for Atlanta. As was the custom, the driver had been deputized by the police department so he got out with arms spread, trying to push back the onlookers. His passenger was medical intern Dr. Edwin Paine Lochridge. Before paramedics, they would send young interns out in the ambulances.

Dr. Lochridge knelt to the ground to check the woman's vital signs and through the bloodied face he recognized her! It was Peggy Marsh, a friend of his mother's since her youth. Lethea Turman Lochridge and Peggy Mitchell had been friends since their youth. Dr. Lochridge had known Margaret all his life. Once they got her stabilized the driver helped him get her onto a stretcher and placed in the back of the un-airconditioned car.

As he continued to treat her, he tried to talk to Marsh, who was standing nervously at the open door.

"How did this happen?" asked Lochridge.

"We were going to the movie," Marsh said, still unable to comprehend it all. "And then a car.... And I tried to make her stop, but she just kept going."

Nearby onlookers gossiped about the scene. "It's Margaret Mitchell, the author. She and her husband were on their way to the Peachtree Arts Theatre to see *A Canterbury Tale*."

The Marshes had been crossing the street and both of them, in poor health, walked slowly at best. He was still recovering from heart problems and trudged along. His wife had chronic ankle problems. When the speeding car rounded the corner Marsh tried to pull her back... but, true to her life, she did what she wanted and kept going.

Lochridge tended to the patient, applying pressure to stop the bleeding. About then a police officer arrived and wanted to question Marsh.

"We decided to go to the movie," Marsh explained. "We never made it."

As he talked Marsh began sweating profusely, breathing more heavily. Since the young intern knew them, he was familiar with Marsh's heart problems and recent poor health. Lochridge told the ambulance driver they should get him into the car as well.

The ambulance sped through the night. At the hospital the driver pulled up over the emergency ramp, braked, then swung open the door. Dr. Edwin Paine Lochridge helped carry his family friends inside. After getting Margaret on a gurney, they put Marsh in a wheel chair and someone began checking his vital signs for a possible heart attack.

At Grady Memorial, the city hospital, emergency patients were automatically admitted and the hospital provided health care for low-income people. This would not have been Margaret Mitchell's choice, as she always went to St. Joseph's Infirmary where she had a private room and knew many of the staff, including, in bygone days, her own cousin, Sister Melanie.

Grady was a teaching facility and even though she may not have gone there herself, Mitchell had a connection with the hospital as she funded scholarships for some of the doctors there. In recent years she had worked with Benjamin Mays, the president of Morehouse College to provide anonymous scholarships to Morehouse medical students. One of Atlanta's first black pediatricians, Dr. Otis Smith, was the recipient of her generosity. None of that mattered now as she was being attended to at 8:30 p.m. on that Tuesday evening; admitted as one more patient injured in a drunk driving accident, a problem that had escalated in Atlanta at the time.

According to Wilma Fowler, the nurse who took care of her that night, Margaret Mitchell was taken to the third floor, Ward "F," and occupied one of the three single rooms on that floor. Because the patient was admitted as Margaret Marsh, Wilma Fowler did not immediately realize who she was, but soon learned it was the famous author.

"The night supervisor informed me that we were getting a female patient," said Fowler, at the time a 21-year-old nursing student who would be graduating the next month. "I was told I would be taking care of her all night."

She undressed the patient and then the doctor came in to examine her. In the hall, John Marsh, whose vital signs had checked out, paced the floor. Soon a gurney was set up for him, though mainly as a precaution against another heart attack. Although worried about his wife, Marsh complied. Hospitals then were not air conditioned and it was a very hot night. The small room held only one bed, a small dresser and a straight, hard chair. Marsh, not allowed in, stayed on the stretcher right outside the door. He knew the situation with his wife was critical, as she had not regained consciousness.

Atlanta went to bed not knowing that one of its most beloved citizens lay near death. Only one visitor came that night. Mayor William Hartsfield, a friend, who received a call from the police. Marsh looked up, saw the mayor and felt a sense of relief.

"What happened?" the mayor asked, seeing Marsh on the stretcher. "I thought it was Peggy."

"Bill! Thanks for coming!" Marsh replied, feeling somewhat calmed. "It was Peggy. She was hit by a car. She suffered head injuries and internal injuries. They just put me on this because they were worried about a heart attack, but I'm fine. I'm just so worried about Peggy. I ... can't lose her."

Marsh explained what had happened that night, about their cancelled dinner plans and then their last-minute decision, with Mitchell feeling better, to go to the movie. The theater was very close to their home and also near one of their favorite dinner spots, The Piedmont Driving Club. They'd had drinks at the Club, Marsh added, but never made it to the movie.

The mayor nodded sympathetically. Hartsfield and Marsh were quiet. The nurses and doctors came and went. Finally Hartsfield broke the awkward silence. "She's going to come through this," he reassured.

Marsh nodded, silent, grateful the mayor had rushed over. Just seeing Mayor Hartsfield reminded John of happier times when they'd been together on so many occasions, both as the mayor and as a friend. When Atlanta was the scene of the Hollywood Premiere of *Gone With The Wind*, Mayor Hartsfield had proclaimed a three-day festival. He'd celebrated with the Marshes and all of Atlanta when the movie stars, including Clark Gable, Vivien Leigh and the others, came to town.

The mayor was here, everything would be OK. He stayed a few hours until eventually Marsh fell asleep. The next day, Atlanta woke up to radio reports and newspaper headlines that Margaret Mitchell was clinging to life at Grady Memorial after being hit by a car. The medical team was assembled, but the patient showed no signs of improvement. She suffered pelvic fractures and massive head wounds, along with internal injuries. Outside, a crowd was gathering. Once word got out about the famous patient, the hospital had to bring in extra employees, nurse Fowler recalled. They had already set up twenty-four-hour police protection, but more security was brought in to keep the crowds out of the building.

"We had extra people answering the phones," said Fowler. "It was one of those old switchboards with the wires. Calls were coming in from all over the country and the operators could not handle them all so they brought in extras."

Movie stars were calling. *Gone With The Wind* producer David O. Selznick telephoned. Everyone wanted to know how she was doing.

Fowler had checked her vital signs every fifteen minutes since taking over as the in-room nurse for Mitchell after her shift began at 11 p.m. the night before. The vital signs were normal. Blood pressure was normal.

But the injuries were life-threatening and the patient had not regained consciousness.

Fowler left her shift on August 12th at 7 a.m. and walked out the door. She noticed that Marsh, who had been there most of the night, was not on the stretcher. Margaret's brother Stephens Mitchell had come up and the two were talking elsewhere.

Stephens Mitchell had been in contact with the police department and found out that the twenty-nine-year-old driver of the car was jailed on charges of drunk-driving, speeding, and driving on the wrong side of the road.

Marsh went home for a while and was tended to by Bessie Berry Jordan, their long-time maid of twenty years. She had been there when Margaret Mitchell filled hundreds of boxes and sent them to soldiers during World War II. She had seen her do work for the Red Cross and raise money for the Navy. Now, knowing that her mistress may be dying, was a great burden on her yet she did her best to take care of Marsh.

Marsh was in anguish, with his wife in the hospital bed. He wished he could have helped her. In his heart, however, he knew there was no telling Peggy Mitchell what to do. That was one of the things he loved so much about her. She had always been as determined a woman as the strong-willed young lady he had dated—the 'new woman' flapper in the Roaring Twenties.

Wilma Fowler, whose future husband drove an ambulance at Grady, though not that night, felt concerned for her patient. Her condition was not improving.

There were different eyewitness accounts and those who knew her or had learned about her had differing opinions as to exactly what happened, but one thing known was that the driver, Hugh Gravitt, an off-duty taxi cab driver, had been cited for bad driving more than twenty times in the previous ten years, and after Stephens Mitchell found out the driver had been drinking, he was furious. He could not believe that his sister, who had been such a force in his life, was lying helplessly in the hospital bed because of an accident caused by a drunk driver.

Elsewhere in Atlanta, Richard Harwell read about it in the newspaper. He was shocked to learn that his friend Margaret Mitchell had been hit by a car. Harwell, a historian, author and close friend of both John Marsh and Margaret Mitchell, had talked to John only the day before. After he read the paper, he called his brother Ernie and told him about the tragedy.

"They had plans to have dinner with my brother that night," explained Hall of Fame baseball announcer Ernie Harwell. "Richard had been captain of a mine sweeper in World War II and still had affiliations with the Navy base, so they were going to have dinner at the Officer's Club. John called that afternoon and said Margaret was not feeling well. Just think, if they had been on the Navy base with Richard, that car might not have hit her."

Marsh went back to the hospital, to his spot in the hall and waited for updates. As he hoped and prayed for Margaret's recovery, he thought about the many times each of them had been hospitalized; and suddenly he missed Sister Melanie, who Mitchell's great-aunts had known in her younger years as cousin Mattie Holliday, before she entered the convent.

Before she passed away, in 1939, Sister Melanie, who was old and had lost much of her eyesight, knew just the right words to say. When Peggy had asked Sister Melanie if it was OK if she named a character in her book after her, the cousin had smiled and said, "Only if she's a good person!"

When nurse Fowler arrived for work the next night at 7 p.m. she was amazed…. "So many people sent her flowers. They came in from around the world. I was not assigned to her room after the first night, but I stopped in every day and asked how she was doing. Unfortunately, she never regained consciousness."

In 1949, Grady Memorial was at a slightly different location. As Fowler recalled, it used to be at the corner of Coca-Cola Place and Butler Street, about six blocks from St. Joseph's Hospital. Florists in Atlanta, running out of flowers, sent orders to other shops. Flowers then were not kept very long in the rooms but were set out on display the day the patient received them, then moved to the hall. Margaret Mitchell received so many that they were taken to other areas of the hospital. Many were driven to neighboring hospitals so others could enjoy the flowers the famous recipient would never see.

Clark Gable sent a floral arrangement. Fowler saw the card. Marsh and Stephens Mitchell tried to look at all of the cards so that they could acknowledge them. Margaret Mitchell had always made such a point to write back to every single person who wrote to her, so they wanted to be able to thank as many of the people as they could. The Marshes' secretary, Margaret Baugh, was devastated. She offered her services to John and asked the nurses if there was anything she could do. Baugh would write the thank you notes, getting the names off all of the plants and arrangements before they were moved.

Louise Durden, handling hospital public relations, was called in, and Frank Wilson, the superintendent, was in constant contact. As the days passed, more friends of the Marshes volunteered time answering the phones. Lethea Turman Lochridge, the mother of the young intern who had helped Margaret, was one. She found out about the accident from her son almost immediately after they had gotten Mitchell into the hospital bed. Lethea arrived with a bouquet of pink and red roses. A waitress called when Lochridge was manning the phones. Her customers at the restaurant were asking about Mitchell's condition. Stephens' wife, Carrie Lou Reynolds Mitchell, came to see about her sister-in-law. But there was still no change in Margaret's condition.

The employees had never seen anything like this. Some knew who Margaret Mitchell was, but had not read the book or seen the movie. Others felt they had a friend in that hospital room. Both the book and movie had become such a success that Mitchell was an icon in Atlanta.

David O. Selznick, who had just married his second wife, actress Jennifer Jones, a month earlier, could not believe the tragic news. He'd had his problems with the author while filming the movie, but Selznick had a warm affection for her since it was her novel *Gone With The Wind* that led to his film winning 'Best Picture' at the Academy Awards in 1939. He had personally won the Thalberg award for creative producing on the movie that year also. The remarkable story, penned by her hand, captured the nation's attention and hearts. Selznick had enjoyed meeting Mitchell at the Atlanta Premiere of *Gone With The Wind* ten years earlier.

He called his former executive assistant Marcella Rabwin—who had been closely involved throughout the making of the movie—reaching her at her home on Ocean Front in Del Mar, California, where she lived with her husband, Dr. Marcus Rabwin and their family. Marcella loved the movie and was of course saddened.

Marcella, retired from her job with Selznick, was a full-time homemaker. She put her children down for their naps and went outside. She walked along the beach, looking out at the horizon, and memories began to flood her mind. It had been one of the best years of her life and also one of the worst. There were casting problems, directing problems; and just general problems in getting Margaret Mitchell to cooperate, yet *Gone With The Wind* was always something close to Marcella's heart. Later, as one of the last surviving members of the production team, she spoke to groups, signed autographs, and published a memoir, *Yes, Mr. Selznick, Recollections of Hollywood's Golden Era.*

Marcella Rabwin, who had been omitted from the credits, as was every other assistant in those days, never forgot in her heart how much she loved the movie and for that she mourned the death of the book's author.

Four days later, Carrie Lou Mitchell joined several of Margaret's closest friends in a waiting room down the hall. John Marsh had visited with his wife earlier in the day and there had been a sense of optimism, so he felt comfortable leaving to go home and take a nap.

Shortly after he left, things began going downhill. They were letting family members into her room for short visits that day, and all of the comings and goings gave her friends in the waiting room down the hall reason to worry. Something was happening. Something very bad.

Three of Peggy Mitchell's doctors were present. There was much conferring between them and the nurses nearby. The newspapers reported that the hospital operators continued answering the calls with brave faces saying she was "critical."

When Stephens Mitchell arrived, newspaper reporters informed him that his sister had taken a turn for the worse. This was the day they were to operate on her and, he had been hopeful that surgery might save her, Stephens went straight to her room.

Later, when he opened the door and emerged from his sister's room, his face was pale and sad. Carrie touched his hand and slowly entered the room, the last time she would visit her sister-in-law. Upon request of the family, all photographers were removed from Grady Hospital and the parking lot.

Stephens stopped to speak to the reporters, giving them her full name. He wanted them to realize that to him, she was more than Margaret Mitchell the author, she was Margaret Munnerlyn Mitchell Marsh, his sister; a daughter and a wife.

Nineteen forty-nine was a different era. If a person of Margaret Mitchell's celebrity had been hit by a drunk driver and died, the paparazzi nowadays would be all over the story, but the photographers who had been asked to leave the parking lot at Grady Memorial knew why they were being asked to leave, and they complied. No pictures were taken of her body being removed.

Bessie Berry Jordan had been told of Mitchell's death, but Stephens Mitchell had asked her to fix a nice lunch for Marsh and be sure he was resting before he was told. She prepared his lunch and did her best to be pleasant as she served it even though her heart was breaking. A few minutes after noon one of Margaret's doctors, along with Stephens Mitchell went to the Marsh home and told the husband that his wife had died.

President Harry S. Truman called Marsh at his home and offered condolences. Newspaper and radio reports went nationwide and throughout the world.

In response to the thousands of fans internationally who wanted to honor her, the Mitchell family established a fund for Grady Memorial Hospital. Out of the tragic death of one who had helped so many would come the new Margaret Mitchell Emergency Ward.

For Margaret Mitchell, who had brought to the world Scarlett O'Hara, Rhett Butler and the rest of the unforgettable characters of *Gone With The Wind*, tomorrow would not be another day. She'd had those nightmares of being in a car accident and just as Scarlett O'Hara had had nightmares of running through the fog. At the end of both of their stories, their nightmares had come true.

Margaret Mitchell's tale….

The basic story of *Gone With The Wind* revolves around a Civil War family and a young girl's vow to survive at any cost. Scarlett O'Hara is the daughter of Irish plantation owner Gerald O'Hara and his wife Ellen Robillard O'Hara. Traditional Southerners, they live on a plantation known as Tara. Along with Scarlett there are two other daughters, Carreen and Suellen, as well as slaves and an overseer. The story, with its epic backdrop, is set in the time just before the Civil War through the Reconstruction days of the Old South.

As the book begins we meet Scarlett O'Hara as she flirts with the Tarleton Twins on her front porch. We learn of the upcoming barbecue, see Mammy's relationship with the family and are introduced to Gerald, his wife, Ellen, and the daughters.

In her carefree, youthful way Scarlett is in love with neighbor Ashley Wilkes. Early in the story it is revealed, much to the dismay of Scarlett, that Ashley is going to marry his cousin Melanie Hamilton. As they said in the book, "the Wilkes always marry their cousins."

The grand barbecue at the Wilkes plantation, symbolizes the carefree, happy days of the South in 1861, soon to mark the start of the war. At the barbecue, Ashley announces his engagement to the sweet, good-hearted Melanie which horrifies Scarlett.

Mention of Ashley's upcoming nuptials sends the sixteen-year old Scarlett into a tailspin. Throughout the story, Ashley appears conflicted, knowing what is proper, decent and most of all honorable—yet ever on that conflicting edge. Scarlett proclaims her love to Ashley, in the Wilkes' library and he gives her a glimmer of hope—but marries his cousin anyway. In this scene Scarlett has her first encounter with Rhett Butler, a good-looking stranger she spotted earlier in the day. He is taking a nap and wakes up in the room to overhear the private conversation between Scarlett and Ashley—a conversation he will bring up to Scarlett in the future on numerous occasions.

Ashley marries Melanie and the Civil War starts, both events changing Scarlett's life forever. Out of spite Scarlett marries Melanie's brother, Charles, who, shortly after the wedding, goes off to war. Soon she learns she is pregnant (with their son who would be called Wade

Hampton Hamilton, after Charles' commander who was his father's best friend) and then Charles dies of pneumonia due to the measles. (Two of Scarlett's children are left out of the movie, which follows the book very closely except for a few characters and events.)

Scarlett grows bored with the thought of wearing the black "widow's weeds" and with her life on the plantation, since there are no men to flirt with in the County—they've all gone to war. As a way to cheer her up, her mother suggests Scarlett go to Atlanta to visit her sister-in-law, Melanie. Melanie is living with her Aunt Pittypat since Ashley is off at war. Sarah Jane "Pittypat" Hamilton had raised Charles and Melanie since their parents died when they were very young.

Rhett Butler, the exciting, tall, dark and handsome man who originally overheard Scarlett trying in vain to win Ashley's heart before Ashley married Melanie—comes into and out of Scarlett's life. He is in love with her, but too proud to let her know at first, as he knows her heart belongs to Ashley. He drops in occasionally to look after the women at Aunt Pitty's house while Ashley is away.

The kind-hearted Melanie donates her time at the hospital, nursing the sick and injured soldiers. Scarlett works there, too, but hates everything about it. She longs to go home to her mother at Tara, but Melanie is pregnant with Ashley's child and it is too dangerous to travel.

The Yankee invasion is imminent and cries of "The Yankees are coming!" erupt everywhere, and all Scarlett can think of is getting back to the safety of Tara. She tries to leave with Aunt Pittypat, but Dr. Meade persuades her she can't leave until after Melanie has her baby, and Scarlett has promised Ashley she would take care of Melanie. Melanie is a sickly girl and once she has baby Beau, she is near death. Scarlett sends the young slave girl, Prissy, to Belle Watling's house to find Rhett Butler and ask him to help them get back to Tara. Belle is the high classed madam Rhett Butler spends time with.

Rhett helps Scarlett and Melanie escape by getting them a horse-drawn cart. He starts out on the trip with them. They leave against the backdrop of fire in the Atlanta skies as the Confederates' ammunition is being blown up before the Yankees can get to it. The cynical Rhett Butler, it turns out, has another side. He stops the carriage at a fork in the road and gets out to join the Confederate army.

Scarlett is terrified to be left behind but makes it through a treacherous trip home, with Prissy in the back looking after the still-ailing Melanie and baby Beau. As they come upon the Wilkes plantation, they see it has been burned and Ashley's father is dead. They arrive to see Tara, still standing, though everything around it is in ruins. Scarlett's mother is dead. Her sisters have scarlet fever. Her father is delirious. The majority of the slaves have been set free, but, out of loyalty to the O'Haras, Mammy, Pork, and Dilcey have chosen to stay. (Dilcey is only in the book.) They are as useless as Gerald, however, because of the shock they've just been through. Everyone, including Melanie, Carreen, and Suellen, now depend on Scarlett to tell them what to do. Pork reminds her they are 'house workers' and don't know about field servant's work. There is no food, and everyone is hungry. Even Mammy, who was once such a force in her life, helplessly asks, "Miss Scarlett" what are they going to do?

Scarlett decides to go searching for food at the Wilkes farm. She goes out back to the slaves' garden, digs up some radishes and eats the muddy roots. She throws up, and this becomes a turning point for her as she vows to do whatever it takes to "never be hungry again!"

To save Tara, she goes to Atlanta to ask Rhett Butler for the money needed to pay their taxes, but her plan fails. Once she runs into her sister Suellen's boyfriend Frank Kennedy and sees he has money, she comes up with an idea. She makes up a story that Suellen has been unfaithful and in essence steals her sister's boyfriend for her own husband. Soon Scarlett O'Hara Kennedy writes the check, and Tara is saved. Rhett eventually loans Scarlett the money for a saw mill and soon working and making money takes over her life.

Frank Kennedy and Scarlett have a daughter named Ella Lorena Kennedy (again, not mentioned in the movie), but Frank is killed while leading an attack involving the Ku Klux Klan. The Klan is left out of the movie, yet the incident is implied. She later marries Rhett Butler and now she finally has the wealth that will save Tara.

The two take a fun honeymoon to New Orleans where Scarlett is treated to anything she wants: the finest food, new clothes, travel, sleeping late. But one night she wakes up screaming from a terrible nightmare.

She tells Rhett about it, admitting she always has the same dream: she is running through the fog yet does not know what she is running toward. He comforts her, assures her she has nothing to be afraid of now.

Rhett gives her everything she wants, including the huge mansion, but there is always the boundary of Ashley in her heart; a man she will never have and who does not love her in the way she wants to be loved. At times Ashley displays his weakness by not being more firm and open about his love (or non-love) for her. In Scarlett's mind, Ashley always seems to leave the door open.

Scarlett gives birth to a daughter with Rhett and they decide to name her Eugenie Victoria (same basic name as one of Margaret Mitchell's aunts). But when Melanie remarks that the child's eyes are as blue as *The Bonnie Blue Flag*, which was the name of a popular song, Rhett proclaims that the child will be known as Bonnie Blue Butler.

Rhett and Scarlett never seem able to communicate the love that they really have for each other. Holding out hope for Ashley, she decides she does not want any more children with Rhett. After a while she begins to see Ashley as a weaker person and on the day of his surprise birthday party they are caught in a friendly embrace that is mistaken for more. Rhett hears about it and forces her to show her face at the birthday party that night even though they all think she was with Ashley. Later that night, a drunken Rhett carries Scarlett up to his room and the next day she is basking in the warmth of the night, but his apology ruins the feeling.

When Scarlett becomes pregnant again she is afraid Rhett will not be happy, so she speaks of it sarcastically. Equally sarcastically he tells her to cheer up, maybe she will have "an accident," and with that she loses her balance and falls down the stairs, suffering a miscarriage. In bed, recovering and in a feverish state, she cries out, "Rhett, Rhett," but no one hears her. He is hurt that she did not call for him, though actually she did and neither realizes it.

In one last effort, Rhett encourages his wife to give up her businesses, but she will have nothing of the idea. Scarlett wears Rhett's spirit down and by the end of the story he seems to fall out of love with her, staying with her only for the sake of Bonnie.

Then the little girl dies in a horse-riding accident. For a brief period

Rhett loses his mind, and will not allow anyone in the room with him and his dead daughter. He refuses to bury her because she is afraid of the dark.

Finally, Melanie, weak and sick yet staying up late with him, calms him down. She tells him she is expecting and he is happy for her. As she emerges from the room and informs Mammy that they can have the funeral the next day, she passes out. The doctor had told her it would be life threatening if she were to become pregnant again.

Melanie dies in her own home, but not before asking to see Scarlett. As she emerges from Melanie's deathbed, Ashley is in the hall, and Scarlett sees how upset he is. It is then she realizes how much he did love Melanie.

She looks around for Rhett, but he is gone. Finally it dawns on her that it is Rhett Butler she has loved; that she was only in love with the romantic idea of Ashley, not the real man.

Meanwhile Rhett observes Scarlett comforting Ashley, and thinks they will get together now with Melanie dead. Rhett is tired of it all and realizes he has lost his love for her and heads home to pack. Running through the fog, she reaches their home and begs him not to go, telling him she loves him. But he is adamant. She asks him what she will do if he leaves and he delivers the most famous line in the book (as he steps out into the fog): "My dear, I don't give a damn." The movie adds the dramatic, "Frankly," to that declaration.

Rhett leaves a heartbroken Scarlett behind. But after she cries for a moment, she summons up her courage and delivers the lines which define her character throughout the story— "I'll think of it all tomorrow.... After all, tomorrow is another day."

Margaret Mitchell's book is about survival, and at times it seemed that was the theme of her own life; though in the end she was not able to survive.

Chapter Two
Scarlett O'Hara

Margaret Mitchell dreamed she would die in a car crash and she did. Dreams had always played a part in her family's lives. They believed in their outcomes. Her mother had told her about a dream great-grandmother Ellen Fitzgerald had in the 1860s which came true—recurring nightmares of the Yankees coming, and in the end they did!

When Margaret Mitchell wrote *Gone With The Wind* she included two recurring dream sequences. Bonnie Blue Butler has nightmares of being in the dark, and most prevalent, Scarlett O'Hara's recurring dream of running through the mist (or fog). She dreamed it in New Orleans, and Rhett Butler tried to calm her fears, assuring her that once she realized she was safe, the nightmares would stop. As it turned out, the dream was about running through the mist away from Ashley Wilkes and towards Rhett. That dream does come true, but in a negative way just as in the other Fitzgerald-Mitchell dreams.

Including the dream sequences in the novel is only one of the ways Mitchell puts herself and her family in the book.

Scarlett O'Hara had a seventeen-inch waist, the smallest in three counties! Her creator had one almost that small if she'd have cared to measure. Both Scarlett and Margaret Mitchell were short—Mitchell was just five feet tall—and shared delicate features, as well as easy laughter and an Irish heritage. Mitchell had a loveliness to her in her youth with her silky smooth complexion and bright smile.

Peggy Mitchell's eyes were as vivid as Scarlett O'Hara's, though Peggy's were blue-gray, and Scarlett's were green. Peggy Mitchell, by all accounts, liked to laugh and people enjoyed her.

Actress Ann Rutherford who played Carreen in the movie got the chance to meet her and found her very likeable.

"She was the dearest lady," Ann said. "She was so sweet."

Everyone who met Peggy Mitchell thought she was a character, with a personality twice her size. And in her younger days, the flirty Mitchell, captivated more than her share of men with her charm—just as in the first sentence of the book, she says Scarlett did.

On the fifth line of the book, in describing Scarlett, she also directly describes herself, using the unusual term of "square jaw." In a letter Margaret Mitchell wrote to her cousin Lucille Stephens Kennon on June 21, 1938, never before published, she is replying to her cousin who has sent her some pictures of her great-grandmother Ellen Fitzgerald (Philip's wife.)

"I see where mother got her large blue eyes and where I got my thick eyebrows which are not mates," she says in the letter. "I am afraid my square jaw came from the same lady."

As Scarlett O'Hara's life was intertwined with her relatives, so was Margaret Mitchell's. Scarlett O'Hara had moved in with her deceased husband Charles' family and then went home to help her own family save their farm. In the book and movie there was a home base, Tara. Scarlett O'Hara's life revolved around that home and her family even though she did not have a good relationship with members of her family at times and was often away.

The events of Scarlett O'Hara's life play out mostly in Clayton County where Tara is situated, or in Atlanta, where she lives for much of the story. It has been written that Mitchell's Grandmother Annie Fitzgerald Stephens' life very much paralleled Scarlett's. Observers have long seen the obvious connections between Scarlett O'Hara and Margaret Mitchell, but there are also many similarities with Margaret's grandmother, who (for better or for worse) was a major influence on her life. Mitchell spent much time with her and at least on two occasions they lived in the same house.

In writing *Gone With The Wind*, Margaret Mitchell, according to family members, applied many of her grandmother's personal traits and experiences. Margaret's family immediately recognized the similarities between Scarlett O'Hara and Annie Fitzgerald, as evidenced by the written history in her cousin Lucille Stephens Kennon's scrapbook. Lucille was Annie Fitzgerald's niece and Margaret Mitchell's first cousin once removed. Kennon wrote about her Aunt Annie's "overbearing ambition (and) need and love of money, willfulness, and, at times, just plain revenge."

As with the fictional Scarlett who loved money and wanted to see others "pea green with envy," the real-life Annie Fitzgerald, according to her own family, displayed the same basic goals. The real person and the character were basically the same age during the Civil War. They did not care much for school or reading the classics yet both fell in love with men who did, and both were tough businesswomen who rode around in their own carriages without a male chaperone—a practice which, as Aunt Pittypat would say, "was simply not done!"

It has also been written that another person may have provided some background in Margaret Mitchell's mind for the character of Scarlett: Martha "Mittie" Bullock Roosevelt, the mother of Theodore Roosevelt. Martha, born in 1835, lived through the Civil War. A 1981 book, *Mornings on Horseback: The Story of an Extraordinary Family, a Vanished Way of Life and the Unique Child Who Became Theodore Roosevelt*, by David McCullough, mentions the Mittie Bullock-Scarlett O'Hara comparisons.

There may be bits of Bullock as well as story lines from her grandmother's life, but the author apparently enjoyed putting a little of herself in this willful rebel, Scarlett, whom she initially called Pansy. Pansy does sound a little bit like Peggy.

Peggy Marsh was born in Atlanta on Nov. 8, 1900, to Maybelle and Eugene Mitchell. There was a cluster of houses owned by her grandmother, Annie Fitzgerald Stephens, and the house Margaret was born in was a house her grandmother had built. Among other businesses, her Grandmother Stephens was involved in real estate; buying property and collecting rents. Just as Scarlett would not tolerate late payment at the Kennedy store, Annie Fitzgerald Stephens allowed no one to be late with their payments.

In 1902 Maybelle and Eugene moved to another of the family homes at the corner of Jackson Street, a Victorian style house with twelve rooms and a big front porch. There was also an upstairs porch.

Maybelle Mitchell had both a tough side and a tender side. An oft-told story has Maybelle driving a young Margaret out to the country and explaining to her the importance of an education and the will to survive any situation. Maybelle drove her out to the roads of Jonesboro, pointing out the ruins of once great houses. She told Margaret all about Sherman's army and how people who had once led a comfortable life suddenly found themselves in desperate situations. This could happen to Margaret some day, she said, and encouraged her daughter to gain an education and not take her easy life for granted. She wanted her daughter to be in a position where she could survive anything.

Maybelle, a suffragette, was known to hold women's organizing meetings in her living room; yet, with her soft side, she loved to garden and planted many flowers, including geraniums and lilies, in the yard. The Mitchell yard was full of flowers, with violets along the sidewalk leading up to the house; and they had a large backyard, big enough for the family pony and cow.

From a young age Margaret loved to ride her pony around the neighborhood.

One warm, spring evening in 1906, when Margaret Mitchell was six-years old, she was out on her pony riding around town with one of her best friends, an old white-haired man who had fought for the Confederacy. Margaret wore boy's pants as she rode. The little girl was fascinated every time she rode horseback with the old soldier because along the way they would pick up his various friends. This day was no different and soon the men were engaged in stories of 'the war'; and Margaret bump, bump, bumped closely beside them, listening to their stories. One of the men who had joined the group hurled an insult at the others and soon they were cussing and yelling—all quite entertaining to the young girl who hung on to every word.

Margaret's mother Maybelle had encouraged her to ride along with the old soldiers; their families liked the idea of having the little girl ride along, each thinking that one would be looking out for the other. The young girl was learning not only how to be a better rider but all about the Civil War—and how to cuss like a Confederate soldier, too!

Margaret Mitchell and her family also rode at Rural Home. She was adventurous like her Grandmother Stephens, and horse-riding accidents were a way of life. Horses had been a big part of Margaret Mitchell's own childhood, and were a big part of her book.

In *Gone With The Wind*, Scarlett's father Gerald liked to ride fast and jump fences, and he died jumping a fence. After Rhett and Scarlett's daughter Bonnie got too big to ride in the same saddle as her father, they bought her a pony and, just as Margaret Mitchell had learned to jump at age five, they started teaching Bonnie to jump fences. In the movie, Bonnie also died from a jump that went bad.

Maybelle and Eugene, Margaret's parents, were married in 1895, about thirty years after the War Between The States ended.

"I remember the wedding so well," wrote Margaret's cousin Lucille Kennon in her scrapbook. "I was a little girl and it was a first for me for several things: chicken salad and all the ice cream I could eat, red slippers and a blue dress!

"Aunt Annie outdid herself as usual (for Maybelle and Eugene's wedding)," wrote Lucille in the scrapbook. "The house was turned upside down with decorations. Banners of flowers and ferns graced the parlor, library and hall, stair rail, and conservatory and dining room.

"I had crowded among the guests standing in the dining room so I saw that part, if not the actual ceremony. Jean Mitchell (sic) [Eugene Mitchell] was just out of law school at the University of Georgia. He had no practice even started, but he had been an excellent student, had good prospects and was considered a good 'catch'. The Mitchell family lined up. I knew them, below us on Harris or Ivy Street. There were several daughters, Miss Julie, Ora Sue, Irene, Alene and three sons, Eugene, Gordon (with whom he would eventually share a law practice) and Robert. Then Mr. Mitchell [Eugene's father] married the second time, and had another family. I never knew them but Alene and I were great friends through school.

"At first Mabelle (sic) and Jean lived at home with Aunt Annie but after the first baby came and died, Aunt Annie realized it was not best to mix young ladies, children and young married folk so she built a small cottage around the corner and moved Maybelle there. Stephens and Margaret Mitchell were born there."

Then in 1904 the Mitchells moved to their home at 179 Jackson where Margaret spent much of her childhood. She attended North Boulevard School and Forrest Avenue School for her elementary schooling.

Margaret suffered burns in a fire accident when her skirt caught fire from a nearby fireplace she was watching. Shortly afterward she began wearing pants, rather than skirts, to avoid the possibility of the accident happening again. As a little girl, Margaret Mitchell enjoyed stories, real and imagined.

She liked putting on plays with her friends and playing with her brother Stephens, who was older. They made home-made ice cream, drank lemonade and had parties with the neighbors. There was a big vacant lot nearby where they played ball and flew kites, and raced ponies.

Margaret had a horseback riding accident in 1911 where she fell off, hitting her face on the gravel and hurting her leg. Then when she was in the 10th grade, the family moved to a large Colonial-style house on the east side of Peachtree Street just north of 17th Street.

During Margaret's childhood the Mitchell family made frequent trips to Jonesboro to visit their great-aunts, Mary and Sarah, on their farm. Both were well-respected members of the Clayton County community. Sarah was Sarah Jane, as in Sarah Jane "Pittypat" Hamilton, the aunt in *Gone With The Wind*. Mary was Mary Ellen, named after her mother, just as was Suellen O'Hara in the book. Known as Miss Mamie and Miss Sarah (or Sis, or sometimes Sadie), the spinster aunts ended up raising several of their siblings' children. After leaving home to live in Atlanta for a while, they wound up in the old house in which they grew up with their parents, Eleanor (Ellen) and Philip Fitzgerald.

When Margaret and Stephens went to the Rural Home, as the old homestead was called, they enjoyed running around as children do, and then at the end of the day they joined the family in the living room for the evening prayers. The tradition had started with Ellen Fitzgerald and continued after her death with the aunts leading the family in prayers. Before the Civil War, when Ellen led the prayers, the house servants would come in to participate. In later years, the employees participated. These prayer sessions were mentioned in Lucille Stephens Kennon's scrapbook.

In *Gone With The Wind*, Ellen O'Hara led the family prayers. Though the family's heads were all bowed, Scarlett O'Hara could not keep her mind on the prayers; it was racing with thoughts of how to get Ashley Wilkes' attention. Ambivalent feelings about religion were something both the author and her character shared. Margaret Mitchell's real-life mother Maybelle continued with the Fitzgerald's religious heritage, but evidently it did not interest the daughter.

As a child, Maybelle spent more time at Rural Home than she might otherwise have done. During her formative years, her mother Annie Fitzgerald Stephens became involved in business in Atlanta; thus Maybelle was placed with her aunts at Rural Home (much as in *Gone With The Wind* when Scarlett left her children with their aunt—her sister—Suellen). According to a family scrapbook, Maybelle lived ten years at Rural Home with her aunts and other various relatives who lived there. Annie Fitzgerald had six children, but Maybelle seemed to be the family favorite according to the scrapbook. The aunts were very generous and raised several children of one of their sisters who had died—along with having Annie's children off and on.

Catherine Fitzgerald, Katie as a child, was a sister of the aunts. She married William Stephens and they had four children. When Catherine and William died young, their children, Lucille (scrapbook author), Mamie, Isabelle, and Merle Marie, went to live at Rural Home with Maybelle. It might seem Annie Fitzgerald Stephens displayed about as little concern for her children as did Scarlett O'Hara. Maybelle was a sickly but pleasant child and the aunts loved her dearly. So Lucille, who kept the scrapbook, was raised with Maybelle, giving added credibility to her knowledge of the family.

"They spoiled her [meaning Maybelle] and petted her," wrote her cousin Lucille in her scrapbook. Margaret Mitchell used similar words near the end of *Gone With The Wind* (page 1030) when Rhett Butler talked to Scarlett about how much he had loved her. He said he wanted to take care of her, spoil her, and to "pet" her.

Annie Fitzgerald would return to Rural Home occasionally, apparently not so much to visit her children as primarily for business reasons. Most of the time, she was off in Atlanta running her enterprises. That was another characteristic she shared with Scarlett O'Hara.

Annie Fitzgerald Stephens and Scarlett O'Hara shared many characteristics, but the most obvious thing they shared was living through many of the same experiences.

"After supper everybody went out to sit on the front porch," said Mitchell cousin Sara Spano in her book, *I Could've Written Gone With The Wind, But Cousin Margaret Beat Me To It*, a compilation of Spano's most popular newspaper columns.

According to Spano, many of the stories passed on were similar to those told by Margaret Mitchell in her book. She said the Fitzgerald 'girls' (Mamie, Sis, and Annie) would recall memories of "their girlhood on the plantation before the war and all the things that occurred in the years during and after the conflict. Sara and Mary Ellen had been on the plantation when Sherman came through and Annie had been a young matron in Atlanta, so the picture was pretty complete."

Sara Spano's former daughter-in-law, Mary Lucy, remembered the family talking about 'the story'. She was married to Spano's son, since passed away, but Mary Lucy recalled many conversations.

"I remember when the grandchildren were visiting grandmother at 'Tara'," Spano said, referring to Rural Home as Tara, as the family knew that Margaret Mitchell based the tales on happenings at Rural Home. "Margaret would listen to the stories her grandmother told while my former mother-in-law would go climb the trees."

Saundra Voter, who helped type Sara Spano's book for her talked to Sara about her having the same family as Margaret Mitchell.

"I believe Margaret based Gerald O'Hara on her grandfather Fitzgerald," said Saundra. "Sara didn't seem to be upset at all about so much of the family history being in the book. In fact, I think she was rather proud of it."

"When Margaret's 'little book' (as they called it) came out, Sara's mother told her, 'You see there, you see there? If you had been sitting there listening, you could have written this book'," said Saundra. "I'm not sure that Sara would have, though. Sara was an excellent writer. Margaret just had a special way with her descriptions."

Margaret Mitchell attended Washington Seminary. It was lucky they had moved to the Peachtree house because all three houses the Mitchells had previously lived in burned in the great fire of Atlanta in May, 1917.

The fire started near the house the Mitchells had lived in on Jackson at the corner. A large wind came and soon the fire spread for twenty blocks all the way down to Ponce de Leon Avenue.

The fire was so big, and so many homes were lost that a refugee center had to be set up at the Municipal Auditorium. Margaret Mitchell went down to the auditorium with her mother to help. This episode in Mitchell's life may have contributed to the Confederate hospital scenes as she, like Scarlett, went to volunteer. Mitchell, unlike the book character, actually wanted to help.

It was a stressful time. Everyone was concerned about family members who lost their homes. The Mitchells' extended family lost thirteen houses in that fire. Grandmother Annie Fitzgerald Stephens' house was among those destroyed and she soon moved in with the Mitchells.

The year ahead was filled helping the family members, and moving her grandmother in. Margaret's senior year in high school also included parties and activities and then shopping for all that she would need as she prepared to leave for Smith College in Massachusetts the next fall.

Margaret's Aunt Edith lived in New York; so by choosing Smith, out east for her daughter, Maybelle felt she was leaving her at a good college and with a relative not too far away. Taking her daughter to college, Maybelle planned a fun trip, including a quick stop off in New York to visit Aunt Edith. Mother and daughter had an enjoyable time on their trip. Later it would be written that Margaret disliked her aunt, though it remains unclear whether she disliked the aunt at the time of the trip or whether those feelings came out after this aunt allegedly threatened to sue her over the book.

Maybelle Mitchell, a busy woman, had not been the type to spend pleasurable time with her daughter, so this trip would stay with Margaret for a long time. Most of Margaret's memories of her mother later would be of her imparting wisdom and teaching her lessons, rather than going shopping or talking about boys. Perhaps that is why Margaret made Ellen O'Hara so busy throughout her fictional life. She was so busy running the plantation. She had to work on the books after firing the overseer so she could not go to the Wilkes barbecue with the rest of the family. She did, however, take the time to have a 'motherly' talk with her after Charles Hamilton's death.

That tender conversation was one of the last times Scarlett O'Hara saw her mother. The trip to college was also very special for Margaret, as it was a rare occasion when she was able to spend quality time with her mother. Unfortunately, like Scarlett, it was the last time the teenager saw her mother alive. Both the fictional character and the author arrived back home shortly after their mother had died.

Margaret Mitchell included her mother's name in her novel with the character, Maybelle Merriweather. It seemed as if Margaret's college education was doomed from the start. In the ten months she was away, she suffered the deaths of two people she loved, her mother and a boyfriend, Clifford Henry. She spent the one year at Smith College but did not return after her freshman year.

Clifford Henry was a young man she was dating before he went off to war. By the fall of 1918 it seemed peace was coming as soon as the Americans joined the forces, bringing the Allies closer to winning the war against the Germans. Young women kissed their patriotic men goodbye, waving flags as they went, but unfortunately for young Margaret, Clifford did not return. He was killed during the first American round of fighting in World War I.

Clifford had been one of the many servicemen the Mitchells entertained at their home on Peachtree. Maybelle and Eugene Mitchell opened their home to the young servicemen as a way of thanking them for their service to the country. They gave many parties to entertain the men before they left for war.

Cliff liked to dance and also enjoyed the same poetry and classical books as Margaret, so they got along very well. It has been written that they became engaged before he left for the service. They had shared letters when she was at Smith that first semester and she'd even gotten to know his parents, who lived out East. Clifford Henry went off to war about the same time her brother Stephens went. Clifford's death was a shocking blow to Margaret, the first close friend who had died. Previously her life had been one social occasion after another; now the war had claimed someone dear. Margaret had other boyfriends in Atlanta and at college, but Clifford Henry's death broke her heart and she had a hard time getting over it.

About the same time, another enemy struck— the Spanish Influenza.

The Influenza epidemic of 1918, though hardly mentioned in textbooks, killed more people than all the fighting in World War I. An estimated 675,000 Americans alone died—ten times more than those killed in the War.

There had been an earlier epidemic, but the September-October outbreak was brutal for the entire world. In Northampton, Massachusetts, Peggy and her classmates felt the effects as Smith College was put on quarantine and classes suspended.

Back home in Atlanta, Peggy's mother Maybelle was tending to those around her who were sick, including Margaret's father, Eugene. Soon she, herself, became sick with influenza; and by the time Margaret got the news about how sick her mother was, it was too late. This scene from Mitchell's real life was played out in *Gone With The Wind,* as Mammy blamed the Slatterys for Ellen O'Hara's death because she had been taking care of their family when they caught typhoid fever. Scarlett, too, arrived just after her mother died.

After the death of both mothers, the fathers seemed unable to cope, at least for a time. Eugene Mitchell had trouble accepting his wife's death but after a while he came out of it unlike Gerald O'Hara who seemed to crumble after his wife died.

Gerald O'Hara's character was not patterned after Eugene Mitchell, but that episode certainly was. She may have given Gerald and teen-aged Scarlett the close, loving relationship that she wished she had with her father during those years.

For a while, after his wife died, Eugene Mitchell spent many days in bed, unable to deal with the loss of his wife; but one day he called Margaret into his room and urged her to go back to Smith and finish the year. At the end of the year she moved home to keep house for her father and he encouraged her to abandon the idea of Smith and stay home in Atlanta. Eugene Mitchell seemed to need his daughter as much as Gerald O'Hara needed Scarlett.

Margaret Mitchell is the only one who truly knew whether she was a victim of her father wanting her back in the house after her mother's death or whether she was simply using it as an excuse for why she did not go back to Smith. She could have attended college in Atlanta, however, when discussing education she always brought it back to insisting that she had to come home to "keep house." She once wrote to a friend from Smith, Allen Edee, expressing her ambivalence on how she felt about staying home or going to school. During this time of confusion she confided to him that she felt she had a lot of potential, like a "dynamo going to waste."

Later, Mitchell would say she had wanted to become a doctor. In an autobiographical sketch in the *Wilson Bulletin,* in September, 1936, she wrote, "I hoped to study medicine but while I was at Smith College my mother died and I had to come home to keep house."

Whether an excuse or an unfulfilled dream, she did not take any other classes after returning home from Smith.

Clifford Henry was not her only boyfriend who served in the military. Henry Love Angel, a childhood friend from her neighborhood, was among those who had vied for her attention and won. Angel and Courtenay Ross were also neighbors and good friends; but the relationship between Angel and Mitchell rose to the level of romance, according to letters published in *Lost Laysen,* edited by Debra Freer.

Her friendship-turned-romance with Henry Love Angel came to light when Angel's son found letters written by Margaret to his father, as well as pictures and a short novella by Margaret called *Lost Laysen.* He donated the pictures, letters, and book to the Road to Tara Museum in Jonesboro; later, author Debra Freer combined it all in a 1996 book, *Lost Laysen.* According to Patrick Duncan of the Clayton County Convention Center, the letters are no longer at the museum.

In previous biographies on Margaret Mitchell, Henry Love Angel was mentioned as one of five boys visiting in her hospital room when she was sick. She had written about this occasion to Allen Edee, her Smith friend. There are pictures of Mitchell and Henry Love Angel holding hands and arm in arm in Freer's book, which also contained loving letters.

For two years starting in the summer of 1919 Margaret, Henry, and their friends would visit a place called Shadowbrook Farm in the countryside of Suwanee, GA, according to *Lost Laysen* (page 22).

Peggy and her friends enjoyed hiking, horseback riding, and swimming. The tension in the Mitchell house caused by her grandmother and father's apparent desire to control her grew so great that the younger Mitchell used any excuse to go out of town with her friends.

In letters to Angel she mentions other boyfriends by name, including Winston Withers (referred to as Winston "Red" Withers,) Berrien (also called "Red") Upshaw, and "Dr. Morris," a man with whom she attended a costume party at a country club, though she left with Upshaw.

In 1920, Margaret had another bad accident on a horse, re-injuring her leg and ankle; an injury from which she never seemed to recover.

The early 1920s, although a time of chaos in the Mitchell household, were mostly fun and exciting for the thrill-seeker Margaret. At the same time, she was doing things her grandmother looked down on. Her father was constantly trying to reckon with his rebellious daughter, and there was no mother in the house to buffer this tension. Her older brother Stephens generally stayed out of the way.

Her life mirrored the times. It was the Roaring Twenties and people were having fun. Whether going to debutante parties, out of town excursions, horseback rides or just being with her friends she had a happy-go-lucky time. She had experienced the new freedom of going away to college and continued living her life on her own terms, even with the constantly disapproving eye of her grandmother and father.

Margaret had many boyfriends, sometimes at the same time. Peggy Mitchell was known for being a flirt and— not unlike her created flirtatious character of Scarlett O'Hara— she loved being the center of attention surrounded by boys.

In 1920, the year after Peggy Mitchell came home from college, Prohibition started. The 18th Amendment went into effect and the making, sale, and transportation of liquor became illegal. This didn't stop people from drinking; they merely had to be more creative. 'Speakeasies' in the North and 'Clubs' in the South were created, and the partying set continued on.

During the prohibition years, Peggy frequented Clubs and dated a bootlegger who would become her first husband. It seemed as if she craved the attention she got by bucking the system; going against the 'norm', and generally having a good time doing as she pleased.

"Margaret Mitchell was a fascinating person," said *Gone With The*

Wind collector and expert John Wiley, Jr. "I would have loved to have met her. She was not a saint, but she certainly wasn't as bad as she's been portrayed, either."

Mitchell loved telling jokes, at times very crude, employing the vocabulary she'd learned from the Confederate soldiers she rode with as a child. Though new for women, she also enjoyed smoking and drinking in public,

"Those weren't bad characteristics in the Fitzgerald family," said Marie Nygren, the daughter of Margaret Lupo, Margaret Mitchell's cousin. "Yes, she smoked, cussed, and drank alcohol but in our family that was just how the women were. The women were strong and those qualities were not seen as a negative."

"She had a great sense of humor," explained Wiley, who produces *The Scarlett Letter*, an informational newsletter for GWTW fans.

Mitchell used that sense of humor to gain the friendship and admiration of many young men and like Scarlett O'Hara, she was always surrounded by doting suitors. Scarlett did not share all qualities with Mitchell, however. Scarlett grew bored with conversations about books or art. Margaret Mitchell had read the classics and could quote them.

"That's how we were all raised," said Nygren. "We were raised to be independent, strong, capable women. Even from the days of Annie Fitzgerald Stephens the women in the family were expected to own your own business and go to college."

Margaret did not own a business, although it could be argued that *Gone With The Wind* turned out to be her business. She did, however, have her heroine as a business owner since Scarlett bought a sawmill and ran the store once she married Frank Kennedy.

"The notion of a 'Southern Belle' was a 'no-no' in our family," said Nygren.

Marie Nygren was carrying on the family tradition by owning a real estate development, including a bed and breakfast with her husband, Steve. It is a beautiful countryside complex, called Serenbe, in Palmetto, Georgia, not far from where she grew up in Atlanta.

It was suggested to Marie Nygren that Scarlett became strong and capable after she lost everything and had to rebuild.

"Scarlett was always strong and capable," she said. "She may have been flirting with the men but she knew what she was doing. She knew what she was trying to get."

The 1920 census lists Margaret Mitchell living with her father Eugene, her 23-year old brother Stephens, and her grandmother Annie Fitzgerald Stephens. Annie was sixty at the time. Margaret invariably enjoyed listening to her stories and had great respect for all she had accomplished, but she did not like the way the woman was always trying to interfere in *her* life. Anne felt that since Margaret's mother had died, she needed to step in. They were always butting heads. And as Annie grew older, she became more combative with her granddaughter.

Nineteen twenty was also the year Margaret began dating Berrien Upshaw, her future husband. She had known him for a while through her friend Courtenay Ross. It was also the year she and Courtenay were introduced as debutantes. They got their picture in the Atlanta Constitution with the rest of the debutantes. Peggy Mitchell's life in the early 1920s consisted of going to parties, clubs, and entertaining friends.

Her future second husband, John Marsh, had recently moved to Atlanta to work as a reporter for the William Randolph Hearst newspaper, *The Daily Georgian*. Although they were not immediately exclusive, once she met Marsh he was a constant among the men she was dating. Peggy Mitchell spent part of the spring of 1922 in Birmingham, Alabama, with her friend Augusta Dearborn. Peggy volunteered at the newspaper where Augusta worked. In March of 1922, Peggy wrote to Angel telling him she would be home soon and ended it by saying, "I've missed you. Love, Peggy."

Later that spring, "She was back in Alabama staying at a 'plantation' owned by her boyfriend, Winston 'Red' Withers," according to *Lost Laysen*, p.55. Though she was at the Withers' family farm, on Saturday, June 24[th,] she was writing a love letter to Angel and when she left Withers' place she headed to a rendezvous with Upshaw. From her time at Winston's she went to her friend Augusta Dearborn's sister's home, where she joined a group of young people, including Upshaw. At the same time she was dating John Marsh. Since Peggy Mitchell was a well-known socialite in

Atlanta, gossip spread around about her many boyfriends. There was actually a mention in the newspaper of the Marsh-Upshaw-Mitchell love triangle.

Somewhere in the midst of all her boyfriends, by the end of the summer of 1922 she settled on Marsh and Upshaw as her two main suitors; however, there was never a time, for more than a few weeks, that she was dating Upshaw exclusively.

Suddenly (only a month after visiting Winston Withers' plantation, and only weeks after going out with Marsh), Peggy announced her engagement to Upshaw and they married on September 2nd. Winston Withers was in the wedding and John Marsh stood by her as the "best man." Shortly after their honeymoon, Peggy wrote a loving letter to Angel wanting to get together with him.

Peggy and Red Upshaw lived in the Mitchell family house on Peachtree with her father and brother, and she got a job at the Sunday Magazine section of the *Atlanta Journal*. It was a short-lived marriage and her father helped her get a divorce.

Once she married John Marsh, the Marsh newlyweds moved into a small apartment and she seemed to have settled down. Everyone who knew the Marshes knew how devoted he was to her and she seemed to completely settle into married life. Not too long after the wedding to Marsh, Peggy suffered yet another injury to her ankle—the same ankle she'd injured several times earlier.

Things were not looking good during the spring of 1926 at the Marsh apartment. Due to injury, Peggy Marsh was practically confined to her home, and being a fun-loving, active person she was not very happy about it.

"Peggy was hobbling around the 'Dump' (the nickname the Marshes gave their apartment) on crutches," said Ann Taylor Boutwell, a docent at the Margaret Mitchell House and Museum in Atlanta. "She had injured one of her ankles—the same one injured twice before. Once when she was eleven-years-old, she fell from a horse while living in the old Victorian gingerbread house in Atlanta's Old Fourth Ward; and there was that time in 1920 when she injured her foot riding in Athens, Georgia. Her doctor warned her to stay off the ankle, 'give it a rest'.

"She gave *Atlanta Journal* Editor Angus Perkerson her resignation. A few weeks later, she received her last check, dated May 3, 1926."

Peggy and John had been married less than a year, having said their vows on July 4, 1925. Less than four years earlier she had been a happy-go-lucky flapper who enjoyed dancing, parties, and surrounding herself with many different boyfriends. Now, as her husband left for work every day, she was confined to her apartment.

"Although John was extremely busy with his advertising and public relations job at the Georgia Railway and Power Company and his moonlighting for the Community Chest," said Boutwell. "He was deeply concerned about Peggy. She was getting bored and was not in the best of moods. 'I'm about as pleasant to live with as a porcupine or a snapping turtle', she told a friend."

In the days before television, she could not sit in bed and channel surf. It was also before computers and the internet, so she could not check her e-mails or 'instant message' friends. There was no Facebook or Twitter. Besides the radio, her housekeeper Bessie Berry was the only contact she had with the outside world on a regular basis. Peggy was getting depressed and it was even playing into the dynamics of their marriage, as John got up and went to work every day while she had confined herself to the boredom and solitude of their one-bedroom apartment.

"John knew when she was happy, he was happy," said Boutwell. "Every other day he lugged library books back and forth on the Peachtree streetcar. One September evening so the story goes, he returned to the Dump with a surprise—a secondhand portable Remington typewriter. The early birthday present from John launched the beginning of her new career."

He suggested she write a book, and after thinking about it awhile, she decided it might help with the boredom and depression she was feeling by not being able to go out with her friends. It would be fun to try to write a book.

What would she write about, she asked her husband.

"Write what you know," he told her.

One thing Margaret knew a good deal about was the Civil War. She would write a book set in that time period, and tell the story she'd heard so many times before: the dreadful time when Sherman and his army came through Clayton County and lives were lost or changed forever. Yes, her own great-grandfather Philip Fitzgerald's farm and what happened to his family would give her the background she needed to get started.

Chapter Three
The Family Scrapbook

Rural Home was the name of Philip Fitzgerald's plantation. Throughout much of her life Margaret Mitchell had relatives who still lived there, and the old farm was where she heard a lot of the Civil War tales.

When *Gone With The Wind* was published, her relatives recognized pieces of their lives in it. They were excited for her and excited to see the similarities in the book, but something happened shortly after the book hit the stores. Mitchell and her husband, John Marsh, began denying that any of the book was based on actual events. During the time she was writing it she had good relationships with her aunts as well as her cousins, though she'd always had a stormy relationship with her Grandmother Stephens. Throughout the years since the book was written, those who knew the family thought Annie was the basis for her character Scarlett O'Hara.

Scarlett Fever by William Pratt and Herb Bridges is one of the books that mentions this. A recently discovered family scrapbook gives a closer look at the real people and events behind *Gone With The Wind*. Mitchell used her skill as a writer to take stories from the Fitzgerald family, and some from her own life, blending them with her own creativity to fashion many of the stories in her book. She also traveled, talked to people and did library research.

Many families throughout history have had a strong woman who helped her family survive a devastating time. Mitchell knew about her own. Given that so many people pointed to her grandmother Annie as a possible model for Scarlett, it is hard to imagine that Margaret Mitchell did not write about what she knew.

The fun comes in trying to determine what real people the characters emerged from. Since *Gone With The Wind* was published there have been hundreds of books and magazine articles written about the author, book, movie, and actors who appeared in the movie. What is it that keeps *Gone With The Wind* alive and creates so much enthusiasm with fans over all these years?

Many credible authors have written about Margaret Mitchell and speculated on how the stories came about. Unfortunately Mitchell is not around to give us the real answer.

It is interesting, however, to be able to read straight from the scrapbook of a cousin who actually lived in the home with the elderly aunts. Lucille Kennon Stephens was raised by her aunts and lived with Maybelle Mitchell, Margaret's mother, for years. She did not have a reason to make stories up because she was not going to profit or lose anything by the success of the book. She wrote notes in her scrapbook and specifically stated that she was writing it down so the truth could be known. Her version of the story is that at the time she wrote the scrapbook there had been a veil of secrecy concerning the possible ties to the Fitzgerald family stories.

It has long been rumored that Mitchell "stole" a family diary. First of all, what would have been wrong with using family information in parts of her book? Any history book, no matter how scholarly, is originally written by a person who did research and ultimately based it on the findings or the knowledge of another. In this case, Mitchell's family was there. They saw the Battle of Jonesboro, so why not draw on their expertise?

Some say this diary is in a private collection, some say it is stored in a collection at the University of Georgia, and at least one historian doesn't believe there is a diary but rather a memoir. Either way, Lucille Kennon's Scrapbook is an interesting look at a Civil War family and some of the things that happened to them before, during, and after the war.

And it definitely contains incidents from their family that could have triggered Margaret Mitchell's imagination and been used in her book. It also tells of a book written by Mitchell's mother Maybelle that had all of the family stories in it, so Margaret may never have had to steal a diary if a book was handed to her by her mother.

The scrapbook mentions several prominent families in the area, including the Crawfords, Venables, and Dorseys among others, as friends of the Fitzgeralds, and the Hollidays as cousins. The Harpers and Dicksons were also Fitzgeralds' friends. Solomon Dawson Dorsey was the head of the Dorsey family who lived during Philip Fitzgerald's time. His grandson, Hugh M. Dorsey, became Governor of Georgia. The Dorsey property was near the Crawfords. Thomas Shanklin Crawford, who married Dorsey's daughter Althea Frances Dorsey, was also a friend of the Fitzgeralds. Lucille's scrapbook mentions the socializing they did with the Crawfords, Dorseys and others.

Margaret Mitchell had good relationships with her relatives, including cousin Lucille Stephens Kennon, and this is evidenced in a long, friendly letter Margaret wrote after Lucille had sent her a picture.

"You were so very nice and thoughtful to let me have a copy and I appreciate it so very much," Mitchell wrote to her cousin in June, 1938, after *Gone With The Wind* had come out. This letter and the scrapbook were kept together by family members after Kennon's death, and no problem of discontent or conflict between the two was mentioned to Kennon's granddaughter. Thus we can presume she had no grudge against Mitchell and that there is no reason to discount the scrapbook entries. Lucille's mother was raised with Mitchell's grandmother.

"All fiction comes from nonfiction," said Marie Nygren, Lucille's granddaughter, who recently discovered the scrapbook. Marie's mother, Margaret Lupo, was Margaret Mitchell's cousin. Margaret Lupo, who once owned Mary Mac's Tearoom in Atlanta, was in the same generation as Mitchell. Mitchell kept in touch with her relatives, known as the "Fitzgerald / Stephens" relatives on her mother's side of the family.

In 2007, while going through some of her mother's things, Marie noticed an old scrapbook filled with pictures from the 1800s.

"My grandmother wrote and put it together later in her life when all of her children were grown as a way of recording family history," said Nygren.

Nygren, who does not have first-hand knowledge of Mitchell's relationship with her mother, discovered the scrapbook in the presence of the author of this book. As they started reading it together they realized the amazing information they had right there in their hands. Never before had the public been able to read actual writings from someone who knew both Philip Fitzgerald AND Margaret Mitchell.

They were all in the scrapbook: the elderly aunts Mamie and Sis; Philip Fitzgerald and his wife Eleanor; and the rest. There are pictures from the 1800s of the family members, including a picture of a family-owned saw mill. There are stories that when you read them, ring a bell with *Gone With The Wind* fans.

To put it all into perspective, the author of the scrapbook was Lucille Stephens Kennon, Nygren's grandmother. Lucille's mother was Catherine (Katie) Fitzgerald, a daughter of Margaret Mitchell's great-grandfather, Philip Fitzgerald. Catherine and her husband died at a young age and their children were raised by their aunt in Atlanta who later returned to Rural Home.

With the scrapbook was another note which basically told the story again, except in different words.

"She did a rough draft," guessed Marie Nygren, when asked why it was written twice. Lucille Stephens Kennon must have felt so strongly that the story be handed down that she wrote two versions of it, and they exist today.

She seemed not to be writing it out of spite or bad feelings, but to set the record straight for her family and anyone else who read the scrapbook. With permission from Marie Nygren, below is an uncorrected excerpt from the scrapbook—keeping the scrapbook author's own spelling and grammar.

In Her Own Words

I am not writing these memories in any spirit of criticism of Margaret Mitchell as author of "Gone With The Wind"—I am sure she is the author—

I would just like to accord to her author's tale the love, appreciation, and acknowledgement to her mother, and grandmother! The stories Mabel (sic) said she was writing down for her children—Stephens & Margaret—the memories Aunt Annie regaled her grandchildren with are all Fitzgerald happenings and are scattered through the book.

Aunt Annie was Annie Fitzgerald—one of the seven daughters of Philip and Elenor (sic) Fitzgerald. They lived near Jonesboro and Fayetteville. The eldest daughter had been sent four years to Charleston to a convent finishing school, but when it came time for Annie and Agnes, the next line girls to go to school, finances were beginning to fall so they were sent to a young ladies academy in Fayetteville, GA. Up to that time the girls had gone to a plantation school maintained by the neighboring plantations.

…Annie became engaged to a young man in Augusta, GA at a very early age for to be unmarried after eighteen years marked a girl as an old maid. She and Aunt Mamie came to Atlanta to visit some relatives and friends and buy materials for the truseau (sic). As was the custom at the time their friends (the Holliday cousins) gave a "social," night party and invited all the eligible young men for Aunt Mamie to meet. Among them was a newly arrived dashing, black eyed, gentleman from Ireland. His name was John Stephens and was old enough for Aunt Mamie.

…But Annie was not going to let Mamie have the new beau in the Immaculate Conception Parish—she, as they said then made a dead set for him, and went home engaged to him. The trousseau was bought but used for another bridegroom. Grandfather was horrified. A promise of marriage was as good as the ceremony to him, but Annie threatened to run away and marry in the "big road" in front of the house so he agreed.

…And so they were married! He, an intelligent polished traveled man of the world, and she young, pretty, untutored, untrained, self-willed and stubborn and at times kind, generous and thoughtful and always devoted to grandma, and "home." It must have been a gala wedding—the first of Mr. Fitzgerald's seven daughters to marry. I have the red linen table cloth Grandma used at all the wedding breakfasts. It is worn thin in places and there are some broken threads. The long fringe is gone, but it is still real Irish linen. I am sure the neighboring gentry were present—Bennets, Blalocks, Venables, Crawfords, and Stewarts and Dorseys.

... Maybelle was the oldest daughter. She married Eugene M. Mitchell in 1893 (sic). I remember the wedding so well I was a little girl and it was a first for me in several things—chicken salad—all the ice cream I could eat— red slippers and a blue silk dress! Aunt Annie outdid herself as usual. The house was turned upside down—with decorations. (Throughout) the parlor, library and hall, stair rail, conservatory and dining room were banners of flowers and ferns. The porches and old long school room were enclosed in heavy ausinberg and festooned with vines and tables set out for supper.

Wurms orchestra provided music, and to my eyes the girls were gorgeous. Maybelle came down the stairs with Uncle John looking lovely in while satin and veil. Uncle John's white hair and beard made him look distinguished and handsome. I had crowded between the guests standing in the dining room door so I saw that part if not the actual ceremony.

Jean (sic) [Eugene] Mitchell was just out of law school at the University of Georgia. He had no practice even started but he had been an excellent student, had good prospects and was considered a good "catch." The Mitchell family lined up. I knew them, below us on Harris or Ivy Street. There were several daughters, Miss Julie, Ora Sue, Irene Alene and three sons, Eugene, Gordon and Robert. Then Mr. Mitchell (Eugene's father) married the second time, and had another family. I never knew them but Alene and I were great friends through school.

At first Mabelle (sic) and Jean (sic) lived at home with Aunt Annie, but after the first baby came and died, Aunt Annie realized it was not best to mix young ladies, children and young married folk so she built a small cottage around the corner on Cain street and moved Maybelle there. Stephens and Margaret Mitchell were born there and the other girls, (Maybelle's sisters) Eugenia and Edith thus had the big house and grounds for entertaining by themselves. It takes a young lawyer a long time to establish a practice and they got impatient with Jean (sic) and Maybelle.

Now I must go back many years to find some of the facts for contributing to the disintegration of Aunt Annie's family besides her overbearing ambition, need and love of money, willfulness and just plain revenge at times.

...The need for more money for the growing family drove Aunt Annie on—(but) the desire for moderation and economy animated Uncle John. And finally the knowledge and constant reminder that (all of) the property

belonged to his wife proved the last straw. He left home.

I had all this part of the story from Aunt Sadie, who lived many years with Aunt Annie, and loved both her sister and brother-in-law. She rode each day with the older girls to Miss Hannah's School, took lessons there herself, then taught the young children Latin. This was all before the advent of public schools.

Aunt Annie was on her own, She had been running a dray [dray is a cart used for hauling] service from the back lot and had her own carriage house and she had a "dog cart" and horse of her own to drive. So she started collecting rents, doing repairs, running the draying service continually, running a saw mill outside Atlanta and being her own boss generally. Eventually she got involved in land titles, mortgages, lawsuits and loan sharks.

…Every so often Aunt Annie had to return to "Rural Home" with her mother gone, and it was a frightening sight to see her driving to Jonesboro alone in a carriage.

The children absorbed the stories grandmother told of her childhood and old home, and came to know intimately those roads and people along them. As well during their own childhood, as from Aunt Annie and Aunt Mamie, of this during the terrible time of Sherman's march, and dreadful reconstruction days.

But Maybelle had not been entirely unoccupied! She told a friend of mine—Claire O'Conner—in about 1917 that she was writing some of the family stories for her children and she wanted Claire to read them to give an opinion of them. Claire was a newspaper woman herself, and promised to do so, but Mabelle (sic) died in the first flu epidemic.

Margaret herself told me of the pile of books on the telephone chair that she used to sit on when she was too little to reach the table!

(Shortly after Gone With The Wind came out) She was asked about Rhett Butler. … "How do you know?" they asked. "I ought to… He was my own grandfather" she replied.

But something happened. I heard Edith [sic] and Eugenia (these were Margaret's aunts, Maybelle's sisters) threatened defamation and law suits. There was trouble again for Jean (Gene, Mitchell's father) and Margaret Mitchel (sic) never again publicly acknowledged her own mother.

I have no doubt she wrote the book, but the help she got from her grandmother, her mother, and her father remains unacknowledged. They gave her freely, and would have been proud of her. So I think even at this late date the truth should be told.

...All of this story from Sadie who lived many years with Aunt Annie and both her sister and brother-in-law.

...The above taken from Lucille Stephens Kennon's scrapbook, written approx. 1939

Relationships:

- Lucille Stephens Kennon to Margaret Mitchell's first cousins once removed.
- Margaret Mitchell to Margaret Lupo—second cousins.
- Margaret Mitchell to Marie Nygren (Margaret Lupo's daughter) second cousins once removed.
- Annie Fitzgerald Stephens to Catherine (Lucille's mother) sisters.
- Sadie (Sis or Sarah), referred to above, was one of the elderly aunts referred to in Mitchell biographies that Margaret and her brother Stephens used to visit. She is also Annie's sister.
- Maybelle Mitchell (Margaret's mother) was a first cousin to Lucille Stephens Kennon and they were raised together for much of the time.
- Marie Nygren is the 4th generation down from Philip & Eleanor (Ellen) Fitzgerald, the great-great grandparents who lived during the battle of Jonesboro and the Civil War.

Chapter Four
Rhett and Scarlett – Star-crossed Lovers

As Margaret Mitchell recuperated from her ankle injury and started writing her book, she may have recalled a story about an Irish girl and a man named Rhett from South Carolina that has been retold in print in recent years. She had enough people in her own life to base characters on, but if this story had any connection to *Gone With the Wind* it may be because it was based on star-crossed lovers.

In the novel, Rhett Butler and Scarlett O'Hara were as star-crossed as Romeo and Juliet. Rhett was confident, forceful, and thought he could get everything he wanted; and when he could not get Scarlett he wanted her even more. At first it is the fun of the chase but later he grows to love her, even deeply. Scarlett is immature and thinks only of Ashley. She does not understand that she is more in love with the idea of loving Ashley than with the person he had grown to become.

Scarlett develops a deep friendship with Rhett Butler that eventually turns into love, but her childish game-playing prohibits her from realizing it. After Melanie's death, Scarlett finally understands that Ashley really did love Melanie, and not her. Suddenly she seems to realize the love she has for Rhett, but alas it is too late.

But what if Margaret Mitchell actually knew what happened to "Rhett Butler" after he left?

When Margaret Mitchell wrote the book she was young and naïve about the publishing world. The problems she was besieged with after producing such a successful book seemed to change her. It appeared that she got only limited support from her father, who has been quoted as saying he begrudgingly read the book once and would not read it again. He was there to help form the corporation needed to protect her legally, but there is nothing to show he supported her writing and encouraged her to write another book.

We will never know if she would have written another book about Scarlett and Rhett, because she was not afforded the luxury of living her life as she would have envisioned it. She was plagued with problems, illness, and then died before turning fifty. One thing we do know is the one book she did write—the classic that lives on some seventy-five years later ends when Rhett Butler leaves Scarlett O'Hara.

What if there was a strong handsome man from South Carolina who fell in love with an Irishman's daughter? And what if the fates would never allow them to fully love each other? That would be a star-crossed lovers idea and it might be a storyline to go with Mitchell's Civil War setting.

The determination of a young woman to rise above the devastation of the Civil War would have been interesting, but not as interesting without that 'star-crossed lover' element. There are some who say Mitchell wrote a love story with the backdrop .of the Civil War, while others say she wrote a story about the Civil War and threw in a love story.

An article in a newspaper and a chapter in a Christian book both claim her two protagonist characters came out of the love affair between a real person named Rhett (only his name was Rhett Turnipseed) and an Irish girl—who they name as Emelyn Louise Hannon.

Just as Margaret Mitchell may have based the character of Belle Watling on a real-life madam named Belle Brezing, using the same first name, she may have chosen the name Rhett because of this Rhett Turnipseed. If she did use the story as her first stop in the writing process, she did not use much of the story; and actually, if true, the part she left out was the most interesting—but it involved religion and that was something Margaret Mitchell admitted she did not have.

That Margaret Mitchell "stole" the story of *Gone With The Wind* was a claim made in the *Washington Times* on Sept. 25, 1991, by editor Wesley Pruden. He wrote it twice; the first time when the sequel *Scarlett* was due out in 1991, and most recently when the second "sequel," *Rhett Butler's People,* came out in 2007.

The two articles contained sarcasm, but nowhere in either of them did it say it was not true; so the reader assumed, coming from the editor-in-chief, that he had gotten it somewhere. Pruden retired in 2008 after fifteen years as the editor-in-chief of the *Washington Times* and continued on with political columns as editor-in-chief emeritus.

An entire chapter of the book, *A Dance With Deception; Revealing The Truth Behind The Headlines,* by Christian author Charles Colson, was devoted to this story; and when contacted through the Prison Fellowship Ministries, he said he got his information from the *Washington Times* article. Colson was the Nixon aide who served time in prison for a Watergate-related charge. He became a Christian and started Prison Fellowship Ministries donating royalties from the more than twenty books he has written for the ministry. His books are best-sellers and once that chapter on *Gone With The Wind* appeared in *A Dance With*

Deception, it became fodder for sermons by ministers all over the world.

The Rev. Melvin Tinker, Vicar of St John Newland Church in England, was one of the ministers who picked up the story and mentioned it in a sermon, in December, 2000. He agreed to have parts of his sermon reprinted here:

They say that truth is stranger than fiction. And that is often so. Take for example the case of the book "Scarlett," sequel to the book and film "Gone with the Wind" which is now a cinema classic. Immediately on its publication, the book sold 900,000 copies. What many people don't realize is that the original novel was based on real people and what happened to them is far more interesting than what happened to the fictional characters.

There was a Rhett Butler whose actual name was Rhett Turnipseed. And there was a Scarlett O'Hara, though her name was Emelyn Louise Hannon. Rhett did leave her to join the Confederate army, and it was what happened after the Civil War, which makes the story so interesting.

Rhett became a drifter and a gambler, eventually ending up in Nashville. And it was there on Easter morning, 1871, that Rhett attended a Methodist revival meeting. He was so moved by what he heard that he became a Christian. Soon after, he attended Bible college and became a Methodist minister. Once he had taken up pastoral charge of a church, he heard that one of his flock had run away and had become a prostitute in a house of ill repute in St Louis. And so off went the Reverend Rhett on his horse.

As the story goes, when Turnipseed gets to St. Louis, he is surprised to see that the woman who answers the door of the brothel is none other than his old love Emelyn Hannon. In her determination to do anything for money, she has become a madam. After they talk for a while, Rhett asks her to release the girl he's come to save. When the strong-willed woman says no, Rhett uses an old familiar tactic—card playing.

And so Rhett challenged the Madam to a game of cards on the understanding that if he won, the girl would walk free. Well, he did win, with a straight royal flush.

Had the story ended there, that would have been marvelous enough, but it doesn't. The young girl eventually married into a leading family in the state. And after her encounter with the new Rhett, Emelyn gave her life to Jesus Christ and eventually opened an orphanage for Cherokee Indian children. She died in 1903, a much loved and respected Christian woman.

What is the moral of that? It is this: God saves the no-hopers. A drifter and gambler. A woman living off the proceeds of prostitution. Those who society might well write off as life's inveterate losers, are the very ones God seeks out.

"I saw the article in Charles Colson's book, A *Dance With Deception*," said the Rev. Melvin Tinker from his church in England. "I took it to be true."

After Rev. Tinker's sermon that Sunday morning, his church posted it on their internet site as they do other sermons he preaches. One day he got a surprise.

"I received an e-mail from a descendent of Emelyn Hannon," he said. "She was interested in the fact that I knew the story. The email came in 2006. I wrote back to her. She said she had known the story before seeing my sermon, and even pointed out one or two things involving the exact accuracy of the story."

After Rev. Melvin Tinker communicated with the Hannon descendent, he lost contact with her.

"The person is out there somewhere," said Rev. Tinker, "and she knows the story."

Tinker did not save that e-mail. How could he have known that the topic would surface a year later? The article in the *Washington Times* said that Rhett Turnipseed became a circuit-riding minister in Kentucky. Margaret Mitchell's husband, John Marsh, grew up in Maysville, Kentucky, so it is even in the realm of possibility that his relatives could have actually come across him.

Through genealogy and the magic of the internet, a real live person named Rhett Turnipseed was found in 2007. As luck would have it, he lived within a half-hour of Clayton County where *Gone With The Wind* took place: right down the street from Philip Fitzgerald's grave in fact! A phone call was placed, a message left, and to the surprise of this author, a retired journalist called back and said he was Rhett Turnipseed. (For clarification we will call him Rhett IV and his great-grandfather, the man the story is about will be referred to as Rhett.)

When checked out, it was found that the current Rhett Turnipseed

(IV) is an award-winning journalist in Atlanta and Washington, D.C., enshrined in the Georgia Broadcaster's Hall of Fame. He spent years working for the Voice of America (VOA) in Washington, D.C. before returning to Georgia. He said he had heard the story and though he did not know it all, he did not discount it. He was interested in helping uncover the story.

During the time Margaret Mitchell spent her childhood summers in Jonesboro, there were Turnipseeds whose ancestors were Rhett Turnipseed's cousins. William and Mathew Turnipseed moved to Clayton County in 1860 and according to the census, Mathew Turnipseed owned six slaves. Their descendents were there in the early 1900s.

The original Rhett Turnipseed was born in Richland County, South Carolina, in 1851, to Julius and Martha Dubard Turnipseed. Rhett's given name was Barnwell Rhett Turnipseed, but he as well as the three generations that came after him went by the name of Rhett. Rhett Butler was also from South Carolina: Charleston.

Rhett Turnipseed and his brother lived with their grandparents, Adam and Katherine Dubard after his mother and sister died of Typhoid Fever and his father passed away when he was ten.

The Dubards raised cotton and Adam Dubard took the cotton to nearby Columbia to sell it. He worked hard and had little time to entertain grandchildren; consequently Rhett spent much time getting scolded by his grandparents, as they were very set in their ways. Grandmother Kate wanted order in the house and expected Rhett and Edward to spend quiet time reading and studying. They would use any excuse to escape the quiet house and ride their horses.

The year Rhett's father died, his cousin Sarah Dubard in Grenada, Mississippi, also died. The trip to visit the relatives in Grenada ended up being great fun for the Turnipseed boys as they got to be with their Dubard cousins and be introduced to a life they never knew existed.

Rhett relished the freedom that his Mississippi cousins experienced. They stayed for only a short while that time, but they would visit back and forth over the next few years.

During the Civil War, Rhett, who was a teenager, was always trying to get something going to make money.

"He was a sort of an entrepreneur, and a raconteur." said his great-grandson, Rhett IV. "He was full of stories."

If Turnipseed joined up with the Southern forces in the Civil War, it would have been late in the war, as he was a teenager. Back then there was no age restriction for enlistment, as now, with eighteen being the minimum age.

Education was important to Grandpa Adam Dubard who wanted the boys to follow in his footsteps of getting a college degree. He sent Rhett to Wofford College where one of his teachers, James H. Carlisle, went on to become the college president. During the school year he lived in a boarding house with seventeen other college students and his grandfather sent him money.

Rhett's life took another tragic turn while he was away at college, when he received word that his grandfather had been killed. According to a Turnipseed family letter, Adam was "robbed and murdered on the highway leading to what is known as Crane Creek Swamp. The robbers and murderers thought he had money on his person as he had just sold his cotton in Columbia. They did not know that he had sent the money to Rhett at Wofford College before starting home."

Rhett realized that if his grandfather had not sent him the money, maybe he could have given it to the robbers and the old man would still be alive.

After attending his grandfather's funeral and finishing up with school, he headed down to Grenada to visit his cousins in an attempt to outrun his pain. Grenada was an exciting town at that time. The Mississippi Central Railroad was completed in the 1860s making Grenada accessible by train. Grenada was a growing region; a railroad town and a commercial center for the area. It was a river-boat town on a river which connected to the Mississippi, making it an easy ride to New Orleans. There were card games, gambling on the steamboats, an abundance of alcohol and all of the other things that took place during this time. It was so unlike the structured life in the Dubard household in South Carolina.

The Dubard cousins (including William and his wife, Nancy Nipper Dubard—whose brother and sister lived in Clayton County, GA) would have introduced him to the "excitement" of the river, including poker (also enjoyed by Rhett Butler) at which many people were trying to make money; some more successfully than others.

Nancy Nipper Dubard's siblings John Nipper and Barbara Nipper Turnipseed had moved from their hometown area of Richland County, South Carolina, and landed in Clayton County, Georgia, at the same time that Philip Fitzgerald lived there. Research also places Rhett Turnipseed himself living in Clayton County for a short time, but the date is unclear. The Nippers, Turnipseeds, and Dubards were a close family and visited each other and exchanged letters.

About this time, according to the story, Rhett would have met Emelyn Hannon. Though connections with Hannon's relatives have not been established, genealogical research finds an Emeline Hannon in Mississippi and an Emma Hannon in Alabama around that time.

The biggest problem in trying to locate a person through the old censuses is that the census takers misspelled names and wrote sloppily much of the time. Margaret Mitchell's own relatives had their names spelled several different ways, so the girl's name could have been anything from Emelyn Hanson to Evelyn Hammon. But everything seemed to fall into place with Turnipseed.

In both stories, "Rhett" was unable to win his lady's heart, so he took off. The articles say Turnipseed drifted through New Orleans and the "mean, hard places in the Reconstruction South."

As Margaret Mitchell may have heard it, the story ended with Rhett helping Emelyn when she asked for it. Alas, the realization set in with Rhett that she would never love him so he left her, unaware that she had realized too late that, indeed, she did love him.

That is where Rhett Turnipseed and Rhett Butler's lives separate. The story which was portrayed by the ministers all over the world contained the message that Rev. Tinker had said: *"God saves the no-hopers. A drifter and gambler. A woman living off the proceeds of prostitution. Those who society might well write off as life's inveterate losers, are the very ones God seeks out."*

It was well known among Mitchell biographers that Margaret Mitchell had shunned her family's religion. If the story did happen, it would be understandable why Mitchell ended her book with Rhett leaving—before he became a Christian.

After Mitchell died, John Marsh had a conversation with actress Ann Rutherford who played Carreen O'Hara in the movie. Marsh said Mitchell had written other things but that she would not have wanted them seen in the condition they were in. Marsh was showing her his collection of *Gone With The Wind* books in foreign editions and Rutherford asked him where the other books Margaret wrote were and he said, "I burned them!"

According to Rutherford, Marsh said, "I had boxes of stuff she had been working on but she hadn't polished it up. She didn't like to have anyone read her work until she had given it the final polish."

I said, "But in her case wouldn't it have been better to have put it in a safe storage for fifty or one hundred years? If it had been fifty years we could have had lots more Margaret Mitchell. Somebody else could have polished it pretty well. I was just horrified," (that he had burned all of her papers).

The article in Charles Colson's book, *A Dance With Deception*, talks of Rhett Turnipseed becoming a Christian on Easter Sunday 1871 and then taking Divinity classes. This is believable according to Nashville history, as divinity classes were being given and works were underway for a school where Methodist Ministers could be trained.

Bishop Holland McTyeire, who had connections to Rhett through his roots in Richland County, South Carolina, was in the process of starting a Methodist college in Nashville.

"Nashville was a hotbed for the Methodist Church at this time," said a Nashville Library research assistant.

Rhett's old college professor, James Carlisle, a friend of Bishop McTyeire's was working with the bishop in establishing the college for young ministers in Nashville.

Beth Boord, the Assistant Dean of Development and Alumni Relations of Vanderbilt Divinity School, was consulted regarding the story and she said, "Vanderbilt University came into being in 1873, so it is quite possible that he attended Vanderbilt to become a minister.... We did train ministers and we were affiliated with the Methodist Church at the beginning of our history. It would have taken two years of study to become a circuit rider minister."

Boord said they do not have records of attendees at that time.

Further supporting evidence of his church training comes from an obituary for Turnipseed in the *Christian Neighbor* that said "his influence in the Church in the town where he lived did much to strengthen the organization and to encourage its members."

Back in those days, the best way to spread the Gospel was by horseback. Rhett Turnipseed's son, Dr. B. Rhett Turnipseed II, who became a very well respected Methodist Minister, started out as a circuit rider.

Rhett Turnipseed soon met Matilda Turner, a highly moral woman from Grenada, Mississippi, and she offered him the love he was looking for.

They were married in 1873 in Grenada and Mathew and Barbara Turnipseed traveled from Clayton County, Georgia to celebrate the occasion. Rhett and Matilda had three children; a daughter and two sons. The sons both became Methodist Ministers, with his namesake Rhett Turnipseed (II) becoming very well respected in his field.

According to Rhett's great-grandson, the stern Matilda would not have approved of the plan to go to St. Louis to rescue the girl from the brothel; but he went anyway, leaving his family behind.

The article says he ran into Emelyn at the brothel in St. Louis. After that, Rhett returned to Mississippi and eventually packed his family up and headed back to South Carolina to resume the life his grandparents had helped him achieve by putting him through college, according to the census.

Rhett Turnipseed IV does not discount the story. "My cousins and I are now thinking about the fact that not much was ever said about great-grandfather Rhett. Maybe they thought his life was too much for their conservative tastes," he said.

Rhett had left his wife and children behind to come to the aid of another woman, and perhaps that was the reason his family did not talk about him. And maybe his tender feelings toward Emelyn who had become a prostitute caused Margaret Mitchell to have an empathetic madam in her book.

Mitchell could have gotten the story from her aunts who would have known Turnipseed's cousins. Or she may have gotten the story herself from William Turnipseed, who was born in 1850 in Richland County, South Carolina, and moved to Jonesboro. According to the census records he was still there in 1930, during the time Mitchell was working on *Gone With The Wind* and spending time researching in Clayton County. William was the nephew of William Dubard and Nancy Nipper Dubard.

"I had read that (my great-grandfather) Rhett did some post war wheeling and dealing that we don't see in his preacher's and teacher's Godly obits," said Turnipseed. "It is obvious that he traveled about a good bit in his young adult days. This career as described in his obituary does not go against the idea of going to rescue the maiden at the house of ill repute in St. Louis."

Rhett IV has a copy of the original obituary in the *Christian Neighbor Newspaper* that said about his great-grandfather: "In church work he was as true and unceasing as in the (work he did in the) school."

It also said, "What more can one be than an obedient child of God, and a tender, faithful friend?"

He would have demonstrated that faithfulness to an old friend in riding to St. Louis to retrieve that girl and also in taking the time to share his Christian faith with his long-lost love.

The original Rhett Turnipseed died in 1886.

"After he died, Matilda (my great-grandmother) really didn't talk about him," said Rhett IV. "I think the family became so staunch in their church that they did not want to be associated with him and recalling his wilder days."

Emelyn Louise Hannon supposedly ended up in an orphanage for Cherokee children in Talequah, Oklahoma. There actually was such a place, but unfortunately a fire destroyed many of the records of the Cherokee Nation, including the inhabitants of that orphanage. The graves in the small cemeteries in the Talequah area (some in the middle cow pastures), are hard to read.

Could Margaret Mitchell have gotten the idea for her star-crossed lovers from this Rhett and Emelyn?

Rhett IV had several connections to Margaret Mitchell, having grown up in Gainesville, Georgia, about a half an hour from Atlanta.

Located on the shores of Lake Lanier at the foothills of the Blue Ridge Mountains, Gainesville was a town Margaret Mitchell felt comfortable with. We've seen in her letters that she sought refuge there at least once in her life so she may have had friends there.

What a coincidence that Mitchell fled to the very same town where the grandson and great-grandson of Rhett Turnipseed were living. The story could have even come directly from the Turnipseed cousins in Clayton County or from someone Margaret knew in Gainesville.

In 1939 Rhett IV's mother Leone went to the Premiere for *Gone With The Wind.*

"My mother and her sister and some friends were outside the Loew's Grand Theater, watching all the festivities," said Turnipseed IV.

"Mom got a glimpse of Clark Gable and Vivien Leigh and others as they went by," he said. "It was a mob scene on Peachtree Street. My mom and her friends had heard it would be a grand experience with spotlights and all of the famous people. They weren't disappointed."

Wouldn't it be strange to think that Leone Turnipseed was actually at the premiere of a movie that was inspired by her husband's grandfather? The current Rhett Turnipseed ended up marrying a woman from Fayetteville, Georgia—quite a coincidence. Rhett and his wife Jane Turnipseed who is a teacher, were living in an area not far down the road from the land the Fitzgeralds walked on, and very close to the cemetery they are buried.

Looking at the genealogy of the Turnipseed family, we see another thing in common with *Gone With The Wind.* Back in the 1800s, the Turnipseeds, like the Wilkeses, married their cousins.

Chapter Five
Rhett Butler

Many have suggested that Margaret Mitchell's first husband, Berrien Upshaw, was the model for Rhett Butler. In his book, *The Irish Roots of Margaret Mitchell's Gone With The Wind,* David O'Connell, Ph.D., writes, "It is probable that Mitchell drew the inspiration for Rhett Butler from a number of experiences that she had had with her first husband, Berrien "Red" Kinnard Upshaw...."

O'Connell adds that Mitchell might have been afraid of a lawsuit from Upshaw and decided to change his appearance, making Rhett Butler look completely unlike Upshaw.

Although Berrien Upshaw has been seen as at least a partial model for Rhett Butler, several other names have been tossed around. Claims of research have been made public and may have good merit. Margaret Mitchell was really the only one who knew for sure, but it is fun to look at the possibilities.

Sir Godfrey Barnsley's name has been mentioned as an inspiration for Rhett Butler's character, but according to the historian who has extensively researched him it was actually his son-in-law who would have been an inspiration for Rhett Butler.

The story of Sir Godfrey Barnsley's life could well have provided some of the research information Mitchell used. Barnsley, one of the wealthiest antebellum plantation owners in the area, built the beautiful Barnsley Gardens which still exists today as a resort with a museum in Adairsville, Georgia.

"Margaret Mitchell went there to visit with an older woman [while she was researching her book]," said Terry Lynn Crane, widow of Fred Crane, who played Brent Tarleton in the movie. Fred and Terry Lynn also visited Barnsley Gardens and talked to its historian, Clent Coker.

The older woman Mitchell visited with was Addie Saylor, Barnsley's granddaughter; and she went there more than once, according to the historian in charge.

Coker, the Barnsley Historian and Founding Director of the museum at Barnsley Gardens, has done some interesting research which he included in his book, *Barnsley Gardens at Woodlands: The Illustrious Dream*.

"I've spent a lifetime researching the Barnsley project," said Coker.

According to him, Margaret Mitchell, known for reading every book she could get her hands on, read a book which piqued her curiosity.

"Augusta Evans Wilson, the author of the best-selling book *St. Elmo* which was first released in the 1860s used Barnsley Gardens as the setting," said Coker, whose family history is connected to Barnsley dating back to the Civil War.

Sir Godfrey Barnsley lived through the Civil War and suffered severe financial losses. His daughter Julia Baltzell and her second husband took over the property.

"Julia was a strong-willed woman and taught the women on the plantation how to survive," said Coker.

Addie Saylor, who died in 1942, was Julia's daughter [Barnsley's granddaughter]. According to Clent Coker, after Mitchell had read *St. Elmo*, she went to Barnsley Gardens several times.

St. Elmo was the *Gone With The Wind* of its time. It was a hugely successful book which sold a million copies within four months of its appearance and remained in print well into the twentieth century. It contained a strong woman in Southern society. Augusta Evans Wilson was the author of nine novels—all about Southern women.

"*St. Elmo* was so popular it was re-released several times," said Clent Coker. "Margaret Mitchell read it and wanted to see Barnsley Gardens, so she came and visited with Miss Addie Saylor and asked questions. Barnsley Gardens was a showcase of the South, one of the most flamboyant estates in the area."

Julia's husband has been compared to Rhett Butler, as he was a blockade runner during the War Between The States. Mitchell might have asked Addie Saylor about him.

Another person mentioned as a possible Rhett Butler model was the one-time Confederate Secretary of the Treasury, George Alfred Trenholm. Born in Charleston, South Carolina, he eventually became a blockade runner.

Dr. E. Lee Spence wrote about it in *Treasures of the Confederate Coast: The "Real Rhett Butler" and Other Revelations.* Spence, an internationally recognized shipwreck expert, found many similarities between Rhett Butler and Trenholm. At the end of the Civil War, Trenholm was a very rich man, and that was definitely something he had in common with Rhett Butler.

Cornelius Vanderbilt, Jr. mentioned another possible Rhett Butler model in his 1956 book, *Queen of the Golden Age: The Fabulous Grace Wilson Vanderbilt.* He talked about a Vanderbilt uncle, Richard T. Wilson, a blockade runner who ran cotton.

The Georgia-born Richard Thornton Wilson was raised on a farm and became successful in business. According to his obituary in the *New York Times*, Nov. 27, 1910, Wilson applied his business ability to the Confederacy when the war broke out. The article said that when it was over he came out $500,000 richer. After the war he moved his family to New York and one of his daughters became Mrs. Cornelius Vanderbilt. Margaret Mitchell would have had to research blockade runners and those who made a profit on the war to get her facts straight, so any of them may have served as models.

Even Margaret Mitchell's grandfather John Stephens could have provided a small part of Rhett Butler's character. The most famous line of the book and movie is spoken by Rhett Butler as he leaves Scarlett, his wife, behind. According to Mitchell's cousin, Lucille Kennon's scrapbook, she may have heard those words before. Parts of her description of Butler resemble Lucille's description of Margaret's grandfather, John Stephens.

Lucille described Mitchell's grandfather as *"a newly arrived dashing, black-eyed, gentleman"* and *"an intelligent, polished, traveled man of the world."* In Lucille's written history, she told of how, in a time of crisis, John Stephens and his brother had signed their property over to their wives with the understanding that when things got better they would give them back. His brother's wife signed the property back to his brother, but Annie refused. Annie Fitzgerald Stephens was so strong-willed and became so obsessed with money that her husband left her:

"He left home. Moved to the Markham house and lived there many years," wrote Lucille in her scrapbook. *[See family scrapbook- Chapter Three]*

So Annie Fitzgerald, who did not believe in divorce, watched her husband walk out the door. To avoid the scandal of a divorce, they just lived separately.

Did Annie beg him not to leave? Did she ask him where she should go and what she should do? (As Scarlett says to Rhett at the end of *Gone With The Wind*.) Did Margaret Mitchell's grandfather look at his wife and tell her, just before walking out into the fog, that he didn't 'give a damn'?

According to Lucille Stephens Kennon's scrapbook, "Before the 'great silence', she (Margaret Mitchell) told a group who asked if Rhett ever came back to Scarlett, 'Certainly' …'How do you know?' they asked. 'I ought to ... He was my own grandfather', she replied."

At first Clark Gable was conflicted about playing the role of Rhett Butler, but once he got to know more about him—after he finally read the book—he wrapped himself around the character.

"I would like to ask Miss Mitchell where she met a man like Rhett," said Gable during the premiere. "I'm just guessing, but to me he must have been the real thing, with very little fictional embroidery."

Rhett Butler was the exciting, handsome man who would appear wearing expensive tailored suits and bearing lavish gifts and then mysteriously disappear for days at a time. He came from a prominent family, was expelled from West Point, and provided the young Scarlett O'Hara with daring, almost dangerous excitement. Much of the above could be said about the man who would be Peggy Mitchell's first husband, Berrien "Red" Upshaw.

At one point in Peggy's young life, her love affairs seemed to be about as mixed up as "poor" Scarlett, as she once called her. There are those who saw some of her husband, John Marsh, in Rhett Butler. Where he says he wanted to spoil her and pet her, that was how Marsh was to Mitchell. He would do anything for her, just as Rhett would do anything for Scarlett. Rhett, after all, had loved Scarlett through two marriages. John only had one to wait through; he had served as Best Man at Margaret's first wedding.

Though she may have given a few of Marsh's admirable qualities to her fictional hero, it has been more widely written that Margaret Mitchell patterned much of the character of Rhett Butler after her first husband Berrien "Red" Upshaw.

Upshaw's life may have provided some attributes for Rhett Butler, but by no means did she pattern the entire character after him. The story of Berrien "Red" Upshaw offers some interesting insight into the whole mindset of the young Peggy Mitchell.

As a teenager, Peggy, like Scarlett O'Hara, was "boy crazy." She loved being the center of attention, surrounded by boys. In one of her most favorite and chronicled episodes of her young life, Berrien Upshaw was one of five suitors who courted her in her hospital room at the same time one day. It would not have been hard to have talked the nurses into letting them into Peggy's room, as she was a frequent visitor to St. Joseph's Hospital, and it was also the same hospital to which her cousin, Sister Melanie, was assigned. None of the boys knew the others would be there so it put Peggy in a situation— but a situation she enjoyed.

Peggy had been accident prone all her life and she spent many a night at St. Joseph's. Sister Melanie was an older woman when Peggy knew her, having been born in the mid- 1800s. In 1880—just a few years before Sister Melanie entered the convent—the nuns from Sisters of Mercy started St. Josephs, which was Atlanta's first hospital. At the time Margaret Mitchell went there it was located on Courtland Street, later the site of the Marriot Marquis Hotel. Sister Melanie was with the Sisters of Mercy and during that time they trained their nuns to be nurses.

Maybe this is why Melanie Wilkes worked so hard for the Confederate Hospital in *Gone With The Wind.* And in the Hollywood movie, David O. Selznick had her wear the head covering that looked like a nun's habit.

St. Josephs has since moved to the suburbs and has grown into a large hospital, but at the time Peggy Marsh was going there it was a small, private hospital. With all the moves and the privacy laws, there is no way to retrieve any medical records for her during these many illnesses, so we must rely on what has been handed down.

By 1919 Peggy's mother had died and she lived with her father, brother Stephens, whom she called Steve, and her Grandmother Annie Fitzgerald Stephens. None of them came to visit her on this trip to the hospital—only the five boyfriends.

One of the suitors, Winston Withers, told her they were "fellow sufferers" united in a common goal. In a letter to her friend Allen Edee she said she "loved 'em all" and that they had all kissed her goodnight, but that she had no intentions of matrimony with any of them.

Peggy Mitchell in her hospital bed surrounded by five boys was like Scarlett O'Hara sitting on the rosewood ottoman, under the oak tree, eating "bah-be-cue" at the Wilkes plantation. She had a group of would-be suitors surrounding her. There she sat with her wide brimmed hat and the green-sprigged dress looking coyly up at the boys. It had actually happened in real life to Peggy in that hospital room—without the barbecue.

In both cases, the young girl, enjoying the effect she had on men, had no intention of marrying any of them, but shortly afterward, Scarlett O'Hara married Charles Hamilton, one of the suitors at the barbecue. Peggy Mitchell eventually married Red Upshaw. Both marriages were short lived; one due to death, the other to divorce.

The real life scene did not include John Marsh, another man who was also courting her; and the fictional scene did not include Ashley Wilkes, the man with whom Scarlett O'Hara was in love.

During her dating days when Peggy Mitchell kept several young men on a string—just as Scarlett O'Hara did—none of them seemed to care. They were one big happy fan club, each boy simply waiting for the time he could be alone with her. This was much like Scarlett who flirted with both the Tarleton Twins as well as the other boys of the County.

Red Upshaw received a lot of her attention for a while, and, in what observers looked upon as odd, he ended up becoming roommates with Marsh at the same time they were dating. According to letters, they would both date her the same night, one dropping her off to the waiting arms of the other.

Just as Rhett Butler had a dangerous air, Upshaw came off with an exciting edginess which was what Peggy was after in those days. Peggy thought she loved Red while John looked on; very much like Scarlett thought she loved Ashley while Rhett waited.

Those who knew them thought everything about their relationship was strange, including the fact that they chose John Marsh to be the best man at their wedding. (Ashley Wilkes stood up with Charles Hamilton as he married Scarlett, too.)

Everyone knew something was wrong, including the groom's parents.

"During the ceremony, mother took one look at John Marsh and knew he was in love with Peggy," said Nancy Egerton, Upshaw's half-sister.

Why did Berrien Upshaw seem to have such a hold on Margaret Mitchell?

Berrien "Red" Upshaw was born in Monroe, Georgia, in 1900, the year after his father William had graduated from the University of Georgia in Athens. His mother's name was Annie. William was a successful businessman working for Aetna Insurance and was Superintendent of the Sunday School at their church.

Annie had her hands full with their three boys, Berrien, Edward, and James; and in 1912 the family moved to the East Lake area of Atlanta where William took up the game of golf, playing at East Lake Country Club. They attended church together and William was moving up the ladder in the insurance business.

In 1917, when Berrien was sixteen, he met a girl named Courtenay Ross, and began dating her, according to author Darden Asbury Pyron in his book *Southern Daughter*. He went to several parties at her house and got to know her friends, including her best friend, a girl named Margaret Mitchell. These were carefree days for Berrien Upshaw, and he was a happy-go-lucky teenager, but those days were soon to end.

Aetna offered his dad a promotion with a sizeable raise if he would move to Raleigh, North Carolina. The parents were overjoyed; Berrien was crushed, having to move when he was in high school.

Not long after the family arrived in Raleigh, Berrien's brother Edward was hit by a delivery truck. It was a terrible thing for the family to witness. He was rushed to the hospital and eventually had to be institutionalized for the rest of his life.

The Upshaws tried to live as normal a life as they could even though Berrien seemed unhappy and would take frequent trips back to Georgia to see his friends. His dad, William joined the Carolina Country Club for golf and he tried to get the boy interested, but he had more interest in going to parties than playing golf with his father.

Later that year the influenza epidemic of 1918 hit Raleigh, and Annie Upshaw died in childbirth at the young age of forty. This was a turning point in Berrien's life as all normalcy which had existed before was gone. His mother was dead, his brother Ed was in an institution in New Jersey at the time, and Berrien was graduating from high school. It was too many things happening too fast for young Berrien.

His mind was always racing and he couldn't sleep at night. It was time to figure out what he was going to do with his life. Though his father had tried to have a close relationship with his son, Berrien would not let him in. He grew further and further apart from his father, basically just asking him for money or help when he needed it. He started getting into trouble and developed a terrible relationship with those back in North Carolina.

Friends introduced William to a pretty young woman named Myrtle Miller who was the principal of Murphy Elementary School in Raleigh. They were engaged later that year. Berrien would have nothing of his new stepmother and the new situation taking place at home. He began showing signs that he could not adjust to change.

He signed up for the fall classes at the University of Georgia, Athens, not far from Atlanta. At that stage in his life, the tall, lean, red-headed boy was considered handsome. He was scared to death about all the new happenings in his life but didn't want the outside world to know. He put on the airs of a person who had it all. He strutted around on campus, appearing exciting as he carried himself with the confidence that commanded attention. Since Courtenay Ross liked him, he was admitted into Atlanta's elite teenage social circles.

After two semesters of school at the University of Georgia, Berrien grew restless and told his father he wanted to transfer to the U.S. Naval Academy at Annapolis, Maryland. His father helped him with his application process and in June, 1919, he entered the Naval Academy.

The Upshaws were very well connected. They knew a lot of people and once lived next door to the governor's mansion. Years later William Upshaw's friendship with Senator Josiah Bailey helped him secure a Naval

Academy appointment for another son, Bill, who made a successful career out of the Navy.

This part goes along with Rhett Butler's history of being from one of the finest families in his hometown.

William and Myrtle married on August 30, 1919, and they eventually added three more children to the family (who would be Berrien's half-siblings).

"After Mr. Upshaw married Myrtle they had Mary Bryan," said Alice Hardy a neighbor in Raleigh who eventually bought the Upshaws' house after they moved out. "Then they had Nancy, who married Courtney Egerton, a wonderful and well respected ObGyn; and William (Bill) who graduated from the U.S. Naval academy in Annapolis, Maryland."

Meanwhile, the same year all of this turmoil was happening to Berrien, his friend Peggy Mitchell was in Massachusetts for her freshman year at Smith College. When her mother died also from the influenza epidemic, she ended up coming home at the end of the school year. Red and Peggy reconnected in the summer of 1919 shortly after she got home.

In January of 1920 Berrien left Annapolis and then that fall he re-enrolled at the University of Georgia. Eager to get back into the party scene, Berrien joined the Sigma Nu Fraternity.

"Mr. Upshaw was member #376 at the Chapter," said Michael Barry of Sigma Nu, University of Georgia. "It appears that he had other relatives who were also Sigma Nus, William Francis Upshaw (his father), and James Claud Upshaw (an uncle). We have no other details about Brother Upshaw."

For entertainment on the weekends, Berrien hit the social scenes of Atlanta. It was about then that he began being known by the nickname 'Red' because of his red hair.

"We never called him Red," said his half-sister Nancy Egerton. "No one in his family called him that. It was just something he picked up later. We always called him Berrien."

Courtenay Ross had broken up with Berrien long ago, and when Peggy ran into him, they became attracted to each other. It was very important to her father Eugene Mitchell, a prominent lawyer in Atlanta, that his debutante daughter associate with top quality people. Perhaps it is for that reason that the legend of "Red" Upshaw began.

In a letter to a college friend, Margaret Mitchell described him as 'an ex-Annapolis, ex-University of Georgia football player'.

It was quite a feat to be linked to the Georgia Football team in the early 1920s. In 1920 the team was very good, receiving a great deal of recognition. They had gone 8-1 and were the Southern Conference Champions.

"He never played football that I was aware of," said Nancy Egerton, his half-sister, who is a big sports fan.

It is unclear if Margaret Mitchell described Berrien Upshaw in that manner to boost his credentials or if he misrepresented himself to her.

"He's not listed as a letterman," said Charles Whittemore, the Assistant Athletic Director for the University of Georgia after he checked the records and did not find Upshaw's name anywhere.

"He didn't have an athletic bone in his body, and he wasn't at Annapolis during football season," said Nancy Egerton. "He was very smart. In fact he had a brilliant mind, but he used it in a different way. He never graduated from the University of Georgia, and he was kicked out of Annapolis."

The whole affair with Upshaw was clouded in secrecy as far as the Mitchell family was concerned. When the publicity for *Gone With The Wind* first came out, Peggy's cousin Lucille would later say the family tried to hide the fact that she had been married and divorced before her marriage to John Marsh. This type of publicity would not be good for Mitchell, but once her friend Ginny Morris brought it up in a magazine article, writers and biographers began writing about it. Cousin Lucille also said that Eugene Mitchell did not like Upshaw and eventually saw to it that he was removed from the situation, and took care of getting the divorce.

During the time she was dating Upshaw she had a set of friends her father and Grandmother Stephens did not approve of, similar to Scarlett O'Hara and her 'carpetbagger' friends. In the book Scarlett was told in no uncertain terms by her family and immediate friends that she was behaving in a manner they did not approve of, but that did not make her stop. It made her more determined to live her life on her own terms— like Upshaw did.

Both were fighting for their independence. Their relationship together could have been summed up by Rhett's declaration to Scarlett in the movie: "We're alike. Bad lots, both of us. Selfish and shrewd. But able to look things in the eyes as we call them by their right names."

Peggy Mitchell did not care what her family thought of her new friends. They were fun and she enjoyed being with them whether they were drinking at the Piedmont Driving Club or in her own living room putting on the plays she would write.

Rhett Butler liked Scarlett O'Hara because he saw a little bit of himself in her. The same could definitely be said about what drew Red Upshaw to Peggy Mitchell.

The fictional Rhett Butler had gone to West Point but on page 910 of *Gone With The Wind* it says he didn't graduate.

Peggy had not stayed at Smith College to graduate, either. She was torn between wanting to continue her education and what she was doing at the time. Upshaw was just as ambivalent about his education.

During the day, when the others her age were attending college classes, Peggy Mitchell was directing the family servants as to what groceries to buy, what menus to serve, when and how to scrub the floors, whatever was required to run a successful household for a family of the Mitchells' social prominence in the early 1920s.

She did what was expected of her during the day, but most evenings she would cut loose and go out with her friends or invite them over. With no mother to buffer the yelling and negative disapproval of her father and Grandmother Stephens, and a brother who just stayed out of the way, Peggy Mitchell seemed to completely disregard their wishes.

Eugene Mitchell went round and round with his daughter—not unlike many other parents of teenagers do.

She and Red dated quite a bit although not exclusively. It may have been exclusive for Red, who found her to be a kindred soul and a lighthouse he could cling to during a foggy period in his life, although he did not like the general public to know it. He took what he could get from her and tried to impress her with his fancy car so he could stand out in the crowd.

After being at the University of Georgia, Berrien grew restless again.

With some help from his father, he was readmitted to the U.S. Naval Academy. On his way to Naval summer camp, he stopped through Atlanta and gave Margaret his fraternity pin, but she continued dating other boys while he was gone.

During the time she was "pinned" to Upshaw, she went on an overnight camping trip to Lake Burton with a young doctor, along with several other couples and a youthful chaperone. She met Augusta Dearborn on this trip, who became a close friend. At this time, Augusta lived in Birmingham but was in Atlanta for a while visiting her married sister.

Lake Burton is a beautiful area in the mountains with sixty-two miles of shoreline, some of it used for camping, picnicking, swimming, and fishing. It was just a short trip from Atlanta. Margaret was happy to be able to get out of town and out from the watchful eyes of her father and her brother Stephens. She was growing increasingly restless, bored, and depressed with her situation of being at home.

Peggy loved being in the mountains and being active and generally just feeling free.

The same doctor she was with on the trip also invited Margaret to a costume ball being given at the East Lake Country Club. East Lake was the area where Berrien Upshaw had lived with his family before they moved to North Carolina. He came back from the Naval summer camp and was invited to the same party.

East Lake was a very prestigious country club run by the father of the famous golfer, Bobby Jones. Jones was actively golfing during that time and the year before he had made it to the final round of the U.S. Amateur Open. The prestige of the club did not end there. The athletic program was run by John Heisman, the Georgia Tech football coach for whom the Heisman Trophy was named; and one of the swimming teachers was Johnny Weissmuller the five-time Olympic Gold medalist swimmer who later starred as Tarzan in the movies.

The high society patronized the East Lake Country Club. In fact, it is said that Zelda Fitzgerald, the wife of F. Scott Fitzgerald, once jumped into the pool fully clothed.

Since it was a costume party, Peggy came as an antebellum girl. She ran into Berrien Upshaw, who thought she looked very cute with her curly wig. He asked her to dance.

Just as the recently widowed Scarlett O'Hara caused a stir by dancing with Rhett Butler when she was supposed to be in mourning, the fun-loving Peggy Mitchell left her date to dance with Upshaw, and soon she dumped the good doctor and left the party with Upshaw.

Though he was crazy about her, Berrien did not seem to get jealous of Peggy if she had other boyfriends. He always made himself available to her, just as Rhett Butler was there for Scarlett. With Peggy Mitchell it seemed the other boys accepted that they were going to have competition if they were going to date her.

Red Upshaw intrigued Peggy. He liked to do the things she liked at that time in her life, including riding horses, hiking, and going to the clubs. In order to fit in with the group he had met with Courtenay and Peggy—all girls from wealthy homes—he needed more income than his father was sending him. This is when he started bootlegging.

Berrien enrolled at the University of Georgia again and when Augusta Dearborn invited Peggy to a weekend at her sister's cottage on St. Simon's Island, he was again included in the group. Though he was exciting and a bit dangerous—in a good way to Peggy—her friends and family were apprehensive about him. The biggest thing they had in common was they were rebels out for themselves, out for a good time. They had both lost their mothers and lived their lives in the fast lane.

In *Gone With The Wind (page 189),* Rhett Butler called Scarlett a little rebel. That was part of the attraction. Peggy knew the kind of boys her father wanted her to be dating and she knew Upshaw was not that kind of boy.

On page 99, Scarlett O'Hara spots a handsome stranger at the bottom of the stairs and asks her friend Cathleen Calvert who he is. The friend informs her that his name is Rhett Butler and that he has a bad reputation; a *terrible* reputation. Miss Calvert also informs Scarlett that he is from Charleston and that although his parents are regarded as a great family he seems to be persona non grata back home. Scarlett also learns that Butler was kicked out of West Point.

The same could have been said about Upshaw, substituting Raleigh for Charleston and the Naval Academy for West Point.

In 1921, both John Marsh and Berrien Upshaw were in love with Peggy Mitchell. John Marsh was affected by every move she made even when she was not dating him exclusively.

It was the spring of 1922 and Prohibition was in place. Berrien Upshaw, with his hot rod car, had worked his way into the debutante crowd and he and Peggy both joined a social drinking club called the Peachtree Yacht Club. It had nothing to do with yachts, but was a place where Peggy and her friends could comfortably drink, smoke and impress each other by telling off-color jokes and stories. Harkening back to her youth when she rode horseback with the foul-mouthed story-telling old Confederate soldiers, she could hold her own and was the center of attention when telling stories. She'd learned from the best and now she was the best. Peggy was skilled at entertaining her friends. She was a lively girl and always the center of the party. Almost anyone who knew her spoke of how she brightened up any room. She was fun, loud, and bold, and even her looks stood out as she wore bright red lipstick on her creamy white face.

Berrien Upshaw has been portrayed as unstable and violent, however, he apparently did not display these qualities during the time he was dating Peggy; nor, at that time, did he display the possessiveness often found in a violent person.

"During the times he was with Margaret Mitchell he was a pleasant person," said Nancy Egerton. "My mother liked him then and she liked Margaret, whom she called 'Peggy', very much. He was a very charming person during that time period."

Berrien Upshaw was not motivated enough to sell insurance, the profession his father tried to get him interested in, and his income was questionable. He got more and more into bootlegging and that was how he afforded the flashy car he drove. Just as Rhett Butler provided supplies during the Civil War, Red Upshaw provided alcohol during Prohibition. Both men were secretive about their employment and disappeared for days, returning with money and gifts.

His sports car actually played a part in the bootlegging. Nearby Dawson County Georgia was a haven for bootlegging activity. Bootleggers would get the illegal alcohol and race it back to their destinations.

"We knew Berrien was a bootlegger," said Nancy Egerton. "There was a lot of whiskey produced in the mountains of Georgia, North Carolina, and South Carolina."

As late as spring of 1922 Marsh and Upshaw were both still dating Peggy. She was telling others she wanted nothing to do with marriage but it all came abruptly to an end when her engagement to Berrien Upshaw was announced in the newspapers at the end of that summer. Their wedding would be two months later in September. John Marsh was so upset about Margaret choosing Upshaw over him that he abruptly left Atlanta to take a job offered to him by a friend at the University of Alabama-Tuscaloosa, raising funds for the university. Even though he was devastated, he kept his disappointment to himself and if ever Peggy needed him he was right there for her. He seemed to change jobs with each move Peggy made. The number of jobs Marsh had in a short period of time rivaled the number of times Berrien Upshaw enrolled and quit school.

In a strange move, the couple asked Marsh to be in the wedding, which was September 2, 1922 and he came into town four days early to be the best man. John Marsh went above and beyond what a former boyfriend should do, writing the wedding announcement for the newspaper. Berrien had long ago turned from his family's Baptist religion and Margaret had dropped her family's Catholic religion. Since they had no church, they chose an Episcopal minister. The bride wore a low-waisted dress with pearl trim and carried a big spray of red roses.

"Mother and Daddy went to the wedding," said Nancy Egerton. "They brought my brother Bill with them. Peggy thought he was the cutest little thing you ever saw."

Bill was just a baby at the time and Peggy enjoyed holding her youngest in-law. Little children were cute and fun to Peggy, but she only liked them if she could hand them back to their parents. She had about as much interest in having children as Scarlett O'Hara did, though Scarlett had three.

Something must have upset her Grandmother Stephens at the wedding as she was said to have been crying so loudly that someone asked her to move to the back of the room. For some reason this was the last straw and she severed ties with Margaret after the wedding.

In the Southern culture of the day, the short engagement would raise questions. In Gone *With The Wind* (page 128), Margaret Mitchell, herself, mentioned short engagements when she noted Scarlett's two week engagement to Charles. She said that such a short engagement would have been impossible if it were not for the war, since a normal engagement would have been a "decorous interval of a year or at least six months."

She wore a low-waisted wedding dress rather than the traditional wedding gown gathered at the waist, however, the flappers of the time were wearing this type of dress.

An online genealogy chart done by a fourth cousin of Margaret Mitchell lists a child from the Upshaw-Mitchell marriage. However, it must be noted that people make mistakes on genealogy charts and the only real proof would be a birth certificate, and no such record was located.

According to biographies, Margaret spent much of the time during this new marriage in bed, apparently too depressed to get dressed.

Her former sister-in-law sets the record straight. She was not pregnant.

"Absolutely not," said Nancy Egerton. "I never heard anything about that. I think the reason for the short engagement had to do with Margaret losing her mother."

After one night in Atlanta, the couple spent their honeymoon in North Carolina, part of the time at the famed, luxurious Grove Park Inn in Asheville, North Carolina.

The Grove Park Inn looks much the same today as it did back then. The massive stone lobby boasts fireplaces at each end. New in the 1920s, it was receiving much attention among the rich and famous. There was also the rumor that it was haunted, which tantalized the adventurous Peggy.

Two years before Peggy and Berrien stayed there a young woman dressed in pink fell to her death at the hotel's Palm Court Atrium. She had stayed at the hotel, and there were unexplained accounts of severe cold and chills to people who entered that room, and pink smoke was seen, said to be her spirit. The newlyweds did not stay in that room, but they went there to experience the thrill.

A visit to the Grove Park Inn today affords guests the opportunity to sit on the very same balcony that Margaret and Berrien sat on, overlooking the lovely green mountainous view. If asked about the Pink Lady that the Upshaws had heard about, the waiters offer assurance that on occasion a woman in a pink ball gown is seen even today. The hotel has enjoyed a long and colorful history with many distinguished guests, including Eleanor Roosevelt, Henry Ford, John D. Rockefeller, F. Scott Fitzgerald, and President Woodrow Wilson.

It was a grand honeymoon like Scarlett and Rhett's had been. After eating the best foods and drinking the best drinks, they visited briefly with the Upshaw parents in Raleigh. According to Darden Asbury Pyron in *Southern Daughter*, the couple vacationed for a month. Shortly after returning from their honeymoon, the relationship between Margaret and Berrien went sour. Part of that reason might have been that Upshaw started his married life living with his in-laws. At Eugene Mitchell's urging, the couple lived with him in his Peachtree Street residence. So basically Peggy and her husband moved into her childhood bedroom—with her father and brother down the hall.

Eugene Mitchell thought his daughter had made a poor choice in husbands. The living arrangements had disastrous consequences as there was so much tension in the house that at one point Eugene went to bed and stayed there for days. Besides their love of parties and drinking, Berrien and Margaret shared something else in common: they each suffered periods of mental instability and depression. Margaret mentioned it in letters to friends. Were her many illnesses, injuries, and subsequent stays in bed due to her depression or was her depression due to the many illnesses and injuries she sustained? Much of the fabric of her life was sewn together with these problems.

And if Berrien Upshaw lived in current times, he might have been treated for a mental condition such as depression or borderline personality disorder. Both of them displayed symptoms that could be attributed to bipolar disease or manic depressive condition, which was not identified as such in the 1920's.

Often those experiencing the pain of mental illness will self-medicate with alcohol and it seemed Upshaw did that. He never held down a job or stayed in one place for very long. With his bootlegging he would be gone for several days at a time.

Alcohol played a big part in several story lines in *Gone With The Wind*. The cover-up with Ashley coming home after supposedly being with Belle Watling, but really being out with the KKK, involved alcohol. Rhett Butler and Ashley faked drunkenness. Scarlett O'Hara drank several times by herself even though it was highly looked down on for a lady to do that in those days. Rhett Butler was drunk the night he took Scarlett up the long steps to his room.

There were violent outbursts between Margaret, Berrien and her father Eugene, with the servants and her brother Stephens looking on. It is curious how they had changed from the fun-loving duo who just could not wait to get married, to completely falling apart as a couple and not being able to last three months in the same house together. The Mitchell family pinned it on Upshaw's drinking and instability.

This episode in Margaret Mitchell's life mirrors one in her book. Once Scarlett O'Hara finally married Rhett Butler they enjoyed a fun honeymoon in New Orleans, but after returning home their marriage went completely downhill.

In real life, after only a month of marriage, Peggy Mitchell Upshaw contacted John Marsh who had been working out of town. He took two vacation days and headed back to Atlanta. Peggy said that despite being married less than a month, she wanted out. John told her that after his temporary job was over, which would be soon, he would come back to Atlanta.

By November of that year, Berrien would leave the house and be gone for two or three days and then return and refuse to say where he had been.

"This is how he was at home," said his half-sister, Nancy Egerton. "He might leave for five days and not tell anyone where he went. He was very erratic. Once he came home and took our father's car and never brought it back. You could say he stole his own dad's car, but Daddy never did say anything about it."

There was much tension in the Mitchell house and very few meals were eaten together as a family. He tried to keep his bootlegging activities a secret, and the days away from home were probably trips to the mountains to get more merchandise. It was shortly before Thanksgiving (November, 1922) and things got so bad between them all that Upshaw left the house for good— at least for awhile.

In an odd twist, Peggy asked John Marsh to intervene between her and Berrien; to help save their marriage. He came to town and talked to Upshaw, but it did not help. Berrien and Peggy talked but could not reconcile.

John Marsh was overjoyed when she told him. It was not long after Upshaw left, in December, 1922, that Peggy started her job at the *Atlanta Journal* newspaper. Marsh moved back to Atlanta and got a job at the newspaper, offering editing help to Peggy. There are different stories as to whether Upshaw came back to the Mitchell house in the winter and spring of 1923, but if he did it would have only been sporadically because he was still bootlegging which took him out of town for long periods of time.

Margaret saw him again, though. There was an incident in 1923 that was so upsetting to both John Marsh and Eugene Mitchell that they both became ill from the stress.

In her divorce decree she alleged that Berrien became unstable and could not control his temper and he harmed her. John Marsh had been trying to help Margaret out of her marriage to Upshaw, but her ambiguity and uncertainty regarding Upshaw upset him so much that he moved out of town again and this time took a job with the AP (Associated Press) in Washington, D.C.

In July of that year Margaret finally decided to end the marriage. Supposedly Berrien came to her house, and when she saw him she invited him in. He had been drinking. No one knows for sure what happened, but according to the divorce papers he "demanded his connubial rights and then beat her."

On page 940 of *Gone With The Wind,* a frustrated and drunk Rhett

Butler also demanded his connubial "rights," though the author used different terms, as he carried Scarlett O'Hara up the stairs. Though Scarlett had mixed emotions the next morning, it was essentially their last night together as man and wife, just as it was for Margaret and Berrien.

Their divorce was final in June of 1924; and with that happy news, John Marsh moved back to Atlanta. That was not the end of Upshaw and his connection to Margaret Mitchell, though. He left town and five years later married a woman who was pregnant with his child. Just like his marriage to Margaret Mitchell, this marriage did not last more than a few months. Berrien left before the baby was born, and went to North Carolina.

His involvement with Margaret Mitchell should have ended with their divorce, but he seemed to obsess about her at times and he was never really able to leave her behind.

Berrien's appearance had begun to deteriorate and most who knew him knew he was looking sickly. He had long been drinking heavily and was beginning to show signs of alcoholism. Soon he began coughing and developed tuberculosis and in 1930 he was in the North Carolina State Hospital (now Dorothea Dix Hospital) listed as an "inmate," according to the census. It was a mental hospital and it also had a section for alcoholics.

"Daddy fought hard to get him into the Dix Hospital," said his half-sister Nancy Egerton. "He was in there for the tuberculosis, but also for something to do with his mind. His mind was not right.

"Daddy said that for all of Berrien's faults, he had one good quality, and that was that he could always pick good wives. Both wives were always on good terms with Mother and Daddy."

As Margaret Mitchell was finishing up her novel, Berrien Upshaw was keeping tabs on her, just as she was keeping in touch with his family. Margaret had a way of continuing relationships with former boyfriends. She sent flowers to the parents of her former boyfriend, Clifford Henry (killed in World War I) every year until she died.

According to *Gone With The Wind* expert and collector Herb Bridges, "Miss Mitchell kept in touch with his (Clifford Henry's) parents. They would come to town to visit on their way to Florida. She gave them a set of Wedgewood demitasse cups one year on a visit to Atlanta."

There were reports of an unannounced visit and some phone calls from Berrien. One of these reportedly caused Margaret to flee to Gainesville.

On June 3, 1936, *Gone With The Wind* hit the bookstores for the first time.

"I'll never forget it," said Nancy Egerton. "Daddy came home and said, 'Peggy wrote a book and it's getting published!' He told us it was in some of the bookstores downtown, but he was excited because it was going to be in the 'Book of the Month Club'. We waited until it came out as the 'Book of the Month' and that is the copy I still have on my bookshelf. We have kicked ourselves several times because we could have had a 'first edition' copy, but instead we have the 'Book of the Month Club' version."

In July of 1936, a month after the book came out, Margaret Mitchell wrote Berrien's dad (William Upshaw) a friendly letter asking about news of Upshaw and how he was doing

"Our father let her know what he was doing, or where he was. Margaret kept in touch with my mother (after their father's death)," said Nancy Egerton. "She always wanted to know how Berrien was."

With the exciting news of their former daughter-in-law's successful book coming out, the Upshaw family was happy for Peggy and they let her know it. Margaret corresponded with Berrien's father regarding the book and he wrote back friendly letters which Nancy Egerton donated to the Margaret Mitchell collection in Atlanta.

Berrien Upshaw was not so happy with her success. In fact he was stunned when he found out that his former wife had written the highly successful and popular book *Gone With The Wind*. He read the book as soon as he heard she had written it, and he, along with the rest of the country, saw the movie. There was nowhere he could go that he did not see the book on display, see someone reading it, or hear about its success. Upshaw heard the line that Charles Hamilton delivered to Rhett Butler after having listened to him downplay the South's chances of winning the war.

Charles ridiculed Rhett Butler about being kicked out of West Point and not being accepted by any decent family in Charleston, including his own.

It must have stung him, as he had been kicked out of The Naval Academy at Annapolis and had not seen his family back in Raleigh in years. Upshaw contacted Margaret Mitchell and asked her if she patterned the strong, handsome character, Rhett Butler, after him.

Margaret was combative with Upshaw on the phone call and he was so upset with her that he sought revenge. He decided he would write a book about Margaret Mitchell, with his version of their life together.

With no writing experience and no clue as to how to do it, the book idea fell apart before it even got started, so he decided a magazine article would be the best route. He contacted *Collier's Magazine* to get his side of the story out there.

"He wanted to write what his life was like with Margaret Mitchell, slamming her," said Nancy Egerton. "He wrote something and turned it into *Colliers Magazine*."

Collier's was a very popular magazine at the time; a rival to the *Saturday Evening Post* in the 1930s. Upshaw contacted William Ludlow Chenery, the editor at the time.

Berrien chose *Collier's* to air his "dirty laundry." He figured they would be interested since Margaret Mitchell had become such a famous author and they printed fiction by popular authors such as Sinclair Lewis, Willa Cather, and Zane Grey.

When William Upshaw found out what his son had done, he was horrified. He immediately contacted the editors at *Collier's* to try and stop it. He talked to an editor who said the manuscript was an unreadable mess, and they decided they were not going to use it. The whole affair infuriated the younger Upshaw.

"Berrien was just an unstable person," said Nancy Egerton. "My parents felt bad that he tried to do that to her. Anyone would feel bad if their son did that to someone."

Everywhere Upshaw turned he saw more publicity about *Gone With The Wind* and its author Margaret Mitchell. She won the Pulitzer Prize and more awards after that, and each time she got nationwide publicity. Berrien could not escape it and stewed about the never-ending success of his former wife. He never quite got her out of his mind, and that is what may have caused Margaret to fear him as has been reported. Based on the friendly letters she exchanged with his parents the whole time, her former sister-in-law does not believe Margaret was afraid of Berrien.

Perhaps it was wishful thinking on his part that Peggy would have patterned Rhett Butler after him. For her part, why would a woman want to glorify an ex-husband, one she had no regard for, in such a worthy manner as a lead character in her book? In any event, in some twisted way it seemed at times that once Berrien Upshaw saw Rhett Butler as himself, he tried to "become" Rhett Butler.

Just as Rhett had gotten to the Civil War late, "Red" was late getting involved with World War II. Just as Rhett Butler's work involved blockade running on ships to get supplies, Upshaw sought a similar career on a boat.

In the spring of 1939, he saw that Margaret Mitchell had paid homage to the Navy by sponsoring the Navy cruiser, "Atlanta." Besides the money she donated she was involved in the ceremonious commission of the ship and presented gifts to the officers. She also visited with the sailors and talked to each one individually and this of course was covered by the press.

That December the movie *Gone With The Wind* came out, making headlines all over the world. Upshaw signed up for the Merchant Marines, and they accepted him

In November of 1942 the Japanese sank the "Atlanta" at Guadalcanal and Margaret led the fundraising to replace the ship. Once again Upshaw saw national headlines involving Peggy. A second 'Atlanta' was launched at the end of 1944. Again Berrien Upshaw saw his ex-wife receiving even more accolades from the Navy, a group he had tried and failed to become a part of.

A year and a half later, when his father died, he was off trying to establish his seaman's career and did not go home.

"He didn't come to the funeral and never came back to Raleigh for the remainder of his life," said Nancy Egerton.

Perhaps Upshaw was mirroring Rhett Butler's feelings one last time. In *Gone With The Wind* (page 766), Butler talks to Scarlett about his father's death, saying he was not sorry his father had died. He went on to talk about how the Butler father and son did not get along, basically blaming the disappointment the son had caused the father.

Nancy Egerton said that the Upshaws were a happy, productive family. "My parents were always nice to him. Our father was always there for him."

But Berrien never lived up to the potential his father had originally seen in him. Though the father would never have said it, Berrien must have been a disappointment to him; and in his heart Berrien knew it. Rhett Butler knew his father disapproved of him and said so. (p. 177.)

Rhett Butler's father had had respectable plans for his son, but the hard-headed Rhett had not followed through. And, frankly, it was an embarrassment to their old Charleston family when he became a blockade runner.

Was it a coincidence that after reading about Rhett Butler, who was a sea captain, running supplies during the Civil War, Berrien Upshaw joined the Merchant Marines? In January of 1946 he was listed on an "Overseas Manifesto" at the Port of San Francisco.

Did Berrien (knowingly or unknowingly) assume the "identity" of Rhett Butler whom he had accused Margaret Mitchell of patterning after him? In 1947, his name appeared on a Manifest from Italy to the Port of New York on the SS Thomas Eakins.

In January, 1949, it was announced in the press that 8,000,000 copies of *Gone With The Wind* by Margaret Mitchell had been sold in thirty languages in forty countries, and that 50,000 copies were still being sold yearly in the United States. A week later Upshaw was dead, an inquest ruling it was suicide. Berrien Upshaw had gone into the Salvation Army in Galveston, Texas and asked for a meal and a bed. The next night he committed suicide by jumping out of the window of the Alvin Hotel in Galveston. No one noticed him and no one missed him. A passerby came upon him at 6:30 in the morning.

Seven months later, Margaret Mitchell was struck by a car. Upon her death, Governor Herman Talmadge ordered the flag over the State Capitol lowered to half-staff until the funeral.

It was in his death that Berrien Kinnard Upshaw finally received his own fame. His grave is on the tour of the Oakwood Cemetery in Raleigh, North Carolina.

"He was sort of a rogue character," said Sharon Freed of the Oakwood Cemetery. "He is not buried in the same plot with his family. His parents are in the 'A' section and he is in the 'Beechwood' section. His grave is on our cemetery tour."

Rhett Butler was a complex character and Mitchell probably took bits and pieces of many people she knew, as well as those she read about. It is possible she took some of her Grandfather John Stephens' looks, and Berrien Upshaw's good qualities as well as some of his bad qualities. She researched blockade running, and as she came upon the Barnsley, Trenholm, and Wilson stories she may have woven them into her character. With a character as complex as Rhett Butler, it's no wonder she would not give out any information as to how she crafted him. It was interesting that the person who studied the character the most—Clark Gable, who played Butler in the movie—thought that from the descriptions she gave and the actions of the character, Rhett Butler must have been patterned from someone she knew.

Chapter Six
Ashley Wilkes

Scarlett O'Hara said it over and over: "Oh Ashley, I love you. I love you…." She never said those words to her first two husbands, and only said them to her third in a desperate attempt when she was about to lose him. Ashley Wilkes was the epitome of the Southern Gentleman, handsome and honorable. His father owned Twelve Oaks, the scene of the lively barbecue which set the tone for the novel. The young, flirtatious Scarlett O'Hara was smitten with Ashley—but he had already arranged to marry his cousin Melanie.

The character of Ashley Wilkes was created by Margaret Mitchell and she may have used influences from people she knew, including Clifford

Henry, the young soldier she met in 1918, the summer before she left for college. Henry did have some of the qualities she gave to Ashley in that he was educated—just graduated from Harvard—and he enjoyed poetry and reading. Two months later, she left for Smith College and he was transferred overseas. It was the last time they would see each other. He was killed before she came home for Christmas break. He was special to her, but so were several others.

Unlike some women who like to flirt and have many boyfriends, Mitchell actually invested a great deal in her men. She developed deep friendships with them, writing long letters and sharing her thoughts and heart with them. In *Gone With The Wind*, Scarlett O'Hara shared everything with Ashley Wilkes. As Mitchell set out to develop Scarlett's character, she may have taken pieces from many of the men she had loved.

While she was at college, she met her friend Virginia "Ginny" Morris (with whom she had a falling out later in life after Ginny wrote an article about her) and a boyfriend, Allen Edee. Peggy and Allen dated during her brief time at Smith and then wrote letters back and forth for at least the next two years; those letters are at the Atlanta History Center.

In the mid-1990s letters were discovered that had been written between Margaret Mitchell and another boy, Henry Love Angel. Angel had been mentioned in previous Mitchell biographies as one of the five boys she wrote about to Allen Edee, who were visiting her in her hospital room at the same time. He was the third in the threesome of Mitchell, Courtenay Ross and Angel, as playmates in their youth. As it turns out, Angel could have repeated the lines that Ashley said to Scarlett at the beginning of the book when he said she'd always had a piece of his heart; that she'd cut her teeth on it.

So while she was flirting with Allen Edee in letters, she was doing the same with Henry Love Angel. The book *Lost Laysen, Margaret Mitchell Author of Gone With The Wind*, edited by Debra Freer, features pictures of Henry Love Angel and Peggy Mitchell holding hands and in loving embraces. The letters start in 1919 and end in 1922.

Another who occupied Peggy's heart was Dr. Leslie Morris. In July of 1921 she went on an overnight camping trip to Lake Burton with him.

They had much in common, as she had said she wanted to become a doctor and he was interested in Georgia's history and poetry.

Morris may have been one of the five boyfriends in the hospital room because she mentions one of them being a doctor. Another boyfriend, Winston Withers, was also there. She had been dating Withers off and on at about the same time.

Though still dating Morris that September, according to *Lost Laysen* she wrote Angel a note that may have been hand-delivered. In it she expressed hopes of seeing him. Interestingly, this was a month after she had left Morris at a dance and gone home with Berrien Upshaw. There were many men in her life who could have served as the basis for Ashley Wilkes.

Some people in Clayton County think Dr. George Crawford, who lived in Jonesboro during the Civil War, might have provided some inspiration for Ashley's character. The whole Crawford family was friendly with the Fitzgeralds, just as the Wilkes were good friends with the O'Haras. We know the O'Haras went to the barbecue at the Wilkes Plantation, and in real-life the Crawfords attended weddings and other social occasions at the Fitzgerald home. The Fitzgerald daughters were friends of the Crawford daughters, whose brother was George. In *Gone With The Wind* it was the O'Hara girls and the Wilkes girls with their brother Ashley.

If it has been assumed by many that Rhett Butler was at least partly inspired by Berrien "Red" Upshaw, then there were many who saw the chivalrous Ashley as having come partly from John Marsh, Mitchell's husband of over 20 years. She gave her fictional character blond hair just as Marsh had. She also gave Ashley the same culture and education as her husband. Though Scarlett never married Ashley, he was in her life longer than anyone. John Marsh, as her second husband, was the constant in Peggy Mitchell's life, too. John Marsh and Ashley Wilkes were both the pillars of their community, well respected by those who knew them.

Marsh had become such a fixture in Mitchell's life that he grew sad after she married Berrien Upshaw, and it was that way for Ashley after Melanie died. Ashley said in *Gone With The Wind* (p.1014) that if he had ever been strong it was because she was behind him. He later said, after her death, that all the strength he ever had was gone.

Both Ashley Wilkes and John Marsh have been portrayed to be soft at times, seeming almost to crumble when the times got tough. After the war, when Ashley came back and the Old South was gone, he became weak in countenance.

After her brief marriage to Upshaw, Margaret seemed to mature. Once she settled in with John Marsh he provided the strength and stability she needed.

"John Marsh worked for Georgia Power," said broadcaster Ernie Harwell, a young man at the time and the paper boy for the Marshes. "He was a solid citizen of the community. He made good money."

Marsh loved the same cultural things she loved and they could have intelligent conversations. Because Peggy enjoyed reading so much, she enjoyed talking about the books with others in an academic way, and Marsh was on her level in that area.

Her brief job at the *Atlanta Journal* had enabled her to interview people and write articles, keeping her mind always working and providing her with a legitimate writing background. Actually, Mitchell had been a writer all her life, having written many, many letters, short stories and plays. The newspaper job gave her a focus and a way to make a living during a tough time, and also gave her a personal credential as a "writer." Although she had not made her mark in the world of academia by obtaining a degree, she was "published" and that put her in the company of the writers and literary types she sought out.

It was during her time as a newspaper writer that John Marsh first worked with her, helping edit stories. She kept in touch with Marsh after she married Upshaw, and he probably knew about Upshaw's shaky finances. Marsh may have been the one to suggest she try for a job in the newspaper business. He was an excellent copy editor and used his corrections as a way of getting next to her and helping Peggy learn. Marsh was totally devoted to her and would do whatever it took to be around her and to be supportive of her.

When Scarlett wanted Ashley to help her run her business, Ashley's devotion to both his wife Melanie and Scarlett caused him to help her. Marsh had helped Mitchell during times she was married because he cared about her. Ashley Wilkes is truly a fictional character, but his good qualities do resemble Marsh's.

Mitchell and Marsh were married in 1925. Unlike her upscale first wedding held in the affluent home of her father, the Marshes chose to have their wedding reception in their new apartment on Crescent Avenue. Just as Scarlett O'Hara's home had a name—*Tara*, and as the Fitzgerald plantation was called *Rural Home* the Marshes named their apartment, The *Dump*. The newlywed couple marked their door with a card written in Peggy's handwriting that said: "Peggy Mitchell and John Marsh."

One of John Marsh's similarities to Ashley Wilkes was that Marsh was far overshadowed by Berrien Upshaw in the early years of their relationship. It was Upshaw whom she first chose and Marsh never really fought for Peggy. In *Gone With The Wind*, Ashley made it clear that he did have feelings for Scarlett, but he did nothing. He neither dropped Melanie in favor of Scarlett, nor came right out and told Scarlett he did not love her and he loved Melanie. In the same fashion, Marsh stood by and watched Upshaw steal the woman he loved. By doing the honorable thing, Ashley let an exciting life with Scarlett go by the wayside, much the same way John let Peggy go, even serving as best man at the Upshaw-Mitchell wedding.

In Gone With The Wind, Ashley Wilkes listened to the one he loved (Melanie) and though he did not want to work at Scarlett's sawmill, he did it because Melanie wanted him to. When Mitchell was married to Upshaw and they were having marital problems, she asked Marsh to intervene and help save her marriage. This was the last thing John wanted to do, but, since Peggy asked, he did it.

John had a great love for Peggy. In fact, he had few interests in life besides her. He would go to work and come home to her. They enjoyed having dinner together, reading, and listening to the radio.

In 1926, while recuperating from an ankle injury, Peggy Marsh was growing restless. She could not walk on it so John Marsh would bring home books to her every day. According to the Mitchell stories, one day Marsh jokingly told her he'd brought her all the books from the library and the only way she would get another one is to write one herself.

As close as Margaret and John Marsh were, and Marsh being a

journalist, the question always lurked…what role did he play in the book? She always downplayed his role, saying he'd not even read the whole thing until it was completed.

In Helen Taylor's book, *Scarlett's Women, Gone With The Wind And Its Female Fans*, she talked about (p. 67) how important it was to Margaret Mitchell to be historically accurate, saying that John Marsh made a seventeen-page glossary of terms to "ensure consistence of dialect."

A seventeen-page glossary of terms—if Marsh did that— would be hard to do for a person who had no role in the book. Mitchell spent many long hours on her book, writing and rewriting. She did much research and interviewed people so that she could get her facts correct. It was a fictional novel, but the backdrop was as historically accurate as Mitchell could make it. If she had questions she could ask her father, an expert in Georgia history. It is amazing to think of the amount of work that must have gone into writing that book in the 1920s, with none of the advantages that writers have today.

Various stories have been told of Marsh's involvement or non-involvement with the book. No one living today was in that apartment when the book was being written. Authors and biographers can speculate or interview people about what they think happened, but the evidence either way went up in flames the day John Marsh burned all of her papers.

Ann Rutherford, who played Carreen in *Gone With The Wind,* was invited to the Marsh apartment sometime after Margaret had passed away. It was when she and Cammie King, (who played Bonnie Blue Butler) were in Atlanta for a *Gone With The Wind* event that John Marsh invited them to his house to see his collection of the book in foreign languages.

"There was one in every language," said Rutherford. "I said, 'But I don't see anything of Margaret's other writings', and he said, 'That's because I burned them! She had boxes and boxes of things she had written but I burned them right there in that fireplace!' I just looked at him. How could a person do that?"

One of Margaret Mitchell's friends said Mitchell came up with Ashley's name as a tribute to her. Tim Lee, a *Gone With The Wind* collector owns several letters and writings from an old friend of Mitchell's, Lillian Ashley

Whitner. Before her marriage, and during the time Mitchell was writing *Gone With The Wind*, Ashley was her last name, and she wrote that it was her last name that provided the first name of Scarlett O'Hara's love. According to Lee, who has done some research on her, Lillian and Peggy attended the same school and both women were newspaper writers.

"Lillian wrote some memories of Margaret Mitchell on the back of an old newspaper article about her," said Lee, referring to one of the writings he owns. "In this note she is referring to the ankle injury Margaret had and has drawn a line to it."

The time period this is referring to would be when she was in bed with the ankle injury, while she was writing *Gone With The Wind* and then after she sold it to *Macmillan* editor Harold Latham. Years after it happened here is what Lillian Ashley Whitner wrote on that newspaper article that Lee still has:

"I had lunch with her (Mitchell) every Thursday while she was in bed—GWTW was scattered all over the room—Several times I would read a page or two—Mr. Latham bet her a case of champagne the book would be made into a movie. All Peggy would tell me about the book was that my name was in it—It turns out to be Ashley Wilkes!"

Both the fictional person of Ashley Wilkes, as well as the real John Marsh, loved books because they came from educated families. Marsh's mother was a school teacher and at least one of his sisters ended up being a teacher.

John Marsh was as awestruck of Peggy as Ashley was with Scarlett. Both men looked with loving eyes at the respective women and helped them whenever they needed it. Though it might not be the popular thing, Ashley Wilkes always did what he thought was the right thing. If there was one quality they both shared it was doing the honorable thing. John Marsh stayed completely by Margaret's side throughout her life. There were weeks at a time when she would be in bed, but he always remained steadfast and did everything he could. He stood up for her at all times. She returned the favor throughout their married life, several times, when he suffered from long illnesses.

"Margaret and John had a real love for each other," said Marianne Walker, author of *Margaret Mitchell and John Marsh: The Love Story*

Behind Gone With The Wind, based in part on letters from the Marsh family as well as on personal accounts from John Marsh's family. "They would play cards together or with friends, or go to dinner at the Piedmont Driving Club, which was across the street from their apartment."

John Marsh would put in long days at the office, and then after dinner he would look over her work, helping to edit it just as he did in her early days as a newspaper reporter. They worked very well with each other, each knowing his/her own role. Marsh saw how happy writing the book made Peggy and he was glad he had suggested it to her. She had been confined to her apartment and bored, but after he came up with the idea for her to write a book everything changed. She had a reason to wake up every morning, in fact at the beginning she could not wait to get started writing every day.

As Margaret Mitchell was struggling to come up with her characters, she was searching for another woman to be involved with Rhett Butler. John Marsh may have suggested just the perfect person. He had first-hand knowledge of a famous madam who would be the perfect inspiration for Belle Watling.

Chapter Seven
Belle Watling

"Margaret Mitchell was apparently afraid she might be sued for libel if she admitted publicly that Belle Watling's character was based on Belle Brezing," said James Kemper Millard, CTA President and CEO of the Lexington History Museum. "Buddy Thompson's book asserts she admitted to friends the true basis for her character."

In 2009 the Lexington History Museum began holding its annual "Belle's Birthday Ball" to commemorate the famous madam's birthday which was June 16th.

For many years the people of Lexington have said Margaret Mitchell's husband John Marsh used his knowledge of Lexington to inspire his wife with both Belle Brezing and a local landmark.

"Tara is a country home that still stands on Manchester Farm behind Keeneland Race Course," said Millard.

According to the website VisitLex.com: "Locals say that the antebellum mansion was the inspiration for "Tara" in Margaret Mitchell's "Gone With the Wind."

Though Margaret Mitchell learned about the Civil War and her family history when she was a young girl, she probably could not draw from family stories when it came to adding a madam character. She wanted to have a character who could be a friend to Rhett Butler yet create some conflict for Scarlett.

For that information she needed to go no further than the town her husband John Marsh once lived in: Lexington, Kentucky. He and many residents of Lexington at the time knew about one of the most famous madams in the country. Marsh may have known her—not because he had used her services—but because of his job as a newspaper reporter in Kentucky.

John Marsh's beat at the newspaper was crime, and madam Belle Brezing was flourishing during his time in Lexington, and so as a good reporter he definitely would have known about her. She was one of the most famous citizens of Lexington, and he was probably in the house on several occasions (as a reporter). She was known for inviting the press and the police into her house and feeding them.

According to the book *Madam Belle Brezing* by E.I. "Buddy" Thompson, she was so famous that "no one could be convinced that (John) Marsh had not furnished his wife with the name and some of the attributes of the character that became Belle Watling in *Gone With The Wind*."

Just the name alone would be quite a coincidence. Take the "B-r-e" out of Belle Brezing's name and insert "W-a-t-l" and you have Belle Watling.

In *Gone With The Wind*, the kind-hearted Belle Watling is a red-haired madam who runs a high-class brothel. Her establishment is first-rate and it is speculated that she has the backing of a wealthy financier. When she tries to donate money to help the Confederate cause, she is turned down because she's a prostitute. Undaunted she goes to the charitable Melanie who gladly accepts it; gold coins—wrapped in one of Rhett Butler's monogrammed handkerchiefs.

When David O. Selznick brought Watling to life on the big screen he toned her down a bit; rather than a brothel, she runs a drinking and dancing establishment.

Belle, sitting in her fancy carriage, with the black driver in front, thanked Melanie for accepting the money. They have a short conversation and Belle Watling confided that she has a child who doesn't live with her. That was the fictional Belle; but the real Belle had a similar story.

From the late 1800s to 1917, a madam named Belle Brezing ran the finest "bawdy house" in Lexington, Kentucky. The comparisons of Margaret Mitchell's dreamed up Belle Watling to the real-life Lexington madam Belle Brezing are too major to be a coincidence.

When her book became so popular, neither Margaret Mitchell nor John Marsh wanted anyone to know she had patterned the character of Belle after a real person, possibly because they were afraid of being sued. Belle Brezing was still alive at the time. When pressed about the fact that he was from Kentucky and may have known about her, Marsh would say no character, Belle included, was patterned after a real person.

According to Ric McGee, Executive Director of Ashland Terrace Retirement Community in Lexington, even today, some of his residents remember Belle. They remember the stories they heard because everybody in Lexington, Kentucky knew "Miss Belle."

When it came time to develop the madam character, Marsh's previous job as a crime reporter for the *Lexington Herald* gave him knowledge of the most famous prostitute in town. If he didn't help with some of the story lines and descriptions involving her, it seems he must have provided Mitchell with how to get the information.

Belle Brezing, born Mary Belle Cox on June 16, 1861, was the daughter of Sarah Ann Cox, of a poor farm family who moved to Kentucky.

Belle's mother Sarah, who some reports said was a part-time prostitute, was living in a relative's house with Belle and Hester, the two children she had born out of wedlock. She could not read or write but liked to sew, so she became a seamstress, taking in the neighbor's sewing and eventually becoming a dressmaker.

Sarah married a man named George Brezing who owned a saloon. Brezing eventually sold his saloon and opened a grocery store near their house on West Main Street in Lexington. Sarah thought she had found a man who could be a father for Belle and her sister Hester, and they took the last name Brezing (shown spelled several different ways on various census reports and even signed differently by Belle herself.) Their happiness was not to last. The marriage did not prove to be a good one; both parents were often drunk and violent.

In 1866 they divorced and Sarah met and moved in with William McMeekin, a local carriage painter. The indecisive Sarah soon left McMeekin, but the memory of seeing the many carriages that he painted stayed with Belle as one of her first childhood memories. She vowed she would one day drive around in one of the most beautiful carriages money could buy.

It really was just a dream at the time because she grew up without money and had very few friends. With the erratic lifestyle led by her mother, Belle was often left to herself. When she went to school, she was shunned by the other children because their mothers looked down on Sarah. As she got older, she craved companionship and this transferred to having several boyfriends.

In 1875 fifteen-year-old Belle got pregnant. She had been with at least two boys: James Kenny and John Andrew Cook. She ended up marrying Kenny.

According to an article by James Flahardy in the Audio/Visual Archives of the University of Kentucky, shortly after the baby's birth a sensational story made headlines in the *Lexington Daily Press*. An article in the paper described the wedding and a little more than a week later the other boyfriend, John Cook, was found dead outside Belle's back gate.

He had been shot in the head. This part plays into *Gone With The Wind* as Frank Kennedy was shot in the head and dragged to Belle Watling's house in the cover-up Rhett Butler staged to save Ashley and Dr. Meade.

In the real-life story, there was a photograph of Belle along with love notes and a lock of hair in his pocket, making it look as if he was a scorned lover who committed suicide. The newspapers weren't buying it and argued it was a cover-up; that it was murder.

John Cook had worked in the same store as Kenney, but it is not known whether Cook and Kenney knew they were both dating Belle Brezing at the same time. There were several articles in 1875 in the *Lexington Daily Press,* still available today, about the sensational story.

The following are the two notes (as she wrote them, uncorrected) from Belle to Cook.

DEAREST ONE—I will be down town at three o'clock look out for me. I will go to the office and by the store. Ma has come, have my pistol for me.
BELLE
Lexington, KY

DEAR ONE—Here it is and I want you to write me when you go and believe me your truly girl as ever, send me yours and don't forget it eather (sic).
Your darling,
BELLE

According to the newspaper reports, Belle was making plans to see him at his shop (the same shop where Kenney worked) at 3 p.m. By 4 o'clock he was found dead, lying at the back gate of Belle's house

The *Lexington Daily Press* printed an article, "Suicide or Murder?" The paper reported: "There is a prevailing sentiment in the community that the young man John Koch (Cook) who was found dead in an alley between Main and Short on Thursday evening did not commit suicide.

Amid the confusion and mysterious circumstances surrounding Cook's death, James Kenney abruptly left town, leaving Belle behind with her baby daughter Daisy May.

The scene in *Gone With The Wind* where Kennedy's body was found near Watling's house is one of the most convincing pieces of evidence that Margaret Mitchell had researched the Lexington madam in connection with her book. Both cases involved a cover-up. The newspaper articles were there, and since both she and Marsh had been in the newspaper business they knew how to look up old articles. These days she could have accessed them through the internet; however, back then she would have gotten it first-hand at the newspaper or from someone who knew about it.

If Margaret Mitchell did not know about Belle Brezing and the dead man who landed at her back door, it was quite a coincidence that Scarlett O'Hara's second husband, Frank Kennedy, would suffer the same fate. Frank Kennedy was really killed in a Ku Klux Klan incident, but to save his and Ashley's reputation Rhett Butler staged a cover-up. He sent Archie out to retrieve the dead bodies of Frank and the other man who was with Ashley.

On page 811 of *Gone With The Wind*, Scarlett suddenly realizes that while Ashley is home, her husband Frank is not with him. She asks Rhett Butler in a worried voice what has happened to Frank. He informs her that he's dead; shot through the head. He further tells her that he was carried to "the vacant lot near Belle's."

The *Lexington Daily Press* reported, when the coroner had arrived on the scene of the murder behind Belle Brezing's house, "he adjourned the inquest until the morning at 9 o'clock," when Belle Brezing had to appear.

In the book, just after Frank Kennedy's death (page 813, *Gone With The Wind)*, it tells of Belle Watling answering the Captain's summons and having to appear before the provost marshal the next morning.

Belle Brezing's mother, Sarah, died shortly after that and Belle and her infant daughter Daisy May were evicted from their home.

She was in no position to raise a baby—sixteen years old, with no home. Elizabeth Barnett, a neighbor, volunteered to take the child. Elizabeth and her husband had two teen-age sons. She was excited to have a baby girl, as her sons were getting older and would soon be out of the house. She also knew her home was a much better environment than the one little Daisy May was born into. Elizabeth's husband was a tailor, and they were looking forward to providing the child with fine clothing, love, and good religious training and morals. Unfortunately they did not get that chance.

As Daisy May began to grow, Elizabeth Barnett noticed things were not right. As it turned out, the child was developmentally challenged and had to be sent to a special institution out of state, where she spent the rest of her life, much to the disappointment of Elizabeth. Each month checks arrived at the Barnetts' house from Belle Brezing to pay for the care of the child who was now called Daisy May Barnett.

Gone With The Wind contains a conversation between Melanie and Belle Watling where Belle tells her she has a son just like Melanie does. When Melanie looks shocked and asked her if he lives with her, she says no—the child is in another town.

Belle Brezing went to work in what was then called a "sporting house" owned by a woman named Jennie Hill. As a matter of historical interest, it was in the same house in which Mary Todd Lincoln grew up.

The 1880 census lists Jennie Hill, who was thirty-three, as the head of the household, with seven other females listed as boarders. Jennie's profession was listed as housekeeper but no professions were given for the other seven. Belle was a friendly person. She kept a watchful eye on Jennie and how she handled the money, trying to learn the ropes of a business at which she thought she could be successful. It was not long before she started her own house on July 1, 1881. She rented a place on N. Upper Street.

The world's oldest profession was against the law even back then, but she found ways to get around it.

According to author Thompson, she would open her kitchen up to the police and reporters covering the crime beat, preparing delicious meals hoping to stay in their good graces. It was said she was indicted more times than any other citizen in Lexington and on Dec. 14, 1882, after being arrested for keeping a bawdy house she was pardoned by Governor Luke P. Blackburn.

The *Lexington Daily Press* carried an article in 1889 saying that citizens were calling for the closure of Belle's house. She decided to move temporarily, but later a multi-millionaire from Philadelphia helped her finance an elegant house.

Like her counterpart Belle Watling in *Gone With The Wind*, Belle Brezing was supported by a gentleman who had money.

On page 658, Scarlett is thinking about Belle and how she could not have made the kind of money needed to run such a nice place. She guessed that Belle must have had a rich backer.

Because Rhett Butler had never bothered to hide his relationship with her and because he was the richest man in the area, it was generally assumed he was the one. At the end of the book, he admitted to Scarlett that he had "invested" in Belle.

Belle Brezing's benefactor was said to have been William M. Singerly, a wealthy Democrat from Philadelphia who had run for governor of Pennsylvania in 1894. William Singerly helped her buy a two-story house which was decorated much the same as Belle Watling's house was described in Mitchell's book. It was a sprawling two-story building; clearly the nicest house on the street.

Belle Brezing's house eventually caught fire. When it was rebuilt, Belle made it even grander and one story taller, and men from all over the country came to her house.

Horse racing was big and men with money came to Lexington. Those who wanted the very best went to Belle Brezing's at 59 Megowan Street.

"When the trotters were in town, the girls needed to be dressed in fancy clothes for the horse people," said Ethel McQueary, an octogenarian from Lexington.

"I was raised next to the horse race running track in Lexington," said McQueary. "We also had a trotting track, The Red Mile, which is still in operation. When the moneyed trotting people came to town Belle would have her girls in their best."

Brezing wanted her girls to look as fine as the gentlemen who came to see them. The horse people were very wealthy and she wanted her establishment to welcome them. Both Belles had kind hearts. Brezing remembered how lonesome she used to feel after her mother had died and she had no home. She treated her girls to shopping sprees and bought them the finest fashions.

"Belle would call William Embry who owned Embry's Store and he would keep his store open after hours so the girls could shop," said McQueary.

Embry's Store was on Main Street in the heart of downtown Lexington.

Belle Brezing would march her girls past the Lexington Laundry and Angelucci's Men's Clothing to Embry's.

"Embry's had the best fashions and most expensive designers in town at that time," said Ethel McQueary, who actually worked there in the 1950s. "My mother-in-law worked at Embry's in the 1920s."

Just down the street from Embry's was the Ben Ali Theater where Belle would occasionally treat her girls by taking them there. At the time Belle's girls attended, it featured live theater on a stage that boasted a beautiful peacock on the white velvet curtain

And for those cold evenings, Belle shopped at Lowenthal's Furrier for her mink coat. Embry's, still in business in Lexington, later bought the furrier and the Laundromat.

Speaking of Lowenthal the furrier, Jamie Millard, the President of the Lexington History Museum relates this story.

"The son of her furrier relates that his father's biggest single sales day was the day after fake "thank you for your expression of sympathy" cards were sent to many prominent men in the community as a joke after her funeral!"

Belle's was the scene of many lavish parties. She lived the happy, glamorous life and entertained the rich and famous—much like Belle Watling in Atlanta. Belle Watling was having one of her parties the night Prissy came to her establishment looking for Rhett Butler. Butler attended her affairs, just as Singerly attended the parties of Belle Brezing.

"I remember my brother, J.R. Wyatt, loading his first rumble-seat car with his friends and driving back and forth in front of Belle's house on Megowan Street," said Ethel. "He knew where it was because during the day he worked at the Western Union office which was across the street from Embry's. He would bicycle to Belle's house with telegrams almost every day. That's how he got to know where the red light district was!"

Belle Brezing was known for helping those in her neighborhood. Whether it was food or money, she never forgot what it was like to be needy and she tried to help those who were less fortunate than she was.

One more similarity between the two Belles was their concern for the hospitals. According to Buddy Thompson (page 115 of his book), the Protestant Hospital a block away had a fire and put out a plea for sheets. Belle contacted the owner of a store downtown and bought all the sheets and towels in stock and had them delivered to the hospital. The nurses were so grateful, but when they found out who had donated them they returned them because they said it was bought with "tainted money."

Margaret Mitchell used a similar story by having Belle Watling try to donate money to the hospital. Though they desperately needed the money, they turned it down since it was being offered by Belle Watling. Later, Belle pulled up in her fancy carriage and waited until Melanie came out of the hospital. Melanie gladly accepted the gold coins, wrapped in Rhett Butler's handkerchief. The real-life madam Brezing was always looking for ways to help people, especially her own girls. She also took them to shows and put on special parties just for them on the holidays. These special times called for those beautiful gowns they bought. Still, she never escaped the loneliness and pain from her childhood. Brezing developed a great friendship with a doctor and, according to reports, he supplied her with drugs which helped ease her emotional pain.

In 1910 Belle Brezing was in her glory. She was listed in the census as being the head of the household, having a housekeeper and five "boarders," all women in their twenties. She had a ballroom complete with a piano, which was used for the entertainment of some of the wealthiest men in the United States. She traveled to New York to furnish her house and see the latest fashions. Hers was the place where fantasies came true.

It was a mansion beyond even Scarlett O'Hara's dreams, although the home she built after marrying Rhett Butler was close. Brezing's house was furnished with the finest table linens, the most expensive china and "food equal to what Belle had found in New York," according to Thompson. "Furniture and decorations would be the latest, offering comfort to compare to the best men's clubs in the country... the women would be dressed in evening gowns and their undergarments would be of the finest silk fabric with lots of imported lace."

The next few years were good ones for Belle Brezing and everybody knew who she was. When she would go out in public, she was always fabulously dressed and easily recognized.

On page 248 of *Gone With The Wind*, Belle Watling is described as one of the most famous women in town. Everybody knew her by her red hair and "gaudy, overly fashionable" dresses.

Just as she had dreamed as a child, Belle Brezing rode in the finest of fine carriages, brightly painted, better than any she had seen her one-time, stepfather figure William McMeekin paint. Going out in her carriage was like free advertising as far as Belle was concerned, so she dressed the part with the most expensive clothes in town.

She rode proudly around Lexington with her black driver and these images survive (on page 659 of *Gone With The Wind*) as Belle Watling did the same thing.

Just as Mitchell's Belle Watling offered comfort for men during the Civil War, Belle Brezing's house drew World War I military officers from nearby Camp Stanley. Articles ran in the Lexington newspaper about investigations and crackdowns and the Sept. 22, 1917 edition listed Belle's house:

"153 Megowan Street—Bell Breezings (sic)—Six inmates [her 'girls'] Price of house $5. Moerlein's beer sold. Inmates dressed in fancy gowns. No soldiers admitted."

No soldiers admitted that was because only the officers were permitted the luxuries afforded at Madam Belle's house. Though it was a house, Belle sold alcohol, had party rooms the men could entertain in, and offered breakfast to those who were still there in the morning. At times it was like the saloon-type atmosphere portrayed in *Gone With The Wind*.

Once when Rhett Butler is talking to Scarlett O'Hara, Rhett compares Scarlett to Belle Watling. He points out that while both are strong women with successful businesses, Belle stands out because she has a kind heart

One Christmas, knowing her girls would be alone on Christmas night, she decided to have a party for them. She hired a quartet which included a young singer, John Jacob Niles.

"My father was working for the Burroughs Adding Machine Company at the time," said one of his sons, John Edward Niles, a musician in Maryland. "My father knew Miss Belle. How he knew her he didn't elaborate and I didn't ask. On his way home from a business trip once he got a note to stop off at Lexington and go to their courthouse and fix the adding machine."

This was before Niles became a famous musician. He was just a young man making a living by traveling around and fixing adding machines, playing music on the side. It was in 1910 and when he went to Lexington, a friend asked if he could get a quartet together and sing for Brezing's girls on Christmas. He had plans to spend Christmas evening with his family, but he figured if he could do the show in the morning, he would have time to catch a train back to Louisville and be home in time for the holiday with his family.

"He got some people who agreed to do it," said John Edward Niles, "But they chickened out at the last minute."

Ron Pen, the director of the John Jacob Niles Center for American Music at the University of Kentucky, carried on the story. "Having heard of Niles, Brezing invited him to gather a vocal quartet to sing carols at her Christmas morning breakfast. Niles was not above singing in a whorehouse and his notes record that he sang his carols, 'Jesus, Jesus Rest Your Head'. 'The King Shall Come', 'Silent Night', 'Joy to the World', 'O Come, O Come Emmanuel', and 'Go Away From My Window'."

Pen, who was writing a biography on Niles, had access to his private writings. According to Pen, Niles noted "very pretty whores at breakfast" and said they had "good table manners."

Niles kept a diary and made reference to the event. According to Pen, Niles wrote, "Being not yet twenty-one, I thought it would be a lark to sing in one of America's greatest whorehouses. But I knew that I would have to work some kind of modern miracle to trap three others into joining me to sing the Birth of Our Lord and Master in Bethlehem in the confines of a house of ill fame of all things, on a Christmas morning!" As it turned out when he could not get the other three, he showed up alone and offered to play his guitar and sing for the group. When he arrived he was greeted at the door by Belle, who looked lovely in her "Sunday best." Despite Niles being the lone singer, she happily welcomed him. The other girls eagerly waited for him. They, too, dressed in beautiful dresses, looking forward to the concert.

"Miss Belle was there beside me, warning them not to lay a finger on her singer," continued Niles in his diary. "Then it was over, and Miss Belle, who said that her own breakfast was usually very light, sat at the head of the table and I sat on her right. From time to time, the girls, now dressed like great ladies, came timidly and ate ravenously, giggled like boarding school girls and, along with some excellent food, devoured me with their eyes. When Miss Belle rose, everyone else rose."

The women had been pleased with the show and Belle Brezing, showing her gratitude was treating Niles to the big breakfast. She carried on a nice conversation with him as he ate and then handed him an envelope when he left. He was pleasantly surprised.

Niles, who had been a little shy about coming alone, was a struggling musician at the time, without enough money even to buy a coat to wear on that cold December evening.

"She accompanied me to the door and handed me an envelope, which I later discovered to contain exactly twenty-five dollars," said Niles in his journal which Pen is using in his upcoming book.

John Jacob Niles went on to become famous for his songs, including "Wonder As I Wander" and "Jesus, Jesus, Rest Your Head." He was inducted in the Kentucky Music Hall of Fame along with musical greats such as The Judds, Lionel Hampton, and Mary Travers, and eventually even performed at the White House, but he never forgot the kind woman he had once performed for. He always remembered how she was quick to help him when he was struggling. In later years he pointed out her house to his son, Tom.

"I remember it as a solid, red brick building that had clearly seen better days," said Tom Niles.

"Miss Belle had the best food in town," said John Edward Niles. "At her place you not only got her girls, you got the delicious food she served. She had the nicest house and the best food and cooks. She served the food on fine linen table clothes and used good china and silver. Everybody in town knew about her. Everybody."

In 1917 the Army tried to close the brothels down.

"Miss Belle continued to run a smaller arrangement after the big place was closed down," said Niles. "The whole time she was a very well-known person."

In 1938 she was diagnosed with uterine cancer and she died Aug. 11, 1940—less than a year after the premiere of the movie, *Gone With The Wind*. Daisy May, the daughter who lived in the institution, died ten years later, while undergoing an operation for a broken hip. Belle Brezing was so famous that *Time* magazine carried her obituary.

The Lexington newspaper described her as "the colorful character of the Gay Nineties and early Nineteen Hundreds," and "the operator of one of the largest and most lavish establishments south of the Mason-Dixon Line."

"Belle Brezing was the model for Belle Watling and everybody knew it," said John Edward Niles. "When *Gone With The Wind* came out everybody in Lexington knew who it was."

Although not a madam during the Civil War; she was living during Margaret Mitchell's lifetime. Niles had Margaret Mitchell's sister-in-law, Francesca Marsh, as a teacher at Sayre School in Lexington.

"She told us she was John Marsh's sister, that Margaret Mitchell was her sister-in-law," said Niles. "At first I was only in seventh grade so I went home and asked my mom about it. I watched the movie and then read it when I was in the ninth grade. Miss Marsh had autographed pictures hanging in the classroom."

According to Niles, Mitchell had the character down perfectly.

Niles said the other thing that gave Belle Watling away was the relationship she had with the police. She was able to get Rhett out of jail. "She knew all their dirty little secrets," just like Belle Brezing did. Miss Belle (Brezing) was well liked—except by the wives of the town. She knew the dirty little secrets of Lexington. The good women of the Garden Club did not like her, of course, but everyone knew her."

In the scene where the women are sewing at Melanie's house and Ashley comes home drunk after the "political meeting," which the officer knows did not happen; Rhett tells the officer the men were at Belle Watling's. He describes it as a big party with champagne, like the parties Belle Brezing would have thrown, and even implies that the officer had been at Belle's before.

Once it has been established they were at Belle Watling's, Rhett comments that there will be fights between many a couple—that the wives won't be speaking to their husbands in the morning. The next day when they spoke to authorities the men were cleared of the charges, because, according to Niles, Belle Watling, like Belle Brezing, knew too much.

As Belle Watling said (P. 820, *Gone With The Wind*), women in her business knew a lot of things about the wives of the men who visited them. She knew a lot of men and these men did not want it out that they knew her.

"It was common knowledge that she served food to the police and newspapermen," said Niles. "With John Marsh living in Lexington and his sister teaching there, it was obvious she (Mitchell) talked to her husband about her."

"Margaret Mitchell denied that Belle Watling was Belle Brezing," said Niles. "Maybe it was because she wanted to show she was an independent writer and was creative on her own. She was a great writer in her own right."

"Everybody knew Belle and basically everyone in Lexington liked her except the wives of her customers," said Niles. "She was a good businessman, very proper and carried herself well. She was rather a religious woman."

Belle Brezing, like the fictional character, Belle Watling was a good person.

Perhaps that is why the inscription on her tombstone reads: "Blessed are the pure in heart."

Chapter Eight
Philip Fitzgerald—Margaret Mitchell's Great-Grandfather
(Possible Model For Gerald O'Hara)

Civil War survivor Philip Fitzgerald lived to see everything from immigrant deaths on the ocean steamer they came to the United States on, to Yankee troops taking over his plantation, while destroying others around him. He is buried in the Fayetteville City Cemetery in Fayetteville, Georgia. Resting near him in the cemetery is his only son, Philip Jr., who died in infancy. Also in the same area are the graves of two of his daughters who lived to be more than seventy years old, as well as his niece's in-laws, the Holliday family.

In his eighty-two years on earth he lived in three countries. Born in 1798 of a Roman Catholic family in Ireland, he lived for a while in France, and died in Georgia—his life providing the threads that form the fabric of one of the most famous books in the world.

In the early 1820s Fitzgerald and his younger brother James (born in 1791) and James' wife traveled to the United States by boat looking forward to meeting up with their other siblings who had gone ahead of them. As with all overseas travel of the time, the boat ride was terrible. Many did not survive, but the Fitzgeralds did. They were in their twenties with high hopes in their hearts and dreams of acquiring some land, starting a family, and living happy, productive lives.

After arriving in Charleston, South Carolina, plans were changed and they did not join their relatives up North but eventually settled in Fayette County, Georgia. This was the County Seat in 1831, a growing area, so it was a good place to make a start.

In 1838 he married Eleanor (also called Ellen) McGhann, who was like-minded in her religion and valued education. When he met Ellen, her father had just died the year before and her mother was dying.

Philip Fitzgerald was forty years old and Ellen was twenty, making

Mrs. Fitzgerald twenty years younger than her husband. When Margaret Mitchell was creating her characters, she gave a large age difference to the O'Haras also. (Gerald O'Hara was 43 and his wife Ellen was 15 when they married, making Ellen O'Hara 28 years younger than her husband.)

"There was very little (money) left her mother who, too was dying," said Lucille Stephens Kennon in her scrapbook. Fitzgerald, who lived in another town, came to help the McGhann family.

"(Fitzgerald) wanted to come there as promised before she passed on. He buried her and married his bride," she wrote. "He packed up her sister Julia."

They brought Julia to live with them in Fayetteville for the first few years. Family was always very important to Philip Fitzgerald.

He always dreamed of being a planter but started out teaching school. He then bought a store and became a merchant, saving up enough money to buy a house and some land along the Flint River. In 1858, the area they lived in became part of the newly formed Clayton County and their land was actually in two counties.

As the Fitzgeralds unpacked their possessions at Rural Home, they hung their crucifix in the living room near the front door. His great-great granddaughter Marie Nygren still has that cross.

Rural Home, when it was first built, was two stories high with two rooms on each floor, but additional rooms were eventually added. There was a fireplace in each room and they put together a rather extensive library. The furniture was in the American Empire style, popular in the 1840s.

Shortly after the house was built there was a land dispute. Philip felt he owned part of the land which another family said they owned.

According to the family scrapbook Fitzgerald's determination to keep this land caused an incident to happen that was passed down from generation to generation about a gypsy curse having been put on the Fitzgeralds. It all centered around a house some people were living in.

"He told them he had bought the property and asked them to move," wrote Lucille. Evidently he left and when he got back they were still there.

"He told the sheriff and had them arrested," she wrote. "The lady cussed him."

Because of this land dispute the woman became so angry at Philip Fitzgerald she told him she put a curse on him that all his daughters would be widows and his sons would die.

Their children were Annie, Agnes, Mary (Mamie), Sarah (Sadie or Sis), Isabelle, Adelle, Catherine (Katie), and Philip, Jr. Unfortunately, Philip died before his first birthday, so they raised all daughters.

One of those daughters, Annie, married John Stephens, also an Irish immigrant. They provided granddaughters, including Mary Isabelle, who was called Maybelle (and became Margaret Mitchell's mother). This combining of names was used in the book by Mitchell as Scarlett's sister Suellen's name came shortening her name, Susan Elinor; and Carreen's given name was Caroline Irene.

Maybelle would eventually marry Eugene Mitchell, a lawyer in Atlanta, and continue visiting Mary [Mamie] and Sarah [Sis]. Philip Fitzgerald had taught his family respect for land as well as education and the love of books and culture, exemplified by the large library at Rural Home.

While many in Lexington recognized Belle Brezing in Belle Watling, there were those in Jonesboro, Georgia who had heard stories of Philip Fitzgerald and recognized him in Gerald O'Hara. They had similar descriptive characteristics and both were political, Irish tempered, and not caring what they said or did.

According to historian John Lynch, who runs the Holliday-Dorsey-Fife Museum in Fayetteville, Georgia, the Fitzgeralds were very much like the fictional Gerald and Ellen O'Hara.

"Philip Fitzgerald liked to go to the area taverns," said Lynch, whose ancestors knew the Fitzgeralds.

Just as Gerald O'Hara would be out drinking in the taverns with his friends and try to hide it from his wife, Margaret Mitchell's great-grandfather Fitzgerald enjoyed some other common interests such as card playing and jumping horses. Ellen Fitzgerald was known for her strength and business sense, which was like Ellen O'Hara who missed the Wilkes' Barbecue so that she could work on the 'books' for Tara. Both women were quietly strong, but had husbands who could be outwardly volatile.

At the Wilkes house when the men were having their political discussion, Mitchell described Gerald's voice as "raised in furious accents" as he argued with John Wilkes during a lively discussion about the impending war. "Grandpa was loud, angry as all the Irish were," said Lucille of Philip Fitzgerald in her scrapbook.

In the late 1800s Hoke Smith, later a senator and then governor of Georgia, was in Jonesboro giving a speech about an issue unpopular with most of those in attendance. According to a scrapbook from Margaret Mitchell's family, there was much ranting and yelling going on.

"People were muttering things like 'tar and feathers' and 'riding on a rail'," wrote Lucille Stephens Kennon, granddaughter of Mitchell's great-grandfather. Fitzgerald had been standing on the outskirts of the crowd but like the character Margaret Mitchell created, Gerald O'Hara, he wanted to be in the middle of the action—especially when it had to do with politics.

"Let me through boys, let me through," he said as he urged his horse through the angry mob.

In that scene where O'Hara is involved in the heated political discussion with John Wilkes, Mr. O'Hara is right in the middle of it and is not afraid to give his opinions.

It can't be denied that O'Hara and Fitzgerald shared some qualities. In the book and movie, Gerald is seen as a short, gruff, Irishman, fond of drinking, riding horses, and talking of politics. Mitchell's grandfather Fitzgerald has been described as "short of stature," "powerfully built," and as one who had a "formidable aptitude for self-defense." He was often seen coming home late from the taverns and riding his horse around town or jumping fences in the countryside.

In 1831 Fitzgerald's brother James and James' wife Mary Ann had their first daughter, Mary Anne, who eventually married a man named Robert Kennedy Holliday. They had seven children, including Martha Anne, who everyone called "Mattie."

James and Philip Fitzgerald eventually became farmers; planters, as they were called back then. Philip owned slaves. It was said he really did not agree with the concept of having slaves but if not for them he could not have raised all the crops he did. The Fitzgerald Mammy helped raise all the daughters.

In the 1861 Tax Digest for Clayton County, he was listed with 2,527 acres of land and thirty-five slaves. The 1860 census valued his real estate at $61,000, making him one of the richest men in Clayton County at the time. Fitzgerald taught his family the importance of tradition, to value land, and, with the urging of his wife, the family always continued to say their evening prayers just as his family did in the old country. This tradition continued at Rural Home even when Margaret Mitchell visited as a child.

The Fitzgerald daughters went to school in Charleston, except for Annie and Agnes, who studied at the Fayetteville Academy.

The family liked to have fun and had many visits and parties with the neighboring folk, including the Crawfords who lived down the road a bit.

In 1873 Philip Fitzgerald built a large addition to the home; this included the porch, which was to become a central meeting place for grown-ups or children. The house was on Bumblehook Road, since changed to Tara Road today.

Most of the background stories on Gerald O'Hara in *Gone With The Wind* were true for Philip Fitzgerald. Mitchell described O'Hara noting "the small figure on the big white horse galloped up their (the neighbor's) driveways, smiled and signaled for tall glasses in which a pony of Bourbon had been poured over a teaspoon of sugar and a sprig of crushed mint…"

Stories have been handed down of Philip Fitzgerald riding around on his horse after drinking and one of the most often told involved Fitzgerald being so drunk he got on his horse backwards. No doubt he hoped his wife would not find out about his antics, just as Gerald O'Hara tried to keep his from his wife also.

Fitzgerald lived a long life—until 1880. Ellen went on to live until 1893, but she wasn't lonely as she had Sis and Mamie, their two daughters who never married. Though they moved away for a while, they eventually lived out their years at Rural Home; and because Annie was so preoccupied all the time, she left her daughter Maybelle at Rural Home for years at a time, so Maybelle was partially raised by her great-aunts –Philip Fitzgerald's daughters, Sis and Mamie.

Once she was married, every summer Maybelle would bring her children Stephens and Margaret out to Rural Home and Sis and Mamie would tell them the stories of their heritage. Rural Home was always a central meeting place for members of the Fitzgerald, Holliday, Stephens and, finally, Mitchell families. Mary Anne's daughter Mattie, who eventually joined the convent, spent a good deal of time visiting Rural Home.

Chapter Nine
Tara and Twelve Oaks

As Margaret Mitchell worked on her book she came up with a few characters. She chose the star-crossed lovers plot and a basic storyline as she sat at her Remington typewriter planning out the book. Sometimes she wrote in bed, but much of the time she was up and about in the little apartment with the typewriter sitting on a table. She determined the book would be set around the War Between The States. The history heard at Rural Home about when General William Tecumseh Sherman's troops came through and everybody's lives changed forever just kept coming back to her. There were still people who talked about it, and on every trip to Jonesboro she saw the old historic buildings and homes.

Every family in Jonesboro had a story back then. The Fitzgerald family story was that Sherman had spared their home and that Grandmother Annie Fitzgerald Stephens helped her aging father and sisters rebuild their farm—but at a cost. The story that has been passed down through the family is that when Sherman saw the Fitzgerald's crucifix on the wall and when he found out Mrs. Fitzgerald's name was Ellen it all hit to closely to home for him. He thought of his own wife, Ellen, who was Catholic, so he let the home stand. Rural Home survived, but the hungry Union soldiers took all their crops and left the place in ruins.

Margaret Mitchell begins describing the setting of her novel on page four where she talks about the newly created Clayton County.

"The County" has become so identified with Mitchell's epic that in April 1969, when her brother Stephens Mitchell cut the ribbon for the opening of the Clayton County Federal Loan Association's new office building, he gave Clayton County the permission to claim they were "Home to *Gone With The Wind.*"

Visitors have come to Clayton County in search of "Tara." The Hollywood version was a façade—just a front built for the set— and was once moved to Clayton County but is not available to be seen. The real-life Fitzgerald house in Clayton County where many of the episodes that may have inspired Mitchell occurred, has been torn down also, however, the area does serve as a haven to those who want to see the area Margaret Mitchell based her book on. There are several plantation homes still standing which residents think may have inspired the Wilkes plantation and others in her book.

Stately Oaks Plantation, in Jonesboro, is a large, white-columned mansion which is available for tours. Tour guides tell of how Margaret Mitchell would have seen the home sitting atop a hill on her way into town. She described Twelve Oaks as sitting on a hill.

Another plantation that may have contributed to her thoughts of Twelve Oaks was what is known as the Crawford-Talmadge House. This historic house had connections to three different Georgia Governors. Ancestors of Governor Hugh Manson Dorsey who served from 1917-1921, first lived in it, followed by Eugene Talmadge and then Herman Talmadge.

Governor Eugene Talmadge knew the Mitchell family. Eugene's son, Herman Talmadge married his wife Betty Shingler, at the governor's mansion in Atlanta in 1941. Their marriage would endure many storms, both political and personal. While she was married to Talmadge, Betty loved to entertain on the grounds of the plantation. She played bridge with Lady Bird Johnson and hosted luncheons for Pat Nixon and Judy Agnew, wives of President Richard Nixon and Vice-President Spiro Agnew, during the Watergate investigation.

The Talmadges had two sons, Robert, who drowned at Lake Lanier at age twenty-nine in 1975, and Eugene, (Gene) who lives on the property today.

Governor Eugene Talmadge had originally bought the plantation after the last member of the Crawford family died. Talmadge's son Herman and his wife Betty inherited it, and after their divorce she ended up with it. Betty Talmadge called it "Lovejoy Plantation" at the time she owned it, and claimed it was the inspiration for Twelve Oaks. It is now generally referred to as the Crawford-Talmadge House, and, at this writing, remains in the family, still with their son, Gene, living there.

It is a beautiful white-columned house first as a settler's cabin and then added onto as the plantation grew.

Thomas Crawford and his family were among the guests at Annie Fitzgerald's marriage to John Stephens, and some of the occurrences mentioned in the book were said to have taken place at the Crawford's, also.

According to a flyer that Betty Talmadge used when the house was open for private parties, "Legend says that when the Yankees approached Lovejoy's Station on the Macon and Western Railroad, Mr. Crawford filled the tall porch columns with grain to prevent it (the grain) from being captured by the enemy. The lawns of Lovejoy Plantation were the scene of a battle between Confederate and Northern soldiers. Mini-balls were discovered in the walls of the home during the restoration. Battle trenches may still be seen within a mile of the home."

The flyer also points out that the plantation is not far from the spot where "Confederate General Hood paused to regroup his remaining forces after the ill-fated Battle of Atlanta. When Hood's forces went forth from Lovejoy, they left Georgia to face the devastation of Sherman's march to the sea."

When Betty Talmadge was alive she began opening it up for private parties. Her entertaining was reminiscent of the fictional Twelve Oaks entertaining. The Wilkes' barbecue is the scene of Scarlett's conversation with Ashley Wilkes and the introduction of Rhett Butler. Margaret Mitchell described Twelve Oaks as white with tall columns, wide verandas, a flat roof and very beautiful and stately. She also mentioned that it sat on a hill and had French doors and stairs leading up to the porch

Betty Talmadge was so interested in history and in *Gone With The Wind* that she had Rural Home, the original home owned by Philip Fitzgerald, moved to her property and restored. The home had survived the Civil War and had been taken apart and reassembled on her property with the idea of opening it to the public.

Unfortunately, this great treasure of history, so carefully protected by Betty Talmadge, is no longer standing. The Talmadge house, which had been a local curiosity, sits back and cannot be seen from the street. What happened to the old Fitzgerald place?

"It was standing," said Gene Talmadge, Betty's son. "Then that bad tornado that tore up the racetrack came and knocked it off the foundation. It did some severe damage."

On July 6, 2005, an F2 tornado with winds of 150 mph whipped through the Atlanta area causing severe damage to the Atlanta Motor Speedway. Talmadge said he told his son and some friends to take the old building down and store it in a garage on the property.

The historical estate, accessible only by a private road adorned with 'No Trespassing' signs, is surrounded in mystery itself. Because of the news headlines Betty and Herman Talmadge made in the '70s and since in recent years the residence has been the subject of several news reports, local citizens have wondered what it looks like.

They've heard that Rural Home, which some even call "Tara," is there and they wonder what Talmadge plans to do with it. Nothing right now, he says.

"I've had some offers," said Talmadge. "I would consider putting it back up if the right offer came. It meant more to my mother than it does to me."

Betty Talmadge had also bought the facade of Tara from the set of the movie. She had planned on turning the property into a *Gone With The Wind* themed venue, but she died before she got it finished. Just think— the famous "Tara" from David O. Selznick's movie is being stored on the same property as the real-life Rural Home.

"I have the facade of Tara in another garage," said Talmadge. "At one time a long time ago before I got involved, Coca-Cola thought about doing something with it, but they decided not to."

It is a beautiful house, kept up with many flowers and landscaping. There is a magnolia tree in the front yard which actually came from one of Thomas Jefferson's trees. It was given to Betty Talmadge by a White House gardener.

Dr. Donald Stokes tried to buy the Tara movie façade and Rural Home several years back from Betty Talmadge, in his efforts working with the City of Morrow, Georgia to develop "Tara Home," a tourist destination with a model of the movie version of Tara. He has had another conversation with Gene Talmadge about buying it.

"I'm not going to get involved with that," said Talmadge. However, he did leave the door open for discussion. "For the right offer, I might consider it."

"Gene is talking to the City of Morrow about the facade and the Fitzgerald House," said Stokes. "It would not surprise me to one day have access to both. That will be the best opportunity, in my estimation, to preserve and protect those pieces of history."

Everyone who ever lived in Rural Home has died, but the closest relative is Joseph Mitchell, the only living son of Margaret Mitchell's brother Stephens. Joe Mitchell lives a secluded life in Atlanta.

Gone With The Wind enthusiasts are fortunate that these plantation homes and other historic buildings from the Civil War period are still standing in the Jonesboro, Clayton County area.

According to Gene Talmadge, the Crawfords and Fitzgeralds lived about three miles apart, which was an easy horse ride. The Crawford-Talmadge house is so famously associated with *Gone With The Wind* that Butterfly McQueen once visited and Gene Talmadge still has the picture of her.

Many of the stories Margaret Mitchell had heard as a child took place at the Fitzgerald's Rural Home, the Crawford estate, and other homes of relatives and friends. The popular belief is that Margaret Mitchell's descriptions of the plantations were not taken from specific Clayton County homes. Many similar stories happened in these homes, but she turned elsewhere for her descriptions.

There were two houses in nearby Roswell, Georgia that may have inspired her.

"Both Bulloch Hall (the home of Teddy Roosevelt's mother, Mittie Bulloch) and Mimosa Hall of Rosswell have the Greek architecture," said Joseph Moore, the author of *The History of Clayton County, GA, 1821-1983 (compiled by the Genealogical Society of Clayton County, GA)*. "Both houses are still there and Margaret Mitchell had been in the houses as she wrote stories on them for the newspaper."

Other historic houses exist in the Jonesboro area that may have provided inspiration to Margaret Mitchell because, through the old houses that stood, she could get a clearer picture of what the area was like during the period about which she was writing.

The Warren House is an old historic home, instrumental in the Battle of Jonesboro. It was built by Guy Warren, a Northerner who ran the railroad. The original depot was across the street from his house.

During the Civil War, Warren left the area and the house was used as a hospital for both the North and the South, as there were so many casualties there. Handwritten poems and prayers from both Confederate and Union soldiers are said to still be visible on the walls.

"There are still some writings on the walls that the troops had written," said Patrick Duncan, the Head of the Clayton County Convention and Visitors Bureau. "It's now a private residence but we hope someday to have it available to be toured."

Another period home is the Johnson-Blalock House, built in 1859 by Col. J.F. Johnson. The Blalocks were mentioned in the family scrapbook as being friends of the Fitzgeralds. The Ashley Oaks Mansion, built in 1879 was not there during the Civil War, but it was there when Margaret Mitchell came to Jonesboro.

There are so many more historic houses and graveyards (including the Patrick R. Cleburne Confederate Cemetery) as well as the old depot in the area.

"We work together with all of the historic sites in the area," said Duncan. "Our 'Road To Tara' Museum is housed in the old Depot. The original train depot was down the street by the Warren House but was destroyed in the Civil War. This one was rebuilt and holds our museum."

The 'Road To Tara' Museum displays Herb Bridges' collection of

Gone with the Wind memorabilia. Bridges once owned one of the largest collections in the world. He is a respected expert on the subject and a sought-after speaker.

At the time just prior to the Civil War, Clayton County was a newly created county, having just been formed by an act of the state legislature on November 30, 1858. The area had been settled in the early 1820s as part of Fayette County and along with parts of Henry County it became Clayton County.

It is noteworthy that in researching the area around Jonesboro where the fictional Tara and Twelve Oaks are located in the book, depending on what year one is searching for facts it may say Henry County or Fayette County or Clayton County referring to areas right next door to each other. In the early censuses, Philip Fitzgerald's plantation was actually listed as being in Fayette County.

Towns in Clayton County include Forest Park, Jonesboro, Lake City, Lovejoy, Morrow and Riverdale. Philip Fitzgerald's plantation, where the great aunts lived, was listed in some census documents as being in the "Lovejoy" area, very close to Jonesboro.

In *Gone With The Wind*, all of the families in the County knew each other. They held big barbecues and social gatherings, and it was the same in real-life. Unlike today when some people do not even know their next door neighbors, people went outside more; they socialized with, gossiped about, and helped their neighbors.

The Georgia Railroad ran between Macon and Atlanta, making the Jonesboro stop at "Lovejoy Station." Because of the railroad, transportation from Jonesboro to Atlanta was very easy. For instance, that was how the Fitzgeralds and Hollidays visited with their Holliday relatives in Griffin, Georgia.

When Margaret Mitchell was a child, before cars became common, the Mitchells often went by horse and buggy from Atlanta to Clayton County.

Margaret Mitchell chose this area as the setting for her book because she was familiar with it. As she mentioned the red Georgia clay and described the area, that was one thing she did not need to research in books. She knew the area and had heard the great-aunts Mamie and Sis talk about "the war."

"They talked about the Civil War all the time, refought old campaigns, and argued about the tangled, bewildering muddle of politics of the Reconstruction days," she told Medora Field Perkerson on WSB the July that the book came out. "Their remarks about the Carpetbaggers and Scalawags of Reconstruction days were also forceful and of deep interest to me... so how could I help but know about the Civil War and the hard times that came after it? I was raised on it. I thought it had all happened just a few years before I was born."

As Peggy Marsh sat at her typewriter, she had the Civil War setting, a few characters, and the basic plot figured out. After she decided what she wanted to write, she researched every little fact so that it could be as historically accurate as possible, while remaining a fictional novel.

"She was very detail oriented," said John Wiley, Jr., publisher of *The Scarlett Letter*, a nationally distributed quarterly newsletter for *Gone With The Wind* fans. "She checked her facts and wanted to be sure the history was correct."

Writing the book was a long process for Mitchell because she wanted everything to be right. In choosing names for her characters, it has been said that she went to much trouble to be sure none of her characters had names of real people so as not to embarrass the person or to ward off possible lawsuits, but those who knew her family recognized many of the names in the book. Take Gerald O'Hara, for example. It is not very difficult to see where she may have gotten it: Fitzgerald, her own family name.

Perhaps if Margaret Mitchell had been able to talk about the real-life happenings that inspired her, she could have enjoyed the whole process and shared it with her family. She might not have suffered so much after the book came out if she had been able to deflect some of the publicity to her family rather than fighting so hard to deny it.

In Jonesboro, even today, there are rumors that she got some of her stories from the diaries of her relatives.

"It has been said that she read her Grandmother Annie Fitzgerald's diary," said Abb Dickson of Jonesboro. "That diary still exists. It is somewhere in a private collection."

Her cousin Lucille Stephens Kennon's scrapbook from the 1880s tells the history of Lucille's life, some of it including the events that happened in Rural Home and to the Fitzgeralds. The scrapbook is full of pictures from her childhood and her family. She was the daughter of Catherine Fitzgerald, one of the daughters of Margaret Mitchell's great-grandfather Philip Fitzgerald. Katie, as she was called as a child, was a young girl of sixteen when the Civil War started and Fayetteville historian John Lynch noted the similar names of the real-life Katie Fitzgerald and the fictional "Katie" Scarlett O'Hara in a speech he made at the Stately Oaks Plantation in Jonesboro, commemorating Margaret Mitchell's Birthday Celebration in 2007.

Margaret Mitchell, like her fictional family the O'Haras, came from a proud Irish family whose highly regarded reputation was important to them. The women, including her mother, Maybelle, went to private schools and valued education.

After marrying, Maybelle and Eugene Mitchell taught the same values to their children, Margaret and Stephens. The things that seemed to be most important to the Mitchells were books, education, social status, and family history.

Eugene Mitchell, a prominent attorney in Atlanta, was president of the Atlanta Bar Association and former president of the Atlanta Historical Society. He came from a good family, with a Methodist minister grandfather and Civil War veterans. They had lived in Atlanta since its start.

When Margaret Mitchell was growing up in the early 1900s many people who had lived through the Civil War were still alive, including her own elderly aunts in Jonesboro. The war had ended only thirty-five years before she was born. Since her whole existence was so close to the real-life experiences of the War Between the States, it was easy to draw on memories from childhood conversations from those who had survived it. As the old people reminisced, Margaret hung on to every story....

"Art imitates life"

The 1850's were tumultuous for the United States as quarrelling persisted among sections of the country. The North wanted a special protective tariff for its industries, the West wanted free farms for settlers as well as aid for building roads and improvements, and the South wanted to continue in the life they knew.

Philip Fitzgerald was a planter, and Ellen Fitzgerald was busy with their young girls. The Fitzgeralds had a Mammy, and just as Scarlett was a handful for Mammy in *Gone With The Wind*, their daughter, Annie (Mitchell's grandmother), was equally as ornery.

To obtain what she wanted, Annie Fitzgerald often had a complete disregard for others. According to Lucille Stephens Kennon's scrapbook, "I have heard Aunt Annie tell of coming home in the afternoon, going to the [slaves'] "quarters" to slip some "big hominy" the colored mammy was feeding to the 'pic-a-ninnies"—the small negros (sic) too little and young to work. She knew she was going to be scolded when she got to the house but it was too much fun to grab a spoon, and give some child a smart on the head and take her place in line for a bowl."

The wealthy Fitzgeralds' home may not have been a mansion but it was very nice. There was a 'cook-house' in the back. It was a separate building where the slaves cooked the meals over a fire. Later on, the cook-house was connected to the big house as a kitchen, but during the Civil War, the meals were prepared in the building out back.

Both the O'Haras and the Fitzgeralds gave their homesteads names. 'Tara' of *Gone With The Wind* was whitewashed brick. The real-life 'Rural Home' was built of wood, but it did have a porch which was the scene of many leisurely conversations just as was Tara in the beginning of *Gone With The Wind*.

The book starts off with Scarlett O'Hara on the porch visiting with Stuart and Brent Tarleton. The porch had significant meaning for both the O'Haras and Fitzgeralds. The real-life Fitzgeralds also had the slaves' garden out back, and it was in a slave garden that the dramatic radish-eating "I'll never be hungry again" scene took place.

The Civil War didn't begin until 1861, but the political climate of the late 1850's was already volatile. The South had slaves, but at first the North was more concerned about the new territories being explored and wanted to ensure that Congress kept the expanding territories from having slaves. The Compromise of 1850 and The Missouri Compromise were attempts to settle the problems involving slavery.

As new territories developed, difficulties surfaced. The Kansas-Nebraska Act, which established the new territories, left room for legal slavery. The North opposed it. The newly formed Republicans were dedicated to stopping slavery and especially to preventing it from moving Westward. There were those who wanted to end slavery already in force since the 1830s, but once Abraham Lincoln was elected president tensions were heightened.

In his Inaugural Address, Lincoln mentioned that slavery was illegal. Hard feelings led to the secession of the Southern States, the naming of Jefferson Davis as President of the Confederate States of America, and Davis naming General Robert E. Lee as head of the military. On April 12, 1861, the South fired on Fort Sumter in the harbor at Charleston, South Carolina. The war was on.

From the beginning, the North had more resources and Margaret Mitchell used Rhett Butler to explain this (page 110), when the men were talking about war. He reminded the men that there were no cannon factories or any other type of manufacturing in the South.

Rhett Butler also mentioned that there were no warships and warned that the North could take control of their harbors, prohibiting them from selling their cotton overseas. The South's main source of income was the cotton they grew and they depended on the sales of that cotton to the North and overseas. They needed the North for their livelihood.

Ellen and Philip Fitzgerald and their daughters lived on a cotton plantation, just like the O'Haras.

Fitzgerald and his neighbors in Clayton County grew cotton and sold it. They counted on the sale of cotton for the livelihood of their families. If the North were to succeed in their goals of eliminating slavery, the South's whole way of life would change. There were miles of cotton fields and all they could think about was 'How would they harvest that crop with no slaves?' But then, when the South seceded from the Union, where would they sell their cotton since the Northerners had the textile factories and bought the cotton. It was a serious time in the history of the United States.

At the beginning of the war, the call went out for volunteers. The South was united and determined. As the fighting got closer to Georgia, the families in Clayton County talked of war more and more.

Many echoed the sentiments of Ashley Wilkes in *Gone With The Wind* (page 108), where he says he will fight if there is a war, but he hopes there will be no need and that the North will leave them in peace. Others were more eager to fight for the cause.

On March 10, 1862, Georgia Governor Joseph Brown's mandate to gain volunteers from each county caused young men in Clayton County to come running, to sign up for the Confederate Army. Companies from all counties surrounding Clayton met at Camp Stephens just outside of Griffin, Georgia. This group became the 44th Georgia Regiment of Volunteers. On April 4th the new regiment was ordered to Goldsboro, North Carolina.

Mitchell re-enacted a scene like this one in *Gone With The Wind* (p. 144) as Charles Hamilton tells her that President Lincoln has put out the call for volunteers, so the South was answering back.

Just the thought of "Mr. Lincoln" beefing up the North's army caused men and boys from every family to want to sign up. This scene was dramatically played out in the movie as the men ran from the house at the Wilkes' barbecue to sign up.

The story of Tara was the dramatic story of the war and survival which happened to many people of the South. The Civil War and Reconstruction Period happened much as it was described in her fictional novel in the real-life stories of Margaret Mitchell's relatives, especially the Fitzgeralds and those around them. *Gone With The Wind* took place in the newly created Clayton County and some of what happened to the characters really did happen to Margaret Mitchell's ancestors.

"I am not writing these memories in any spirit of criticism of Margaret Mitchell as author of *Gone With The Wind*—I am sure she is the author," wrote Lucille Stephens Kennon in her scrapbook, but she went on to say she would have liked for Mitchell to have given more "appreciation, and acknowledgement to her mother, and grandmother! The stories Mabel (sic) said she was writing down for her children—Stephens & Margaret—the memories regaled to her grandchildren are all Fitzgerald happenings and are scattered thru (sic) the book."

On every visit to Rural Home that Margaret Mitchell and her brother

Stephens took, they were greeted by their two maiden aunts. Is it any wonder she threw a spinster aunt into the mix of characters in *Gone With The Wind?*

Just as the fictional Aunt Pittypat Hamilton raised her niece and nephew, Mitchell's Aunt Mamie raised her sister Catherine's children. When Scarlett goes to Atlanta, she stays with Melanie and Charles' Aunt Pittypat. In the movie, Aunt Pittypat provides comedic value as, throughout the story, she faints from shock.

In *Gone With The Wind*, Melanie and Charles are Ashley Wilkes' cousins. The fictional Wilkes and Hamilton families valued education and reading was a big part of their lives. Melanie's parents died when she was young so they moved in with their father's brother and sister: Henry Hamilton and Sarah Jane "Pittypat" Hamilton.

The Hamiltons considered Melanie and Charles to be their children since neither Henry nor Pittypat (as she was called) had married. Henry, who was not used in the movie, was a lawyer. Margaret Mitchell knew about people moving in with their aunts and uncles. She knew 'Henry' as a familiar name, and she definitely knew about relatives who were lawyers.

Another storyline involves Scarlett stealing her sister Suellen's boyfriend, Frank Kennedy, and marrying him so that she could get money to pay the taxes on Tara. Here is an interesting account from Lucille's scrapbook involving Annie Fitzgerald.

"Annie became engaged to a young man in Augusta, Georgia at a very early age, for to be unmarried after eighteen years marked a girl as an old maid. She and Aunt Mamie came to Atlanta to visit friends and buy things for a trousseau. As was the custom at the time their friends gave a "social" night party and invited all the young men for Aunt Mamie to meet. Among them was a newly arrived dashing, black eyed, gentleman...His name was John Stephens and was (supposed to be) an escort for Aunt Mamie. I'm here to say that most of the Irish young men coming to America at this time were poor and were looking for brides with means. Grandpa's daughter answered this requirement.

"But Aunt Annie was not going to let Mamie have the new beau in the Immaculate Conception Parish—she (was) dead set for him, and went home

engaged to him. The trousseau was bought but used for another bridegroom. Grandfather was horrified. A promise of marriage was as good as the ceremony to him, but Annie threatened to run away and marry in the "big road" in front of the house so he agreed."

So just as Scarlett O'Hara stole her sister's boyfriend and married him in the book, Annie Fitzgerald stole the man intended for her sister and married him, too!

Despite being 'in mourning' after losing her husband Charles (Pitty's nephew), Scarlett works at the Confederate fund-raising event at the request of her sister-in-law Melanie. After Rhett Butler announces he will pay one hundred and fifty dollars in gold to dance with Mrs. Charles Hamilton, and she accepts, Aunt Pitty is out cold. In real life there were two sisters living together. In Mitchell's book there were two siblings, except one was a female and one was a male.

The Harpers, another prominent family in the area, were mentioned in Lucille Kennon's scrapbook. They gave many parties on their plantation, which was in Henry County at the time, and according to Harper descendent Debbie Whittemore they were friends with the Fitzgeralds.

Roderick Henry (R.H.) Harper lived with his wife Francis Ann Crawford Turner and their children.

Philip Fitzgerald was in his mid-sixties and had served in the Indian Wars but was too old to fight during the Civil War so he remained at home with his family, just as Gerald O'Hara did. The Harpers had three family members who signed up: the father and two sons.

According to Debbie Whittemore, this is the family on which Margaret Mitchell based the Tarleton family of *Gone With The Wind*.

It must be mentioned that there are other families in the area who had twins who also felt it could have been their family.

"The colorful Peebles twins, who lived on a neighboring plantation were one family I had heard of for the Tarleton Twins," said historian John Lynch whose own ancestors lived in the area at the time. "They lived near the Fitzgeralds."

As has been pointed out, no one can know for sure, but it is interesting to examine the possibilities.

By the time Margaret Mitchell was writing her book, the Harper family had moved in town to Jonesboro and the generation that she got to know did resemble the Tarletons, and according to Harper descendents Mitchell acknowledged it to them while writing the book. While this may seem questionable since she strongly denied any of her characters were based on real people, she spoke freely about her book for a very short time after it came out.

Both families were large: the fictional Tarletons had eight children, the real-life Harpers, six. They were both in the horse business. The real-life Harpers owned Harper Brothers Horse and Mule, the largest horse and mule company in the area.

In *Gone With The Wind* (page 6), Margaret Mitchell described the Tarletons as having the largest horse farm in Georgia. By the time Mitchell was writing the book, the Harper's horse business had spread to several states. The generation of Harpers that Margaret was familiar with in the early 1900s had sons who fought in World War I and one died.

Both the real Harpers and the fictional Tarletons had at least two sons from each family who went to fight for the Confederacy. The other similarity, of course, was that both families had red-headed twins. The Harpers of the Civil War generation had one set of twins. The next generation—the one Margaret Mitchell knew personally—had two sets. Lon and Al were redheads just like the fictional Stuart and Brent Tarleton.

"My great-grandparents (R.H. and Frances Ann Harper) knew Margaret Mitchell's aunts, and I've heard the aunts were real characters!" said Debbie Whittemore, who heard the stories from her mother Katherine Harper Fordham.

As a young girl, Margaret Mitchell would accompany her aunts to George and Martha Harper's house in Jonesboro. George, one of R.H.'s sons, was older by then and they were friends with the great aunts. He still remembered the war. She loved to hear the stories told about when he and his brother and father (R.H.) fought in the Confederate Army during the War Between the States.

"Margaret used to be over at the house, just talking," said Debbie Whittemore. With fourteen children, including two sets of twins in the family, the house was always buzzing with the excitement.

The Harper Family holds reunions and at a recent one Debbie Whittemore discussed this with a cousin, Sandy Heely who also remembered the story.

"When Margaret Mitchell wrote *Gone With The Wind*, she added the Tarleton twins," Whittemore explained. "They were nineteen-year-old boys patterned after the Harper twins and they even had the red hair! By the time Margaret saw them they were teenagers. She would see them come in together and she thought they were so cute. She always got a big kick out of Lon and Al."

"When she was writing the book, she told our family that story, and acknowledged to them that the Tarleton twins were based after them."

Debbie Whittemore said Mitchell gave the family a signed copy of *Gone With The Wind* since she patterned some characters after them.

When they grew up, the Harper twins that Mitchell knew joined the family horse business their father had set up. Lon and Al, along with Nesbit and the other brothers took the business a step further.

"My grandfather (Nesbit) and his brothers formed Harper Brothers Horse and Mule Business, which among other things supplied livestock for the World War I efforts," said Debbie Whittemore.

In *Gone With The Wind*, Margaret Mitchell describes the Tarletons as being very wealthy, with a large number of slaves to prove it. Mitchell also described the family as a large family, with the largest horse farm around.

The Tarleton twins are not major characters in the book, but their appearance plays a significant part by setting some of the tone. While lounging on the porch of Tara, her father's plantation, the reader sees what a flirt Scarlett O'Hara could be as she toyed with the twins. They also serve to spill the beans about the upcoming engagement of Ashley Wilkes to his cousin Melanie Hamilton and we find out that Scarlett is none too happy to hear that news. It is in this scene that Scarlett is introduced as a boy-crazy, strong-willed 'know-it-all', and here, too, the reader finds out about the imminent possibility of war.

In the movie, Brent Tarleton, played by Fred Crane, the handsome son of a dentist from New Orleans, has the pleasure of saying the opening lines (Scarlett spoke first in the book). Brent is on the front porch at Tara with Scarlett and his brother and he is commenting on the fact that they were expelled from college and what does it matter since there will soon be a war. Scarlett promptly scolds him with her famous line about how all this talk of war is spoiling all the parties this spring.

The scene with the Tarleton twins is also reminiscent of many afternoons and evenings spent at Rural Home, just relaxing and talking on the cool, shaded porch.

If Mitchell used the Harpers as a partial model for the Tarleton family, then she might have combined the Civil War Harpers with the 1920s Harpers. She had access to letters saved from the Civil War sent home by the Harper father.

Roderick Henry Harper enlisted as a private in Company "A," 44th Georgia Infantry, C.S.A. His two oldest sons, George and James, joined with their father. Their mother, Frances Ann, stayed in Jonesboro with their other children. Just as with the real-life Harpers, three of the Tarletons joined up early in the War Between The States. The wives and mothers, left behind, moved in together and families watched out for one another while the men were off at war. Frances Ann's in-laws moved in with her just as Philip Fitzgerald's niece Mary Anne Holliday moved in with the Fitzgeralds during this terrible time.

R. H. Harper wrote many letters home to his family; they were saved and available for family or the neighbors to see. Letters such as these give insight into how terrified the soldiers were to leave their families.

Just as illustrated in *Gone With The Wind*, the men were very patriotic toward the South and were proud to die for 'the cause' but they were very human and concerned for those at home just as the ones left behind were worried about their beloved soldiers. The scene where Melanie greeted Ashley as he returned home for a short three day leave the Christmas after the Battle of Gettysburg illustrates the humanness of the soldiers. The 44th Georgia Regiment lost 10 soldiers, had 49 wounded and 9 were reported missing in the Battle of Gettysburg.

In another scene Melanie is on the front porch with Scarlett and Mammy, when Melanie spots a Confederate soldier walking slowly up the street. Suddenly Scarlett notices (page 515) what Mitchell describes as Melanie putting her hand up to her throat and then running down to greet him.

At first Scarlett is worried Melanie is going to faint but then she sees that the girl begins moving towards the soldier. It's a dramatic scene with her running to Ashley, both having their arms extended towards each other.

A similar story is told by Sara Spano in *I Could've Written Gone With The Wind, But Cousin Margaret Beat Me To It.*

"One story we always wanted told was how Ellen, standing on the side porch one day, looked up and put her hand over her heart and began to run down the lane to meet Philip, who had come home from the war [Indian Wars]. If you remember, Melanie did just this when Ashley came home to Tara.

"This story made a great impression on me and I would often pretend to be Ellen running down the lane to meet her husband. I was always careful about that 'hand over the heart' bit before I started running."

R. H. Harper, homesick and worried about his family, wrote letters home every few days.

"All you have to do is look at the letters that were written back and forth to the soldiers to see the things that happened in Clayton County that also happened *in Gone With The Wind*," said Abb Dickson, Clayton County businessman whose family knew the Fitzgeralds.

These letters are reprinted with the permission of the Harper family descendents. They are copied "as is" with no corrections, keeping in mind that spelling and grammar were different back then.

Goldsboro, North Carolina April the 12

My dear wife and children and parents,

I drop you a few lines to let you know I am well and (I hope) they will reach you all enjoying the same. We got here Wednesday night at 10:00. We are three miles from where there is a bunch of soldiers. They don't think they will have to fight here but else where I don't know how long we will stay here or when we shall go. I have been trying to get a substitute.

But here not yet, more to do I believe I will hear soon. Send my boys by Hill and some paper. I lost mine. Let me hear soon, from you all quick for I want to hear from you all very bad. I want this to do for all I will write in a day or two. I saw your cousin Beall this morning. He is well and starts home

Monday. Kiss the little children for me and pray for me all of your days and nights. Let Pap know when you write. Nothing more. Only I remain your dear husband until death.

R.H. Harper.

Direct your letters to Goldsboro, North Carolina in care of Capt. Peebles 44th Georgia Regt. Company A

(Note: R.H. Harper's commanding officer, Captain Peebles was captured at Spotsylvania, Virginia on May 10, 1864 and then after being exchanged he was wounded and recovered at a Confederate hospital. He was on his way to rejoin the command when the war ended. Ashley Wilkes, who fought in Cobb's Legion, was also captured during the Battle of Spotsylvania Court House in 1864.)

These letters would be similar to Mrs. Tarleton getting letters from her sons or the ones Melanie got from Ashley, which she read aloud to anyone who wanted to hear them.

This was early in the war—the same time frame used with the volunteers from Clayton County in *Gone With The Wind.*

Camp McIntush May the 8th 1862

Near Goldsboro, N.C.

My dear wife and children

I have just got your letter and was glad to hear from you all. I got all you sent me. I reckon this leaves us in good health, we have very firey weather. It is thought we will have a big fight soon somewhere not far from here. I was in the Arkansas Regt. Yesterday. I saw a man that was acquainted with Uncle G. Hanson and Claborn and old John Mckansie and all. The boy, Phil and Sarah are married and that was old John that was killed you was reading about. He was the Preacher but he was fighting brave. Bob was with him and lay behind a log and killed 4 yankees at the time. The one that shot his Paw had become clean. If the Sows and pigs is doing well I think you can spare one and pigs I want some for another year. Do as you think is best, you and Pap . He can tell you what you ought to have for them. Write soon how you all are for I am uneasy as you all have the measles*. So I remain your dear husband and Paw until death. I want you all to Pray for us all. I will write in 2 or 3 days.

Kiss little Fanny for me—R.H. Harper

*Note the mention of the measles. In *Gone With The Wind*, Scarlett O'Hara's first husband, Charles dies early in the war from pneumonia which developed from his having the measles. Measles was a big problem as were other illnesses.

Also notice the salutation, "Dear Wife." This is the same salutation that Ashley used when he wrote to Melanie, as on page 210. It was a sign of the times to use a more generic, polite form—just as Gerald O'Hara called his wife "Mrs. O'Hara."

Dear Wife and children

I drop you a few lines to let you know we are well. Frank has been sick a few days with sore throat but he is well now. He has a sore finger, middle finger. I am feared it's a fever. We was ordered to Petersburg but they stopped us 120 miles farther from home. We got here yesterday morning. I haven't seen Rod and John Jackson since we've been here (unreadable) 3 more out of the Regt. gone on the other side of the river. (unreadable) Jenkins is in town guarding prisoners. They have to stay 24 hours we don't know how long we will stay here. Probably some time.

We haven't had nothing to eat but crackers and fat boiled meat for 2 days like a while ago. Will got a (unreadable) and went into town and give one dollar for 4 fish meat meals. 10 of us we sold $8.00 worth of bacon at 20 cents a pound. When we left Macintosh I understood a bit go that Dock and Waid was on the other side of the river. I don't know whether it's so or not. I think we are in a healthy place for a town or city. I want you and Pap to write to me soon as you get his and I will (unreadable). Write it to Weldon H.L. so the Regt. as before don't delay writing for I want to hear from you all and how you are getting on with the crops. Give my respects to all the kin and Pap will see Uncle Jerry and Aunt. Tell Aunt I haven't forgot her. Kiss little Fanny for me. Children I want you all to be good boys and girls and mind your Ma and grandparents so. I must come to a close. Remember me in your prayers so I remain your Dear husband and father til death.

R. H. Harper.

Unfortunately, R.H. Harper's letters with the touching closing lines, "I remain your Dear husband and father til death," would be all they had of their father as he was killed June 26, 1862, at the Battle of Ellison's Mill near Richmond, Virginia; just several months after enlisting. In the movie, Stuart and Brent Tarleton are also killed shortly after they join the Confederate Army.

The 44th Georgia Regiment that the Harpers fought in suffered greater casualties than any other regiment on the Confederate side. At the end of the war when the white flag went up at Appomattox Court House on April 9, 1865, there were only 62 survivors of the original 1,115 who had left home in 1862 with the 44th Georgia.

Though the Harper's father died in the Civil War, his sons George and James Harper returned safely to their family in Jonesboro. George married a woman named Martha and they had a very large family including Lon and Al and Debbie Whittemore's grandfather, Nesbit.

"My mom is the niece of Al and Lon," she said. "Neither of them died in the Civil War (like the Tarletons did in GWTW.) They lived during World War I, but they continued in the horse business. The Harper Brothers were a large horse and mule dealer with offices in Atlanta, Cuba, St. Louis, and Chicago.

The Civil War hit the folks back home in Clayton County in two ways. First of all their sons and husbands were off fighting, just as R.H. Harper and his sons were, but then as the war moved into Georgia they grew fearful for themselves, that harm could come to them on their own farms.

The North appeared to be growing tired of the war, and in the summer of 1864 the South was stalling in hopes that Lincoln would not be re-elected.

The Union's General William Sherman got the idea to destroy the railroad system from Macon to Atlanta and cut off the South's supplies. On Aug. 18, 1864, the Jonesboro depot was set fire by Union forces and some of the track was destroyed. Sherman realized the Confederate Army had supplies arriving by way of Atlanta so he sent some of his troops south and instructed Gen. Oliver Howard to come in on Jonesboro from the west.

Philip Fitzgerald's niece, Mary Anne Holliday, whose husband Robert K. Holliday was off in another area fighting, sought refuge with her uncle's family at Rural Home during the Battle of Jonesboro. She brought four of her children and they all worried about her two daughters, Mattie and Lucy, who were in Savannah at school.

Tom Barnes, the author of *Doc Holliday's Road To Tombstone* and whose credits include a PBS documentary on the history of Georgia, recreated the scene as he saw it through his research:

"The citizens of Jonesboro stood in their front yards and watched horsemen of the Confederate Cavalry race through the streets and listened to the thunder of war as the battle for the city of Atlanta raged on.

Philip Fitzgerald rode through the confusion, pulled up at the front gate of the Holliday house and called out, 'Mary Anne, Meg hurry and get as many valuables from the house as you can carry, while I hitch the wagon'.

'What does all this mean, Uncle Philip?'

'We're going to the farm tonight. Rumor has it there will be a battle soon'.

Margaret Mitchell's great grandfather, Philip Fitzgerald was right about the battle of Jonesboro. The scene was played out throughout the South. Cries of "The Yankees are coming!" were heard everywhere and then there was the hurried packing and people fleeing their homes in fear of the Union Troops.

On August 25, 1864 the South's General Hood saw that Sherman's army seemed to be retreating. He did not realize they were merely repositioning themselves and that they were headed toward the Flint River. Rural Home was located near the river.

Once Hood realized what Sherman was up to he sent Lieutenant General William J. Hardee with his own corps under the command of Major General Patrick R. Cleburne and Major General Stephen D. Lee's Corps to defend Jonesboro and the fighting began.

Many homes around Jonesboro were being destroyed, yet the Fitzgerald place was left standing. Marie Nygren, daughter of Margaret Mitchell's second cousin, Margaret Kennon Lupo, said the family heard that story many times and still has a prominent piece of memorabilia from that era.

"I own the original cross from Philip Fitzgerald's house, that saved the home," she said.

Nygren says that according to family history, Sherman himself came up to the Fitzgerald door and upon entering the house he spotted the large cross on the wall.

"He saw that they were Catholic," said Marie Nygren. "It was rare at that time in the South and because Sherman's wife was Catholic, he did not burn the house down. The story was that he talked to Philip Fitzgerald's wife and actually had tea with her."

There was another real-life similarity to the book at this point: illness at the time of the Yankees occupying their property. In the book, when Scarlett O'Hara returned to Tara with Melanie and Prissy only to find out that her mother had just died of typhoid fever, she was heartbroken. She then found out that her sisters Carreen and Suellen had caught it also.

According to Mitchell cousin Sara Spano, "My grandmother [Annie Fitzgerald's sister] who was a little girl, and one other sister had scarlet fever and the general gave orders that the house was to be spared. He even stationed a guard around to protect my great-grandmother (Ellen) and her daughters."

The guard also protected Mary Anne Holliday and her family who had taken refuge with the Fitzgeralds. After Philip Fitzgerald had picked them up they spent several days at Rural Home.

As Sherman and his Northern troops sought to destroy everything in their range, Jonesboro was in ruins. Homes were looted and then set afire. Crops were destroyed. Union forces did everything they could to be sure the railroad was destroyed and that no supplies would be delivered and the devastation so bad they would not be able to recover. The Fitzgerald home, just like the O'Hara home in *Gone With The Wind*, was left standing. But everything around it was in ruins.

It was a terrible time for the Fitzgeralds with Union Troops taking control of their property. Mary Anne Holliday worried about her own house and she could not wait until she could take her family home.

During the time of the Battle of Jonesboro, the fictional Scarlett O'Hara was in Atlanta. During this time in real-life, Annie Fitzgerald was married, living in Atlanta, running her businesses. As the horror of the war was upon them, young Annie Fitzgerald longed to be with her family at Rural Home.

When Annie arrived at Rural Home she was devastated at what she encountered, but the most shocking was the fact that the hated Northern soldiers had stayed in the home she had grown up in.

Margaret Mitchell used this exact scenario on page 410 of *Gone With The Wind*. She asked her father why they left Tara standing. Gerald O'Hara looked at his daughter, dumbfounded, and then told her that the Union Troops used Tara as their headquarters. She was shocked and horrified to learn "Yankees" had been in her house.

John Lynch, whose ancestors knew the Fitzgeralds, received permission to search the grounds around the Fitzgerald plantation years ago. He came upon some proof that Union soldiers had been on the property.

"I was searching for artifacts around the Fitzgerald plantation," said Lynch, the director of the Holliday-Dorsey-Fife Museum in nearby Fayetteville. "I found a Yankee cavalryman's buckle and other items associated with Union cavalry. It is a fact that the troops were there and probably used the house as a headquarters. It does show up on old Civil War maps."

According to Harper family history, not too far away, the Harper Plantation was in the same situation. The Harper's quick thinking Mammy tricked the union soldiers by rolling their meat in flour and dirt and throwing it out the window telling the troops it was rotten and they could have it. They didn't want 'rotten' meat, so after they left the Mammy picked up the meat, rinsed it off and the family ate it later.

Margaret Mitchell had Scarlett O'Hara use a similar tactic *in Gone With The Wind*. After Scarlett killed the Yankee, she took his wallet. When the Yankees came through the second time, Scarlett O'Hara hid the wallet in the dirty diaper of Melanie's baby, Beau. After they left and Melanie was changing the child, she noticed it.

Speaking of the scene where Scarlett kills the Yankee, this may have happened, but not at the Fitzgerald plantation. One of the tour guides at the historic Stately Oaks Plantation told guests at the 2007 celebration of Margaret Mitchell's birthday about an incident that supposedly happened at the Crawford home just after the Battle of Jonesboro: one of the Crawford daughters shot a Yankee on the third step.

Genealogy shows that the Crawfords did have a girl named Allie Frances Crawford who was born in 1850, so her age would have been about right.

"Yes, I knew that," said Gene Talmadge, the current owner of the house. "Miss Parker Babb, who was a truant officer and about the most respected citizen in the area at the time, told me when I was a child that a Union soldier was killed when he was coming up the stairs."

Mrs. Parker Babb had known Chuck and Arie Crawford, grandchildren of Thomas Crawford, and it was originally from Arie Crawford that the story came.

Mrs. Babb was Nell Wise Babb who was born in 1892, less than thirty years after the Civil War. She married G. Parker Babb. The other story that has come from Nell Babb was that one of the Crawford daughters had a dress made from the curtains in the house.

Since Nell Babb's husband Parker worked on the Crawford property for a time, she knew the Crawfords. Martha Arie Crawford, one of the daughters of Thomas Crawford, was eighteen when the Civil War started so she would have known about that story and she lived in the Crawford House until the 1930s.

Nell and Parker Babb were married in 1915 and Parker worked for the Crawfords.

"I don't remember Parker Babb when he was the farm manager, but I was just a kid back then," said Gene Talmadge, whose grandparents originally bought the house from the Crawfords. "When I knew him he lived in Lovejoy and Miss Babb worked for the School system and was a truant officer."

Talmadge believes the stories about the girl shooting the Yankee straggler on the steps and the Crawford girl making a dress out of the drapes.

"I believe Miss Babb," he said. "She was not a gullible woman and I believe what she said. She was a smart, able woman with common sense."

Gene Talmadge said he has not seen the blood stain, but that perhaps a forensics expert could find it if the stairs were exposed. The event took place more than one hundred forty years ago, but when Margaret Mitchell was writing her book, people like Arie Crawford and Nell and Parker Babb's family were still alive.

With the invasion of so many Union soldiers, there just were not enough Confederates to stand up to them all. According to the historical marker erected to commemorate the Battle of Jonesboro: "Confederate Forces under Gen. Hardee, endeavoring to defend the remaining R.R. (railroad) to Atlanta against outnumbering Federal troops August 31-September 1 were forced to withdraw to Lovejoy's (station)."

The battle of Jonesboro lasted two days, from August 31-September 1, 1864. The importance of this battle was that it finally caused Atlanta to fall to the Union troops. Sherman figured if he cut off their supplies in Atlanta, the Confederates would have to evacuate Atlanta. His troops cut off the railroad from Macon to Jonesboro.

General Hardee for the South had his forces trying to defend the last railroad to Atlanta. General Hood evacuated Atlanta, but just as in the movie, *Gone With The Wind*, the Confederates blew up their own military supplies on their way out so the Yankees would not get to them.

Margaret Mitchell wrote about the explosions set by the South to destroy their own ammunition before the North could get to it. In describing the fantastic fire scene which was the first scene filmed, it has been referred to it as the "Burning of Atlanta," but Mitchell clues the reader that it was the artillery burning by having Frank Kennedy explain it to Scarlett in the book. Rhett Butler explains it to her in the movie.

The next day, September second, General Sherman and his army occupied Atlanta, ordering all civilians out.

On November 15th the Union troops left Atlanta in flames and headed toward Savannah in what would become known as Sherman's March to the Sea.

Hundreds of unidentified Confederate soldiers who died during the Battle of Jonesboro are buried in the General Patrick R. Cleburne Confederate Cemetery in Jonesboro, Clayton County, Georgia. "The Cemetery still flies the Confederate flag," said Oliver "Sandy" Heely, a descendent of R.H. Harper, who grew up in Jonesboro.

The scene in the *Gone With The Wind* movie where all of the wounded soldiers were laid out was portrayed as Mitchell would have wanted, because the Civil War was such a devastating war. Many lives had been lost in the Atlanta campaign. In Atlanta the Union suffered 3,641 casualties, the Confederates an unbelievable 8,499.

The Battle of Jonesboro saw 1,149 Union and 2,200 Confederate soldiers killed. Originally the soldiers were buried where they fell, but later the confederate cemetery was established and is maintained by the United Daughters of the Confederacy. There is a monument at the cemetery, and, interestingly, the inscription was written by Wilbur Kurtz, the friend of Margaret Mitchell's who went to Hollywood to help with the movie production. He was chosen for his knowledge of the history of Atlanta and Clayton County. The monument reads:

"To the honored memory of the several hundred unknown Confederate soldiers reposing within this enclosure who fell at the Battle of Jonesboro, August 31-September 1, 1864.

"These Soldiers were of Hardee's Corps, commanded by Maj. Gen. Patrick R. Cleburne, Lieut. Gen. Stephen D. Lee's Corps, and a portion of Maj. Gen. Joseph Wheeler's Cavalry Corps. Commanded by Lieut. Gen. William J. Hardee and charged with the defense of Jonesboro though vastly outnumbered by Federal forces they gave their lives to parry the final thrust at the heart of the Southern Confederacy."

Erected by the Atlanta Ladies Memorial Association
1934
Inscription by Wilbur G. Kurtz

Families who could afford it and knew where their loved ones died had graves of their own. Once they received notice of the death of their father, husband or brother some of the families just did not have the money to ship them home and bury them, so they were buried in the confederate cemeteries. Margaret Mitchell mentioned gravestones in *Gone With The Wind.*

Scarlett and her sisters had paid a call on the Tarletons after the father returned home from war and they had lost their sons. She was so sorry for the family until she saw the tombstones they had on their son's graves. It was as if the tombstones were a symbol of having enough money to waste, because Scarlett suddenly decided she didn't feel sorry for them any more. She thought it was so terrible that they wasted the money that many needed for food, so she felt they did not deserve her sympathy anymore.

After observing all of the similarities between the book and the real-life people of Clayton County, it is safe to say that when Margaret Mitchell crafted her novel she probably was inspired by her family's experiences as well as the people she had heard about.

"In the 1800's when Philip Fitzgerald lived, his property was out in the country south of Jonesboro," said local historian John Lynch. "Highway 19/ 41 is the 'four-lane' and Jonesboro is off to the east of it. Running north and south, parallel with the railroad, the highway was built probably in the 1930s. Rural Home was on Bumblehook Road, which is now Tara Road (off of Tara Boulevard which is Highway 19/41)."

According to Sandy Heely, the nearby Lawrence House was used as one of the Confederate Hospitals in Jonesboro. Margaret Mitchell researched the hospitals because of the scenes with the make-shift Confederate Hospital in Atlanta. Mitchell talked to Heely's mother about her book.

"Sandy's mother, Lou Heely, knew Margaret Mitchell and according to Sandy, Mitchell told his mother that she envisioned the Fitzgerald place as Tara," said Debbie Whittemore, his cousin. "The Fitzgerald place was her basis for Tara. Because of the family's close friendship, Sandy Heely has a *Gone With The Wind* original novel that Margaret Mitchell autographed for his mom."

Philip Fitzgerald, who was sixty-five at the end of the war, had to start over again with no field slaves, no food, just his daughters and an ailing wife. Does any of this sound familiar from *Gone With The Wind*? It was the story of many families from the South, but Mitchell's was included in that group.

Margaret Mitchell never knew Philip Fitzgerald as he had died twenty years before she was born, but on every visit to Rural Home that she and her brother Stephens took, they were greeted by those great-aunts, Sis and Mamie.

Margaret Mitchell had heard the story that was handed down through the generations about the gypsy putting the curse on the Fitzgerald family that their sons would die and their daughters become widows.

This could also explain why widowhood played such a big part in *Gone With The Wind*. Her female ancestors had spent much time in the "widow's weeds" of the time.

Katy Fitzgerald Stephens (two sisters married men named Stephens) was pictured in Lucille Kennon's scrapbook in black mourning clothes complete with veil in a photo dated 1898. She had become a widow two years earlier. Katy's sister Agnes and her husband died at a young age, so that would have been another time to wear the mourning clothes. Another sister, Adelle, also became a young widow. According to the scrapbook: "Mrs. A.M. Daly (Adelle), who had lost her husband, came to Atlanta to keep their house and sent her daughter through school." Mamie and Sarah never married, and then there was Annie. She became a widow later in life, though her husband had walked out on her when she was young.

"Margaret modeled Scarlett after her grandmother, Annie Fitzgerald Stephens," said Marie Nygren, the daughter of Mitchell's cousin, Margaret Kennon Lupo. "Everybody knew that."

Lucille Stephens Kennon wrote, "Scarlett was Aunt Annie in many ways. And Aunt Annie was Margaret's Grandmother. She had many admirable traits of character, but self-will and determination were always uppermost."

In *Gone With The Wind*, Rhett Butler teased Scarlett O'Hara that she was the "Belle of the County." The same was said about Annie Fitzgerald.

"Someone remarked that 'those Fitzgerald girls are the belles of Fayetteville'," said Lucille Kennon in her scrapbook, "Whereupon Aunt Agnes replied, 'Yes indeed. Annie is the bell and I'm the clapper'."

After the Civil War, the country was in economic and political turmoil. Congress established the Freedmen's Bureau, which was an effort to help former slaves. Its purpose was to provide schools, food, and medical treatment. Reconstruction was supposed to be a time for the country to heal itself of the many problems it faced. Lincoln had tried to be sympathetic to the black cause, but any sympathy the government had ended when he was assassinated and Vice President Andrew Johnson, Democrat, took over.

This troubling time in American history was called the Reconstruction period. The 14th and 15th Amendments to the Constitution provided citizenship and the right to vote for blacks, who had only recently been slaves on the plantations. The slaves had been freed, and most were overjoyed, but some stayed on the plantations out of a sense of duty to their masters; and in the book, those such as Mammy, Dilcey and Pork stayed on with the O'Haras. Perhaps some of the recently freed blacks felt they had no place to go. During this time they had to figure out where they would live and what they would do with their newfound freedom.

Carpetbaggers and Scalawags, people from the North, tried to form an allegiance with them. During this time the Ku Klux Klan was strong in the South. The KKK was founded in Tennessee in 1866 by a group of Confederate Army veterans. They were afraid of the possible power the blacks might gain with the recent changes in government and they tried to terrorize them with their violence.

Margaret Mitchell acknowledged the KKK in her book; however David O. Selznick chose not to mention them by name or show them in the movie. He was Jewish and felt empathy towards the black race. Mitchell showed the KKK from what she considered the "South's" view.

In *Gone With The Wind*, Scarlett drove to her sawmill and the store, and the route she took was through an area Mitchell called Shantytown.

Margaret Mitchell's grandfather, John Stephens, had also owned a store.

"They may have set Uncle John up in business," wrote Lucille in her scrapbook. *"He soon had a flourishing wholesale feed, grain and seed business and began to buy real estate."*

The real-life Annie Fitzgerald would drive to the store and sawmill she bought, by herself and those who knew about it thought it was a frightening thought to see a woman alone in a horse-drawn cart.

Shantytown was a makeshift "town" where the recently freed blacks had built houses. In the book (and movie) she was accosted by a would-be attacker as she drove through, but Big Sam just happened to be nearby. Big Sam was her friend and former slave from Tara. When he heard her screaming and saw it was her, he saved her. The word got out about the "almost-attack" which she made sound like an attack, and some of the men wanted to "avenge" it.

That night Ashley, along with Scarlett's husband, Frank Kennedy, told their wives they were going to a "political meeting." The other women knew what was happening. Scarlett got mad at them because she did not know they were going out to avenge what they thought was an attack by a freed slave, but it was actually a white man who grabbed her. They were actually involved in the Klan though Scarlett did not know it.

Out of respect for blacks, Selznick did not show it, but tried to keep with Mitchell's story in a round-about way.

Later, in the book, Scarlett finds out that the "political meeting" was really a Klan meeting. When Rhett Butler finally got it out of Melanie where Ashley and the men went, the reader finds out that it was "Out the Decatur road near Shantytown…"

This story is very similar to a real-life happening within Margaret Mitchell's family. Mitchell's first cousin once removed. Lucille Kennon's scrapbook tells the story:

Written in her words from her scrapbook (with no changes):

"During the reconstruction period, the carpet bag government (came) the first need for the 'Kluxers', Uncle John's brother Mike (This would be Margaret Mitchell's great-uncle) must have been a member. There was trouble one night and a man was killed. Mike and the other boys had to be hidden and then gotten out of town for the Federal officers were after them! Aunt Sadie said it was a dreadful time.

Uncle John, the older men, and the boys involved put on disguises and spirited the younger ones out across to Alabama and on to Texas.

Before getting so involved Uncle John, who seemed to be able to play both sides and had business with the occupation forces, made over all of his property holdings to his wife to avoid confiscation, if he were caught. Mike did the same thing and gave his to his wife "Sallie Mike" as I always heard her called. The wives were expected to give back the titles but Aunt Annie never would. Uncle John built some stores on Decatur Street and some negro tenant houses, but the situation became worse from day to day…"

Since Annie refused to give the titles back she ended up owning the businesses her husband had. She became the landlord on the stores and tenant houses.

The stories were so similar and Mitchell even used Decatur Road in the book. According to Lucille's scrapbook, John Stephens must have been a little like Rhett Butler in that "Uncle John seemed to be able to play both sides and had business with emancipation forces."

That story may have also inspired the scene where Tony Fontaine shows up at Scarlett and Frank Kennedy's in the middle of the night. In this story, (page 644) Tony has killed someone and is trying to escape to Texas. His reasoning for the murder was that one of them said something threatening to his sister-in-law Sally. Tony was scared, but he stopped for some brief food and shelter before trying to escape to Texas. "Sally" was the name of Tony's sister-in-law, and in the real story from the scrapbook, "Sallie Mike" was John Stephens' sister-in-law.

The other similarity with *Gone With The Wind* found in this section of Lucille's scrapbook was the sawmill that Annie Fitzgerald ran. She would be seen driving her own carriage out to the sawmill—something that was just not done by women back then:

"So she started collecting rents," said the scrapbook, *"doing repairs, running the draying service continually, running a saw mill outside Atlanta and being her own boss generally. Eventually she got involved in land titles, mortgages, lawsuits and loan sharks."*

In *Gone With The Wind*, Scarlett needed money to pay the taxes on Tara so she went to Rhett Butler. After visiting him in jail and having that plan foiled, she was leaving, and as luck would have it she passed Frank Kennedy, who was engaged to her sister Suellen. Scarlett found out Frank owned a store and planned to buy a sawmill. She realized how much money could be made on a sawmill because of all the rebuilding that needed to be done in Atlanta after the war, so she lied to Frank that Suellen had another boyfriend and she persuaded Frank to marry her. Soon she owned the store and the sawmill, and she was doing things like Mitchell's grandmother had done.

Margaret Mitchell would have known a lot about the importance of sawmills in those days to all the growth in the South. It was right there in her family. Among the pictures in Lucille's scrapbook is one of "My father, William Stephens at his lumber mill in Atlanta…in 1890." William Stephens was Margaret Mitchell's great-uncle. He was the brother-in-law of Annie Fitzgerald Stephens and this may have been the sawmill she eventually owned.

That may be where Margaret Mitchell got the idea for Scarlett to own the sawmill and for Frank Kennedy to own the store, which she ended up running.

"Eleanor [his wife] was from Madison, GA," said Lucille Kennan in her scrapbook. *"When she married Philip they moved to Fayetteville and he ran a store. He owned about 100 slaves at the time they were freed, but he never believed in slavery. It was a thing he hoped to see legally done away with."*

This could explain why Gerald O'Hara was so sympathetic toward his slaves. He had a genuine friendship with Pork, his valet, and he even bought Dilcey so that Pork could marry her and live with his wife.

Lucille's scrapbook also gives us a clue as to where she got the idea for Aunt Pittypat and Uncle Henry to care for Melanie and her brother Charles after their parents died when they were still children. Lucille's parents both died when the children were very young and they were raised by their aunts Sis (also called Sadie) and Mamie at Rural Home—the same aunts Margaret Mitchell visited with her mother and grandmother.

"Aunt Sadie promised to care for us and never has an aunt fulfilled a promise so well," Lucille wrote. *"We stayed on in Atlanta through high school. Then she sent each of us to old State Normal School for several years."*

Lucille's accounts of the stories of the family personalize the stories of Sis and Mamie and their family. Now through this scrapbook we get to hear some of those stories.

When Margaret Mitchell was writing her book, she had no idea it would become so famous and read all over the world. Her family's life experiences were so sensational they were worth a book. She took something she was familiar with and, using her own descriptive writing style, made it into the best-selling book it became. There were some people in Clayton County, including some relatives who felt left out when she would not acknowledge that she had, indeed, taken some real life happenings and used them in the creation of her story.

"I agree that Margaret should have given credit to her aunts and grandmother for the stories and history they gave her," said Saundra Voter, who helped Sara Spano type her book, *I Could've Written Gone With The Wind But Cousin Margaret Beat Me To It.* Spano, Mitchell's cousin, had spent many summers with Margaret at Rural Home.

"Perhaps," Saundra concluded, "She didn't want people to know that so much of *Gone With The Wind* was based on that history."

If this was the case, it becomes understandable why Margaret Mitchell did not want to go to Hollywood and work on the movie even though she was invited several times.

David O. Selznick kept coming back to her asking about the characters.

"Margaret was an exceptional woman and deserves all the accolades and attention possible," said Voter. "It is remarkable that her book and the movie have lasted so long and is so beloved by so many people, including myself."

"Doc" Holliday Connection

While many people in Clayton County recognized the resemblances between Scarlett O'Hara and Annie Fitzgerald, there were also those who knew about the famous Doc Holliday's involvement with the Fitzgerald family. It must be pointed out that the entire Holliday family, including John Henry (Doc), were upstanding citizens. They had professional careers and did a great deal for their community. Many who knew them simply thought things just went terribly wrong for John Henry, but one can assume it was the fame he received from the Gunfight at OK Coral that caused Mitchell and her family not to mention them.

"McDonough Road, Jonesboro and the night Atlanta burned were all part of Margaret Mitchell's *Gone With the Wind*," said author Tom Barnes. "They also had a place in a story I was researching and writing, *The Life and Times of John Henry [Doc] Holliday*. The scene I was working on took place at Jonesboro on the night Atlanta burned and one of the characters involved was Philip Fitzgerald, a great uncle of Mattie Holliday, John Henry's romantic interest in the story."

Mattie's mother, Mary Anne had sought refuge with the Fitzgeralds. Mattie was at a convent in Savannah at the time. Her involvement with her cousin, who would become known as Doc Holliday, may have contributed to *Gone With The Wind*. Barnes' research serves to fill in some blanks from his perspective. According to Tom Barnes, one of Mattie's sisters had letters between Mattie and John Henry that she burned. It was not clear if she was told to burn them or whether she chose to do so.

When the time seemed right, Philip Fitzgerald took the Hollidays home, but when they got there the scene was reminiscent of when Melanie saw Twelve Oaks. It was completely destroyed.

Tom Barnes wrote:

"Mary Anne Holliday and her brood had followed the war news from Uncle Philip's farm. When the shooting stopped they rode back into town. Uncle Philip, on horseback, was leading the way with Mary Anne at the reins of the wagon. As they picked their way through the rubble in the streets they were astonished by what they saw.

Most of the houses were standing with frames and interior walls holding up a finished roof, just the skeletal remains were in evidence. Exterior wood, clapboard, window frames, porch rails, yard fences, barns and outhouses had been plundered for the quickest way to acquire the lumber needed to build breastworks.

Mary Anne looked on with dismay and simply shook her head as she viewed houses of friends, houses where she had been to tea just a few weeks earlier. Homes that only days before would have been looked on with pride, were now without distinction. Missing were the flowers, shrubs, fruit trees and vegetable gardens all trampled or rooted up by desperate men seeking timbers to build a shield against enemy bullets.

When Mary Anne pulled up in front of her house she was sickened by what she saw and lamented to Philip, 'Is there nothing sacred to those people? Have they no respect for the law?'"

Once she saw her home was in ruins, Mary Anne Holliday wanted to get her children away from the devastated Jonesboro area; so they headed to Griffin, Georgia where other Holliday relatives lived. Her other two daughters, Mattie and Lucy, made it safely to Griffin and they were once again together, this time with their Aunt Alice, Uncle Henry and cousin John Henry Holliday.

Barnes' book, Doc Holliday's *Road to Tombstone: The Life And Times of John Henry Holliday* is interesting and this is merely one small part of it. He has also written about it on his "Rock The Tower" blog on the internet.

After General Sherman's troops had set fire to and looted everything that was in their way, food was hard to come by. As with their neighbors, the Hollidays and Fitzgeralds lived on vegetables they grew in their garden: turnips, beets, and collards.

It was that poignant scene in the book and movie that is taken directly from Margaret Mitchell's relatives' experiences where Scarlett is so hungry because "the Yankees" have taken everything. She goes to a garden and digs up muddy radishes and they make her sick as she eats them.

The whole Philip Fitzgerald Civil War story is not complete without a further explanation of the Doc Holliday connection. John Lynch runs the museum in Fayetteville, Georgia which carries the Holliday name, but inside are many historical facts dealing with the Fitzgeralds as the two families were intertwined.

Though Margaret Mitchell never mentioned a Doc Holliday connection in her family and her brother Stephens never mentioned it, recently the Margaret Mitchell House has begun acknowledging it. It is common knowledge in Clayton County and in the historical displays at the Holliday-Dorsey-Fife Museum.

Mary Anne's daughter, Mattie, eventually became a nun, named Sister Mary Melanie, and was called Sister Melanie. Since there is a storyline in *Gone With The Wind* involving two cousins and one of the characters was named Melanie, it is fascinating to examine. The Hollidays and Fitzgeralds were related by marriage. Annie Fitzgerald and her sisters were cousins with Mattie Holliday and in fact Mattie and her family put on a party for Annie when she was engaged to be married.

Writer Tom Barnes believes Mattie had a romantic tie with her cousin John Henry [Doc] Holliday and that this played a part in Margaret Mitchell's book.

His book is historical fiction but Barnes says it is based on facts; facts that he researched for many years.

Author Karen Holliday Tanner does not believe there was a romantic interest between John Henry Holliday and his cousin, Mattie.

An interview with another Holliday cousin indicated that Margaret Mitchell knew Mattie Holliday well and visited her each week when she was older. Once it was established that the possible love connection between Holliday and his cousin Mattie was going to be explored in this book, that cousin said she does not believe there was a romantic interest and asked that she not be included in the book if it was going to mention that possibility. Out of respect for her, that interview and her name have been left out, but she did tell of frequent visits that Margaret Mitchell had with Sister Melanie during the time she was writing the book.

"Some people believe it, some don't," said the curator John Lynch about a possible love connection between Mattie (Sister Melanie) and Holliday.

"I worked with a [still another] cousin of Doc Holliday's, who was a relative of Doc's on his mother's side," said Barnes. "I did a lot of research. Anything I said about the relationship between Doc and Mattie, I stand by it."

Barnes had previously worked on The PBS television series "Georgia's Heritage" as host, narrator, and writer. The last segment featured the Doc Holliday story.

His research led him to question "why Margaret Mitchell didn't wish to discuss her characters with David Selznick." His conclusion: "Autobiographical. She did not want it known how close her story came to real life and her own family heritage."

The Margaret Mitchell House and Museum Visual Arts Collection housed in the Atlanta History Center includes the following names in the Margaret Mitchell collection: Dr. John Henry "Doc" Holliday, DDS; Mary Ann Fitzgerald Holliday; Roberta R. Holliday Moran; Major Henry Burroughs Holliday ("Doc" Holliday's father); Capt. Robert Kennedy Holliday; Sister Melanie/Mattie Holliday; Holliday/Moran relatives.

Barnes said he accidentally came upon some information that raises the legitimate question…was the story of Doc Holliday and his cousin, Mattie, the basis for at least one *Gone With The Wind* storyline? It is a controversial idea. You decide.

John Henry Holliday was born to Alice (McKey) and Henry Holliday on August 14, 1851, in Griffin, Georgia. Henry's brother, Dr. John Stiles Holliday, a prominent physician in Fayetteville, traveled to deliver him. He brought his wife, Permelia.

Four years later, this same Dr. John Stiles Holliday built a home in

Fayetteville, Georgia which still stands today as the Holliday-Dorsey-Fife House and exists as a museum, run by John Lynch. This is an important point, as the house was eventually used as part of the Fayetteville Academy, which later became known as the Fayetteville Seminary. Because the Hollidays knew the Fitzgeralds, Margaret Mitchell's grandmother (Annie Fitzgerald) stayed in this house while attending Fayetteville Academy. John Stiles Holliday served as a trustee to the school, which Margaret Mitchell used as the school Scarlett O'Hara attended in *Gone With The Wind* (p. 495).

According to Karen Holliday Tanner's book, *Doc Holliday: A Family Portrait,* the Robert Hollidays (Mattie's family) had moved to Jonesboro in 1857.

As noted, when the Civil War broke out Robert joined the Confederate Army and his wife, Mary Anne, took her children to live with her aunt and uncle, the Fitzgeralds, for those scary two weeks

When she found out her own house was destroyed, they took refuge in Griffin, Georgia to be with their Holliday cousins.

The Hollidays were a close-knit group and often traveled by horse and buggy or train back and forth from Jonesboro to southern Georgia to visit each other, so Alice and Henry Holliday welcomed them with open arms. John Henry liked having his cousins there.

Eventually Mattie and Lucy arrived safely from school in Savannah, and suddenly John Henry's quiet life changed as the cousins added excitement to the family home. It was during this time that John Henry formed a close childhood friendship with his cousin Mattie. That they were close has not been disputed.

"Little Mattie developed a particular fondness for young John Henry with his blond hair and blue eyes and his quiet personality," said Karen Holliday Tanner in her book (page 28). "She helped to look after her cousin, who was two years her junior. A strong bond of friendship grew between the two that was to last for the rest of John Henry's life."

Though she mentioned their closeness in her book, when she was questioned about a possible love relationship she said she does not believe one existed.

Two years after the Civil War ended, when John Henry Holliday was fifteen his mother died from tuberculosis. Three months later, his father married the neighbor down the street and moved the family to a new home.

Shortly after that, John Henry left home to live with his Uncle John and Aunt Permelia, reuniting him on a regular basis with his cousins.

According to Tom Barnes, the feelings between Mattie and John Henry escalated from a close friendship into a love story.

His blog states: "The storybook romance between John Henry Holliday and Mattie is cut short by disease and family strife. The young dentist is forced to abandon Mattie for life in the West."

Barnes points out their family would have been very much against the situation since they were first cousins and Mattie's Catholic religion did not condone the marriage of first cousins.

After going to Dental School in Pennsylvania, John Henry returned to Georgia and eventually practiced dentistry in the Atlanta area for several years, living with his aunt and uncle again.

According to the Karen Holliday Tanner book, John Stiles Holliday had taken in a young slave girl named Sophie during the Civil War who taught John Henry and his cousin Robert to play poker and that is where he got his first taste of gambling.

John Henry continued his friendship (or possible relationship) with his cousin Mattie, with whom he shared similar interests of books and culture. They were together during the Christmas holidays in 1872. Mattie's father died and was buried in the Fayetteville Cemetery in the same area as Philip Fitzgerald, so John Henry and his family traveled to Clayton County for the funeral.

John Henry began losing weight and showing signs of illness. To his horror, in the summer of 1873 he was diagnosed with tuberculosis, a scary proclamation as his mother died of the same ailment and his brother, Francisco, had just been diagnosed.

John Henry had made plans with his cousin Robert to open a dental office together, but everything changed when he was diagnosed with the tuberculosis. Soon he left town and reportedly headed west where the air was better for his health. There have been other reasons given for why he left, including the possibility that his prominent Catholic family frowned on his relationship with his cousin, but the point is he went out west—stopping off in Texas.

"Margaret Mitchell seems to be mirroring the story in *Gone With The Wind* with a discussion between Ellen and Mammy. A young Ellen was distraught after her former boyfriend (and cousin) Philippe Rollibard died in a barroom brawl. She blamed her father and sisters for driving him away, saying she hated them and never wanted to see them again. Ellen told Mammy she wanted to go away and never see them again."

According to Barnes, Mattie bid John Henry a tearful goodbye and ripped the locket from her neck, placing it in his hand to remember her by. In *Gone With The Wind*, Ellen had given her locket to her cousin Philippe when he left town, also.

John Henry Holliday left and stopped for a few years in Dallas, Texas, where he practiced dentistry. Due to his constant coughing, he was not as successful, so he turned to another lucrative moneymaker: gambling. Those late-night card games with his cousin Robert and Sophie, the young former slave who lived in his uncle's home, were paying off. Soon gambling was his way of life and he picked up the nickname, "Doc." It was also through card games that he came to meet various characters of the Wild West, including Wyatt Earp, who would become his best friend.

In those days, a gambler out west had to protect himself, so Doc began carrying a gun and a knife. He met up with a woman named Kate Elder (aka "Big Nosed Kate," aka Kate Haroney) who traveled around with him. Though she was with him for much of his life out West, some of the time romantically and some of the time just for companionship, he never married her. Did he think he would one day reunite with Mattie?

During the next seven years, Mattie wrote to John Henry from her home in Jonesboro and he wrote her back, according to author Barnes.

He found out about some of the letters Mattie sent to Holliday, and maintains she was always a faithful letter writer and dreamed of seeing him again.

"I know this for a fact, that there were letters between Mattie and Doc," said Barnes. "All through his early times out West there were letters.

From all the research I've done, I know it was one of Mattie's sisters who destroyed the letters so no one would know they had a love story."

John Henry Holliday had two sides to him, it seemed. There was the tough side of him who struck up a life-long friendship with Wyatt Earp. He lived a hard life, and was in such pain from the tuberculosis that it was said he kept the whiskey bottle close. Since he could not make a living as a dentist, late night gambling and seeming to be in the wrong place at the wrong time became the norm for him. The other side, according to Barnes, was the one most people did not see: the sentimental man who was missing his loved ones left behind in Georgia. This side of Doc Holliday was the educated man with the love of books. Kate Elder knew both sides.

No one back in Georgia could believe the John Henry Holliday they knew would have been involved in the Gunfight at OK Corral. At the time, Wyatt Earp was the police chief of Tombstone, Arizona. The night before the gunfight, Doc Holliday was in a bar and supposedly had words with Ike Clanton, who was unarmed. Clanton challenged him to a duel the next day.

Word got around that Clanton had enlisted his brother Billy and also his friends, Frank and Tom McLaury and even Billy "The Kid" Claiborne. Holliday told Earp, who then deputized Doc as well as Virgil and Morgan Earp, his brothers. This was to try to stop the violence from happening.

The morning of October 26, 1881, the "cowboys" as the Clanton side was referred to, walked down Fremont Street in Tombstone. They came upon Wyatt Earp and his group. The shooting lasted only 30 seconds. Morgan and Virgil Earp were wounded, but the McLaurys and Billy Clanton were killed.

Mattie and the rest of the Holliday family read the terrible news in the Atlanta newspaper of their cousin being involved in the big gunfight and were shocked to hear that he was now being called "Doc" rather than John Henry. It was like he was a completely different person.

Despite what they heard, Mattie and John Henry's other relatives were steadfast in believing in him. They always saw him as a tragic figure who just did the best he could with the hand that was dealt him.

A little over a year after the incident at the OK Corral, Mattie decided to enter the convent. The dark-haired, goodhearted Mattie became known as Sister Mary Melanie.

"If you read any of the descriptions of Melanie in *Gone With The Wind*, it was Mattie," said John Lynch, who runs the Holliday-Dorsey-Fife Museum and has pictures and stories of Martha Ann "Mattie" Holliday there.

According to Tom Barnes on his internet blog, "Mattie, desperate in her loneliness, becomes a nun—Sister Mary Melanie. Sister Melanie lives to tell the rest of the story to cousin Margaret Mitchell, and Doc Holliday's legend becomes part of Ms. Mitchell's epic novel, 'Gone With The Wind'."

Though Doc had parted ways with Kate Elder, she came to take care of him when he became weak with his tuberculosis. On Nov. 8, 1887, after he died, she packed his things up in a small trunk and sent them to the address of Sister Mary Melanie Holliday in Georgia. It was the only address she knew; the only person he had kept in touch with from home. That part was known to be true.

According to the Tom Barnes' book, in the trunk, along with some letters and clothes, was a small, gold locket. He stands by the story.

When John Henry left Georgia in 1873, Mattie would have been twenty-four and her Fitzgerald cousins Sis and Mamie twenty-five and thirty-three, respectively. Mattie had spent much time with them in later years at Rural Home. They were about in their fifties when Margaret Mitchell was born. As he had become so famous and was the first cousin to Sister Melanie, Mitchell would have probably talked about Doc Holliday with her family. He died just eighteen years before Margaret was born. As much as Mitchell liked gossiping it would be hard to believe she did not talk to Sister Melanie about her famous cousin.

Margaret Mitchell used to go and visit Sister Melanie at St. Joseph's where she worked and lived. She went against the conventional Catholic thinking (maybe because she herself had turned from her family's religion) and allowed the cousins to marry in her story.

Barnes said that on some of the visits to Sister Melanie's room, when she had retired and was growing ill, Mitchell took notes.

"She would go and visit her after shopping on Saturdays," said Barnes. "Some of the notes were taken on corners of brown paper bags."

This does not contradict what the Holliday cousin who chose not to be involved in this book said about her visits.

Back To The Novel

Before she began writing the novel, Margaret Mitchell wanted to be sure she had everything right in her mind. According to John Lynch, whose great-great grandfather Robert Dickson was a neighbor of the Fitzgeralds and was on jury duty with Philip Fitzgerald, she did some rooting around in Clayton County. She contacted someone she knew would know about it, but who was not in her family.

"My great Aunt Lela Dickson, a school teacher, drove Margaret Mitchell around when she was researching the book," said Lynch. "Aunt Lela had a car and in the 1930s not many women had cars. She drove her around and showed her where things were."

Sister Melanie died in April of 1939, just eight months before the debut of the movie, which featured Olivia de Havilland playing a woman named Melanie, who married her cousin.

The interesting connection does not end there, however. It moves on to Scarlett's parents, Gerald and Ellen O'Hara.

In *Gone With The Wind* (page 52), a young Gerald O'Hara is having a conversation with his valet slave, Pork. Pork, a trusted friend, tells Gerald he should get married, and he encourages him to marry rich. Gerald replies that he has his heart set on one Ellen Robillard and a discussion takes place between Pork and James and Andrew (Gerald's brothers—Philip Fitzgerald also had a brother named James) where Margaret Mitchell lets the reader in on a little background.

Ellen Robillard was of French descent and from Savannah (the same town where the real-life Sister Melanie attended school as a child). Andrew urges Gerald to give up on Ellen; that she is not available because she is in love with her cousin, Philippe Robillard. Ellen and Philippe have been in love for a year despite the fact that their family is against it.

Gerald has hope, though, because Pork had told him earlier that

Ellen's cousin Philippe has left at his family's insistence for the "West." West, in this case means New Orleans, as opposed to the "West" where Doc Holliday went.

Later in the book, after Ellen's death, Scarlett is asking Mammy and Dilcey about her mother. Dilcey tells Scarlett that in her last breath Ellen called out, "Feeleep! Feeleep!" Mammy sternly glares at her but she knows that Dilcey does not know anything about Philippe. Mammy will go to her grave with Ellen's secret.

Mitchell wrote in the book (page 54) about the small box which arrived from New Orleans that Mammy handed Ellen. The package contained a "miniature" of Ellen, as well as some letters she had written to Philippe. When she saw the letter from a priest informing them of her cousin's death in a fight in a bar, she threw the locket to the ground.

"Mattie [Holliday] became a nun, just as Ellen considered doing," said Denise Tucker, of the *Gone With The Wind, But Not Forgotten*, blog. "Philippe obviously lived a rough and tumble life, as did Doc Holliday. Doc Holliday fully expected to die a violent / active death as did Philippe in a barroom brawl. I think there are a lot of parallels between Doc and the character Philippe."

This small story was of such significance that when Donald Craig wrote *Rhett Butler's People*, the second book sanctioned by the Mitchell Estate, he brought it up.

On page 497, Scarlett asks Mammy about Philippe Robillard. Though Scarlett begs the old woman to tell her about him, saying everyone is dead so that it wouldn't matter now, Mammy keeps her allegiance to Ellen.

In *Gone With The Wind* Ellen blames her family for Philippe's death, feeling it never would have happened had the family not condemned their love and had him sent away to New Orleans. She vows she will leave. Shortly after that, Gerald O'Hara arrives on the scene and asks her to marry him and move to Tara.

Mammy is against it and says so, but the broken hearted Ellen threatens to leave or go into the convent. (By the way, the idea of 'going into the convent' was also used when Scarlett's sister Carreen decided to become a nun.)

This same threatening technique was used by the real-life Annie Fitzgerald when she wanted to marry John Stephens. According to Lucille Stephens Kennon's scrapbook, the family was against it but she threatened to run away and marry in the 'big street' so they agreed to let her marry.

In choosing a name for Ellen's lover, Mitchell chose the French version of the name of the relative she, Doc Holliday, and Sister Mary Melanie Holliday all shared: Philip Fitzgerald.

The genealogical facts are there: the parties were related—at least by marriage—and from accounts of Mitchell and Holliday cousins come the facts that Margaret Mitchell did know Mattie Holliday (when she was Sister Melanie), and of course Sister Melanie knew the elderly aunts very well.

Back when *Gone With The Wind* came out, who would have known that the story of the famous gun-slinger Doc Holliday would have had anything to do with Eugene Mitchell's prominent Atlanta family and this debutante daughter, Peggy. No one except maybe the Fitzgerald and Holliday relatives.

Chapter Ten
Margaret Mitchell Writes The Book

Every author has his or her own way of writing a book and often they do not write it in order starting from page one to the end. They sometimes write different chapters at different times, creating outlines to help stay organized. This was the method Margaret Mitchell used.

At the beginning, when she had first gotten the idea to do the book, she scribbled down some notes. Each time something came into her mind about a storyline she would write it down. After she got the basic storyline down in her head, she made an outline of the chapters. That way she could write any chapter she wanted to and not have to write it in order. In fact it is said she wrote the first chapter last.

Saundra Voter had helped Mitchell's cousin Sara Spano type her book, *I Could've Written Gone With The Wind, But Cousin Margaret Beat Me To It.*

"Sara told me there were manila envelopes all over her apartment," said Voter. "She would sit on the couch and it would be lumpy and under the cushion was an envelope."

That was Mitchell's filing system for her chapters. She labeled the envelopes with chapter names. When all was said and done, the book turned out to be very long.

As Margaret Mitchell was working on her book in the late 1920s, the climate in the United States began to go from the 'happy-go-lucky' Roaring Twenties, to the economic disaster of the 1929 Stock Market crash. People were devastated. Many who had invested heavily in the Stock Market lost everything. They had to start from nothing and re-build, much the same as her characters the O'Hara family did in Clayton County, Georgia after the ruins of the Civil War.

The changes in the country's economic situation were similar to the happy times at the beginning of *Gone With The Wind* and then the onset of war and eventually reconstruction. Margaret wrote chapter after chapter and then she would go over what she had written, always checking her facts and making sure she was consistent in both dialect and the facts.

The manuscript was written on various types of paper, most of which had yellowed, and while she worked hard on it in the beginning there were times she would not touch the book for months.

She wrote most of the story between 1926 and 1930 in their small apartment on Crescent Avenue. Their rooms were part of a larger house and they had a back entrance. There were a total of four rooms in the apartment which exists today as the Margaret Mitchell House. The front room, a living room, consisted of a couch, some chairs and a table on which Peggy kept her typewriter. She used a black portable Remington to type her famous manuscript. Sometimes she would work on it in the living room and sometimes in the bedroom, next to the living room. There was also a very small kitchen and bathroom.

They had turned down her father's pleas to live with him in his large house with the full staff of help. "The Dump" almost seemed to represent

Peggy Mitchell's defiance of her father and her complete walking away from the life she had lived as a debutante, although the Marshes did employ household help.

They had to walk through the bedroom to get to the kitchen, which itself was so small there was no room for a table. When they ate meals at home, it would usually be in the living room at a small table they had set up. Both Peggy and John read the newspapers every day and listened to certain radio shows.

There were, of course, no computers for her to use when writing her book. It was truly incredible that she was able to write such a detailed book with so many historical facts on merely a portable typewriter. The only real research tool she had was the library—and only books written before 1930. She could not "Google" terms or e-mail people with a quick question. But she did have the memories of the stories she had been told, and perhaps some information left to her by her mother.

One June day in 1928, she read about the female aviator Amelia Earhart who had flown across the Atlantic Ocean. Charles Lindbergh had done it the year before and was a national hero, but this was the first time a woman had done it, though she was a passenger with two other men.

"That's amazing!" she said to John. For the next few days she looked at the articles in the newspaper about how Amelia Earhart was doing things that no woman had done before. Her mother, Maybelle, had been a suffragette and had worked for women's rights, so she was well in tune with strong, capable women taking the initiative.

Over the next few years she would see Amelia Earhart become a household name. Earhart wrote a book and also various newspaper columns promoting flying for women. For Margaret, Earhart represented the idea of women's survival in a man's world.

Soon Earhart became recognized for the products she was endorsing to raise funds for her flights. Earhart represented a line of clothing which was comfortable and boyish, just the type of clothing Mitchell enjoyed wearing. It was said that during the time Peggy Mitchell was writing her book, she wore men's clothing and a visor as she worked.

The Mitchell and Marsh family continued to visit Rural Home, though once Grandmother Stephens stormed out, there were tensions between those at Rural Home and the Mitchells. Aunt Mamie died in 1926. Grandmother Stephens was still alive, but Margaret had little or no contact with her.

Aunt Sis was over seventy and still living at Rural Home. Maybelle's sister Eugenia Stephens Gress looked after her.

"Eugenia Victoria was the aunt's name," said Abb Dickson, whose ancestors sold half of their land to Philip Fitzgerald and Margaret Mitchell's ancestors. Eugenie Victoria was the name Mitchell used for Scarlett and Rhett's daughter who they ended up calling Bonnie Blue Butler.

Aunt Sis became ill and then died in 1928. Eugenia Gress had been married to Morgan V. Gress of the very wealthy Atlanta Gress family, who donated the Cyclorama to the city of Atlanta in 1898. The Cyclorama, located in Grant Park, is the largest oil painting in the world.

Morgan's father, George V. Gress, who owned a lumber business in Atlanta, was a very charitable man and helped fund Atlanta's first zoo. After Aunt Sis' death the old homestead (Rural Home) became available. Aunt Eugenia shared the same grandfather as Maybelle (Philip), so Rural Home was special to her and she wanted to own it.

"The great-aunts had been alive when Margaret was young," said the historian John Lynch, also related to the Dickson ancestors (neighbors of the Fitzgeralds). "It was from them that she learned many stories about the family and the Civil War. They are buried in the Fayetteville City cemetery. She started *Gone With The Wind* about the time the first aunt died. Was that a coincidence?"

According to the Margaret Mitchell House website, "Recalling the stories told her by her family and Confederate veterans, Margaret Mitchell set to work in secret. Few people knew she was writing a book, and only John Marsh was allowed to read it as it progressed."

Evidently it was such a secret that some members of her own family did not know she was writing it. Lela Dickson, the woman who drove her around knew about the book.

"...*Margaret Mitchell had asked Lela, whose parents had been close neighbors to her own Fitzgerald ancestors, to drive around Fayette and Clayton Counties with her, to point out sites of this Civil War story. Tom*

*and Talula [members of his family] thus knew before it was published (that)
an important book was being written about that sorrowful time. It would
be a book that provided people with not only entertainment and temporary
escape from troubled times, but the hope that they, like Scarlett O'Hara,
could become masters of their world, not victims."*

Lynch, who says "everyone in Clayton County has a *Gone With The
Wind* story," had heard that one of the reasons Mitchell had chosen his
Aunt Lela to drive her around was because she had a car and could drive.
According to Lynch family history, Mitchell was in the passenger seat
making notes of the things she saw. Lynch was not sure why Mitchell did
not have her own aunt, Eugenia Stephens Gress, take her out to see the
sights.

"The house I own in Jonesboro was originally owned by Edith Smith,
who was a historian," said Abb Dickson, Lynch's cousin. "Margaret
Mitchell would come to visit Miss Smith and sit on her porch trying to
tie in the history."

Besides talking to the townsfolk, Mitchell did research in Clayton
County.

Lynch got a chance to talk to another of his relatives, who was in his
90s, about Margaret Mitchell and her research.

"Margaret Mitchell went to Clayton County (and Fayette County)
to research family names so as not to name anyone in her book after
existing families," said Lynch. "That is the official story. I believe that
but I also believe she wanted to know about the Fitzgeralds and their
neighbors so she could at least give them somewhat similar names—and
the appropriate ancestral backgrounds—and she did!"

"She was very thorough with her research," said Lynch. "She was
limited, with no computers, etc., so I think she did a wonderful job."

Mitchell visited the house that later became the Holliday-Dorsey-
Fife House (museum.) "She (Margaret Mitchell) knew that the Hollidays
had lived here and she knew that her grandmother boarded here and she
just wanted to see it and find out what the Fife's [who owned it at the
time] knew."

"My parents told me that when the book came out everyone in town
was saying, 'Who are you in the book?'" said Abb Dickson, owner of a

funeral home in Jonesboro and also an accomplished magician.

During the time Mitchell was writing the book her Aunt Eugenia moved to the Jacksonville, Florida area to a huge estate. Eugenia's brother, Alex, moved into Rural Home. Eugenia would continue to spend limited time there, but the majority of her time was spent at the Florida compound.

Annie Fitzgerald Stephens was listed in the 1930 census as living in the same home in Florida with Eugenia Gress. She was eighty-four years old and never really patched things up with Margaret since storming out shortly after Margaret's first marriage.

Though it is obvious to all that Margaret Mitchell used at least parts of Annie Fitzgerald's life in compiling the character of Scarlett O'Hara, many wonder why she would use someone she did not like. If she did use Annie for Scarlett and if she used parts of Berrien "Red" Upshaw when putting together Rhett Butler, she used two people she had basically thrown out of her life. The very people she seemed to dislike the most in her life contained some of the character elements she would choose in creating some of the most memorable people ever to grace the pages of a book or light up a movie screen. Scarlett seemed to hate Rhett Butler but she could never really let him go.

As Mitchell worked on her book, things were getting cramped in their apartment. John got a raise in 1932 and the Marshes said goodbye to the Dump, moving to a larger apartment on Seventeenth Street just around the corner from her father's house on Peachtree.

It had an extra bedroom, so finally they had a room they could set up as an office. Margaret would not have to be working on the book in the living room.

During the time they packed up their things and moved, the manuscript had been put away. Getting adjusted to the new place gave Margaret other things to occupy her time with and she only worked on the book sporadically. If she had any idea what was to come in 1935 she might have spent more time finishing it up.

Harold Latham of the Macmillan Company had been taking trips around the country looking for new authors. It was really just a fluke that he ended up discovering Margaret Mitchell. He had contacted Angus

Perkerson, the newspaper editor who had been her boss for a time. Angus' wife Medora Field Perkerson turned out to be a great friend to Margaret during and after her time as a reporter for the *Atlanta Journal Magazine*. Medora had been maid-of-honor at her marriage to John Marsh.

The Perkersons were to attend a luncheon at the Atlanta Athletic Club and they had invited Lathan.

At the last minute, Angus Perkerson was tied up with other business so his wife invited Mitchell. Somewhere during his visit Medora told Latham, "If what you are looking for is a novel of the South, Peggy is your best bet." When he asked her if she had something to show him, Mitchell replied, "No, I have no novel."

She had not been working on it for a while and it was in the condition any author's book would be when they were not finished: not ready to show a publisher. There were notes in the margins and some chapters had repeats in them. It was not cleaned up, and she did not have the confidence to show it to him in the condition it was in.

Later she changed her mind after being insulted by a young woman at the luncheon who insinuated that Peggy Marsh would not be serious enough to write a book. That comment was just enough to get her going. She called her husband and then she took the manuscript to Latham. The pile of brown envelopes stacked on top of each other were almost too much for the small, thin, Peggy to carry, but she was determined.

She left the pages with Lathan at his hotel, but as she thought about it later she got cold feet and called him up asking him to return it. He had already started reading it and liked it. He finished it all the way home on the train and liked it so much that The Macmillan Company bought the rights to publish it.

When the book came out in 1936, people could identify with the situations Scarlett and her family experienced because they had just gone through the tough times of the Depression. Readers enjoyed reading about the fun and the parties that Scarlett had at the beginning of the book, as they could identify with that happy atmosphere in the early 1920s. The book was a huge success.

Lucky for Peggy, her brother and father were lawyers so Stephens helped her with the contract. It was from that first day that Stephens and their dad Eugene looked over the initial contract that the "business" of *Gone With The Wind* began. They set up a company which Stephens continued to run until his death. He was always busy because there were lawsuits, foreign rights, and of course the many people who wanted to write "sequels." Much of Stephens Mitchell's lawyer work centered around his sister's one book and all that came from it.

The original contract called for an advance of $1,000—$500 upon signing and $500 upon completion of the book, and royalties on the retail price.

All was not smooth and rosy for the Marshes once Margaret got the book contract. Much work remained to finish up the book. She still had to write the first chapter and she was changing the heroine's name from Pansy to Scarlett. There were other changes to be made such as the original name she had for Tara was Fontenoy Hall and she had not come up with a concrete title for the book.

These were the days when every single page had to be re-typed to reflect the new name. Correction tape and White-Out ® had not been invented back then. Macmillan gave her a deadline and she was nervous she would not be able to do all the work by then. John Marsh ended up taking a leave of absence from his job so they could get it done.

"Every word in the book of 1037 pages is Peggy's own writing, of course," he told Medora Field Perkerson in a newspaper article, "but we both worked night and day getting the manuscript into shape for the publisher."

While Marsh maintained every word was hers, he provided Perkerson with more insight into how she wrote it: "I started reading right from the time she started writing and we would talk about it. As you know, talking things over sometimes makes an idea come clearer. In trying to write it out beforehand, the mechanical labor may get between the writer and the idea."

John Marsh was a well-respected journalist. He had been a newspaperman and then had gone into public relations. Those who worked with him considered him very knowledgeable and an excellent editor.

From the very beginning, the book brought in money. There was the initial book contract and immediately the Book-of-the-Month Club, besides that there were the movie and the foreign rights and subsequent licensing rights. The Mitchell-Marsh family shared in the financial success of the book

Gone With The Wind had been scheduled to be released in May of 1936 so the first edition was printed with "May 1936" on it, but because of contractual arrangements with the Book-Of-The-Month Club, the book actually came out in June. The 10,000 books marked "May 1936" are the first printing of the first edition (true first edition to the collectors), but books marked "June 1936" are also first editions, though they are the second printing of the first edition.

When *Gone With The Wind* came out, according to John Lynch, her relatives were excited for her. But as she began to clam up about the origins of the story, some of them felt left out. They felt she should have given the Clayton County relatives some of the credit. It was not the money they were after as they were all very successful in their own means; but some of them seemed to think they were shut out by her lack of recognition to them.

A relative reportedly tried to capitalize on Mitchell's success by attracting tour buses to Rural Home and representing it as "Scarlett's house."

According to Lynch, when Mitchell heard of this she was upset and contacted her Aunt Eugenia Gress in Florida, who put a stop to it. As Mitchell continued to deny that any of her book was real or based on any real happenings or characters, she grew increasingly out of favor with some members of her family.

According to John Lynch, Aunt Eugenia was angry at her for writing *Gone With The Wind.*

"She was convinced that Margaret Mitchell had found a diary in the attic that had belonged to one of the Fitzgerald sisters and she used it to write the great novel and made a ton of money from it also."

In the 1930s, Margaret Mitchell took John Marsh to Rural Home to see it for the first time, and, according to Lynch, "she was shocked to see her grandmother in the house."

She and Aunt Eugenia were spending winters at the Gress estate in Florida and when it was warm they would visit Jonesboro to be sure they had control of the family land.

"Evidently Mrs. Gress allowed her to live there–after all Annie was her mother, just as she was Maybelle's (Eugenia and Maybelle were sisters)," said Lynch. "If she (Mitchell) was aware of her aunt's displeasure of her, can you imagine how awkward it would be to visit the place?"

"Eugenia Gress did not like Margaret Mitchell at all for exposing the family secrets," said Abb Dickson. Dickson's grandfather Lester Dickson was a lawyer who represented the Stephens-Gress family for years. "She didn't think she should be spreading things around about her relatives. Philip Fitzgerald died in the same way as Gerald O'Hara, in a horse accident."

There have been many writers throughout history who have written successful novels based on true stories. Anyone can write a book about anything. *A Tale of Two Cities* by Charles Dickens is an example of a novel based on real happenings. *Meet Me In St. Louis* and *All Quiet On The Western Front* are other examples.

Lynch said a businessman in Fayetteville confirmed that Mitchell and Gress had had a falling-out. The businessman was doing some work for Eugenia Gress at Rural Home. She was in town from Florida and he offered to take her to the Fayetteville Library which Margaret Mitchell had helped fund, thinking she would enjoy seeing it.

"I don't want anything to do with that woman," said Eugenia Stephens Gress, according to the businessman. "She stole my aunt's diary from the attic of the old home place and wrote that book with it."

"Rhett and Scarlett were real people in her family," said Abb Dickson. "That was the feeling throughout the entire family. She probably was taking several people and events and rolling them together."

When *Gone With The Wind* first came out, Margaret Mitchell gave a speech at the Library and her good friend Richard Harwell was there. She gave him a book and signed it. Days like that were precious because shortly after that she stopped giving speeches about the book and she stopped signing them. She would not do radio interviews and stopped doing newspaper interviews—unless it was with a writer of her choosing.

Why did Margaret Mitchell choose not to discuss her characters or do live speeches or radio shows on *Gone With The Wind*? According to newspaper reports, she did only one live radio show and it was with Medora Field Perkerson, one of her best friends as the host.

"She was more and more embarrassed about it," said Abb Dickson. "She had rolled them all out for everyone to see. It wasn't many years ago we buried the grandson of the tax collector in Clayton County, Joe Mundy. It would have been Mundy to whom 'Scarlett' wrote the check for the taxes on Tara.

"We're real people here. The Talmadge property (Crawford-Talmadge House) was Twelve Oaks. It was the next plantation over from the property that was the real-life Tara. The mill in the opening was (supposed to represent) Mundy's Mill that adjoined the property. It was described just as it was."

If it was Jonesboro's Mundy's Mill that was described in the book, there is another mill, whose owners say provided the location for filming of the mill shown in the movie.

"The mill that was shown in the movie is in North Little Rock, Arkansas," said Pat Sleade, who has been there. "It's a real pretty area and it's open to the public."

According to information at Pugh's Old Mill in North Little Rock, Selznick's crew somehow found the mill, which had been built in 1933 to look like an old mill from the 1800s. When looking for the perfect setting, they chose that mill, but residents of Jonesboro recognized the description as inspired by Mundy's Mill in Clayton County.

Nineteen-thirty-six and thirty-seven should have been a wonderful time in Peggy Mitchell's life, with the publication of *Gone With The Wind* and then the impending contract for the movie, but it turned out to be just the opposite.

The hoopla surrounding the overwhelming success of the book and then the sale of the movie rights to Selznick International did not affect Margaret Mitchell Marsh in the same way as it might have affected the young fun-seeking Peggy Mitchell only years before. She had mellowed quite a bit and did not enjoy or take advantage of the fame.

It was almost the reverse. She was overwhelmed with people wanting her autograph. After a while she finally made a policy not to sign books, so those lucky collectors who own autographed copies know it is a rare treasure. In fact, once she sold her book and it became successful she hated the fame so much that it seemed in a way to ruin her life.

The book had come out in June 1936 and a week later she was so stressed out she left town for Gainesville, Georgia to try and escape. When she got back to Atlanta there was a letter from her publisher telling her that movie producer David O. Selznick was interested in her book. It should have been exciting, but the thought of it was one more thing in Margaret Mitchell's already overloaded life.

According to Richard Harwell's *Gone With The Wind Letters*, in Aug 3, 1936, *Time Magazine* had requested an interview with Margaret Mitchell, and her husband John sent them a telegram with this reply: "Mrs. Marsh sick in bed as a result of strain of becoming too famous too suddenly."

Mitchell had completed the revisions of the book in January of that year and it came out that summer. Just two months later the author was sick in bed with the strain of "becoming famous too suddenly," as her husband had put it. She was sick and complaining of eye strain.

When you look at the picture of Margaret Mitchell with Harold Lathan finding out she won the Pulitzer Prize in 1937, she still looked fashionable with her make-up and sleek hairstyle. Within no time, the pictures of her show a big change from her carefree youthful look to a heavier woman who looked older than her age.

She had many requests for radio interviews but she did only the one, on July 3, 1936. The show was called The Journal's Editorial Hour on WSB and she was interviewed by Medora Field Perkerson. She felt if she did Medora's show she could have control over what was asked.

"Did you take any of your characters from real life?" Medora asked.

"No, not a single character was taken from real life," Mitchell answered her. "In the first place, I wouldn't know how to go about taking a character from life. And in the second place, made-up characters are so easy to handle. They will obey the author and do just what the author wants, whereas characters taken from real people are apt to be obstinate and unmanageable and to insist on having their own way."

Medora Perkerson talked about the characters of Melanie and Scarlett and the circumstances they faced together.

"If *Gone With The Wind* has a central theme, I suppose it is the theme of survival," Mitchell said in the radio interview. "What quality is it that makes some people able to survive catastrophes and others—apparently just as brave and able and strong—go under?"

The book received many good reviews and Mitchell delighted in reading them. The Marshes employed a "clipping service" so they could keep up with all of the publications that mentioned *Gone With The Wind* or its author. With every review, Margaret would take it upon herself to write the reviewer back, sometimes long letters, and thank them, as well as comment to the writers on what they had said in their columns. If she did not like what they said she would tell them and try to explain why they were wrong, hoping for a correction.

By September she was in bed with a black mask over her eyes due to the eyestrain. Whenever his wife was sick in bed John Marsh would do what he could to take care of her. He tried to shield her from the outside world. Just as her family had done when she was a child, he made it okay for her to take to her bed. He never criticized her or chided her to snap out of it. He simply loved her.

Being married to John Marsh was as if she had chosen to live a simpler life. Though she had grown up with money, she did not seem to care about it with Marsh. They chose to stay in an apartment, which was one of the true ironies of Margaret Mitchell's life.

Page 36 of *Gone With The Wind* produces the famous advice from Gerald O'Hara to his young, strong-willed daughter Scarlett that *Land* is the only thing worth living and dying for. It was a theme in her book.

Though she and John Marsh became wealthy beyond belief on the book, the author of those famous words never owned any land herself. She continued renting until the day she died.

One of the things that distressed the Marshes the most regarding the publication of her book was the sale of foreign rights. Her brother Stephens worked day and night on this. In a letter Margaret Mitchell sent to her cousin Lucille Stephens Kennon she talks about this. Mrs. Kennon had just sent her a picture of her great-grandmother Eleanor

(Ellen) Fitzgerald. Here is the never-before-published letter:

Margaret Mitchell
Atlanta, Georgia
June 21, 1938
My dear Cousin Lucille:
I was at Father's house when Kate Edwards called on Sunday, bringing the pictures of Great-Grandmother. I was sorry that I missed her, as I always enjoyed her calls so much.

I haven't enough words to tell you of my pleasure in having the pictures. I am giving one to Stephens to add to the collection of ancestors I am making for his two boys. The other will join the small but excellent company of kindred now on my wall. You were so very nice and thoughtful to let me have a copy and I appreciate it so very much.

I had never seen a picture of Great-Grandmother before. Of course, I had heard so much of her from Mother, who always described her as being a great deal like Aunt Sis, the same eyes and silvery voice and the same beautiful laugh. In fact, the most outstanding impression I have of Great-Grandmother is her gift for laughter. Mother had this same "gift" and that was one of the reasons she loved Great-Grandmother so much. As I look at the picture, I see where Mother got her large blue eyes and where I got my thick eyebrows which are not mates. I am afraid my square jaw came from the same lady.

She is a great-grandmother to be proud of, isn't she? John was so impressed with her face. As John has no kinspeople here in Georgia, he has adopted mine, even unto the fourth generation back, and he was as pleased with the lady as I.

Nearly a year ago a Mrs. Tommie Perkins (who turned out to be Tommie Higgins) wrote me from a Clayton County R.F.D., saying she had a picture of Great-Grandfather, and the old family piano. They came into her hands when the furnishings of the Home Place [Rural Home] were hastily dismantled in that dreadful time after Aunt Sis's death. I have been trying to get down to see her in order to secure the picture, but my life has been so crowded that I scarcely get time to go around the corner and see Father—much less go thirty miles into the country. I intend to go to see her as soon as things settle down, and I hope to get the picture. I believe, but cannot be certain, that it is the one which hung in the dining room. If I get it and if you do not have a copy,

I'll be glad to have a copy made for you.

Kate Edwards came home bubbling over with pleasure at meeting all of you. She liked you all so much and she is such a good describer that I felt as if I had seen you myself. I hope to have that pleasure some time soon, although I do not know when it will be. Things are much quieter now and John and I were able to go off with the editors' convention recently. But we hope soon to be free of all our "Wind" troubles so that we can make visits about the State.

What took up most of our and Stephens's time were lawsuits and contracts for foreign translations. As each country has its own publishing laws, each contract had to be studied with care, and some of them kept us busy for weeks. The lawsuits are all finished now—and happily finished—with the exception of the one now in progress in Holland against a firm of Dutch publishers who printed my book without a by-your-leave. We have been through I-do-not-know-how-many Dutch courts and the final trial should come up at the end of this month. I've lost every case so far, as these publishers have no intention of paying me royalties if they can get out of it. Whether I win or lose I hope to have it all off my shoulders soon.

You are simply a grand person to let me have the picture. But perhaps you knew how happy it would make me and that was why you sent it.

My love to all of you,

Margaret

The "dreadful time after Aunt Sis's death" that Mitchell referred to involved Grandmother Stephens. The two aunts, Sarah (Sis) and Mamie had been living at Rural Home. Sis died in 1926, so when Mamie died in 1928 a decision needed to be made about the house. According to a Jonesboro historian, Annie (who was their sister), left the funeral early and went to Rural Home with a truck and some strong men and removed the things she wanted. Word got back to the rest of the family at the burial and several other members hastily went to the estate and began grabbing what they wanted.

With all her self-put upon stresses, Margaret Mitchell felt the outside world waited to pounce upon her. Clayton County had been a source of happiness in her childhood, and though Hollywood exaggerated its qualities quite a bit, the one thing that satisfied her was to be able to bring to the public the history of her beloved Clayton County. She just never imagined the chaos it would bring into her life.

Gone With The Wind made her a household name worldwide but she preferred to be anonymous, doing very few public appearances or interviews. She had signed a very lucrative contract with the Macmillan Company and then later with Selznick International, but it never changed the way she lived. As a teenager she was used to seeing her name or picture in the newspaper in conjunction with her status as a debutante and then as a young adult writing for the *Atlanta Journal Magazine*. The fame did not impress her; quite the opposite. She just wanted to live a "normal" life. The Marshes still had their name in the phone book, and people would show up at their door unannounced.

"She was a very private person," said Herb Bridges, the author of several books about *Gone With The Wind*. "The fame overwhelmed her. She didn't need it because her family was already prominent in Atlanta and she was very happy with her life as it was."

Since Mitchell would not agree to be interviewed, several articles appeared that she did not appreciate. One mentioned her first marriage, which she had tried to keep out of the press.

As Mitchell relative Lucille Stephens Kennon wrote in her scrapbook, none of that had been mentioned before. Since the article came out before the movie, Kennon must have written it shortly before that.

"Even Margaret's first marriage to William Upshaw's (son) has not been mentioned," she said in her scrapbook. "He [Berrien Upshaw] was a dreadful character—a rum runner, and a dissolute bum. And Jean (sic) had a divorce gotten quietly. Margaret's health was impaired. But that, with all the rest, has been a part of the silence."

The articles and interest in her life caused her to retreat into a shell. When they traveled, she and John would use aliases when they checked into hotels so they could have privacy. While John rather enjoyed being "Mr. Margaret Mitchell," she did not like putting him in that situation. He might have liked to have retired with her magnificent earnings so they could travel, but she encouraged him to continue working. Perhaps that was one way she thought they would keep some 'normalcy' in their lives.

They lived off of what he made, remained very frugal and stayed in their apartment. The question has been brought up about what happened to all of the money she made? Much of it went to charity and some of it was left to her brother and two nephews after she and John Marsh died, but even today there are lawyers being paid as part of the Stephens Mitchell Trust.

People noted that even with all her fame and money, Mitchell continued wearing the same type of modest clothes and clunky shoes she had always worn as an adult, since becoming married to John.

"She was very practical and pragmatic," said Ernie Harwell, whose brother Richard became good friends with her. Ernie Harwell, who is from Atlanta, worked for the *Atlanta Constitution*, before going into broadcasting and eventually entering the Baseball Hall of Fame.

"Just to illustrate how frugal she was, my wife Lulu was at a reception with my brother Richard and they saw Margaret there. Lulu and Margaret had the same earrings on. Margaret noticed that and said, 'Oh look we have the same earrings', and they saw that they did. Then Margaret said 'I bought mine at Rich's for $3!'"

"She and John Marsh always lived in an apartment," said author Herb Bridges, who has had a successful career lecturing and speaking about Margaret Mitchell. "They never bought a fancy home. There was one little extravagance I saw. It was in a picture of her christening the ship Atlanta and I noticed she had a fur coat on. I remember thinking, well, good for her, she finally spent some money on herself."

As with many creative people, she could not seem to stop working on things. By day she would write letters, long ones to every single person who wrote her, plus many who did not. True writers cannot stop writing and though she did not produce a book, her letter writing seemed to be her creative outlet—yet writing the letters proved very stressful to her. They served a purpose both to her and to the people who received her speedy replies, but it caused her great strain. She would wake up in the morning thinking, "I've got to write back to so-and-so," and then the mail would come and there would be more letters to write. Through accident and injury, she always made time to write letters.

Her letters, at first written in longhand, were usually several pages long. She would write so fast that her neck and back would tense up and her hands would hurt from writer's cramp. She finally started dictating and having them typed.

Mitchell appreciated her fans and those who reviewed her book, and genuinely wanted to thank them for their positive reaction to her book, yet she seemed to get bogged down with the chore of letter writing.

People from all over the world would write her and think she could help them because she had written a book of survival. They depended on her for hope, and it was a lot for her to bear. Often the letters were in other languages, so Mitchell employed the services of a translator.

Besides the letters, she became involved with war efforts during World War II and sent packages of food and clothing to England throughout the war.

After VE-Day, she sent packages to her publisher, translator, and agent who were serving the country. She started sending boxes to other soldiers, and soon it became like the letter writing, an obsession to her. She would pile the items and weigh and wrap them to get them ready for shipping on the dining room table of her apartment.

The foreign rights to the book caused Margaret Mitchell so much grief that she often went to bed with cold rags on her head. Many countries began printing the book without paying any rights, doing as they wanted with the cover and content. Even those editions legitimately negotiated caused her problems. The foreign rights caused them headaches, but the Marshes enjoyed collecting each one.

Margaret Mitchell also volunteered with the Red Cross. Her uniform is displayed at the Atlanta-Fulton County Library on the fifth floor where there is a Margaret Mitchell exhibit. Mitchell did much for the Red Cross and helped raise money for the Navy Ship USS Atlanta. At times she felt overwhelmed with the pressures of the outside world brought on by the success of her book. She felt she had to pay the public back for their acceptance of her book.

"What interests me most about Margaret Mitchell were all of her humanitarian endeavors," said Kathleen Marcaccio, a *Gone With The Wind* 'expert' who has been known as the GWTW Answer Lady in online blogs, "Working for the Red Cross, raising money to build a new *Atlanta* naval vessel, working to integrate the Atlanta Police Department, raising money for the French village library, sending care packages to soldiers, helping to establish Grady Hospital to aid indigent persons get medical treatment, and the Morehouse College medical school scholarships. Most people have no idea of her legacy beyond *Gone With The Wind.*"

Another thing she did was participate in what were called "Town Hall" events with the state prison. Mitchell would go out to the prison and talk to the inmates in the prison's effort to bring education and culture to the inmates.

Baseball Hall of Fame Broadcaster Ernie Harwell, who also participated in the prison Town Halls, remembered the events.

"The Town Halls were a way for the prisoners to be able to participate in educational events and be entertained at the same time," said Harwell. "They had to obtain Town Hall passes to participate in the events."

Though Margaret Mitchell did not like public speaking and turned down most requests, she did like talking to the inmates.

"Though she fled a besieging public of strangers, Margaret Mitchell loved people and liked to entertain them, liked to make them her friends," said Richard Harwell, Ernie's brother.

All of this fame she had achieved by writing *Gone With The Wind* had ended up being more than she had wanted. It was nothing compared to what was going to happen next. Within a month of her book coming out, she had been approached by a Hollywood producer and ended up selling the rights to her novel to a company called Selznick International.

Chapter Eleven
David O. Selznick Buys The Movie Rights

Gone With The Wind had just hit the bookstores in the summer of 1936 and the minute Kay Brown of Selznick International's New York offices read it she knew the company had to buy it. She had been first shown the book by agent Annie Laurie Williams. When Brown told her boss about it he was not interested, but once she told the company finance man, John Hay (Jock) Whitney about it, Whitney basically said, "If you don't buy it I will." In July David Selznick offered Margaret Mitchell fifty-thousand dollars for the movie rights and the whirlwind started.

David Selznick was ultimately the person responsible for acquiring the rights, selecting the cast, hiring the crew and for every detail in the movie. Selznick was the producer, but that title does not begin to describe all that he did, Marcella Rabwin was there and saw it all.

"He worked closely with the actors, as well as the crew, and worked with the editing. He was involved in every event that happened along the way," she said. "I was very close to Mr. Selznick. People always said, 'What did you do?' and I say, 'Anything he didn't have time for'. I was involved in every phase of the production of his films from the beginning when you bought the thing to the time when it was finished and you could breathe again."

According to Marcella, the film cost "four million, eighty-five thousand, seven hundred and ninety dollars." Selznick's original plan was for a movie that would last two and a half hours and cost about two million. At that time it was the most expensive film ever made or even imagined.

Thanks to Marcella Rabwin's book, *Yes, Mr. Selznick*, the video and audio tapes saved by her sons, Mark Rabwin and Paul Rabwin; as well as the memories of things she told them, the inside story can be told about what it was really like behind the scenes of this massive production.

Marcella was with Selznick when he got to work and she did not go home until he left the office, which sometimes was in the wee hours of the morning. As his executive assistant at the office, Marcella entertained Louis B. Mayer and other top movie executives who came to see Selznick. She provided coffee to drink or a shot of bourbon, whichever was necessary at the time. She was a sounding board to the boss, and had a shoulder for those to cry on who were frustrated with him. She served as counselor to his wife, Irene; a part-time nanny to his children; and was a necessary part of the studio's daily life.

"People turned to her," said Ann Rutherford, the actress who played Carreen O'Hara. "David (Selznick) valued her judgment."

"*Gone With The Wind* was the finest motion picture, the most complete and perfect motion picture ever made," said Marcella. "But it was utter chaos putting it together."

"We had no idea of the enormous task ahead of us when we took it on," said Marcella. "That book (*Gone With The Wind*) had become such a Bible to so many people—there were 20 million copies of the book sold in the first year. The first time we ran it as a consecutive piece of work it was five hours, and I didn't know how he was going to cut it. Every minute of it was a beauty but still he had to get it down to what it was three hours and forty-five minutes."

In order to produce the length of film that would keep the audience's attention Selznick knew he was going to have to take some of the people and events out of the book. He felt if he kept as much as possible to Margaret Mitchell's dialogue viewers would forgive him for the omissions.

Jock Whitney had owned Pioneer Pictures, an independent studio and Selznick went to him asking him to back his new company, so they basically merged the two, with Selznick getting additional funding from his brother Myron and from Irving Thalberg and his wife Norma Shearer, and a few smaller investors. Jock Whitney had invested in the new 'Technicolor' and so Selznick agreed to do at least six pictures using the new color process.

The newly formed Selznick International Studios had an interesting background. In September of 1918, Thomas Ince bought approximately forty acres of land from Henry Culver to make movies. He had been working with D. W. Griffith and Mack Sennett in the very successful Triangle Film Corporation which produced silent films. After their relationship went sour, Ince founded the new studio, in Culver City, about twenty-five minutes south of Hollywood. There is a road which runs by it today, called Ince Boulevard. Movies have always been made in this area outside of Hollywood, but the term "Hollywood" has always been used loosely when talking about movie productions in this area of California.

Amid mysterious circumstances, Ince had become ill on William

Randolph Hearst's private yacht and wound up dead, reportedly from a gunshot wound. Hearst was hosting a birthday celebration for Ince. Several famous stars were there including (his mistress) Marion Davies and Charlie Chaplin. The story goes that Hearst was jealous of Chaplin's interest in Davies and a gun was fired accidently at Ince who may have been mistaken for Chaplin at the time. Though there was a famous gossip columnist on board, the episode never showed up in the Hearst newspapers and it was never determined who fired the shot. That story in itself has the makings of a Hollywood movie, and it was: *The Cat's Meow.*

After Ince's death, the studio was purchased and rededicated as the DeMille Studios. In order to film *King of Kings* which was released in 1927, famed director Cecil B. DeMille leased some land behind the original property and this back-lot became known as "Forty Acres." This is where DeMille built the biblical city of Jerusalem for the movie.

In 1928, RKO took ownership of the studio to film *The Bird of Paradise.* The sets built would later be used for *Tarzan* movies and even *King Kong.* David O. Selznick was familiar with the studios as he had used RKO for some of his films.

As a matter of interest that same studio became Desilu in the 1950s and still operates today as Culver Studios (Sony). Desilu, of course, was the production company owned by husband and wife team Desi Arnaz and Lucille Ball. Desi and Lucy were acquainted with David O. Selznick and were close family friends of Marcella and her husband, Dr. Marcus Rabwin; in fact Desi was the godfather to their son, Mark Rabwin's son. Some of the greatest movies of all time were filmed in that studio and lot including *Citizen Kane* (1941), the original *King Kong* (1933), and Alfred Hitchcock's first American film, *Rebecca* (1940).

When he started his new company, Selznick remembered Marcella Bannett from RKO and was impressed with her work. As he began assembling his team, he persuaded Marcella to come on board as his Executive Assistant with several secretaries under her. Marcella had recently married Dr. Marcus Rabwin, the chief of staff at Cedars Sinai, who became known as the doctor to the stars. It was to Marcella that David O. Selznick dictated many of his famous "memos," however Marcella hired a staff to do much of the letter writing. Marcella Bannett Rabwin was an extraordinary woman in her own right. She sat in meetings and stayed late in the night, listening and adding her suggestions to major decisions made by the producer.

"She was very bright," said her son, Mark Rabwin. "She skipped several grades in school and entered college at 16 years old."

Marcella had worked for Warner Brothers, and then went to work for Myron Selznick, David's brother. Her primary job was to go back to Warner Brothers and sign up writers and directors not under contract at Warner Brothers. She was so successful and valuable to Myron Selznick that he was paying her more than anyone at the agency. Myron had asked her to take a pay cut so she would be making less than his male agents, and she quit.

"Our mom called that, 'two steps forward, one step back'," said Rabwin. "And she wasn't going to do it."

At that time she went to work at R.K.O. as Selznick's secretary, and then later he hired her as his executive assistant at Selznick International. "David Selznick was very good to my mother," said Mark Rabwin. "He was known to be difficult to work with, but he treated her very well."

Once production started on *Gone With The Wind*, there was so much work and pre-production involved that it took several years and much money before the filming even started. As soon as it was determined they would be doing *Gone With The Wind*, David Selznick dispersed people to travel throughout the South. He wanted to find genuine talent for the cast, and he wanted to learn all he could about the South.

He had selected the talented George Cukor to be the director. Cukor was also his best friend and many said they looked alike. Cukor was among those sent to Atlanta. Cukor contacted Margaret Mitchell and various people she suggested to help get a good feel for the South. While he was traveling, he scouted for actors.

The *Gone With The Wind* advance team scouted many areas. Among places mentioned in the Margaret Mitchell House and Museum Visual Arts Collection are: Jonesboro, Georgia; a plantation in Arlington, Mississippi; the Caldwell House near Atlanta; a plantation in Auburn Mississippi; a house in Roswell, Georgia; The Keeler House in Marietta, Georgia.

Selznick wanted his sets to look as authentic as possible and he wanted to be sure Cukor knew about plantations of the South. Cukor was sent out hastily and had many jobs including finding out about the area as well as searching for southern acting talent.

"It was the most chaotic film ever attempted," said Marcella. "The casting was crazy. We sent people all over the world, especially in the South, and they went into every little theater, college, and acting class. The South had produced very little besides Alicia Rhett and several others."

Alicia Rhett played Ashley Wilkes' sister India. In the book and movie, she was always jealous of Scarlett for flirting with her boyfriend Stuart Tarleton when they were young. Rhett had been doing local theater in Charleston, South Carolina, and when George Cukor was searching the South for actresses Alicia tried out for the part of Melanie, but after Olivia de Havilland was cast, Cukor offered her the role of India Wilkes.

"Alicia Rhett was a very good actor," said Ann Rutherford, who played Scarlett O'Hara's sister Carreen. "She was also quite a called-upon portrait artist."

Another actress from the south was Evelyn Keyes who played Scarlett's sister Suellen. While Rhett was found in a South Carolina theater, Keyes, from Atlanta, was employed by Paramount and had been in a few movies before Gone *With The Wind.*

The part of Melanie was a coveted part and Olivia de Havilland wanted the role. She was under contract to Warner Brothers and there were a few contractual problems with Jack Warner and David Selznick. Warner wanted Bette Davis to play Scarlett and they said they would loan Bette Davis if they would also take Errol Flynn to play Rhett Butler and they wanted to take one fourth of the picture in profits.

"Olivia was caught in the middle of all of this," said Marcella. "One of her friends was Jack Warner's wife, Ann Warner. She went to her and said, 'If they will let me play this part I will be worth so much more to the studio. I'll be a really important star. This is a terrific part'. Ann Warner told her husband to let her out of her contract to play Melanie. And that was that."

Olivia de Havilland was the only legitimate candidate for the part that anyone involved with the movie had wanted. On the set, she was well liked by everyone.

When it came time to hire Scarlett's little sister, Carreen, David Selznick knew who he wanted. Ann Rutherford was already a successful actress, having been in many movies, including her recurring role as Polly Benedict in the Andy Hardy movies with Judy Garland and Mickey Rooney. He ran into her one day, and suddenly it clicked. Years later he told her, "When I saw you that day, I had just signed Barbara O'Neil to play Ellen O'Hara. I looked down at you and you had a nose just like hers. I went back to the studio and told them to call MGM."

Rutherford was working for MGM at the time. Louis B. Mayer called her into his office and informed her that his son-in-law wanted her to play Carreen in *Gone With The Wind*. She got very excited because the book was so popular at the time that everyone in Hollywood wanted a role. Mayer, who had great respect for her and thought she should be playing a lead role, told her she could not do it.

"I was shocked and said, 'Why not?'" remembered Ann Rutherford. "He looked at me and said, 'It's a *nothing* part'."

She had been in more than thirty movies, some with leading roles, including *A Christmas Carol* where she played the Ghost of Christmas Past. Mayer thought the role was a "come down."

She did not care that it was not the "lead," she just wanted to be in the movie because of her high regard for the book. She cried and he finally let her do it.

"We had all read *Gone With The Wind* and we just loved it," she remembered. "Everyone just wanted to be part of the project."

Another person who wanted to be in *Gone With The Wind* was Hattie McDaniel.

"She was thrilled and delighted to be in this movie," said Carlton Jackson, author of *Hattie: The Life of Hattie McDaniel*. "She adored Clark Gable and was fond of Vivien Leigh. She became a sort of 'Mother Confessor' to all those in the movie. At first Susan Myrick was a bit distant, but after Hattie served a 'home-cooked' meal for the cast, she was in!"

While there were differences in the movie from the book, the setting and descriptions of the houses seemed to be a big concern to Margaret Mitchell. Though David O. Selznick was adamant about using Mitchell's dialogue, he sought to glamorize the Southern plantation. He knew glamorizing it as only Hollywood can do, paired with the new technique of Technicolor, would attract the fans to the movie.

He had a vision of the large, lovely, white-pillared plantations and thought the viewers would take to the romanticizing of the homes. Selznick was right, but it caused headaches for Margaret Mitchell, who knew it was a far cry from the way the houses actually looked in Clayton County at that time. She had described the plantation homes with square posts and they were changed to rounded ones for the Hollywood production.

Perhaps it was the downplaying of Tara, which upset her relatives. They saw her as trying to distance herself from the homes of Clayton County. Mitchell was also upset about the way the movie portrayed Twelve Oaks.

Putting pictures of Philip Fitzgerald's "Rural Home" and David O. Selznick's "Tara" side by side, one can see their descriptions differed. If Fitzgerald's one story posts had been changed to two story columns and if the house had shutters, they would look more alike. It's not known if Selznick's people had the advantage of seeing Rural Home, but they did come to Clayton County to do research and the house was still standing at the time. Pictures show there was shrubbery near both homes and a large tree in the front yard just to the left as you walked outside, so it is conceivable that they did photograph Rural Home and try to incorporate it.

"I think that when she (Mitchell) said that Tara shouldn't have round columns, she meant the massive round columns found on many deep South plantations, especially those on the coast," said John Lynch of the Holliday-Dorsey-Fife Museum. "Of course Rural Home had columns but they were considered more as 'posts' rather than columns. Most all of the older houses had porch 'posts' and banisters or balusters as they were sometimes called.

"The larger columns found on plantation type houses were much larger and usually didn't have banisters in between. A lot of them were 'fluted' like the ones here and most all were hollow and not a solid piece of wood."

Lynch said there were Greek Revival-type homes with columns around the Clayton County area, so he does not feel it was inappropriate for Hollywood to have used that type.

"Margaret Mitchell herself visited the Holliday House (now the Holliday-Dorsey-Fife Museum) when the Fifes lived here and made the comment that "this house would make a good shot in the *Gone With The Wind* movie I'll tell Hollywood about it," said Lynch.

Mitchell complained that Hollywood glamorized the plantations, but according to Lynch there were some nice homes in the area.

"It may be that she kept Rural Home in mind, even thought she said it was not Tara," said Lynch, "And she tried to keep the embellishments at a minimum so as not to make the place more lavish than it really was."

Twelve Oaks was portrayed in the movie as a very large mansion with a winding staircase. Much of the reason for this exaggeration was due to the use of Technicolor. Selznick wanted to take full advantage of this new colorizing technique. Twelve Oaks provided the perfect opportunity. It was the backdrop for the barbecue, which was a happy time before the war, and Selznick used this time to create splendid visuals through the use of a magnificent setting and vivid colors.

The brightly colored gowns the women wore to the barbecue helped in this endeavor. The spacious foyer and large, rounding staircase provided the space for the ladies to be shown all together in their hats and dresses.

"There were a lot of large plantation owners in this area that did not live in huge plantation houses," said Lynch. "Clayton County had nice homes, but modest. You would have to go to Savannah, Charleston, Vicksburg, or Virginia (Arlington for example) to even come close to what Twelve Oaks looked like in the movie."

The Fitzgerald home sat on the Flint River, five miles from Jonesboro just as the fictional Tara did. Though Philip Fitzgerald's was a nice house, it was wooden and crudely built and originally located at an intersection of two roads, with a smaller front lawn. The sensational look of Tara and

Twelve Oaks went hand in hand with the entire production of *Gone With The Wind*. Selznick had a magnificent goal and he spared nothing or no one to achieve it.

Historian Wilbur Kurtz, also an artist who could draw the things he was trying to explain, provided enormous help with researching the antebellum homes. He worked with William Cameron Menzies who was hired as the "Production Designer."

Selznick wanted to transcend the typical "Art Director" title by having one person in charge of the entire physical appearance of the film. This was ground-breaking territory.

"Bill Menzies was just a brilliant idea man," said Marcella "He (and his staff) drew the entire film. This was the first time this had been done. There were thousands of sketches, not just one picture for a theme; but every portion of that scene. They call it 'storyboarding' and this was the first time it was ever done."

Lyle Wheeler, who was the art director for Selznick International worked with Menzies. All in all there were about seven artists who drew watercolor sketches. Each sketch showed a camera angle, and when all was said and done there were more than 1,500 pictures sketched for the storyboard of *Gone With The Wind*.

Both Wheeler and Menzies would end up winning Academy Awards for their work.

The pre-production phase involved everything from deciding on the costumes, sets, and scenery, to hiring the actors and scouting the plantations. Selznick never dreamed he would use so much money up just in the pre-production—before filming had even started!

He went to his father-in-law, Louis B. Mayer, to get some cash. Mayer made the deal that gave Selznick the money he needed in exchange for distribution rights, which is why the credits say "in association with Metro-Goldwyn-Mayer." MGM shared in the profits and would loan Selznick some of its talent, including Clark Gable. From the time Selznick had purchased the screen rights to *Gone With The Wind* in July 1936 until production actually started on the movie in January of 1939, the country was abuzz about who would star in the movie, and Selznick's people were determined to find the best.

"Selznick had to go out on a limb and mortgage everything for *Gone With The Wind*," said Mark Rabwin.

As the other actors continued being hired, the search was on to find the perfect actress to play Scarlett O'Hara. The Selznick public relations machine was in action using this as a year-long vehicle for publicity about the upcoming film. It worked because the public was dying to know 'who was going to play Scarlett?'

There were many names thrown out as possibilities, including Bette Davis, Lana Turner, Joan Crawford, Irene Dunne, Loretta Young, Claudette Colbert, Jean Harlow, Margaret Sullivan, Paulette Goddard, Jean Arthur, and Carole Lombard, who was the girlfriend of Clark Gable at the time.

"The South wanted Tallulah Bankhead or a Southern girl," said Marcella. "The North wanted Katherine Hepburn, the West wanted Joan Fontaine."

Jean Arthur, who screen-tested for the part, was an old friend of David Selznick's. She did an adequate screen test but David was looking for the perfect one and it did not matter that she was his friend. He let everyone try out, but he knew in his heart what he was looking for and he was not going to stop until he found her.

Rabwin had a close personal friendship with Lucille Ball and she wanted her to get a chance.

"Lucy and Desi were very good friends with my parents," said Mark Rabwin. "And Lucy really wanted it, so mom arranged the audition."

Before the audition, she worked with a Southern dialog coach, but all of the work was for nothing As Lucille Ball later said the reading with Selznick "was a disaster."

With all of the beautiful, talented stars and starlets vying for the coveted role, most people did not know that at one time during the search, David Selznick had actually considered giving it to his executive assistant, Marcella.

"She did a studio test for Scarlett," said Mark Rabwin. "They had had trouble casting Scarlett. The studio test may have been early in the search or it could have been later when David Selznick became frustrated."

Marcella, who was from the South herself and was a stunning beauty, had photos made in cocktail gowns to go with the screen test.

"In the end, it was just not something she wanted to do," said her son. "She never wanted to be an actress."

Marcella read three newspapers on Sunday, the *San Diego Union*, the *Los Angeles Times* and also the *New York Times* (which her son says she thought was the best paper in the country) as well as *Variety Magazine* each week, and felt her role was better suited off camera, but it was flattering that her boss brought it up.

"She actually did wear one of Scarlett's gowns, though," said Mark Rabwin. "The occasion was a costume party—an Antebellum Party. We still have the picture with her and Lucy, Desi and my dad. Everyone in the picture was in Antebellum South costumes."

Margaret Mitchell was asked to be a consultant on the film, which she turned down. Selznick wanted her input, but he had to settle for hiring consultants to fill the west coast team in on what they needed to know about the South and the Civil War … the dialect, proper clothing, whether or not Gerald O'Hara should be wearing a riding suit at all times he was on a horse, the correct plants and even the right colors for the furniture.

The consultants were chosen by Mitchell—people she felt knew a great deal about the people of Georgia and the history of the South. She chose Wilbur Kurtz, a local historian, and Susan Myrick, a newspaper writer from the Macon Telegraph. Margaret Mitchell did not want to be involved—but she did not want to be left out either. Sending two people she knew gave her the best of both worlds.

Myrick and Kurtz kept her up to date on the goings on in Hollywood. She knew more about what was happening than Selznick realized, but it did not help the production. She may not have liked a picture of Scarlett wearing a hat in one scene and mentioned to Myrick, but since she didn't give her input to Selznick she provided very little input for the production.

By the time the production phase started most of the actors and actresses had been selected. Every role was coveted because the book was so popular that everyone was familiar with all of the characters so it was just a thrill for most of them to be in the movie. As they reported to the studio most of the cast bonded immediately.

"I felt I knew everyone on the set!" said Ann Rutherford. "Because we all loved the book so much, we knew the characters. We immediately connected with one another —and because we knew the characters, we felt like we knew each other better."

Famous movie stars were not the only ones to test for the role of Scarlett. Em Bowles Locker Alsop was an actress who had screen tested for the role of Scarlett O'Hara in 1938. The Richmond, Virginia native appeared at a forum put on by *Gone With The Wind* collector and editor of The Scarlett Letter, John Wiley, Jr.

"She became one of the women—and the only amateur—who tested for the role," said Wiley. "She was a student at Vassar College at the time and made her screen test in New York with actor Richard Carlson in the role of Ashley Wilkes. Though she didn't make it, Selznick remembered her and at his request, she attended the film's Broadway premiere on December 19, 1939. When the film opened in Richmond that February, she led the grand march at a *Gone With The Wind* ball at the Hotel John Marshall."

Russell Birdwell, Selznick's publicity man, seized every opportunity he could to do a press release. Sometimes he went too far and would release something Mitchell felt she should have been told about. A few times it surprised Margaret Mitchell and made her angry, but Birdwell did not seem to care. By the time she complained the incident was over and *Gone With The Wind* was in the minds of all Americans. There finally came a time when Selznick thought he had finally found his Scarlett.

"Paulette Goddard was the closest we could get to a perfect Scarlett," said Marcella Rabwin. "Scarlett was really the first 'women's libber'. She could fight her way through the world and win."

"They thought Paulette Goddard would be Scarlett," said Paul Rabwin, another of Marcella Rabwin's sons. "They were so sure they were going to use her that when they shot the 'Burning of Atlanta' scene, they used a body double for Paulette Goddard. There was a big problem with her though."

Paulette Goddard was having an affair with silent picture star Charlie Chaplin. They had been involved both in a romantic and professional relationship and were living together. In fact they lived right across the street from Selznick.

With the onset of 'talkies' the motion picture industry sought to develop an ethical code to live by so as not to have the talking picture industry become corrupted. The Hays Code, or the Motion Picture Production Code of 1930, was developed. According to the code, it was "to govern the making of talking, synchronized and silent motion pictures." It was adopted by The Association of Motion Picture Producers and The Motion Picture Producers & Distributors of American in March of that year.

Part of it said: "Motion picture producers recognize the high trust and confidence which have been placed in them by the people of the world...." It also said they "recognize their responsibility to the public because of this trust and because entertainment and art are important influences in the life of a nation." Movie directors had to be very careful with the moral overtones of a production because of the Hays Code.

"This (the Goddard and Chaplin affair) was a big source of discussion," said Paul Rabwin. "The studio had to be very cautious about getting their picture distributed if Paulette Goddard was involved in the movie at the same time she was having an affair."

Time and time again they tried to get Chaplin, who had a reputation as a ladies man, to say if they were married or just living together. Though she had the inside track in Selznick's mind, the unwillingness to clarify their marital status prohibited Paulette Goddard from getting the part.

"Unmarried, living 'in sin' with one of America's most famous but suspect personalities, she would never be acceptable to the prudish American public," said Marcella Rabwin.

There had recently been a big spread in Photoplay Magazine about the high number of unmarried couples in Hollywood and then there was that business about Chaplin's involvement in the mystery of Thomas Ince's death on William Randolph Hearst's yacht several years earlier. Selznick did not want that kind of negative publicity.

The irony was that the actress who eventually got the part of Scarlett was also having an affair with a famous star. They saw to it that he was not in the same town or at least the same area during the whole time the movie was filming.

"We must have had readings by at least ten thousand people," said Marcella. "They cut the list down to 500 and then down to a film with about 150 of the most promising."

David O. Selznick knew exactly what he wanted and he was not going to settle for less than the Scarlett O'Hara he envisioned.

"Margaret Mitchell's book was very explicit," said Marcella. "But there were a lot of things we don't know. We didn't know what shape Scarlett's nose was. There were a lot of things you don't know just by reading the book. Come to think of it, I didn't even know what was on her barbecue plate!"

All of this "who will play Scarlett" talk was great for Russell Birdwell, but it was time to start shooting and David Selznick was getting desperate to find a Scarlett.

"During this time, David wrote me one of the most insulting letters I've ever gotten in my life," said Marcella. "He said 'we've got to do more about finding a Scarlett! This is what I consider to be the worst failure of my entire career'."

Why Selznick could not just walk into her office and talk to her about this was one of the quirks about David Selznick. He wrote memos to everyone, including his wife.

Some people, including George Cukor, did not like receiving all the memos. Cukor asked Selznick several times to talk directly to him or to call him up on the telephone, but the memo was Selznick's preferred style. In fact, he carried special cards in his pocket which he took notes on and then later when he got back to his office he would use these cards to remind himself to write to someone. Ann Rutherford had a good story about Selznick and his memos.

"I was on a train once, walking from the dining car back to my car and I saw David coming towards the dining car," said Rutherford from her home in Beverly Hills in 2008. "I waited for him. I had some advice I wanted to give him."

This was before she had been cast as Carreen O'Hara. Rutherford had performed in many movies already, including her recurring role as Polly Benedict in the Andy Hardy films, so Selznick knew her.

It was during this chance meeting on the train that he noticed her nose was the same shape as Barbara O'Neil's, the actress signed to play Ellen O'Hara. Rutherford told him that the make-up for the upcoming movie should be different than usual. For a normal movie the make-up artists would pluck the actresses' eyebrows and apply rouge.

"Look at me," she said. "Look at my eyebrows. They have almost grown back but the minute I get to the studio the make-up man will start tweezing my eyebrows. As you are working on *Gone With The Wind*, remember it was the 1800's and they didn't have tweezers. They didn't even have rouge back then, the women pinched their cheeks."

Selznick listened to what she was saying and then reached into his pocket, pulled out one of his famous Memo cards and started writing.

"You're right, you're absolutely right," he said. "I'm so happy you told me that."

During the search for Scarlett, Selznick looked at every single audition tape. While the casting search was going on, other things occupied his time.

The first thing Selznick needed to do was make room on "Forty Acres" for the various sets of Tara, Atlanta, and the train station.

"One of his production people came up with a brilliant idea," said Mike Heimos, an actor who was involved in several television productions, "David O. Selznick needed to shoot the 'Burning of Atlanta' scene, and they also needed to raze "Forty Acres" to build their sets. Why not film the 'burn of all the burns' on the old sets on the back-lot? And so they did. They dressed Cecil B. DeMille's old sets from *King of Kings, Garden of Allah* and *King Kong* and set them ablaze and that's what you see when you watch the 'Burning of Atlanta' scene in *Gone With The Wind*."

"They burned the set, but you can't see any of the original pieces when you watch the movie," said Mark Rabwin. "The filming of the fire actually started after most of the structures were burned beyond recognition."

Art Director Lyle Wheeler talked to Selznick about it. The event was going to be such a big deal they decided to allow personal guests and there were 200 invited guests there to watch it. They could only burn it once so they had to get it right.

"The fire was burning, raging madly," said Marcella Rabwin. "We had all the fire departments from Los Angeles, Culver City, and Pasadena. They thought the world was on fire!"

It has been said that on the night of the big fire David O. Selznick found his Scarlett, and it was on his own brother's arm that she was delivered to him. Myron Selznick was the agent for Laurence Olivier, who was dating Vivien Leigh. She had mentioned the possibility of playing Scarlett O'Hara to Myron Selznick who brought it up to his brother. Myron invited Vivien and Laurence to come to the studio to watch the fire. According to Marcella Rabwin, Myron Selznick wanted to make a dramatic entrance with Vivien, who had worn green eye make-up to draw out her green eyes, and was dressed in a tight-fitting dress with a belt to accentuate her tiny waist. She was hoping David Selznick would see Scarlett when he saw her.

They went to dinner beforehand and Myron stalled so they would not be upstaged by the fire. He had to get there at just the right time. The night sky was lit up in red as they drove to the studio.

In dramatic fashion, with the flames raging in the background Myron Selznick presented her to his brother.

"I'd like to introduce you to your Scarlett O'Hara," Myron Selznick said, presenting the fur-clad, bejeweled Vivien Leigh.

David Selznick's eyes grew large. He knew it was her the minute he looked at her.

"I knew it!" he said, "She looks the way I've always imagined!"

"Mr. Selznick said to me, 'She is everything I ever dreamed of'," recalled Marcella Rabwin. "Now if she can only act!"

They brought her in to do some screen tests and Selznick was a happy man because he felt like he finally found his long-awaited Scarlett O'Hara.

Although Vivien Leigh and Laurence Olivier were dating each other, they were both married to different people. So Selznick made sure they stayed away from each other during the filming. By this time, Selznick knew he had to get on with the production so he decided to overlook their affair. At least they were not living together as Chaplin and Goddard were.

Dr. Christopher Sullivan knew Marcella Rabwin and remembers her talking about Olivier and Leigh's love affair.

"Marcella had strong memories of Vivien and Larry Olivier and their passionate affair when she was filming the movie," said Sullivan.

"Vivien Leigh was just so perfect for the part you couldn't believe the good luck!" said Marcella in a taped speech saved by her sons. "Can you imagine how thrilled we were when this girl showed up?"

Leigh was put through many tests and photo sessions. They tested her, silent tested her, wardrobe tested her.

"She was just the most glowing, vibrant, dynamic woman I'd ever met," said Rabwin. "I loved her as Scarlett. I loved her beauty. I loved her talent, and I loved that she represented something that women were not at that time: strong, persuasive, determined. She clawed her way to the top in that movie just as she had in the book."

Mickey Kuhn, who played Beau, and later appeared with Leigh in *A Streetcar Named Desire,* got to know her.

"She was the most wonderful person that I ever met," he said. "She would take the time to talk to you. When I was eighteen years old and on the set of *A Streetcar Named Desire,* she would ask me things like, 'Where do you go to school?' 'Are you planning on continuing with acting as a career after this?' And she would listen to the answers."

It would come out later that Vivien Leigh suffered from mental illness, but Kuhn said he never saw signs of it.

"Think about it," he said. "She was a two-time Academy Award winning actress. If she can do that in front of a camera, she can hide those demons from the people around her."

"Vivien worked so hard," said Ann Rutherford. "She was in so many of the scenes. She worked virtually every day."

Though it has been documented that Vivien Leigh had the mental problems later in her life, it is not clear if she was being treated for the illness during the shooting of *Gone With The Wind.*

"Nobody can say anything negative about her to me," said Kuhn. "I know she had her problems, but my association with her was magnificent. She was such a nice person she didn't deserve the mental illness. No one does. She just had everything going for her, and then she had this terrible problem. She worked very hard to hide it from the outside world."

Selznick set Vivien up in an apartment near the studio while he found work for her boyfriend, Lawrence Olivier in a Broadway show in New York, keeping them as far away from each other as possible. For a while, Vivien Leigh felt hostility toward Selznick because here she was in America, with her family in England, and now her boyfriend had been sent out of town. She had not counted on being separated from Olivier as part of gaining the role of Scarlett O'Hara. Around the time the filming started, there were tensions escalating between her homeland of England, and Germany and they eventually went to war. She was always worrying about how things would turn out.

Once Selznick had Vivien Leigh signed on as Scarlett the actors began working on their lines. According to Marcella Rabwin there were problems galore with the cast and she said she felt like a "Girl Scout leader" trying to counsel some of the cast members.

"Olivia (de Havilland) and Vivien got along, but there were other problems," she said. "The cameraman was upset with the director, the director was upset with somebody else. One of them disliked David Selznick because he was a Jew. There were all kinds of motivations and all kinds of disruptions. One of the biggest problems was everyone was worried to death because we kept running out of money."

If the salaries were known, then it would be easy to see why some of the players might be unhappy. Clark Gable was reportedly paid $117,917 and Vivien Leigh who appeared in almost all of the 700 scenes in the movie received $30,851. Selznick claimed the five most important people in the movie were Gable, Leigh, Olivia de Havilland, who was said to have made $25,370; Leslie Howard, $76,250; and Hattie McDaniel, $6,459.

"Those five names are those David Selznick deemed the most eligible for a laurel wreath," said Marcella Rabwin.

Clark Gable had a lot going on just before he got involved with *Gone With The Wind*. Separated from his wife, Ria, Gable was involved in a very public affair with Carole Lombard. There was the lingering fear if Gable divorced Ria, she would demand half his earnings. The executives at MGM were in negotiations on how to handle this because while they were still married, everything he was making was potentially going to be split with her.

"Ria was his second wife," said Marcella Rabwin. "She was an older woman who was very helpful and protected him. He was a straight, macho man and he needed help. Not just to look after him, but to really push him.

"He wanted to get rid of her because he wanted to marry Carole Lombard. The problem was Ria wouldn't have any part of a divorce. He was frustrated and just wanted to take a vacation with Carole. Gable was the most popular choice to play Rhett Butler but did not want the role. He didn't want to be making a picture, especially not *Gone With The Wind!*"

"Carole Lombard was a friend of mine," said Rabwin "So I knew a little more about their affair than maybe some people. He was married to Ria, but he was in love with Carole. It was a very, very passionate, beautiful, exciting love affair."

Clark Gable had been sending money to Ria, as well as to his father each month, and did not want to part with the money that MGM had been keeping for him—something he thought would happen if he got a divorce. All of this money haggling was taking up valuable time with MGM in getting the deal signed for him to play Rhett Butler. Mayer sent his man Eddie Mannix to discuss the terms for the loan of Rhett Butler to Selznick International.

"L. B. Mayer said to Gable's wife Ria, 'If you divorce Clark we'll give you half a million dollars'," recalled Marcella Rabwin. "Then in turn she was to tell Clark the only way she would give him a divorce is if he played Rhett Butler."

Much of the wrangling at this point was between Selznick and his father-in-law, L.B. Mayer. Both men were hard-headed, but the one thing they agreed on was they wanted to make money on the film. MGM loaning Clark Gable to Selznick would accomplish that goal. Selznick would get the "King of Hollywood," the biggest box office draw of the time in exchange for concessions they finally agreed on. Mayer's company, MGM, would end up sharing in the profits and everyone was happy—at least in theory. But Gable was not happy.

"First of all, Clark Gable did not want to do the picture," Marcella said. "He wouldn't read the book. He didn't want to look at the script. He had a lot of reasons for objecting seriously to doing it."

One of the reasons was a picture he had made in 1937 called *Parnell*. Gable wore costumes and he hated them. The movie was about an Irish politician's struggle to free his country from English rule. It centered on Charles Stewart Parnell's struggles in prison and his relationship with Katie O'Shea which threatened to ruin his plans. Maybe it was just the O'Hara name being Irish that did it, but he associated *Gone With The Wind* with *Parnell,* and part of it was because of the costumes.

Another of Gable's problems was that he was afraid of the role. He knew that everyone who had read the book had an idea in their mind of what Rhett Butler would be like. He was afraid he would not live up to their expectations; afraid he didn't look like what people thought Rhett Butler should look like

He also thought Scarlett's role was going to be emphasized; that it was HER picture. According to Rabwin: "Here was the man who was THE biggest star in Hollywood. He didn't want to be second fiddle to anybody, including and especially 'Scarlett O'Hara', this created character. They didn't even know who was going to play her when he started, so it wasn't Vivien Leigh he was worried about. It was 'Scarlett O'Hara'."

Finally Gable agreed to read the script.

"He read the script," said Rabwin. "And then he sent it back with a little note attached. The note consisted of two words: 'It stinks'. That was more than enough reason not to do it. If you don't like and respect the script, then you don't want any part of it."

David Selznick was not going to let that stop him. He said he would re-write the script until Gable liked it. As long as it went along with the book, Selznick was willing to do anything Clark Gable wanted to make his star happy. Selznick worked hard to get a script he liked, but still Gable was not happy on the set.

Gable's original fear that so many people had just read the book, that it was fresh in their minds, turned out to be a problem for Selznick in many areas. Clark Gable's attitude needed to be addressed and Carole Lombard felt she was the person to step in.

"There was a strong, strong tie between these two people," said

Marcella. "The thing about Carole was, she was a prankster. She could be a devil."

Rabwin went on to tell about one of the jokes she played on Gable. Because he didn't want to do the movie—he was grumbling around that he didn't like the part, he didn't like the costumes, didn't like anything—she wanted to do something to ease the tension.

"She hired an airplane, and had pamphlets made," said Marcella Rabwin. "The airplane circled the set where they were working and dropped the pamphlets. On the pamphlets were two words: 'Remember Parnell!' From that moment on, he straightened up."

Pulling jokes on Gable was nothing new for Lombard who had sent an extra large pair of pink ballet shoes and a tutu to the studio of his previous film when it was decided he should learn to dance for the movie.

Selznick had the monumental problem of taking a book that was over a thousand pages long and making a movie which could hold viewers' attention.

He hired the highly qualified scriptwriter Sidney Howard for the task, assuming Mitchell would be eager to work with him. According to Alan David Vertrees, author of *Selznick's Vision*, "…She refused to cooperate in any part of her novel's dramatization." Mitchell always maintained that since the novel had become such a beloved book, she did not want to be responsible to her fans if the movie disappointed them. She wanted nothing to do with the movie and she made it very clear to anyone who asked.

"Trying to involve Margaret Mitchell was ridiculous," said Marcella Rabwin, Selznick's executive assistant. "You couldn't get her to do anything. She was so aloof about the whole thing. She wrote a letter that said, 'I don't care what you do with my story, just be true to the history'. So in order to be true to her beloved Confederacy, we brought in Wilbur Kurtz, the great historian."

They had to take out some scenes from her book when making the movie, but Selznick refused to add scenes. Even if it was something he might have wanted to do differently, he urged Howard to stay with Mitchell's words.

In a memo published in *Memo From David O. Selznick*, compiled by Rudy Behlmer, Selznick wrote to Sidney Howard. "… we will be forgiven for cuts if we do not invent sequences."

"I had heard Margaret Mitchell was difficult to work with," said Mark Rabwin, son of Marcella Rabwin. "But you have to realize these were two people who were hard to work with individually. David was a very strong personality and so was she. They both wanted it their way."

Richard Harwell in his book *Gone With The Wind As Book And Film*, related a phone conversation between Kay Brown, Selznick's east coast representative and Margaret Mitchell. In the conversation, Mitchell talks freely about scenes from the book, including one involving Belle Watling and Rhett Butler; however, she closes up when Selznick asks about the character of Melanie.

Author Tom Barnes, who has done extensive research on the Margaret Mitchell-Doc Holiday connection storyline, found Margaret Mitchell's unwillingness to talk about Melanie intriguing. In his blog (Tombarnes39.com) he wondered why she would not talk to Selznick about Melanie.

Since her own cousin Sister Melanie knew she was using her name in the book, maybe it was hitting too close to home for Mitchell at this point. In mulling this over, Barnes figured, "It had to be something and I was curious about why she wouldn't work with Selznick on the screenplay."

"Why would a writer not wish to talk, or at least communicate in some way, with the producer who was doing an extension of her work?" Barnes asked. He was one of the first authors to pinpoint Margaret Mitchell's family's relation to Doc Holliday's family and he hypothesized that the real-life Sister Melanie went into the convent after the Gunfight at OK Corral, realizing he was never coming home. He first noticed the storyline of Philippe Robillard and Ellen Robillard (O'Hara) in *Gone With The Wind* as being autobiographical to Margaret Mitchell's family.

Another blogger who has written about the Philippe Robillard/ Ellen O'Hara storyline in conjunction with Doc Holliday is Denise Tucker on her blog Gone With The Wind But Not Forgotten at www.denise-tucker.com/wordpress:

"For those familiar with the book, the character of Philippe Robillard has striking similarities to Doc Holliday. We are not given a physical description of Philippe Robillard; in fact, we are given very little information about the character as a whole. But by looking at the situation, piecing together the few bits of information we are given, we learn that Philippe (like Doc) left Georgia and the cousin with whom he was in love (Scarlett's mother, Ellen Robillard) and headed west according to his family's wishes. We know that he died in a barroom brawl.

"Like Philippe, Doc Holliday was in love with his cousin, previously identified as Mattie Holliday. The family frowned upon their romance. That discouragement coupled with the issue of his health, caused Holliday to leave Georgia for the west. However, he never forgot his first love, just as Ellen never forgot Philippe, even on her deathbed. Doc Holliday and Mattie corresponded throughout the rest of his life. It was she who was notified of his death in 1887."

The Doc Holliday / Sister Melanie story may have contributed to several story lines, including Scarlett's little sister Carreen. Ann Rutherford, who played her, was told that the storyline of Carreen going into the convent could have been based on a real person. She was asked if it would have mattered to her if she had known that at the time.

"I would have been enchanted," she said. "It makes more sense to have characters that actually lived."

Selznick could not understand why she did not want to cooperate with him since he wanted to make the movie as true to the book as possible. There were times that Selznick wanted descriptions of how she imagined her characters. He wanted to give the movie version of the characters the most depth he could, but her reactions confused him.

Paul Rabwin is a Hollywood producer today. He co-produced *Life on Mars* in 2009, *October Road* in 2007 and 2008 and was a producer of *The X-Files* and *ChiPs* television shows and *The X-Files Movie*.

"With the litigious society in which we live, there are always lawsuits going on," he has noted. "Every project is scoured. Let's say there is mention of a doctor in a certain town with a certain name. We have people who will actually check the phone books and come back with 'recommend changing last name'."

Rabwin's mother Marcella was involved in many meetings with Selznick when he would be frustrated with Mitchell because of her lack of interest in the Hollywood project. Selznick wanted to stick with her dialog as much as possible, and he wanted the characters to be just as she had envisioned them.

"Most authors want to be involved," asserts Paul Rabwin. "If they feel they've developed and nurtured their characters, they don't want to lose that control."

He cited the very popular Harry Potter books as examples.

"J.K. Rowling was very heavily involved in the Harry Potter movies," he said. "She was protecting the franchise. Authors want to be involved and the more powerful and well-known the author is, the more they want to be involved."

Selznick wanted to be sure the film was historically accurate; that the accents and phrasing were correct, so he relied on Susan Myrick and Wilbur G. Kurtz.

"Susan and Margaret were best buddies," said Susan Lindsley, Myrick's niece who was named for her. "They had met at a Press Association gathering. They spent a lot of time together and enjoyed talking and gossiping."

Lindsley, a journalist in the process of writing a book about her famous aunt with the working title *Myrick, GWTW*, was born the same year *Gone With The Wind* was published.

"As I grew up I got to hear all the stories from Aunt Sue," she said. "She came to dinner every Sunday and spent holidays like Christmas Eve night with us. Aunt Sue taught us all to swim. She was a fun person like Margaret Mitchell."

Mitchell knew she would get the straight scoop from Myrick, but beyond that Myrick was an award-winning writer. Part of her job involved watching the production and offering suggestions on how to make it more realistic, as well as coaching the actors on having the correct "southern accent."

"Aunt Sue knew a lot about that," said Susan Lindsley. "Part of it was from her experience of growing up in the South, and part of it was that she worked at the newspaper and once covered the women's pages."

Myrick sent articles back to the newspaper while she was in Hollywood.

"I know she really enjoyed her time out there, but it was frustrating for her," said Lindsley. "She would see something that was wrong and tell them, but sometimes they did nothing about it. They would insist on doing things their way."

Wilbur Kurtz was a gentleman and generally did not engage in gossip about happenings on the set, much to the dismay of Mitchell, but she traded some lively conversations with Myrick, wanting to know all the inside dirt.

Selznick and Howard, along with input from Kurtz and Myrick and many writers came up with a movie which, though it had the same basic story as the book, had to be different because, as noted, a thousand page book would not hold the attention of moviegoers. The book offered detailed information about Gerald O'Hara and his wife Ellen in their early days which was not included in the movie. The film version leaves out two of Scarlett's children and somewhat simplifies her life. The KKK and other social issues are left out of the movie; however, anyone who read the book could see the KKK episode implied. The 'n' word was also omitted from the movie.

"The 'n' word as Margaret Mitchell used it was historically appropriate," said *Gone With The Wind* collector, author, and expert, Herb Bridges, "but it would have been inappropriate in the movie."

"Wilbur Kurtz and his wife came to California," recalled Marcella Rabwin. "He examined and re-examined every inch of that film to be sure that historically it was absolutely accurate. I don't think anyone has found anything they can criticize about the movie's historical accuracy."

The book provided brilliant descriptions of the characters and scenes and that was what made it so successful. Selznick wanted the movie to embellish Mitchell's descriptions by bringing the vivid colors from our imaginations to our eyes.

The beautiful pastel dresses worn at both the Wilkes barbecue and the Confederate fundraiser (where Scarlett, though dressed in her mourning black, danced "for the cause" with Rhett Butler) stay in our memories. David Selznick's idea was to make the most of the visuals and create unforgettable costumes, which he did. Selznick's costume people had Melanie looking like a nun as she nursed the sick soldiers. Melanie wore a head covering, yet Scarlett did not. Selznick could not have known about Tom Barnes' claims about Melanie being patterned after "Sister Mary Melanie" who had worked in a hospital, or could he? Barnes thinks he may have known the story.

Selznick sent Walter Plunkett, his costume designer, to Atlanta to meet with Margaret Mitchell and Wilbur Kurtz. As it turned out he became sick on the trip, but was able to do a little work. Kurtz knew local Civil War history so he may have known the story She would not give any hints as to how she had envisioned her characters, but she did refer him to some history books so that he could get the costumes correct to the period of the book.

"Selznick had some pretty good information coming out of researchers from Georgia," said Barnes. "I met Wilbur Kurtz, one of Selznick's researchers, while I was doing a series on Georgia's Heritage. He might have heard of some of this."

Kurtz consulted with Plunkett on the costumes, and according to Barnes it could have been he who suggested it. Was it a coincidence that Melanie's head covering in the Confederate hospital scenes resembles a nun's habit?

Costume designer Plunkett toured the Southern states, asking old people questions about what it was like during the Civil War 70 years earlier. He wanted to know all about the clothes they wore. He wondered if Gerald O'Hara would go to the barbecue with his riding clothes on, or if women rode horses in hooped skirts. Selznick sought perfection and spared no expense on the costumes. It seemed David Selznick was as intent on the accuracy of his movie as Margaret Mitchell was with her book.

Actress Ann Rutherford thought he was spending way too much money on the costumes. She could not believe the details in the costumes, including layers and layers of real lace on the slips under the hoop skirts. She mentioned to him that no one would even see their undergarments so he did not need to do them up so expensively. The producer's reply was that SHE would know. His theory was if a person is playing a wealthy plantation owner's daughter, she ought to feel like one. So he kept the expensive costumes.

Selznick did the same thing with the plantations, both inside and out. For the inside furnishings from "Miss Ellen's portieres" (the green velvet curtains), which were used to make Scarlett's dress, to the luxurious interiors of Scarlett's bedroom, Selznick just wanted the production to be magnificent. Tara was a romanticized plantation; an image that has come to identify "the Old South."

So important was the aesthetic beauty of the plantations and the emphasis of the love of the land, that Selznick employed a full-time horticulturist to ensure the authenticity of the botanicals. Florence Yoch, a leading horticulturist and artist of the time, had worked on the sets of the 1936 Selznick-produced movie, *The Garden of Allah,* and the George Cukor-directed *Romeo and Juliet.*

Selznick understood how the landscapes in *Gone With The* Wind played an important part in the central meaning of the book. As with the aforementioned movies, California's climate was different from the movie's southern setting and Florence Yoch could not use plants from that area. She had to understand the landscape of Georgia.

According to *Garden Design Magazine,* "Hundreds of fake dogwood blossoms were tied to the bare branches of California trees; the big oaks framing Tara's facade were constructed of wooden framing, chicken wire and plaster. Clusters of leaves dangled from gut wires running from the ground to the top of the house to cast believable shadows across the foreground."

Selznick employed artists, painters, scene designers and architects all working together to produce the tremendous detail that *Gone With The Wind* had in its costumes and sets. Two live magnolia trees were brought in along with bushes and vines indigenous to Atlanta. A whole crew worked day and night building oak trees. The authenticity, outstanding costumes, and scenery were major reasons for the movie's success.

One of the tricks played with the scenery was the magnificent mansion that Scarlett and Rhett built when they were married. In the big scene where they all walk up the sidewalk (Prissy says, "Lawsy, we sure are rich!") the lovely garden and lawn was actually the lawn in front of Selznick International Studios. It is still there today. The offices look very much like Tara, and though many people see the building and think it is the facade for Tara, it was not used in the movie. For the mansion, Selznick had them remove the white office building from the picture and replace it with the picture of another mansion and kept the sidewalk leading up to it.

The magnificent color of the sets and costumes come from the entire movie being shot in Technicolor. Herbert T. Kalmus was one of the founders of Technicolor. His wife at the time, Natalie Kalmus, had come over from *Wizard of Oz* to work on *Gone With The Wind*.

"*Gone With The Wind* was huge for Technicolor, and a gamble for Selznick," said Cammie King Conlon who played Bonnie Blue Butler. "It was enormously expensive. The studio had to use special Technicolor cameras and cameramen."

She knew a lot about Technicolor because in later years Herbert Kalmus became her stepfather.

Visitors to the Marietta *Gone With The Wind* Museum Scarlett on the Square where Dr. Christopher Sullivan's *Gone With The Wind* collection is housed are surprised when they see the color of Scarlett O'Hara's honeymoon dress, known as the Bengaline gown.

"Bengaline is a fabric composed of silk and wool threads," explained Sullivan. "In the movie it looks bright white, but the actual dress is a beige color, often referred to as ecru. A costume of that shade, when filmed in Technicolor, will photograph white."

According to Sullivan, if the costume were actually white, it would glare when filmed. Also, the front panel of the dress is one shade lighter than the rest of the dress.

"Walter Plunkett did this on purpose with many of his female costumes," said Sullivan. "This lighter panel in the front makes the dress film in a more three-dimensional manner, and has a slimming effect on the actress."

As soon as Cukor finished *Camille* in 1937, he started the preproduction process for *Gone With The Wind*, which included the scouting for actors and locations. He was very busy as he also worked as intermediate director across the lot at *Wizard of Oz*. Even though he never filmed any scenes there, he was involved at the beginning of the production. Cukor was largely responsible for some of the appearances of the characters in *Wizard of Oz*. After the first director was fired, Cukor made a visit to the film's set and gave some directing suggestions, (such as removing Judy Garland's blonde wig) which were used in the film. In the long-run, it was a coincidence that Cukor had worked on *Wizard of Oz* and Victor Fleming ended up being the director, because the same basic thing happened with *Gone With The Wind*.

Cukor spent over two years on *Gone With The Wind* in pre-production, doing casting, scouting locations and background research. He worked with Sidney Howard on the story, William Cameron Menzies on the production design, and Walter Plunkett on the costumes.

Just before the main shooting began in January 1939, David Selznick decided to throw a party for the cast and crew. According to Gene D. Phillips in his book *George Cukor*, Selznick jokingly said the party would be given "to celebrate the last time when we're all talking to each other." Unfortunately that turned out to be a sign of things to come because three weeks later Cukor was out the door and some of the cast and crew were at each other's throats.

Chapter Twelve
January 1939—Filming Finally Starts

George Cukor directed one version of the opening scene with Scarlett O'Hara sitting on the front porch of Tara, talking to Stuart and Brent Tarleton. In this version Scarlett is wearing the green sprigged dress that she would wear to the Wilkes Barbecue. But for some reason the pace was slow.

"Scarlett's dress was too low-cut and too elaborate for the opening shot of an innocent 16-year-old on Tara's front porch with the Tarleton twins," Marcella Rabwin wrote in her book, *Yes, Mr. Selznick*. "But in addition, the color on the whole film was too dim, the pacing of the scenes too slow; there was no vitality in the picture so far."

George Bessolo had been hired to play Stuart Tarleton, along with Fred Crane as Brent (though the credits have it backwards.) Selznick decided to simply have them be brothers and not emphasize that they were twins, as they were in the book. By the time production ended Bessolo changed his name to George Reeves.

George Cukor was having a lot of his time eaten up by the special attention he was giving the young actors Reeves and Crane. He felt they lacked experience and needed extra coaching but at the same time he felt he should be spending most of his time with Vivien Leigh.

One of Cukor's strong points was that he would take the actors aside and work with them individually. He would explain what the scene meant in relation to their part. He felt the actors should know how the scene related to the rest of the story and its importance to it. Although in retrospect Cukor was one of Hollywood's great directors, for some reason his directorial expertise was just not clicking with *Gone With The Wind.*

"You couldn't believe that the vigor of the film didn't somehow get into the director, even by osmosis, but it didn't," said Marcella Rabwin, who was there. "Though George Cukor was a wonderful director, everything he turned out in those first two weeks just was not up to his usual. The timing was off. It was just obvious it was not working."

Selznick did not like the first scene and later decided to throw it out, opting for a new take with a new, white, ruffly dress for Scarlett.

Cukor continued spending much time with the actors trying to get the most out of each one. In the scene where Melanie is having labor pains, Cukor, just out of the camera's range, was said to have been pinching her toes very hard to give her the sensation of pain. So intent on having that scene seem real, he went to great lengths in preparation.

Melanie's son was born Beauregard Wilkes, and called Beau. It took several days to film as Selznick and Cukor wanted it as real as possible. They hired a real obstetrician and had him on the set to give his input on the authenticity of the scene. Though it looked like it was an empty house with just Scarlett, Prissy and Melanie, there was a flurry of excitement going on behind the scenes.

Beau Wilkes was the first "Technicolor baby" ever born! He was born in front of a large crowd. The production crew, along with Susan Myrick, were there to oversee it and offer her suggestions, as well as many invited guests who were really just gawkers who wanted to be there.

One of those onlookers was Leslie Howard who played Beau's father Ashley. He was not in the scene as Ashley was away in the war, but the crew kidded him about being a "nervous father" pacing the floor.

Olivia de Havilland had researched giving birth as she had not had a baby yet in real-life. She talked to the doctor extensively about childbirth and Cukor, a perfectionist, gave her extra help on this scene. As skillfully as the actors pulled it off, no one could tell that a storm was brewing— literally.

The Santa Ana Winds were blowing in and stirring up trouble just as the filming of *Gone With The Wind* started. A stormy relationship was brewing between once best friends David Selznick and George Cukor. Clark Gable was pouting on the set, and all of this played a role in what was going on. Though Cukor was Selznick's favorite director, it was not working on this film and everyone knew it. Clark Gable was contributing to the problems, and when the big star is not happy something has to be done.

It must be pointed out that any problems Gable was having were with Selznick and Cukor, but he got along well with the other actors in the movie. According to an article in the Record-Courier by Colin McEwen, Ann Rutherford told a group she spoke to at Kent State University in 2009 that she thought Clark Gable was "gorgeous" and that he was well liked by the cast and crew.

Just nineteen days into the actual shooting of the film, Selznick fired Cukor over disagreements on how filming should proceed. Cukor did not get to see the film to its conclusion and received no mention in the credits.

"My mother was a big fan of George Cukor's," said Paul Rabwin. "She talked about him and said she liked him. It was well known that he was gay and that he worked well with women. That may have caused some discomfort for Clark Gable. And he felt like he was being ignored at times with Cukor."

Cukor did work well with the women, specifically Olivia de Havilland and Vivien Leigh. The day they found out Cukor was being fired they went to Selznick's office in their 'widow's weeds' costumes. Marcella greeted them and closed the door, letting them vent their frustrations. They felt Selznick was not taking their feelings into consideration. They both complained with anger and cried with sadness that Cukor was gone. In their black mourning outfits they looked as if they were filming a scene.

Because Leigh and de Havilland had worked so well with him, they each contacted Cukor and took extra practice at his house. Vivien Leigh was working hard and under a lot of stress so she would often stay out at Cukor's house and swim in his pool or take naps in one of the lounge chairs.

What had gone wrong? Why had there been such turmoil on the set among the biggest stars, the producer and the director?

Shortly before Cukor left the production, he did not seem to be himself and Clark Gable was seen moping around the studio. No one could pinpoint the problem but *Gone With The Wind* was falling behind schedule and the production was falling apart before it actually started.

Marcella Rabwin figured it out before anyone else. One of the biggest reasons Clark Gable had been so unhappy on the set was that he had problems with Cukor.

"George Cukor was one of the finest directors in the industry," she said. "But he was always considered a 'woman's director'. He had done wonderful movies with very sensitive and romantic portraits of women. It just came down to this: Clark did not want to work with George."

Cukor had known Gable in his younger days (before he became famous) and for some reason Gable was uncomfortable around him. It was no coincidence that Gable's old hunting buddy, the very 'manly' Victor Fleming was hired to replace Cukor.

Gable had gone to Louis B. Mayer and said, according to Marcella Rabwin, "I'm not going to make this picture if he is going to direct it. Let me out of my contract. I don't care what you've done, I want out."

This caused a major headache for Selznick because Cukor was his best friend.

"David O. Selznick had to fire his best friend!" said Rabwin. "We hired Victor Fleming, who was Clark's idol. He was a great macho, tall man. He was gorgeous. He was taken off *Wizard of Oz*, they were almost finished anyway. He had directed it, but just assigned another director to help finish it up and he came over as a favor to Gable."

According to Selznick's obituary in the New York Times, June 23, 1965, "As a producer, Mr. Selznick was preoccupied with quality, and his perfectionism led him to many fights with directors." Though *Gone With The Wind* had started with George Cukor directing, he was replaced by Victor Fleming.

Though Selznick had fired his friend, their friendship did not end, according to Marcella Rabwin.

"George was always invited to the Selznick's best parties and their witty and loving verbal exchanges went on," she said.

Rabwin also said Cukor was very generous, saying, years later in 1999, "George continued, as he had in the past, to send me elaborate Christmas gifts, including the enormous cashmere woolen shawl from Switzerland which I continued to wear even sixty years later."

"Selznick was not a very likeable guy for the people working around him at the time," said Marcella's son, Mark Rabwin. "This is not to say he was a 'bad' guy, he was just a task master. He was a genius, and hard on everybody. He was goal oriented; nothing was going to get in his way. He was going to keep his star Clark Gable happy and finish the film, so he called on Fleming. Vivien and Olivia took private instruction from Cukor for the rest of the movie."

"It was no secret," said actress Ann Rutherford. "George Cukor was amazing. He understood the situation. They would come straight from the studio and he did it for no pay. He just loved the property. Everybody did."

"Those around him may not have agreed with his decision," said Marcella. "But this will tell you what kind of man David Selznick was. He did not fire George until he lined up another movie for him to direct."

Bob Rosterman, who had worked for MGM's Chicago distribution office for almost twenty years and then for 20th Century Fox, got to know Cukor.

"Selznick went to L.B. Mayer and asked him to set George up with the upcoming movie, *The Women* and he did," said Rosterman. "It was a good fit for him. Despite the firing, Selznick and Cukor remained good friends."

Though he directed many other films, throughout his life, Cukor was always asked about *Gone With The Wind*.

"I could sense he grew tired of talking about it," said Rosterman. "He always tried to make light of it, like 'I survived, I'm still here'."

Dr. Christopher Sullivan talked to Marcella about the Cukor firing.

"I asked Marcella once how she thought *Gone With The Wind* would be different if Cukor had finished directing the film, instead of Fleming. She was very certain that Cukor would not have done justice to *Gone With The Wind*. The fact is, Cukor was not good at giant epic films that had to show the scope of war…. Fleming had experience with war films, battle scenes, and could film the epic concepts.

According to Marcella, Gable's intervention with the directors caused friction with some of the actors for a time.

"Clark Gable was a nice man, a kind man, he really was," Marcella Rabwin remembered. "But (at times) on that picture nobody wanted to work with him. But for all of the problems, Clark Gable gave the performance of his life. He did a wonderful job, and deserved the Academy Award. He was the only one who did not win an Academy Award, but he did deserve one."

In any other year Gable probably would have won, but 1939 produced so many great movies; he was up against Laurence Olivier in *Wuthering Heights*, Mickey Rooney in *Babes in Arms*, James Stewart in *Mr. Smith Goes to Washington*, but the winner was Robert Donat from *Goodbye, Mr. Chips*.

Clark Gable later explained the reason he was so disagreeable for a time on the set. He said it came down to one simple thing: at the beginning he was afraid of the role. He came up with every excuse in the book, but the truth was Gable had never even read the book. By the time they had come to Gable about the role, *Gone With The Wind* was extremely popular throughout the world.

After he got about half-way through the book, he realized what everyone else was saying about the book and became a fan.

For all of Gable's problems at the beginning of the production, those who knew him personally thought he was a good person.

"He was not spoiled," said Ann Rutherford to Katherine Nichols of the Honolulu Star Bulletin newspaper. "He did not fancy himself a large star."

Things were in a state of flux during the time Gable was being indecisive and Cukor got fired.

Selznick chose Lee Garmes as cinematographer. Garmes, who had started as a painters' assistant at Thomas Ince Studios had risen to the ranks of one of the most respected cinematographers in the business having won an Academy Award and been nominated for several when he came to *Gone With The Wind*. He would be in charge of the cameras—their shots, camera placement. Garmes worked with Cukor and filmed a good number of scenes and is remembered for the ground-breaking railroad scene.

According to Variety Magazine (variety.com) "his resume included conceiving the boom shot in *Gone With the Wind*."

There were several others involved in planning that highly acclaimed scene, including Val Lewton who was responsible for writing the scene.

Garmes was known for his 'artistic' filming where he usually went for a soft effect. Selznick began clashing with him because he was going for harsher, brighter colors. Some of his shots were used in the movie, including the railroad yard scene. Though he had done some major scenes, Garmes ended up leaving the production and was not credited.

He was replaced by Ernest Haller, who ended up winning the Academy Award for his work. Haller joined the production and worked with Ray Rennahan who shared the award. Rennahan had worked with Technicolor on several movies already. The new three-color technique was tricky to work with but along with Menzies and others from Selznick's production team, they would create one of the most visually memorable films ever shot.

One of the most amazing things about *Gone With The Wind* was that even with the revolving door of people who worked on the production but were not credited, many of the ones Selznick chose to stay with ended up being recognized for their work. In all the confusion, the producer seemed to have a clear vision, which in the end turned out to be genius.

It was mid-February in 1939 and plans were being made for the big premiere to take place in December. It was just ten months away but while they were planning for a big premiere, they still had a movie to shoot. Selznick and company had to get the movie on tape, edit it, and finish it up—and they didn't have much time to get it done.

Victor Fleming had been well-liked by actors in *Wizard of Oz*, as they, too had gone through other directors before Fleming arrived.

"Victor Fleming was a very nice man, and he was nice to everyone," said Mickey Carroll, who played a Munchkin in *The Wizard of Oz*. Carroll was interviewed for this book in 2008 and passed away at the age of 89 in 2009.

"He actually went back and forth for a time," said Carroll. "He worked at *Wizard of Oz* and also at *Gone With The Wind* at the beginning."

Carroll related a story that in an unexpected way, he and Judy Garland might have ended up appearing in *Gone With The Wind*. The studios were just across the parking lot from each other and Mickey and Judy, who knew each other from their days in vaudeville decided to go exploring. They saw the door was open and both knew that when the door was shut, no one could go in. Judy was only sixteen and Mickey eighteen, so with their youthful curiosity they went in search of Clark Gable and the rest.

According to Carroll, they peeked inside and saw a bunch of chaos going on so they went on in.

"We didn't realize it at the time, but it was a mob scene and they actually were shooting," said Mickey Carroll, an octogenarian who was living in St. Louis, Missouri at the time this book was written. "Once we were in the middle of the mess, we realized we should not be there so we hurried out, but were told later we made it on film."

And with all the cuts, they landed on the cutting room floor.

Mickey Carroll, one of only a few Munchkins still alive in 2009 had performed on the same stages with Judy Garland in the past, including the Worlds Fair in Chicago.

If not for filming *Wizard of Oz* Judy Garland might have been considered for a role in *Gone With The Wind.* She had a personal relationship with Marcella Rabwin, so she could have gotten a screen test.

"When my father was younger [before he became a doctor] he was in the movie distribution business in Minnesota and he delivered movies to Frank Gumm, her father, who also lived in Minnesota and owned a movie theater," said Mark Rabwin. "They became very good friends and after my parents moved to Los Angeles, he persuaded the Gumm family to move out there also."

Marcus Rabwin went to medical school and when he was a medical student, Frank Gumm approached him with a personal issue. His wife, Ethel, was pregnant with their third child and they thought it would be too much so he asked Rabwin what he thought about her having an abortion. Rabwin, who years later became Dr. Marcus Rabwin, 'doctor to the stars', persuaded him not to do it. He told them they would love her as much as they loved their other two daughters.

"That daughter turned out to be Judy," said Mark Rabwin.

Mickey Carroll said it was because of his childhood friendship with Judy Garland that he agreed to be in *The Wizard of Oz.* Victor Fleming was on the search for 'little people'. According to Mickey Carroll, Hitler's regime in Germany was after them just as they were after the Jews, so the studio was able to go to Germany and get a group who were just happy to get out of there.

Carroll was not in that group. He was living in America and working in vaudeville.

"Who wants to be a Munchkin when you can make a lot of money like I was making as an entertainer in vaudeville," said Carroll. "The only reason I did it was because Judy asked me to. I stayed at her house for a week while we were shooting."

He said Victor Fleming was one who made him feel at home on the set, even though he arrived several weeks late due to an automobile accident.

"During the day, after we had just filmed, the Munchkins would be sitting on the set," he recalled. "We sat near Victor Fleming. He was a good director. I realized that from the beginning. He got a lot out of us and treated us just like a father."

The actress who played Bonnie Blue Butler worked with Victor Fleming on *Gone With The Wind*. "Mother said he was kind to me," said Cammie King Conlon, who was four at the time. Her mother told her a story about a day when she had forgotten her lines.

"One day I forgot my lines and the set got very quiet," said Conlon. "Victor Fleming, the director came over and knelt down by me so he was at eye level. He said, 'Cammie, I have a little girl your age and the reason I come to the studio and work so hard is so that I can take care of my little girl. Cammie, do you see all these men around the set?' And I said, 'Yes, Mr. Fleming'. 'Well they all have families too, with boys and girls and that's why they work so hard. Cammie, when you don't know your lines we can't do our work'. Oh, how did I ever survive that?"

Later Cammie went to school with Fleming's daughter, Victoria Fleming. "She and I wound up in the same freshman class at Marymount; then Vicky transferred to Marlborough. I occasionally see her younger sister, who is fabulous."

Cammie had to take horseback riding lessons for her role as Bonnie. Her father would take her to some stables in Bel Air where she learned to ride a pony side-saddle, a horse English style, and she could even ride bareback on a Circus Pony.

"Though I'd worked so hard to learn to ride, you don't see me much on the horse," she reported, "I had learned to jump. I could have jumped. In the scene where I am to die and I'm in my long blue-velvet riding habit—I really thought I was pretty special in that outfit and I'd swish around the set—Mother says I came back to her and said, 'Mother there's a little girl over there dressed just like me smoking a cigarette!' And it was a small man, we called them midgets back then, he was a small person. He was like a thirty-year old man in my outfit and long curls. It was a wig. He was waiting to take the horse over the jump and take the fall and then he would wind up back on the ground."

Back on the *Gone With The Wind* set, it was said that in the beginning, after Cukor left, Vivien Leigh was unhappy and difficult to work with.

"She was English, and not used to the way we do things here," said Mickey Carroll. "But Victor Fleming had a way with people."

Ann Rutherford respected Vivien.

"She was in practically every scene," said Rutherford. "She worked very hard. You could see Vivien Leigh from beginning to end. At the beginning she was just a kid, but you could see her as she matured."

The next problem that arose was the script. Fleming had not liked it from the beginning.

Though Sidney Howard had been working for two years on it, and then Selznick had re-written so much of it at the insistence of Clark Gable. Fleming had looked at the script, and according to Marcella Rabwin declared, "This is terrible!"

"He said, 'It's a cheap romantic novel'," she recalled. "He said it was not a good, strong picture like *Red Dust* or the types of pictures he had directed."

Fleming had come straight from one movie to another with no rest. There was chaos on the new set and he was unhappy with the script, so he contributed to the negativity. He thought it was going to be easy walking into *Gone With The Wind*; but what he hadn't counted on was the micro-managing of Selznick. His first scenes were no better than the first scenes Cukor did.

"His first scenes were disappointing and stolid," opined Marcella Rabwin. "Selznick proposed to lay out every scene himself. Fleming was insulted. The atmosphere on the set became so tense it was almost palpable."

"A few weeks of contention followed, David dictating, the two girls protesting, the crew ill at ease, and the director close to revolt."

Walter Plunkett, the costume designer worked very hard on the costumes, and there were many. He had started his career as an actor, but became more interested in the Hollywood costumes and began working in 'wardrobe' in the 1920s. He was an excellent costume designer and was noted for his skills in 'period' costumes.

One of Plunkett's problems came when Vivien Leigh put on the low-cut green sprigged dress that she wore to the barbecue. She was not well endowed and the ruffles sagged down. Victor Fleming noticed it and didn't like it. He wanted her to show her cleavage, but she did not have a lot to show. He told Plunkett to have her bind her breasts with tape, which proved to be very uncomfortable when she took it off.

Fleming may not have meant any harm to Leigh as he ordered her breasts bound, but she took offense and things like that fueled the fire between them.

Perhaps it was because she had so many scenes and such long hours on the set, or perhaps their personalities just did not gel, but according to Marcella Rabwin Vivien Leigh and Fleming went round and round. Their conflicts often left Vivien in tears in Marcella's office or Fleming in a temper tantrum. At one point reportedly Vivien made Fleming so mad he stormed off the set and did not return for two days.

Fleming ended up having a nervous breakdown and leaving the show for two weeks. Questions circled the 'nervous breakdown' and those around him wondered if he just wanted a break when the times got stressful, because once Sam Wood came on to direct and things were going smoothly, Fleming came back.

"Fleming basically went home and sulked during his 'break down'," according to Marcella Rabwin. "Then when he came back, the picture was so far behind schedule that we kept the interim director Sam Wood for several months. He did portions of the film while Fleming did other portions of it. That's the way we finally got it done in five months. It would have taken five years if we'd done it with one person."

Throughout the revolving door of crew members, Selznick worked continuously on the production.

"It fell to David Selznick," said Ann Rutherford. "He was an amazing man. He not only was around great things, he caused them to happen."

Finally after Fleming came back, things seemed to calm down and he got along better with Vivien Leigh and she ended up taking direction well from Fleming.

There were many requirements in the deal Selznick had made with MGM, and one initially was that Gable's name had to come before the title. Clark Gable's name is punctuated in the credits by putting "And A Visitor From Charleston…Rhett Butler….Clark Gable."

The Wizard of Oz was filmed entirely on a sound stage, unlike *Gone With The Wind*, which filmed both indoors and outdoors. The sets for both movies were adjacent to each other. In those days the "back-lots" backed up to each other.

"They were right next door," said Mickey Carroll. "We even shared make-up people."

"Old Hollywood was different than Hollywood is today," said Mark Rabwin. "The studios were very close knit; it's not as personal now. They shared actors and loaned actors back and forth between the studios. Nowadays you would not find an actor like Clark Gable in a large room sharing make-up artists."

"There would be about 30 make-up people," Mickey Carroll said. "You would go into a room with mirrors on the wall and chairs in front of the mirrors. The worst thing about being in a Hollywood movie was you had to get there at five a.m., for make-up."

According to Carroll, everyone on both movies who was shooting on any given day was expected to be in make-up starting at five a.m., causing long lines. Carroll got to the filming of *Wizard of Oz* late, due to a serious car accident which kept him in the hospital. When he finally arrived, he was not familiar with the protocol and he arrived on the set late for make-up one day. Something happened that he will never forget; another actor was also late for make-up that day.

"Clark Gable and I sat in the same make-up room," he said. "And we talked. As a matter of fact, he was working on lines for the day where he said his most famous line. He started telling me he was going to say a curse word and wondered if they would leave it in the movie."

Many years later, in a three-hour special television event on CBS hosted by actor Pierce Brosnan, the American Film Institute's committee of 1,500 film artists, critics and historians selected Clark Gable's celebrated line, "Frankly, my dear, I don't give a damn!" as the most memorable movie quote of all time.

The production finally started to have more of a focus once the actors and actresses were in full swing with the production shooting. The original scene that Cukor had directed with Scarlett wearing her green and white dress was tossed out in favor of a new one where Scarlett wore the white dress. Selznick wanted more costumes and more emphasis on the happy-go-lucky innocence of Scarlett at the beginning of the book and movie.

It seemed that green-sprigged dress caused quite a stir. Susan Myrick, a consultant on the production, became frustrated during this time.

"She was supposed to tell them when something was not right," said Myrick's niece, Susan Lindsley, "But when she did, they sometimes did not listen. In the barbecue scene, they shot it with Vivien Leigh's dress cut too low. My aunt knew she would not have worn it like that. She kept after them to re-shoot the scene, and in the end they had to re-call some of the cast (including the Tarleton twins) for the re-shoot."

Leslie Howard [Ashley Wilkes] was almost as much of a malcontent on the set as Clark Gable, according to Marcella Rabwin. He had served on the front lines in France during World War I and it was said that he had returned to England shell-shocked. After some recuperation, he rethought his future and decided to go into acting. Acting was a good choice because he was very successful both on the stage and the screen.

Howard had worked with Clark Gable before and also with David Selznick. Like Gable, he just simply did not want to do the part. Howard felt he was too old to play Ashley, even though he was the only one Selznick had ever wanted. He felt it was too bland a part. He also didn't like the costumes.

"Like Gable, he didn't want to read the book, he didn't want to read the script," said Marcella. "He said, 'I feel like the pansy doorman at the Beverly Wilshire hotel in that Confederate costume!' And his lady love Violette was there every second that he was."

Howard would rehearse his lines with his girlfriend, Violette Cunningham, and frequently asked Selznick for advances on his salary. He never read any of the script except the parts that had his own lines; and after his scenes were finished he rushed off the set to get back to Violette.

"The only way we could get Leslie Howard to do *Gone With The Wind* was to promise him he could direct a picture," said Marcella Rabwin. "He never blended with the cast. Nevertheless, he put forth a brilliant performance."

Susan Myrick mentioned Violette in her letters back and forth to Mitchell, which are printed in the book, *White Columns in Hollywood, Reports from the GWTW Sets by Susan Myrick*, edited by Richard Harwell. Evidently there were some on the set who were upset with him for bringing

Violette Cunningham to the set everyday when Laurence Olivier was prohibited from even seeing Vivien Leigh.

Myrick really enjoyed working with Leslie Howard. Whereas Rabwin had to deal with his not wanting to be in the film and not wanting to wear the costumes, it was Myrick's job to work with him on his Southern accent. He worked hard on his accent and was very pleasant to her. When working together, he invited her to his home and served her dinner.

Susan Myrick told her niece, Susan Lindsley, about the fun times she had in Hollywood during that period. She also told her about how she would keep her friend Peggy posted on the goings-on.

During the time *Gone With The Wind* was filming, Carole Lombard was searching for a home for her and Gable, hoping they would be able to get married. Unlike the other women he had dated or the two he had been married to, Lombard, who was a beautiful star herself, wanted to live in Gable's world. She was a good athlete and liked hunting and fishing, and even tagged along on some of his hunting trips.

She found a farm not too far from Hollywood, but just far enough to give them some privacy and the outdoor peace they longed for. As luck would have it, there was a period of time during the shooting where Gable would not be needed for a few days, so with the help of Gable's friend and MGM publicist Otto Winkler, they went to Kingman, Arizona, and eloped. They returned to their farm several hours later for a press conference. It was great publicity for *Gone With The Wind*, and it made Clark Gable a much happier person and easier to deal with on the set.

The filming had started early in 1939, and by April the production needed more money. Once again David Selznick turned to his friend and financier, Jock Whitney, who helped out to avoid Selznick having to give it all up to MGM. MGM had wanted to put in more money for 100 percent ownership of the movie. Whitney believed in the movie, having persuaded Selznick to do the picture in the first place. They ended up getting a bank loan with Whitney as the co-signer.

The production looked like things were going to be sailing along smoothly for a while. Gable loved working with Hattie McDaniel. She was a hard working actress who spent much time with Susan Myrick learning the dialect of a Southern slave. According to Warren G. Harris' book, *Clark Gable, A Biography*, Gable played a good natured joke on McDaniel while filming the scene after Bonnie's birth. Rhett Butler was offering a drink to Mammy, and they had so many takes that McDaniel complained about having to drink so much of the colored water. During a break, Gable had the glass filled with straight scotch and when she took the big swig, she got the unexpected shock of a whiskey burn. He got a big kick out of her reaction, and she took it in the manner it was offered as they had been friends long before *Gone With The Wind*.

"The next morning he had the audacity to whiz past me and holler, 'Mammy, how's the hangover?'" Hattie McDaniel was quoted as saying in Harris' book (page 203).

It would be hard to imagine the role of Mammy being played by anyone but McDaniel, but before she got the role there were many vying for the spot. People had been bothering Margaret Mitchell in Atlanta, saying they had the perfect person to play Mammy.

The national attention to the movie was so huge that when President Roosevelt's maid Lizzie McDuffie contacted Mitchell telling her she wanted the part of 'Mammy', Margaret wrote to Kay Brown to see if she would get it. Mitchell knew McDuffie as she was from Atlanta. Though she wanted to stay out of it, she just could not help giving her opinion on some of the parts.

Since Clark Gable had such a high regard for Hattie McDaniel he mentioned her, and another person who stepped in on her behalf was Bing Crosby. He was friends with McDaniel's brother and he casually mentioned to Selznick that she would be a good choice. Luckily for everyone involved, the part fell to McDaniel.

Cammie King's mother accompanied her to the set every day for her role as Bonnie.

"She did my hair every morning," said Cammie, who published her memoirs in 2009. "Selznick said he didn't want 'Shirley Temple' curls, but not to worry. I have stick straight hair and only mother's persistence and spit made me have curls for filming. While she set my hair, she taught me my lines for the day. My father used to say, 'Cammie will have curls as long as Eleanor's spit holds out!'"

In the movie (and book) Ashley and Melanie Wilkes' child was Beau.

Because of the age progression it took several different children to play the part of the one little boy.

"Patrick Curtis played Baby Beau after the war," said Faye Bell, the owner of Gone With The Wind Memories Store in Plant City, Florida and a friend of Curtis'. "He was in the scene when Melanie had Beau on her hip. And then Mickey Kuhn was Beau when he was a little older. He was Bonnie's little playmate."

Greg Giese played the newborn baby, Beau. And Gary Carlson and Rick Holt played Beau in various stages. Patrick Curtis said that when he was old enough to realize he was in the movie, it was confusing as he watched the show to see the older 'Beaus' who did not look like him.

Mickey Kuhn received the on-screen credit and he was the only Beau who had lines. He got to work with Clark Gable and Vivien Leigh, but even though he was Melanie's son he did not appear in any scenes with her since she was dying at that time.

"Clark Gable was a very nice man, fun to work with," said Kuhn. "I had a scene to do with him and Bonnie. I had three words…Hello. Uncle. Rhett. That's it. How hard is that? Three takes it took me to remember that his name was not Clark. He would walk in and I'd say 'Hello Uncle Clark'. After the third time I messed up he called me over to him and said, 'Mickey, my name is Clark, but in the scene, my name is Rhett'. I said, 'Yes sir, Mr. Gable'. So we went through and did it and it came out fine."

Gable had a way with kids. Looking back on her role as Bonnie Blue Butler, Cammie King Conlon feels she was lucky.

"Mickey Kuhn has told me that Rhett kissed Bonnie more than he kissed Scarlett in the film. When my mother's friends would ask, 'What was it like to kiss Clark Gable?' I would say, 'His mustache scratched!' Later when it was on television I watched it as a young married woman …. All of a sudden as a woman I saw Gable holding me, kissing me, putting me to bed. I thought to have been held and kissed and put to bed by Clark Gable, at the age of five, was a cruel trick!"

Faye Bell, as a collector and store owner, became friends with many of the stars from the film. The film came out in 1939, but at the time of this writing there were several stars still living. When the movie was celebrating its 70th Anniversary it's clear that the youngest baby in it was at least seventy years old.

In July of 2006 Bell attended Olivia de Havilland's 90th birthday party celebration held at the Samuel Goldwyn Theater and sponsored by the Academy of Motion Pictures Arts and Sciences.

"All of the 'Beaus' were there and they got their picture taken together," she said. "Cammie King was there, too."

At the time of this writing Ann Rutherford, Cammie King Conlon, Mickey Kuhn, Patrick Curtis, and Greg Giese were still very active and popular guests at *Gone With The Wind* events around the country. Rutherford was a special guest at a *Gone With The Wind* event in Hawaii in the spring of 2008. All four, plus Fred Crane who played Brent Tarleton were in Marietta, Georgia at the Marietta *Gone With The Wind* Museum celebrating *Gone With The Wind* on July 4, 2008. They signed autographs and attended a dance that evening. Fred Crane, who had celebrated his 90th birthday in March, was out on the dance floor several times. Shortly after that they found out that on the same weekend, in California, Evelyn Keyes [Suellen] had passed away from cancer at age 91. A month later, in August of 2008, Crane died.

The stars who travel around to *Gone With The Wind* events offer a new perspective to the story of the making of *Gone With The Wind*. For years there have been stories about Vivien Leigh, Clark Gable, Olivia de Havilland and the others, but only recently have the younger actors spoken out.

"I have great memories of Victor Fleming," said Mickey Kuhn. "They were wondering how they were going to get a seven year old kid to cry, but Victor said 'I'll get him to cry'."

He took Kuhn away from the set and began talking to him.

"He said things like, 'how would you feel if your parents died?' And 'what if you had a puppy and it died?' I was getting so sad I started to cry so he carried me back to Leslie Howard (Ashley) to do the scene."

The boy performed the scene perfectly, complete with crying, but at the end of the scene he could not stop crying.

"Victor Fleming took me in his arms and walked me around and calmed me down. A Victor Fleming biographer told me that maybe the reason he was so good with me was that he had a great relationship with his own father and was familiar with the good father-son relationship."

On the subject of crying, ever since he had first read the script, Clark Gable was dreading the day he had to do the scene where Scarlett had a miscarriage from falling down the stairs and he had to cry. He thought it was unmanly to cry and said he would not do it. Finally after both Carole Lombard's pleading with him and Olivia de Havilland's talking to him, Fleming had an idea. He suggested they film the scene two ways: the first as Gable wanted to without the crying, and the second one with the tears. Once Gable looked at both versions he agreed the one with the tears was the best.

Mickey Kuhn said there were no playrooms on the set, so he spent a great deal of time in his dressing room, taking naps or doing his homework.

"We had to go to school for four hours and we could only work for four hours," he said. "You would go do your scene and then meet with your teacher who was there at the studio. She would write down the time I got there. If they called me for another scene, I could not go until I had completed my four hours. You could not go to school for three hours and fifty-nine minutes. They were very strict. It had to be four hours."

One of the most surprising things about Mickey Kuhn is that while he was the son of Melanie and Ashley, he never met Olivia de Havilland during the time they filmed the movie. She was not in the scenes with him, and because he was such a good actor he did most of his scenes in one take so he was not on the set for long periods of time.

"I have met her since then," he said. "I was grown up and I wrote to her. When I met her I told her I played her son in the movie. She was very nice and it was a thrill that she knew who I was."

Olivia de Havilland, who turned ninety in 2006, lived for years in Paris and was still active. Recently she had been living in California. Still beautiful, with white hair, she was gracious with the press and public.

At the time this book came out, Alicia Rhett was not doing appearances or interviews and preferred being known as an artist as opposed to having been in *Gone With The Wind*. She was polite if someone came upon her and there are some lucky collectors who have gotten her autograph, but not many.

Carroll Nye, who played Frank Kennedy (Suellen's boyfriend who Scarlett ends up marrying), had been acting since the 1920s. Most of the main actors were older than the characters they played. Nye was born in 1901, so he was 38 in real life and marrying Scarlett, a seventeen-year-old in the movie. An exception to this was Thomas Mitchell who was actually younger than Gerald O'Hara was supposed to be.

When production started, actor Robert Gleckler was cast as Jonas Wilkerson, the overseer of the O'Hara's plantation. On January 28, 1939, the scene where Ellen O'Hara confronts Wilkerson about Emmie Slattery's baby was shot with Gleckler. Gleckler had been in five movies in 1938, including the Shirley Temple movie, *Little Miss Broadway*, and then three in 1939, but a month after shooting that first scene he died.

Victor Jory was recast for the role and the scene was re-shot. He was one actor that Susan Myrick did not have to work with on his accent because he played a Yankee overseer. Jory's character and his association with the "poor" Slattery family is a far cry from the Shakespearian acting he had done previously.

Though the actors all went on to do many more things with their lives, playing in *Gone With The Wind* gave them a certain publicity beyond anything else they did. In the seventy years since the production, any bad memories of problems on the set have been replaced by the success the actors have had in their lives because of the movie. It must be pointed out that the conflicts Marcella Rabwin spoke of were mostly with the producer, directors, and top four actors. Most of the actors and actresses reported to the sets, did their jobs and had a great camaraderie with each other.

The script had been a source of frustration throughout the production. When Selznick first got the rights to the book he contacted the Pulitzer Prize winning novelist Sidney Howard, who agreed to write the script but preferred to work from his farm in Massachusetts.

"He was such a good writer for this movie because he had such a respect for Margaret Mitchell's book," said Marcella Rabwin of Howard. "He would not allow a line of dialog that wasn't hers. Once the movie started shooting, it took five months to shoot."

According to Marcella Rabwin, with Howard in Massachusetts and Margaret Mitchell not of any help, it was no wonder the script was difficult to write.

Selznick wanted it perfect. On this project he would become more demanding than he usually was in his quest for the perfect movie. He could not wait for Sidney Howard, so he hired writers of the caliber of F. Scott Fitzgerald and Ben Hecht. Still, he was never satisfied.

"It took two years to prepare the script," said Marcella Rabwin. "We had plenty of brilliant writers try their hand at it, and in the long run, guess who wrote the final script, even though Sidney Howard got the credit: David Selznick.

"The script that was satisfactory was just hell on wheels," said Rabwin. "He had eight writers. Can you imagine re-writing F. Scott Fitzgerald?"

The scriptwriting consumed Selznick's time, but that wasn't all. An autonomous producer, he was literally in on every decision made—even when the actors tried on their costumes.

"While I was being fitted for my dress one memorable day, David was watching," said Ann Rutherford. "He turned to the designer and said, 'I told you not to add anything to the costume'. And the designer said, 'I didn't'."

"Well, believe it or not, David Selznick was noticing a little accessory that Ann was wearing.

"'Where did you get that necklace?' he asked me. I had on a pretty, heart shaped necklace. I said, 'I got it for being a bridesmaid in a friend's wedding'."

Selznick stepped back and looked at Rutherford in the necklace.

"Keep it in there," he said. "It looks good."

For the producer of a major movie like *Gone With The Wind,* to notice something as small as a necklace showed the uniqueness of Selznick.

Most of the movie was shot at the studio, but a few scenes were shot at different locations. The barbecue at Twelve Oaks near the beginning of the movie was shot at Busch Gardens in Pasadena, an estate (built by the Busch brewing family) which is no longer in existence.

The cotton fields of Tara, as well as the scene where Gerald O'Hara takes his first horseback ride, were shot in Northern California, about eighty miles north of Sacramento.

For the 'Shantytown' sequence, the shooting was moved to Big Bear Lake area in California. Yakima Canutt, who was Clark Gable's stand-in, played the renegade soldier who tried to attack Scarlett.

Throughout the filming, Margaret Mitchell kept tabs of what was going on. She wrote letters to Katherine (Kay) Brown (Selznick's east coast representative with whom she had dealt in selling the rights to Selznick) and continued her contact with Susan Myrick in Los Angeles.

Marcella Rabwin tried to keep in touch with Margaret, sending her still pictures of the costumes and scenery. Selznick thought that if they kept in contact with her she would offer them some assistance or insight into her vision so that Selznick's could be the same as hers. Margaret was appalled when she noticed, on the pictures Marcella sent her, the white fences where she had split-rail fences in the book, but she did not tell this to Marcella, choosing instead to comment on it only to Myrick.

"I had heard she did not want to be involved in the movie in case any changes were made," said Bob Rosterman, a movie expert who has written for *Playbill Magazine* and worked for both MGM and 20th Century Fox in their Chicago distribution offices. "If people did not like the movie, she wanted to be so removed from it they could not blame her."

Clark Gable understood Mitchell wanting to stay out of the movie business.

"I found upon investigation that Miss Mitchell—and most intelligent of her—didn't care a hang what Hollywood was going to do with her book," he said at the time. "All she wanted was peace and quiet. She wrote a book because it was the thing she liked to do, and having innocently caused more excitement than any author in memory asked only to be left alone behind the wall she built around her home."

Gable felt a certain kinship with Mitchell when he found out how much she had protested any involvement in the movie.

"I'm sure we would have understood one another," said Gable in an interview, "for after all, Rhett has caused more than a little confusion in both our lives."

Mitchell seemed to enjoy watching the difficulties Selznick was having with the script from afar. Myrick told her of the many different script writers Selznick had hired to work with Sydney Howard. She was excited to hear F. Scott Fitzgerald was even called in.

Mitchell would chuckle to Susan Myrick about the script not being finished or about Selznick getting the costumes wrong for a scene.

Wilbur Kurtz's wife had evidently told Margaret about the bazaar scene with Scarlett and Rhett dancing together, telling her that Scarlett wore a bonnet and veil.

"In the name of God, what was she doing with a hat on at an evening party where everybody else was bareheaded and wearing low-cut gowns?" Margaret asked Susan Myrick.

Still, as Marcella Rabwin observed, Selznick had expected more help from the author. Near the end of shooting, Selznick decided the opening scene with Scarlett and the Tarletons had to be re-shot. After the re-shoot, the producer looked at the tape and told Vivien Leigh she looked "too old" and they would have to do it again. She was to be a sixteen-year-old in the opening scene. When they first shot it, she was enthusiastic and happy to be working with Cukor, but now Selznick wanted her in a different dress. By the time they shot the scene again, she had been worn down by the separation of miles from Laurence Olivier and the conflicts on the set, as well as the long hours.

David Selznick told her to take a vacation with Olivier and be sure no one found out about it. When she got back, she was relaxed and refreshed and she finished up the scene.

"She was so darling with those wonderful apple cheeks," said cast mate Ann Rutherford. "At the beginning of the filming, she looked like a sixteen year old girl when she was sitting with the Tarleton twins on the porch. She wound up working in every scene of the movie. There are very few scenes where she was not there. As a result she was there from dawn until dark—totally dark. She had all this dialog to learn, all these situations to know, and then she continued driving up to George Cukor's house for help."

According to Ann Rutherford, Vivien lost weight while working on the film.

"At least once a week they would take in her gowns at the waist," she said. "When she finished the picture, she really did have a 17-inch waist. She didn't have time to eat much. She just was the hardest worker and the least temperamental person I've ever seen. She was special."

"So the 'take' they used as the opening scene was actually one of the last scenes shot. By the end of the shooting, Vivien Leigh was happy to be finished. Even though the entire film was shot in less than a year, it seemed to her it was an eternity.

But even though production was over, David Selznick was just getting settled in for the task of post-production. The movie would be scrutinized by those who wanted to be sure morals were upheld, as well as those who wanted to oversee the racial aspect of the movie. The treatment of the black race in the movie turned out to be a public relations challenge but Selznick was up for it.

Chapter Thirteen
Mammy and Prissy

The black actors in *Gone With The Wind* were among the best actors in the business and gave awesome performances, yet in some cases were criticized for appearing in the movie. The period of history relevant to Margaret Mitchell's book is over and there is nothing anyone alive today can do to change it, but we can learn from this history as we progress toward the future.

"When the movie first came out there were some difficulties," said Carlton Jackson who wrote *Hattie: The Life of Hattie McDaniel*. "The Black press generally scorned it as being too friendly to the mindset of Reconstruction America."

Once word got out that Margaret Mitchell's book was going to be made into a movie, the controversy began. The book had just come out and everyone knew it contained racial epithets and dealt with a horrible time in our nation's existence.

Carlton Jackson spent a long time researching Hattie McDaniel.

"Hattie recognized right off that this was going to be one of the most important motion picture experiences in history," he said. "It came at a time during Hitler's Germany. This was no time, she argued, to use black stereotypes as had so often been the case in the past. She helped to eliminate the "n" word from the movie, although 'darky' was used."

Hattie McDaniel won an Oscar for her performance as 'Mammy' and David Selznick, the director, felt she was one of the five most important actors in the movie. He had her picture, along with the four other stars, printed on the program for the World Premiere in Atlanta in 1939. The programs were shipped to Atlanta and once they were looked at he was told due to the racial climate of the times they could not have her on the program. They had to be re-done.

"There had been rumors for weeks in the Black press that Hattie might receive an Oscar," said Jackson. "So there was a huge amount of tension, electricity, edginess, expectations, all mixed up into one great emotion. When Hattie's name was called by Fay Bainter and Frank Capra, the crowd of 12,000 went wild."

Jackson adds, "Here in many ways was America's answer to Hitler and Emperor Hirohito. Hattie was barely able to complete her Acceptance Speech before breaking into tears of joy and pent-up nervous tension. She resolved here to be a good citizen and spokeswoman for 'her people'. At that time she probably thought 'her people' meant her fellow African-Americans. In reality, 'her people' meant every citizen in the United States. She was a wonderful spokesperson for the human race."

Though she wore a maid's outfit in the movie, McDaniel was far from a servile person. She had incredible strength and advanced herself while advancing others, all the while remaining a devoted Christian.

"She came from a modest but very talented family," said Jackson. "Her talents took her far; and in a strange sort of way, from time to time she suffered guilt because of this. 'Why me, Lord?' she always wanted to know."

Many Southern plantation owners in the 1800s owned slaves, and

Margaret Mitchell wrote about the subject in her book. It was what it was.

She started writing *Gone With The Wind* in the late 1920s from the frame of reference she had at the time. Her ancestors had been plantation owners who had slaves. Society today knows slavery was wrong. However, to Margaret Mitchell, she was merely depicting history; what was going on in the South in the late 1800s from her family's frame of reference.

When Hattie McDaniel was criticized by other blacks for accepting the role, she replied that she would rather be paid to play a maid in a movie than be paid to be one in real life.

Mitchell wrote things in her book that if taken out of context seem stronger than perhaps she meant them, such as on page 409 when she called the servants "stupid," saying they did what people told them to do.

Just taking that one sentence out of context it seems she (or Scarlett) disliked the black race, but really it was the opposite. When Aunt Pittypat's life-long slave Uncle Peter has his feelings hurt because 'Northerners' had been insulting him (p. 673), Scarlett, who at times seems to care about no one but herself, soothes him, saying, "What do you care? They aren't anything but damned Yankees!" She comforted him and stood up for him.

In the book, the use of the "n" word was from slave to slave, and when a white person called a servant that name it brought the black person to tears. It was said Mitchell was careful to do research in this area. She also created different dialects for different slaves.

When Uncle Peter was upset because the 'Northerners' said he was not to be trusted, it really hurt him. Scarlett could not bear to see his sadness and she told him that they could not have made it without him and that no one except "the Angel Gabriel" could have done better than he did.

Several brief exchanges with the slaves were actually the few times Scarlett O'Hara seemed to show that she had a heart. A key theme throughout the book was illustrated at the bottom of that same page. Uncle Peter says to Scarlett basically that the Northerners don't understand "us Confederates." Margaret Mitchell was writing a book from the perspective of a Southern plantation owner; a Confederate plantation owner.

In her book, Mitchell wanted to portray a whole different mindset in the South at the time of the Civil War. Even Belle Watling knew it. Melanie said she was a good person for helping them, but Belle summed it up by saying she was just a Confederate like everybody else.

In the Fayetteville City Cemetery in the same section as her great-grandfather Philip Fitzgerald and great-uncle James Fitzgerald, is a grave marked, "Grace (Fitzgerald) Colored servant of the Fitzgerald's." In those days the slaves would be put in graves completely separate from the families they worked for. It was not normal to have a slave buried with the family.

Grace was a freed slave from another family who came to the Fitzgeralds. Even though she was 'freed' she did not have anywhere to go, so she asked James if she could live with them and he let her. She acted as a "Mammy" to show her appreciation, and to further show her affection she asked that she be buried in the Fitzgerald area, which she was.

This interaction between James Fitzgerald and Grace may have been where Margaret Mitchell came up with the idea of Dilcey coming to live with the O'Haras. She asked if she could come (through Pork) and then, when the slaves were freed, she stayed on. The character of Dilcey was in the book, but not in the movie.

Margaret Mitchell lets the reader know (p. 674) that Scarlett trusted blacks more than she trusted most "white people," and definitely more than she trusted Yankees. When Scarlett's father Gerald O'Hara died, she gave his favorite slave Pork, his watch. Pork was very appreciative, but Scarlett realized that her father would have wanted him to have it.Children growing up in the United States today have the advantage of seeing the many positive contributions and advancements made by blacks, in the history books and celebrating Black History Month in February. They learn about strong, successful black men and women who have accomplished much with their lives. The movie and her other acting roles enabled Hattie McDaniel to live a very comfortable life and bring many of her relatives to California and provide a nice life for them, too. Hattie had a long friendship with Clark Gable before the movie and it continued afterward. Her role as Mammy brought her much fame, love, and an Academy award.

During the time Margaret Mitchell was writing *Gone With The Wind*, Atlanta was segregated. It has been widely reported that the Piedmont Driving Club was one of her favorite restaurants, in fact she had drinks there the night she died. By their own website they regard themselves as having "a reputation as one of the most prestigious private clubs in the South." During this time, as with most country clubs, blacks were not welcome.

Although she had been around the black race all her life it was mostly through her family's domestic workers; whether in her parents' house, her own home, or the workers at Rural Home.

Her father employed various workers, including cooks, housekeepers, and a 'washerwoman'. As a grown-up, she and her husband John Marsh employed Bessie Berry (who later became Bessie Berry Jordan).

Bessie Berry Jordan loved her bosses and was a trusted friend as well as an employee and Mitchell also welcomed Berry's daughter Deon into her home. Mitchell took care of both of the women when they were sick; and after Margaret Mitchell published *Gone With The Wind*, Bessie Berry wrote an article for the *Atlanta Journal*; a tribute to her boss, which she asked them to run again after Mitchell's death. Mitchell gave Bessie and Deon gifts and trips, and tried to be very generous with them.

Mitchell privately funded scholarships for young black medical students. Dr. Otis Wesley Smith, a graduate of Morehouse, was the first practicing black pediatrician in the state of Georgia and Margaret Mitchell had funded his education. He spoke publicly many times about her humanitarian works. He served as a founding member and former board chairman of the Margaret Mitchell House and Museum.

A page on the Margaret Mitchell House and Museum's website talks about Mitchell and the black race. It tells about Dr. Smith and then adds:

"Her interest in Atlanta's black community was again made evident when it was also revealed that she supported the early efforts to desegregate the city's police department."

Though it might have helped her in the black race's eyes to have let the public know what she was doing in conjunction with helping with desegregation in the police department, she did that as she did other charitable work in private. Today, she might have hired a public relations person to send out a press release that she was doing work on behalf of blacks, but that was not Margaret Mitchell. She did not like to be in the spotlight that *Gone With The Wind* put her in, and she did not want or seek publicity for her endeavors this way.

To truly understand Margaret Mitchell's treatment of the black race in *Gone With The Wind*, one must read the book in its entirety; not merely see the movie. The movie, which includes a slightly different slant on the slaves than Mitchell wrote, is complete with Hollywood's version of the slaves as providing comic relief and Mammy in her kerchief. Though some of the characters were changed a bit, David O. Selznick had respect for the black race and said he tried to do the best he could in the filming. Selznick, being Jewish, did not want to make a movie that would be offensive to members of a race, so he went to what he felt were great lengths when it came to treatment of the blacks.

According to the Jill Watts' book, *Hattie McDaniel, Black Hollywood, White Ambition*, "When it became public that Selznick had optioned *Gone With The Wind*, African Americans throughout the nation reacted with alarm."

Selznick, while sticking with Margaret Mitchell's book, wanted to honor the black race so he pledged that one way he would honor them was by selecting the best actors he could to play the parts.

One of those actors was Butterfly McQueen. She had been a stage actress and trained in dance, and had appeared in the stage production of "A Midsummer Night's Dream" in 1935. Butterfly McQueen had been conflicted about playing the part of Prissy, especially because of the type of character she was.

Later in life she gave speeches regarding her time in *Gone With The Wind*. One time she was going to be speaking at the University of Charleston in Charleston South Carolina and as she passed through Georgia, she stopped at the historic Crawford Talmadge house in Clayton County, Georgia. While there, she discussed her role as Prissy with Betty Talmadge, the owner at the time. According to Dee Rowan,

Betty's assistant, who currently works there for Betty's son Gene, "She discussed the stereotype of Prissy."

"When I was handed the script, I was surprised," Butterfly McQueen told Betty Talmadge. "I had the idea that in 1939 they would want to show the advances blacks had made."

The movie went by the book so the script called for her to play the part just as Margaret Mitchell wrote it.

"I was happy I did it," McQueen told Talmadge. "It was part of history."

Letters began coming in during the production with questions concerning how the blacks would be portrayed in the movie. According to his executive assistant Marcella Rabwin, David O. Selznick wanted so much to do it right that he contacted Walter White, the executive secretary of the NAACP (National Association for the Advancement of Colored People) from 1931-1955. He was recognized as a spokesman for blacks in the United States at that time.

At first, Selznick told Walter White he would hire a black consultant, but after hiring historian Wilbur Kurtz from Atlanta, he decided to just use Kurtz' expertise on the treatment of blacks during the period around the Civil War.

Marcella Rabwin was heavily involved in this. She asked Kay Brown, Selznick's east coast assistant, to talk to Walter White. They did not want bad publicity generated among the black newspapers around the country.

The handling of the black race in the movie was controversial, but according to Rabwin, Selznick and his people did everything they could.

"But still, we got a lot of complaints about the treatment of the blacks in the movie," said Marcella. "They were 'servile' but they were affectionate and they were loving. They were loved. And they were very important parts of the household. This was the attitude back then. Scarlett loved her 'Mammy' very much."

Selznick was criticized for trying to manipulate White, by not hiring a black consultant—and many of Hollywood's prejudices were revealed. It was a difficult subject because the question was does Selznick stay true to Mitchell's book which would upset White, or does he change the story around to portray the treatment of blacks in a better light?

Kay Brown met with White and she must have been convincing in what she said because in the end they stayed with a lot of what Mitchell wrote. White became involved in the process and came to the studio to watch the goings on.

"Mr. White called in a wide assortment of critics," Marcella recalled. "Walter White was the Jesse Jackson of the day. There were about seven of his men, and they started telling me how terrible this was and how Mr. Selznick has to cut this, and he's got to cut that. They would say 'you've got to change that character' and 'you can't have Pork doing that'. I turned to Mr. White and said, 'Mr. White, do you agree? You've read the book, you've talked to me on the phone, do you agree with all of this?' And he said to me, 'No, this is history'. And there was no more discussion about changing anything because we had the blessing of Walter White.

"We had Susan Myrick and we had Wilbur Kurtz. We had everyone to help tell what were the relationships between the blacks and the whites at the time of the War Between The States."

They felt that as long as they were true to the history—and Mitchell claimed she tried to get all of her historical facts straight— then they were doing their job. The historians were all Southern historians and they had the same frame of reference as Margaret Mitchell. That may be where some criticism arises, but once Walter White said 'this is history', David O. Selznick moved on to the next topic, feeling he'd done the best he could with a difficult subject.

Unfortunately it wasn't the end of it. Earl Morris of the Pittsburgh Courier published a negative piece. The public relations department at Gone With The Wind got rolling and soon the black actors were being interviewed. Hattie McDaniel did a lot to calm the fears of blacks. She was very loyal to Selznick and was criticized for it; even for a time by fellow (black) cast member Butterfly McQueen.

It seemed the only way that Gone With The Wind would have escaped criticism or controversy with regards to race was if Margaret Mitchell had completely left the blacks out of the book. She didn't do that and neither did Selznick, so the book and movie stand on their own merits.

"I think Blacks today are more accepting of Gone With The Wind than they were fifty years ago," said biographer Carlton Jackson, University Distinguished Professor Emeritus at Western Kentucky University. "We have a new generation of African-Americans, many of whom are interested in the history of the Civil Rights movement which, among other things, taught large chunks of non-violence within a historical setting. Often I ask my students if they believe things are better now than a generation ago. Most whites say "yes," and the answer that an increasing number of blacks tell me, as well, is "Yes."

Chapter Fourteen
The People Behind The Movie

Mary Anderson

Mary Anderson got her start by auditioning for the role of Scarlett O'Hara. Though she did not get that role, she did so well she was cast as Maybelle Meriweather. She was sixteen and it was her first film. Following Gone With the Wind Anderson continued on in the movies and appeared in many television shows.

Eddie Anderson- Uncle Peter

Eddie Anderson played Aunt Pittypat's favorite slave, Uncle Peter. Aunt Pittypat was so helpless she depended on Uncle Peter to help raise Charles and Melanie when they were children. Anderson was a comedic actor who was born into a circus family. The year before *Gone With The Wind* he appeared in *Jezebel* and has many movies to his credit including *It's A Mad, Mad, Mad, Mad World* in 1963.

Anderson is most remembered for his role on *The Jack Benny Show* as " Rochester," Benny's sidekick, first in radio and then in television. He was admitted to the Black Film-Makers Hall of Fame in 1975, and was inducted into the Radio Hall of Fame in 2001.

Ward Bond- Tom the Yankee Captain

Ward Bond, who played Tom, the Yankee Captain became a popular actor, playing among other roles, "Bert" the police officer in *It's A Wonderful Life,* as well having a lasting role on the NBC television show, *Wagon Train.*

Bond got his start after playing football at USC when he and his teammate, John Wayne got roles as extras in a silent film in 1928. Bond continued his friendship with Wayne and as John Wayne became a famous star, Bond acted in some of his movies.

"Generally if John Wayne was in a movie, you'd see Ward Bond," said GWTW's Patrick Curtis whose father was friends with both of them. "Ward Bond was a good actor, but he was also a really nice guy."

Curtis also remembered Bond as a character. Curtis' dad was involved in an incident on John Wayne's yacht where Bond showed his practical joke side.

"A bunch of them were on Wayne's yacht, the 'Wild Goose' playing cards," recalled Curtis. "Ward Bond bet John Wayne that he could stand on one corner of a napkin and Wayne could stand on the opposite corner and he could not hit him."

So the men took bets on whether or not John Wayne would be able to take a slug at Bond or if Ward Bond could duck his punch.

"Ward Bond put the napkin down in a doorway and shut the door!" said Curtis. "I can just imagine a very large fist coming through that door and cold cocking Bond!"

Bond played Seth Adams on the show Wagon Train from 1957-61. Because of his great friendship with John Wayne, Bond saw to it that he had a bit part on the popular television series. Wagon Train was the network's top-rated show when Bond died unexpectedly of a heart attack.

Rand Brooks- Charles Hamilton

The first husband of Scarlett O'Hara, Charles Hamilton was the timid, boring brother of Melanie, who Scarlett married just to make Ashley jealous. Charles ended up dying of pneumonia while he was in the war. He didn't get to die a more rugged death at the hands of the

Yankees, he actually caught the measles and it turned into pneumonia.

Brooks said he did not like the role of Charles and wished he could have played a more macho role.

"It was an asinine part," he was quoted by the Associated Press in his obituary in 2003, as having said.

Away from *Gone With The Wind*, Rand Brooks held the distinction of being the actor that gave Marilyn Monroe her first on-screen kiss. It was ten years after playing Charles when he starred in the low-budget film "Ladies of the Chorus." He starred in many movies and played roles including 'Lucky Jenkins' in the *Hopalong Cassidy* films and 'Corporal Randy Boone' on *The Adventures Of Rin Tin Tin* (1954-1959).

At one time Rand Brooks was married to Lois Laurel, the daughter of Stan Laurel, of Laurel and Hardy fame. They ran a successful ambulance service. He later married his second wife Hermine and lived on a ranch in Santa Barbara.

"Rand was a lifelong friend," said Patrick Curtis. "He was one I could always count on to be a presenter at the Golden Boot Awards, of which I am the producer. I could call Rand at the last possible moment, if someone got sick, or was on location."

Everett Brown- Big Sam

Everett Brown is remembered for playing Big Sam the foreman in *Gone With The Wind*. Someone shouted "quittin' time!" But he shouted back that since he's the foreman it's not quittin' time until he says it is. Brown's character served as Scarlett O'Hara's friend when he later helped her escape from the would-be attacker in Shantytown.

The same year GWTW came out he had a small part as Bongo in the Spencer Tracy movie *Stanley and Livingston*. Over his long career he was in at least 28 movies, including *I Am a Fugitive From a Chain Gang*, a controversial movie from 1932 which was nominated for Best Picture. It was done before the codes and many felt it showed the legal system in a bad light. The movie was banned in the state of Georgia because of the way it portrayed prisons. Brown played Sebastian Yale, an uncredited part.

He was also in *Tarzan and His Mate, Kid Millions, The Plainsman, Congo Maisie,* and *White Witch Doctor*.

Yakima Canutt- A Renegade Soldier (and stunt double for Clark Gable)

Enos Edward "Yakima" Canutt got his nickname during his days with the rodeo. His experience in the rodeo led him to become a stuntman. Canutt served both as credited actor and stunt man in *Gone With The Wind.* His acting role, the renegade solder (who tried to attack Scarlett in Shantytown) had a stunt in it as he fell off the bridge.

Actor Julia George's grandfather was Art Felix, a stuntman who worked with Yakima.

"Grandpa (Art Felix) and Yakima would often work in the same movies together," said George, who appeared in a two-hour NBC movie. "Yakima was more often the one who'd get the credit and billing in the film as stuntman, perhaps because he was more well-known.

"In those days there was lots of bickering and throat cutting among the stuntmen for who'd do the stagecoach/lasso stunts for the least pay. Back in late '20s and 30s (pre-Screen Actors Guild) stuntmen would bid on how much they would want for doing certain stunts. They would all be out there on the lot saying 'I'll do it for $500', another 'I'll do it for $300', another ended up getting the gig who said he'd do it for $200. Of course, the $200 guy would get hurt, or killed, and the next guy would say, 'Okay, well, now I'm not doing it for less than $1,000' and on it went."

Yakima Canutt was known for taking the biggest jobs. One story that Felix told was when he went in to Central Casting at age 65—yes he was still doing stunts at that age. They asked him if he could film as a 35-year-old.

"Hell, yes!" he would say but then when he got to the set they would say, "You're no way 35!" And he'd say, "Hell, I'm riding by on a horse, put me in costume, nobody's gonna know how old I am!"

Canutt felt as comfortable on a horse as he did walking on the ground. In the big fire scene, he was driving the buggy and had to control the horse who was getting spooked by all the light from the fire. He also had to dodge the sparks. They only had one chance to shoot that scene and he had to do it perfectly, which he did.

"He was one of the very best among the early day roughstring riders," said Patrick Curtis (young Beau) who knew him. "He was reared on a ranch and couldn't recall when he was ever without a horse. When he was 11, he rode his first bucking bronco... one that had just thrown his older brother... and 'made a good horse out of a bad one'. At 16, he won the five day Colfax County Fair bronco riding, his first such event."

Canutt worked with Curtis' father at Republic Pictures in the 1930's and was one of the "cowboys" who would frequent the Curtis house for Saturday afternoon card games. Being friends with Yakima Canutt has left Curtis with many fun and funny memories, but the one that stands out the most is that it was Yakima who taught him to ride a horse. Unlike a person who learns to ride at a stable, Curtis was learning from the best stuntman in the business, so needless to say he learned to ride hard and fast.

In the mid-1980's Curtis was happy to see him win "The Golden Boot Award" at the awards ceremony that he produced.

Children In The Movie
Cammie King, Mickey Kuhn, Patrick Curtis, Greg Giese and others

Gone With The Wind celebrated its 70th Anniversary of the premiere of the movie in December of 2009. Any actor who was in his or her twenties when the movie was filmed would be in the nineties as this book went to press. There are a few characters who are younger, because they were children in 1939. Some of their memories are from their days on the set but they also have thoughts and experiences about the movie taken from after it was over. All agree they enjoy reminiscing about *Gone With The Wind* and have happy thoughts attached to it.

Mickey Kuhn- Beau Wilkes

Mickey Kuhn, who was born in Waukeegan, Illinois, had moved with his family to California as a child. It was during a shopping trip at Sears that his mother got some information that led to his big break.

"My mother was talking to a woman in Sears Roebuck on Santa Monica and Western one day," said Kuhn, who now lives in Florida. "The other woman said, 'I'm taking my daughter to 20th Century Fox to audition for a movie and they need twins. Your son looks so much like my daughter maybe he could try out'."

Kuhn's mother took him out to Fox, and though he did not end up in the movie with the twins, he was picked to appear in *A Change of Heart*. He was only 18 months old, and thus began his career as a child actor starring in the movie with Ginger Rogers, Shirley Temple and Janet Gaynor. Also in Kuhn's first movie was Jane Darwell, who would be a castmate of Kuhn's in *Gone With The Wind* as Dolly Merriweather. The day he tried out for the role of Beau he was tired and a little crabby.

"I was only seven," he said. "And I was working on another movie and I'd worked all day. About 4:00 my mother said, 'Come on, we have to go now, we're going over to Selznick Studio for an interview'. I said 'Oh mom!' Now remember I was seven. We were working in the San Fernando Valley and the drive from the San Fernando Valley to Selznick Studios was about thirty minutes. I was a kid and as such I was trained, if your mother says you have to do something, you have to do it.

"We got to Selznick's Studio and I opened the door to the casting office. I wanted to cry. It was wall to wall parents! I turned to my mother and said, "Please, I don't want to stay here. Please mommy!" And she said 'Ten minutes. Give your name to the casting agent. Ten minutes and then we'll go'. So I went in to the casting director and I'd no sooner given it to her than a lady came back to the window and said, 'Oh Mickey! Thank goodness you're here! We've been waiting for you! Come on in'. So I went and got my mother and we were in the outer office. This lady put her head out and said to the other kids, 'Thank you all for coming, the part has been cast'. Needless to say I lost a lot of friends. All the kids played together, they'd waited for hours! I didn't know what movie it was. It was just one of those things."

Mickey Kuhn appeared in many other movies with the biggest name stars including Joan Blondell, Betty Davis, and Marlon Brando; but he was most proud that he was in both of Vivien Leigh's academy award winning movies, *Gone With The Wind* and *A Streetcar Named Desire*. Back then, there was a group of child actors who went from movie to movie and he was in that group.

Kuhn remembers his time on *Gone With The Wind*. He had a great relationship with Victor Fleming, who took him aside and gave him special help when he needed it.

Cammie King- Bonnie Blue Butler

Cammie King Conlon played the adorable Bonnie Blue Butler, the daughter of Rhett Butler and Scarlett O'Hara. She was the lucky one besides Vivien Leigh, because Cammie also got kissed by Clark Gable.

The little girl who broke everyone's heart when she fell to her death in a horse jumping incident in the movie would continue off screen to have a full life and in fact at the time of this book publishing, was still out in the public—speaking about her experiences on *Gone With The Wind*. Though many of the actors from the movie had strange things happen to them in real-life after the movie, Cammie King Conlon had just the opposite. She lived a relatively normal life, away from acting, and would have happy memories of her time in *Gone With The Wind* even writing a book in 2009.

Her parents divorced not long after the movie ended and she lived with her single mother and enjoyed a "regular" childhood.

"*Gone With The Wind* had absolutely no part in my life during most of these years," Cammie said. "We never talked about it at home. That's why I neglected to ask my mother so many questions I wish I had."

Since Conlon was so young when she did the movie and with no family video cameras available to capture her every move at the studio, understandably she would not remember everything about her days on the set. Then fifteen years later it came back into her life.

"In 1954, MGM, which still owned the movie, had a 15th year anniversary in Atlanta," Cammie remembered. "Ann Rutherford, who played Scarlett's sister Carreen, and I were sent with George Murphy (later Senator George Murphy) as Hollywood's ambassadors."

"I'm so glad my mother decided that I shouldn't continue with movies because I had a *great* childhood," she said. "I grew up in the heart of Los Angeles in a neighborhood where we played on the sidewalks and lawns, and bicycled everywhere."

"Movie matinees every Saturday; we had two neighborhood theaters where you spent the whole afternoon with two features, cartoons, newsreel and a serial. My girlfriends and I could take the Wilshire Boulevard bus to the first-run theaters. MGM musicals were our favorites. Esther Williams was my idol because she was tall."

Cammie graduated from Marymount High School in Los Angeles. Cammie's mother had a career of her own with two books, a syndicated King Features column, and classes and lectures on personal improvement. She married Herbert T. Kalmus, the founder and president of Technicolor when Cammie was fifteen.

"She didn't meet him on the set of *Gone With The Wind*," said Cammie, "But she remembered seeing him there one day."

Although her childhood was normal, "my teenage years were pretty dazzling," said Conlon. They moved to Bel Air and took exciting trips to Europe, spent summers on Cape Cod and had friends in the movie business.

"We would have screenings in Pops' home theater," she remembered.

Pops was the name she had for her step-father, Kalmus, who had a Ph.D. and was a scientist. Together with his partners, he had developed Technicolor. Because of that he became involved in the Hollywood scene. Kalmus introduced many "Hollywood type" friends to Cammie and her mother.

"He basically disliked Hollywood," she remembered, "But there were some celebrities we entertained: Dorothy and Merian C. Cooper (producer of the first *King Kong*) were our dear friends. Irene Dunne was a close friend of mother's. For a while Italian movie people were in and out."

Just like Margaret Mitchell, she spent her freshman year at Smith, but then returned to California to major in telecommunications at USC.

"I had wanted to work in the production end of television," she said. "I worked at CBS television for a while until I got married. In those days you generally didn't do marriage and a career."

She married Ned Pollock and they adopted two children: Matthew and Katharine.

"We had eleven wonderful years," she said of Pollock, who died of cancer at age forty. After that, Cammie worked in public relations and married and divorced Mike Conlon. She decided to get away from the Hollywood scene.

"In 1980 I 'ran away from home' and settled on the spectacular

Mendocino Coast in Northern California," she said.

In 1989 *Gone With The Wind* came back into her life again.

"Ted Turner decided to replicate the 1939 three-day premiere in Atlanta," said Cammie. "What a change I saw in Atlanta since 1954. Ted Turner brought nine of us from the film: Ann Rutherford, Butterfly McQueen, Evelyn Keyes, Rand Brooks, Fred Crane, Mickey Kuhn, Patrick Curtis, Greg Giese and me. He treated us all like movie stars with our own limousines. It was a gala celebration."

Gone With The Wind anniversaries and Giese celebrations began springing up all over the country and Cammie was invited to attend. She was amazed at how the popularity of *Gone With The Wind* seemed to increase with each new DVD and collectible produced.

People who meet Cammie at events are always excited to see how beautiful she is and how gracious she is to the fans, always taking the time to talk and sign autographs.

Greg Giese- Beau Wilkes, as newborn; Bonnie as newborn

When Melanie Wilkes first has her baby (Beau), and then later in the scene where Scarlett is taking Melanie, Prissy, and Melanie's baby Beau back home to Tara, Greg Giese played the newborn infant, Beau Wilkes. There were just a few times the baby's face was on screen. In other parts of that scene, with the rain, etc., a doll was used for Giese's safety.

He also played the infant Bonnie Blue Butler in the famous scene where Melanie takes one look at the baby and comments on "her" eyes being as blue as the "Bonnie Blue Flag."

In real life, the eleven-day old Giese did not even have blue eyes, they were brown. He might never have been in the movie except for Selznick's great attention to detail.

"They had wrapped the movie," said Giese who at the time this book was written lived in Belleville, Illinois. "And had screened it at two 'sneak previews'. One of the comments was that the infants looked too old."

Selznick sent a representative to the Rice Maternity Hospital in Los Angeles, California to find the perfect newborn. As Greg Giese slept in his crib his parents Cleo and Eugene filled out the necessary papers.

"I became the youngest person ever to get a social security card," said Giese who was the oldest of a family of four boys and two girls. In 1939, Social Security cards were generally not obtained until a person was about to get a job. His parents signed his contract when he was eleven days old.

"They (Selznick International) sent a limousine to the house with a nurse and a social worker," he said. "My mom did not go to the set. The nurse and social worker stayed with me all day. I could not be under the lights for more than twenty seconds."

With the twenty second light rule, the scene had to be completely ready and the lights tested out before the baby was brought on.

One of Giese's on-screen mothers, Olivia de Havilland, kept in touch with Giese's real-life mother.

"Every so often a letter would arrive in the mail from Olivia de Haviland," said Giese. "She was a very nice lady. The first time I met her (as an adult) she looked at my eyes to see if they were blue."

They met at a *Gone With The Wind* reunion. After *Gone With the Wind*, Giese moved to Belleville, Illinois with his mother. He attended what was then called Belleville Township High School and later moved back to California where he spent his career in the insurance business.

"One day my secretary heard they were having a 40th anniversary reunion," he said. "She called them up and said 'my boss was a baby in *Gone With The Wind*', and they said 'We'd love to have him!'"

Just as the others, he enjoys getting together with the group from GWTW whenever he can.

"My involvement with *Gone With The Wind* was sort of like the little baby who survived the Titanic," he said. "We were there for one of the biggest things to happen but we don't remember it."

Two years ago Greg Giese moved back to Belleville and he works at a nearby horse racing track.

"I really enjoy being back with my old friends from high school," he said while dining at Fishers on West Main Street, a local restaurant that has been there for years. "Once I was with my friends and everyone got to talking about how young they were when they got their first job. I said, 'give me a break, guys, I started to work at eleven days old!'"

Greg Giese remembers when the Belleville News Democrat ran a story about the "Movers and Shakers' of the 20th Century from the St. Louis area in the 1960's, Belleville is across the river from St. Louis, Missouri and considered in the St. Louis area.

"They listed me at the top, Ike and Tina Turner second, and Miles Davis third," he said. "That tells you how big *Gone With The Wind* was."

Patrick Curtis, Beau Wilkes as a baby

When Melanie's baby began to grow a little and sit up, Patrick Curtis played the role of Beau. He was ten months old.

"My Mom was good friends with the original director, George Cukor, who apparently hired me in the womb," said Curtis, who is also popular on the *Gone With The Wind* circuit. "When Cukor was let go and replaced by Victor Fleming, I stayed hired, as Mr. Fleming was a motorcycle riding buddy of my Dad's."

Curtis does not have memories of his days on the set, since he was a baby, but has been told much of it by his mother. He claims to remember one thing, though.

"I really do remember Clark Gable holding me up in front of him, and blowing 'raspberries' on my tummy."

Curtis' father, Daniel was the comptroller at Republic Studios, and ran the production side of the business under owner, Herbert J. Yates. Being friends with Victor Fleming led to his father becoming good friends with Clark Gable and they often played poker at the Curtis house.

One hot Saturday in June of 1949, sticks out in Patrick Curtis' mind involving Clark Gable. In the movie, Gable's character Rhett Butler said that Curtis' character Beau Wilkes' mother Melanie was the only really kind person he had known. In real life, Gable was also a kind person, and one day he was a hero to a little boy.

Every Saturday, Curtis' mother Helen would set up two card tables and his father's friends would come over to play poker. Ward Bond, who played a Yankee captain in *Gone With The Wind* and "Bert" in *It's A Wonderful Life*, along with Victor Jory who played Jonas Wilkerson, the O'Hara's overseer in *Gone With The Wind*, were among the regulars.

They arrived a little early one day so Patrick's mother had him go get his father.

Just as he was walking out the door, he saw what he described as "the most wonderful car he'd ever seen." It was a dark green Jaguar convertible.

"It was a Jaguar XK 120, six cylinder, roadster," Curtis remembered. "It was brand new, the first one in California, and the driver was smiling and waving to me as he pulled in."

It was one of those childhood memories he would never forget; so memorable he is including it in a book he is writing and agreed to let it be used here. The "King of Hollywood" pulled up and when Curtis told him he was on his way to get his father, Gable said "hop in."

Curtis' story is written as a Western with himself as "the Crossdraw Kid" and his bicycle as "Trigger." His voice in the story is filled with the same childhood wonder as the narrator in the famous movie, *The Christmas Story*, about Ralphie and the Red Ryder BB Gun.

He got into Gable's new Jag and instead of going straight to the restaurant up the street where Curtis' father was, he took the boy out for a spin. They were going so fast the young Patrick Curtis (aka the Crossdraw Kid) was scared. In the story he wrote:

"Normally, it was three blocks from The Kid's house to the restaurant. But as soon as the slick roadster headed for the hills, The Kid knew this detour was going to be the ride of his life. Mr. Gable told The Kid that he had just picked up the car that morning and wanted to see what she would do. What she would do was scare The Kid to death! This was nothing like his mom's '49 Chevrolet! As they roared faster and faster along treacherous Mulholland Drive, The Kid, terrified…way, way beyond the ability to scream, did the unthinkable, the impossible, the unbelievable…The Crossdraw Kid…peed in his pants!!"

Curtis remembered how embarrassed he was, but Gable did not say anything. Long after the boy grew up—and he knew Clark Gable until he died—he remembered the ending to the childhood story:

"Without saying a word about The Kid's embarrassment, Mr. Gable threw him his soft leather sports coat and said quietly, "Put this on Kid, it's gotten cold and I don't want your mom mad at me." (Let's see, the

Kid's mom mad at Clark Gable… Yeah, sure.) It was around 400-degrees to the Kid, but he gladly donned the jacket to cover his humiliation. "I'll be right out with the others, you take care of the car," said Mr. Gable, as he disappeared inside.

"…. Many, many years later, when the film they had appeared in together, *Gone With The Wind,* was honored as the classic motion picture of all time, people would often ask what he remembered about Mr. Gable. Since he was just a baby at the time of the filming, Crossdraw would tell the story of the speedy, dark green Jaguar, and Mr. Gable's great kindness… to the Crossdraw Kid."

Throughout his childhood, he was in many films. Besides movies he was on some of the *Leave It To Beaver* episodes on television.

"I worked doing production on *Leave It To Beaver* when I was a teenager," Patrick added. "When they needed a kid to say 'can the Beave come out to play?' they would just ask me to do it."

He was involved in one of the most famous episodes of all time: the one where Beaver fell into the coffee cup on the billboard.

"Remember when the Beave got stuck in the coffee cup?" he said. "I was one of the kids down below egging him on."

Patrick Curtis may have been best known as a child actor, and he was just a baby when he appeared in one of the most famous movies ever to be produced, but he grew up to date two very famous women before marrying his current wife, Annabel. In the 1960s he was engaged to Linda Evans of *Dynasty* fame, and then from 1967-1972, he was married to actress Raquel Welch.

He produces the 'Golden Boot Awards' which honor the Cowboy Heroes of our Youth. It is held every year at the Beverly Hilton Hotel, and money raised from the event goes to the Motion Picture and Television Fund.

Other Children In The Movie

Because of the time that passed in the movie, the children had to be played by different actors. It was easy to use make-up to make 16-year old Scarlett O'Hara look older, but it is not so easy to make an infant grow to a seven year old. Kelly Griffin played infant Bonnie Blue

Butler. Phyllis Callow played Bonnie when she was two. Gary Carlson, and Rick Holt also played Beau Wilkes at different times. Because Beau was Melanie and Ashley's son, he had a more prominent role and needed to be included in many of the scenes. It took a total of five actors to play Beau Wilkes.

Fred Crane

Fred Crane delivered the opening lines of the movie as Brent Tarleton. In the book, Margaret Mitchell had Scarlett deliver the first line and Brent came in second. According to an obituary by London journalist Tom Valence (Independent, Sept. 2, 2008) "The casting director, hearing Crane's smooth Southern accent, introduced him to the producer, David O. Selznick and to the director, George Cukor, the latter declaring his voice 'just perfect'."

Years later when told there was some evidence that Mitchell had patterned the Tarletons after a family she knew in Clayton County, Crane's widow, Terry Lynn was surprised.

"Fred never did get to meet Margaret Mitchell," she said. "We had always assumed that the Tarleton Twins came from a book called *The Charleton Twins*. It was an Antebellum-type book set in that time."

Terry Lynn Crane owns that book, and with the way Margaret Mitchell loved to read and do research, she very well may have gotten the idea for the name or some other information from it.

"My wife Mary and I knew Fred," said Ron Kenner, a book editor in Los Angeles and the editor of this book. "He was a very sweet guy. It's interesting that Fred Crane, who in the opening scene downplays the importance of education, was in the real world a highly cultured guy. This is another reminder that actors don't always live their parts in real life."

Crane, who attended Tulane University and Loyola University in New Orleans went on to have a successful career in broadcasting.

"For years he was an integral part of the classical music station KFAC in Los Angeles," remembered Kenner.

Crane started working at KFAC in the 1960's and then in 1987 several of the older employees at the station were let go with no notice.

"After that, Fred was involved in an age discrimination lawsuit with the station," according to Kenner. "He (along with several others) ended up suing the station saying he was let go because of age discrimination and he won."

He continued working in radio and later Fred and Terry operated Tarleton Oaks, a Bed and Breakfast based on *Gone With The Wind.* They were working on a book called *From Tara to Tarleton Oaks, A Gone With The Wind Scrapbook* at the time of his death.

In March of 2008, the same weekend a tornado hit Atlanta causing the NCAA basketball game to be postponed, Terry Lynn Crane had assembled a group of friends to surprise Fred for his 90th birthday. The high winds seemed appropriate as many of the "Windies," as some *Gone With The Wind* fans call themselves, gathered to raise a toast to Crane.

Then on the Fourth of July in Marietta, GA five actors met for a *Gone With The Wind* Celebration put on by Connie Sutherland and Dr. Christopher Sullivan of the Marietta *Gone With The Wind* Museum, Scarlett On The Square. This proved to be his last appearance and the last interview Crane did, as he passed away a month later.

"I know Fred felt rejuvenated attending the event," said Dr. Christopher Sullivan whose *Gone With The Wind* Collection is featured at the museum. "Especially with the four other actors there (Ann Rutherford, Cammie King, Mickey Kuhn, and Patrick Curtis) and seeing so many people happy to see him. He told me he loved me like a son for all the get-togethers we have had over the years, all due to this *Gone With The Wind* hobby. He was very sincere, and I think he realized he did not have a lot of time left and this might be the last time we saw each other."

At that event Fred Crane shared memories of the movie and talked about George Reeves who played his brother. He said they were as close as brothers at one time.

"George Reeves and I were the best of friends," said Crane "George was best man at my first marriage."

"I remember Fred telling a story of when he and George, dressed as the Tarletons, were to go out to Huntington Gardens in Pasadena to shoot exteriors for the barbecue scene," said Sullivan who knew him well.

"Somehow their transportation got fouled up. Olivia de Havilland was being driven in a limousine to the Gardens—so Fred and George, not knowing enough to be intimidated because she was a famous star, asked for a ride. Of course she said yes, and Fred and George serenaded her the entire car trip with romantic songs."

Laura Hope Crewes

Laura Hope Crewes played the silly Aunt Pittypat who was always in need of her smelling salts as she was prone to fainting spells. In the movie, the character was self-centered but Laura Hope Crewes was far from it.

Clark Gable was working as a tie salesman in a department store when he met Crewes, who reportedly encouraged him to pursue his career in acting.

Susan Myrick, the hired set authority on Georgian culture, was very fond of Crewes and said she was the nicest one on the set.

"She is cute as hell," she told Margaret Mitchell, "And more fun than anybody except you and John."

Myrick thought her voice was perfect already but Crewes wanted to change it for the picture, so she asked Myrick to work with her. Crewes was so intent on learning from Myrick that she wanted to record her voice. After treating Susan Myrick to lunch they went to a recording studio where Myrick spoke into a microphone for several minutes and they made it into a record for Crewes to use as a study tool.

An interesting story regarding Laura Hope Crewes involved the home she bought using her earnings from *Gone With The Wind*. It was a colonial-style white mansion with a rounded driveway in front.

"Lana Turner was a later occupant of that home," said Chris Sulllivan. "It was the same home where her daughter Cheryl Crane stabbed Lana's boyfriend to death."

The death was ruled a justified homicide and the girl was sent to a home for girls at the time. Laura Hope Crewes died at age sixty-two of kidney failure while appearing in *Arsenic and Old Lace* on Broadway.

Jane Darwell- Dolly Merriweather

Jane Darwell played Dolly Merriweather, one of Aunty Pittypat's gossipy friends. Years later she was "The Bird Woman" in Walt Disney's *Mary Poppins*. She had retired in 1959 and was living at the Motion Picture Country Home in Woodland Hills, California, when approached by Walt Disney Pictures to play The Bird Woman. She at first refused but Walt Disney, himself, was so set on having her in his film that he personally visited her and persuaded her to take the part.

Darwell, known for her role as Ma Joad in *The Grapes of Wrath*, is also recognized from the many Shirley Temple movies she appeared in. She played the same type of gruff matronly woman, usually the mistress of an orphanage or an old aunt or grandmother, who made life difficult for little Shirley. It was that type of person she played as Dolly Merriweather in *Gone With The Wind*.

Harry Davenport

Harry Davenport was born in New York City the year the Civil War ended. In *Gone With The Wind* he played Confederate physician, Dr. Meade.

"He started in Vitagraph shorts and other silent films as well as early stage appearances," said GWTW collector Dr. Christopher Sullivan. "He free-lanced mainly and was never under a studio contract."

Davenport was co-founder of the actor's union—the Actor's Equity Association.

Harry Davenport was a popular actor at the time and had planned to attend the Atlanta premiere, but due to a mix-up he did not attend.

"I have a telegram at the museum from Selznick upset that the Atlanta premiere festivities had not been finalized to properly invite certain actors," said Sullivan. "He specifically scolded Howard Dietz that Harry Davenport had given up jobs so as to be available...and then was not invited to the premiere."

Davenport's son Ned was also in *Gone With The Wind*, playing the one armed soldier who accepts Melanie's wedding ring at the Atlanta Bazaar.

Five years after playing Dr. Meade, Davenport was the Smith's grandpa in *Meet Me In St. Louis*. He was also in *Little Women*, and over 25 movies. His last film was *Riding High*.

Olivia de Havilland- Melanie Wilkes

Olivia de Havilland as Melanie, was sickly and one of the characters who died in the movie. However in real life she was a vibrant person who would live a long life. At the time this book was written she was spending her time in California. She celebrated her 90th birthday in 2006 with birthday parties in Paris and Hollywood, with a number of guests attending both events. The Paris event included live music, and was attended by many of her friends, since she had been living in Paris for years.

The Los Angeles event was staged by the Motion Picture Academy in her honor. Always the glamorous movie star, de Havilland was beautiful as a ninety year old, with that lovely white hair and the smile she did not get to use very much in *Gone With The Wind*.

"She is magnificent," said Mickey Kuhn, who played her son in Gone *With The Wind*. "I'd keep in touch with her about once a year, and saw her at her 90th birthday party in Los Angeles. Even at ninety-years-old she was just bouncing along, talking to everyone and posing for pictures."

Victor Fleming

Victor Fleming, who won best director for his work on *Gone With the Wind* was the only director to receive screen credit, although he was one of at least five who had input in the movie. Controversy surrounded his hiring, as the female actors liked working with George Cukor. Fleming was very different from Cukor because of his rugged love for the outdoors, hunting, fast cars, motorcycles. He had even worked as a car mechanic at one time. Cukor's softer side was more attractive to some actresses and some on the set of *Gone With the Wind* felt Clark Gable had twisted Selznick's arm to get Fleming to leave *Wizard of Oz*, the movie he was directing at the time, to come over to GWTW.

"Looking back on it," recalled Selznick's executive assistant Marcella Rabwin in a speech years later, "Fleming was the right man for the job."

"What I liked about Victor Fleming is his enormous vitality and authenticity," said Michael Sragow, author of *Victor Fleming, An American Movie Master*. "A lot of Hollywood legends are half-real, half-ballyhoo, but Vic was the real thing. Although the clichéd view of him is as a 'man's man', he was just as successful directing women and children."

Fleming directed child actor Jackie Cooper in *Treasure Island* and according to Sragow's book, Cooper liked the director because (unlike many other directors he had worked with) Fleming would "speak to me like an adult. He would talk to me about the scene. I felt like he respected me."

Mickey Kuhn agreed with Cooper. He remembered Fleming taking him aside (as Beau Wilkes in *Gone With the Wind*) and explaining the scenes to him.

"Someone once told me that maybe the reason he was so good with me was that he had a great relationship with his own father and was familiar with the good father-son relationship," said Kuhn.

Fleming and his wife, Lu had two daughters who he loved very much. Despite having friends like Jimmy Durante at family events, according to conversations Sragow had with Fleming's daughters he tried to give them a normal upbringing, safe and protected.

"His own core of feeling came from his early experience of family tragedy (his father's death in an orange grove when he was four) and the love of a quietly indomitable mother," said Sragow from his home in Baltimore after the book came out. "That and his own devotion to parenting fed into his skill at films like *Captains Courageous* and *The Wizard of Oz*."

Stories have been told about Fleming and Clark Gable's friendship. They were buddies away from the movie studios and both enjoyed the need for speed. Fleming had originally dreamed of becoming a race car driver and even raced in one race, but made his name in films, once working as a photographer for President Woodrow Wilson, a cameraman in the movies, and eventually a major director.

Fleming directed some of the best actors in the business including Gary Cooper in *The Virginian*; Gable in *Red Dust*; Jean Harlow in *Reckless*; Spencer Tracy, Hedy Lamarr, and John Garfield in *Tortilla Flats* (and Tracy won the Academy Award for best actor when Fleming directed him in *Captains Courageous*) and Ingrid Bergman, the woman he would have an affair with during filming in his last film, *Joan of Arc*. One of his favorites actors was Douglas Fairbanks, Sr. whom he had directed in

When The Clouds Roll By (1919) and *Mollycoddle* (1920). Fleming had worked with Fairbanks as a cinematographer on several other films.

David O. Selznick always had a high regard for Fleming, but the stress of making *Gone With the Wind* seemed to pay a toll on their relationship. It has been written that Fleming did not attend the movie premiere in Atlanta because he was upset with Selznick, but according to *Victor Fleming, An American Movie Master*, Fleming "made plans to participate in the premiere" which was to take place Dec. 15, but when Douglas Fairbanks, Sr. had a heart attack his attention turned to him and the plans were changed. Fairbanks died on Dec. 12th, so whether he had changed his mind about attending the premiere or it was a convenient excuse, Fairbanks had meant so much to Fleming and he wanted to be there.

One odd thing about *Gone With the Wind* was that in 1939 everyone associated with the picture was on top of the world and ten years later, many of the principals—including Fleming would be dead. Victor Fleming died in 1949, the same year as Margaret Mitchell.

"Victor Fleming never met Margaret Mitchell," said Sragow, "But he and Mitchell's friend, Susan Myrick, hit it off pretty well, even though she had been a George Cukor loyalist. Vic always stated his goal was to be as faithful as possible to the book while making it into a good movie—his library contained a well-worn and heavily-notated copy of it."

That was one vision he shared with Selznick: be true to Mitchell's book; and together they did that.

Clark Gable

Once David Selznick nailed down the "King of Hollywood" to appear in *Gone With The Wind* he knew it would be a success. Yes, he already had a best-selling novel to work with, and Vivien Leigh put forth a magnificent acting job, but Clark Gable was a box office sensation. Women loved his dreamy looks and men loved his ruggedness. Even today the Clark Gable Foundation serves as a place fans can go, view the memorabilia, and remember the great actor, whose most famous role was Rhett Butler.

"Clark Gable was born in Cadiz, Ohio at 138 Charleston Street in a very small upstairs apartment," said Nan Mattern, the executive director of the Clark Gable Foundation. "When his mother became very ill they moved back to Medville, Pennsylvania, where she passed away, then his father William came back to Hopedale, which is eight miles east of Cadiz for work. There he grew up and went to school until about sixteen years old. Many people around town knew him. Clark was raised with a stepmother and of course his father."

Gable's father was a big part of his life and once Clark achieved stardom, he sent money to him on a regular basis. Even though he was so famous, Clark Gable had another side of him that most did not see—the family side. This is one reason why he fell so hard for Carole Lombard. She offered him a chance to be himself, away from the adoring fans.

When Carole Lombard married Gable, they became in current jargon the "it" couple of Hollywood. Lombard was a huge star in her own right. She was a comedienne and known off-camera for her foul mouth and love of fun. They bought a house several miles outside of Hollywood where Lombard enjoyed doting over her husband, who she called "Pa" and he enjoyed everything about his wife, "Ma."

Though Carole Lombard had wanted the role of Scarlett, she never displayed any sour grapes. As Mrs. Clark Gable, she did everything in her power to make his life happy. Whatever Clark wanted, Clark got, and she was happy to do that.

The mystique of Clark Gable was just something that he lived with. He had been voted 'the King' of Hollywood by a magazine and lived up to the billing. When David O. Selznick told the actors they would be meeting with the voice coach to learn their southern accents, Gable announced that he would not be using a southern accent.

"Clark was very much the star," said Mark Rabwin. "It is much the same today; they just have to work around the stars."

Despite the widely publicized problems he had George Cukor and his demands for Victor Fleming as the new director, Gable acted professionally on the set and there were few problems as far as the actual filming once it got started. Susan Myrick did end up working with Gable on his Southern accent and said she thought he was a very kind person. She had not liked him as an actor before she met him, but once she got the opportunity to work with him she liked him very much.

Clark Gable's appearance as Rhett Butler sent his already successful career soaring. A humble man in real life, he would rather spend time with Lombard than attend Hollywood parties. She was so devoted to him that she learned to shoot a gun so she could go hunting with him, a sport he loved. She had accompanied him to the premiere of *Gone With The Wind* in Atlanta in 1939 and was a very popular figure in the Hollywood entourage.

Seven years later she was dead at the age of thirty-three. Carole Lombard was returning from a tour selling war bonds—she'd raised over two million dollars— when the plane she was in crashed into a mountain outside of Las Vegas. Killed along with her were her mother; Otto Winkler, an MGM publicist; and fifteen soldiers and fliers who were reporting for duty. Lombard had been very patriotic and had encouraged Gable to join the army. After her death, he finished the movie he was working on with Lana Turner and then enlisted in the Army Air Force, flying combat missions in B-17s out of Peterborough, England.

It was said that when he returned home, Clark Gable began drinking heavily and sat up during long, lonely nights watching re-runs of Lombard's old movies. He would eventually pick himself up, continue acting, and marry two more times. When he died of a heart attack at age 59, he was given a small military funeral and was buried next to Carole Lombard at Hollywood's Forest Lawn Cemetery.

In 2001 he was honored posthumously at the Golden Boot Awards, a Hollywood awards ceremony produced by *Gone With The Wind* actor Patrick Curtis for Western television and movie stars. Curtis surprised Gable's son, John Clark Gable, by honoring his father with many of the living actors from *Gone With The Wind*.

Leslie Howard- Ashley Wilkes

In the movie, Ashley Wilkes was played by the English actor, Leslie Howard. It had taken some coaxing to get him to take the part, but he was the only actor Selznick had wanted for the role. As noted, Howard felt the part was bland and the costumes were demeaning, but with the promise of a movie after it was over and a chance to co-produce that movie (*Intermezzo*) he reluctantly agreed to do *Gone With The Wind*. He took the role seriously and was very businesslike in his approach.

Susan Myrick worked with him to transform his British accent to a Southern one. Myrick noted, in her book *White Columns in Hollywood, Reports from the GWTW Sets,* the coincidence that she was trying to teach him the proper way to speak with the Southern dialect, and he had played Professor Henry Higgins in *My Fair Lady*. Higgins was an expert in such things and taught Eliza Doolittle how to 'be a lady' by losing her cockney accent. Howard was a willing student.

One of his complaints about being in the movie was the blond hair. They lightened his hair up and he did not like the way it looked. He wanted to change it but could not persuade the make-up people or David Selznick. Mitchell had created Ashley Wilkes as a blond and whoever played him was going to be blond.

Howard was the only one of the main actors (besides the black ones) who did not attend the premiere. He was also the first one to die, when the plane in which he was flying, a commercial airliner, was shot down during World War II in 1943.

The character of Ashley Wilkes was said to have represented the Old South as he fought the war bravely but found himself confused and without direction afterwards. In real life, Leslie Howard was focused and driven by his political convictions. It was rumored that Howard was engaged in secret war work at the time of his death, as the KLM Royal Dutch Airlines flight he was on was shot down by a German Junkers Ju 88 over the Bay of Biscay near Spain.

In July of 2009, Leslie Howard was to be honored as a war hero along with those who died in that plane crash. The Royal Green Jackets association and Spanish author Jose Rey Ximena, who has written about Leslie Howard's involvement, issued a statement announcing the monunment which would contain a Douglas DC-3 propeller replica similar to the ones on that plane.

The Associated Press (April 18, 2009) reported that Jose Rey Ximena said "Howard's contribution to wining the war is in danger of being forgotten," and that the Royal Green Jackets association wanted to "pay tribute to a man who put his fame and communicating skills to work combating Nazi propaganda."

According to Ximena, Leslie Howard should be remembered as a war hero because of the evidence that Howard was targeted. The tribute to Howard is in Spain near the site of the plane crash.

Howard C. Hickman- John Wilkes

Howard Hickman played Ashley's father, John Wilkes. Hickman spent some years as an actor but eventually turned director and the Director's chair was where he spent most of his career. Hickman had started in movies with the famed producer Thomas Ince, so when it came time to do *Gone With The Wind*, he was familiar with the production studios as he had worked there when they were owned by Ince.

His wife, Bessie Barriscale was also an actress and they were in several movies together.

Victor Jory- Jonas Wilkerson

Jory, who started his acting career in the Will Rogers, Janet Gaynor movie *State Fair* in 1933 played Jonas Wilkerson, the O'Hara's overseer in *Gone With The Wind*.

Susan Myrick mentioned Jory in her book saying (page 290), "He played in stock for ten years and has played in almost every one of the Shakespearean dramas."

He played Captain Keller (Helen Keller's father) in the 1962 movie production of The *Miracle Worker* with Anne Bancroft as Anne Sullivan and Patty Duke as Helen Keller. He continued acting until the late 1980's, playing in movies and in guest roles on television.

Jory was known to be a family man. He and his wife who was an actress, took time to have dinner each evening with their two children. His son Jon Jory became a director and spent 31 years running the Actors Theatre of Louisville (Kentucky) before joining the Drama department at the University of Washington. One of the performance spaces at the Actor's Theatre of Louisville is named after Victor Jory.

Evelyn Keyes- Suellen O'Hara

Evelyn Keyes played the bratty Suellen O'Hara who often got into spats with her sister Scarlett. In *Gone With The Wind* Scarlett stole her boyfriend and she was afraid she was going to be an old maid; in real life she had several very famous husbands: bandleader Artie Shaw and Directors John Huston and Charles Vidor.

"I met Evelyn Keyes," said Dr. Chris Sullivan, "I asked her that since she was a native of Atlanta and went to the premiere in Atlanta if she had a chance to talk to Margaret Mitchell when she attended the premiere. She admitted that she was so in awe of the author, and that no, she did not talk to her other than pleasantries during introductions. She said she was just a foot or two away from her and was too intimidated to talk to her. She regretted her lost opportunity."

In 1977, Evelyn Keyes wrote a book, *Scarlett O'Hara's Little Sister.* Some other movies Keyes appeared in are *Wicked Stepmother, A Return To Salem's Lot, Around The World In Eighty Days,* and *One Big Affair.*

An interesting Evelyn Keyes and *Gone With The Wind* story is that she had left the production and moved onto her next movie, the Cecil B. DeMille film, *Union Pacific,* but was called back. She'd been told her part was finished but with all the script re-writes, David O. Selznick called her back. It was for the famous line about Scarlett having had three husbands and she was going to become an old maid! She walked on the set and recited that one line and left again.

Keyes' last role was in the Marilyn Monroe film, *The Seven Year Itch,* in 1955. She played the vacationing wife.

"In her later years, she was well taken care of in a lovely facility near Santa Barbara, California," said Faye Bell of Gone With The Wind Memories. "Her good friend, Tab Hunter, looked after her affairs while she was there."

Evelyn Keyes passed away on July 4th, 2008.

Vivien Leigh- Scarlett O'Hara

Vivien Leigh, the British actress who played Scarlett O'Hara was having a love affair with her future husband, Laurence Olivier at the time she got the part. She came to America with him, hoping to land the part, and when David Selznick laid eyes on her he knew he had to have her for the role

As noted, Leigh became very close to Marcella Rabwin.

"Vivien Leigh used to go into my mother's office and talk to her," said Marcella's son, Mark Rabwin. "They became very good friends; my mother became her confidante." Known for being the strong-willed, free spirited Scarlett O'Hara in *Gone With The Wind*, in real life, Leigh suffered from manic depression and bipolar disease, and this became more apparent shortly after she attended the world premiere of the movie in Atlanta. Though she battled with her illness, her love for and subsequent marriage to Olivier could not survive it. In 1960, Olivier could not live with her any longer. He had been the big love of her life, and she of his. She never seemed to recover from the loss and died seven years later of tuberculosis at the young age fifty-four.

Interestingly, while Margaret Mitchell wrote about a strong-willed heroine, both Mitchell and the woman who played Scarlett in the movie were plagued by depression, physical illness and injury. Mitchell and Leigh shared another trait. Both were raised as Catholics and later told people they shunned their childhood religion. In another odd coincidence, Vivien Leigh also shared some commonalities with her character as she and Scarlett O'Hara both suffered miscarriages after falling, and both seemingly demonstrated little interest in children, leaving their children in the care of others for long periods of time.

"I had a chance to interview Vivien's secretary, Sunny Lash before Sunny died," said Dr. Christopher Sullivan. "Sunny set the groundwork—I could ask her anything about Vivien EXCEPT about her illness. I spoke to her as a fan, not a writer, but we spoke for two hours on the phone."

After she won her Oscar for *Gone With The Wind* in early 1939 she left for England later that year as World War II was starting in Europe.

"She did not want to travel overseas with her Oscar," said Sullivan. "So Sunny held onto it—on her fireplace mantel—for more than ten years until Vivien came back to the United States to film *A Streetcar Named Desire*."

Sullivan's collection has been exhibited in different places and in 2009 it was being displayed in The Marietta *Gone With The Wind* Museum.

He has many items including some Vivien Leigh treasures.

"Our prized possession," said Connie Sutherland, who runs the museum, "is the original Bengaline honeymoon gown worn by Vivien Leigh in her role as Scarlett. It was borrowed by Turner Classic movies in 2005 for their *Lights, Camera, Classics* exhibition. It is truly breathtaking and worth the price of admission alone."

The surviving actors from the movie agree that Vivien Leigh was the hardest working actor in the movie as she was in almost all of the scenes. She worked so hard that it took a toll on her looks; she lost weight and her face tightened up. The transformation worked out well because she was supposed to go from a young carefree teenager to a more mature woman who had gone through hard times and was determined to rise above it all.

Leigh Mills runs the Vivien Leigh website www.Vivien-Leigh.com. The site contains pictures, stories, and information on upcoming movies she was in.

"The Vivien Leigh Society was a fan group for Vivien in the 1960s," said Mills who is a collector. "The Society President printed newsletters and journals and sent them out to members during the year. I have a couple in my personal collection."

According to her website the organization has disbanded, but one of the members, Joanne Armando told a story in a newsletter, of something that happened to her that she will never forget. She had been a big fan of the actress and kept scrapbooks with pictures and articles in them. When Vivien Leigh was in her hometown for a performance she brought one of her scrapbooks with her and afterwards went behind the stage to try and get her autograph.

An assistant collected programs, pictures, and Armando's scrapbook and took them backstage to have them autographed. A short while later she came out and asked, "To whom does the scrapbook belong?" Joanne Armando could not believe her ears when she was escorted backstage to meet the movie star. Vivien Leigh had thumbed through the scrapbook and landed on a page titled "Shakespeare with the Oliviers" and was very interested in one of the pictures.

As the story goes, Vivien later wrote her a letter requesting to see the scrapbook again and eventually asked for a copy of the picture.

"She thanked me profusely for the picture," said Armando. "How can one truly describe Miss Leigh? Everything I had read and heard about her was true. She was very beautiful and she was wearing a green print silk blouse which highlighted her beautiful expressive green eyes…"

Hattie McDaniel- Mammy

According to Marcella Rabwin, David O. Selznick had a high respect for Hattie McDaniel and thought she was an excellent actor and the perfect choice for Mammy. McDaniel had started as a child in vaudeville. She traveled with musical ensembles and minstrel shows, and progressed as a stage singer. Once she got into the movies, she seemed to be typecast playing similar characters. Because of that the NAACP got on her for reinforcing stereotypes. Her answer to them was, "I'd rather play a maid for seven hundred dollars a week than be one for seven dollars a week."

She might never have been cast as Mammy except for having some famous friends. Selznick wanted her, but Director George Cukor was not so keen on her and Susan Myrick the consultant from the South did not think she would be right. A popular black actress, Louise Beavers, was being highly considered, but several stars intervened and Hattie was chosen.

McDaniel made many strides for the black race in the movie industry. In her later roles as a maid she insisted that her character would not speak in dialect and made sure she could make changes to scripts that she did not agree with.

She appeared in more than one hundred films (and possibly up to three hundred if you include the many uncredited roles she did), including Shirley Temple's *The Little Colonel, This Is Our Life,* and *Song of the South.* In 1934 she sang a duet with Will Rogers in the movie *Judge Priest.*

In 2006 Hattie McDaniel was awarded posthumously when the United States Postal Service issued a stamp in her honor. The first African-American to win an Academy Award, she is depicted on the thirty-nine cent stamp wearing the dress she wore when she won the award for Best Supporting Actress.

Among the honored guests at the postal stamp ceremony were cast members from *Gone with the Wind,* including Ann Rutherford, Patrick Curtis, Mickey Kuhn, and Cammie King Conlon.

"One of the happiest occasions of my life was being involved with this," said Ann Rutherford. "I got to present the stamp to her relatives. To think it actually came to pass in my lifetime! In 1939 they would not even permit a black to come to the Premiere.

"When I got home I had a package and it contained a large, framed replica of the stamp," said Ann Rutherford. "It was such a wonderful tribute I felt I should not keep it all to myself. I knew it needed to be displayed in a museum for all to see, so I shipped it to Herb Bridges, who is a collector, and it is now on display at the Road To Tara Museum."

"Hattie's fame from *Gone With The Wind* no doubt contributed to her appearing in other films, including *Since You Went Away,* in which "she played dignified roles," explained McDaniel biographer Carlton Jackson. "Then in 1946 she jeopardized her standing in the Black community when she played Aunt Tempey in *Song of the South.* She spoke some dialect, an anathema at that time to African-American reformers. In fact, she lost a number of movie roles as a result of this Walt Disney feature."

Hattie McDaniel died of breast cancer at the age of sixty. Although her dying wish was to be buried at Hollywood Memorial Park, she was buried in Rosedale Cemetery because blacks were not allowed at Hollywood Memorial Park. Thousands of people attended her funeral with many limousines following her body to the graveyard. Years later when the Cassity family bought Hollywood Memorial Park, renaming it Hollywood Forever, they built a monument as a tribute to Hattie McDaniel, and though her relatives did not want to move her body, as invited, they were thrilled with the tribute.

Butterfly McQueen- Prissy

Butterfly McQueen appeared in a 1935 production of *A Midsummer Night's Dream,* and danced in the Butterfly Ballet. Since she did not like her given name of Thelma, she took on the stage name "Butterfly" McQueen in the process. Although in *Gone With The Wind* her character was portrayed as silly, she was far from it.

She attended the 50th Anniversary "Gala Re-Premiere" sponsored by Ted Turner in Atlanta in 1989. According to Curtis, while she liked her fans she could not stand to be touched, and this was a big problem because all of her adoring fans wanted to touch her.

"She hated to be touched," Curtis said. "Her friends and fellow cast members had always known this and tried to inform the proper people at each event."

McQueen told David Selznick she did not want to be hit in the scene where Scarlett was angry with her on the steps. Though it appeared that Scarlett struck her, actually she did not. Butterfly McQueen had spoken up and said, "I will not be hit."

Butterfly McQueen was a beloved person. Unfortunately the only parts she got were stereotypes because her role as Prissy made her so identifiable with a maid or servant. She decided that was not what she wanted so she quit the business in 1947, but then returned for a television series called *Beulah* in 1950. Her old co-star Hattie McDaniel played in the television show, which lasted two years, and she continued working in radio and television.

Butterfly McQueen died in December, 1995, reportedly when a kerosene heater she was trying to light exploded.

Thomas Mitchell- Gerald O'Hara

Thomas Mitchell, who played Scarlett O'Hara's father Gerald, had a very busy year in 1939. He acted in five movies that year (*Stagecoach, Mr. Smith Goes to Washington, Only Angels Have Wings, The Hunchback of Notre Dame,* and *Gone With The Wind*). He won Best Supporting Actor as John Wayne's co-star in *Stagecoach*, and is also remembered as Uncle Billy in *It's A Wonderful Life*.

Mitchell, who played a man in his sixties in *Gone With The Wind*, was actually a young-looking handsome man of forty-seven at the time. The make-up department did a good job of making him look the age he was supposed to in the movie. According to consultant Susan Myrick, one day when Thomas Mitchell walked into make-up in his street clothes he saw Vivien Leigh being made-up. He said hello to her and she answered with a polite "How do you do?" as if she didn't know him. Then, after doing a double take, she realized it was him.

According to Myrick she said, "This is the first time I ever saw you without your make-up, and I have thought all this time you were an old man!"

Ona Munson- Belle Watling

Ona Munson, who played the madam Belle Watling, started her career in the musical, *No, No, Nanette* before working on *Gone With The Wind* as Rhett Butler's trusted friend.

Ann Rutherford, who played Carreen O'Hara said that the first time she saw Munson on the set she knew she was Belle Watling because she had the little earrings with bells on them.

"I took one look at her and knew she was Belle!" said Rutherford. "She was perfect!"

The character Belle Watling may have been inspired by the famous Kentucky madam, Belle Brezing and ironically One Munson's life took on the same ending as the real-life Brezing's.

Brezing developed cancer, and spent the last several years of her life heavily medicated on morphine, eventually becoming addicted and dying in her home on Aug. 11, 1940, of an overdose of sleeping pills, less than one year after *Gone With The Wind* premiered. She had been so heavily sedated she may not have ever seen it.

Ona Munson, who had been in ill health and heavily sedated herself for the last several years of her life, overdosed on sleeping pills at age 51.

Carroll Nye- Frank Kennedy

Carroll Nye used his middle name, as his full name was Robert Carroll Nye. He was born in 1901, so was 39 when he played the role of Frank Kennedy. Nye was married to a comedic actor named Helen Lynch.

In 1938, the year before he got the role, Nye had done six movies, *City Girl, Hold That Co-Ed, Safety In Numbers, The Main Event, Kentucky Moonshine,* and *Rebecca of Sunnybrook Farm* (with Shirley Temple.) He had such a strong voice that in five of those movies he played radio or television announcers.

Nye had also been a newspaper man, working at the Los Angeles Times. He died in 1974 of kidney failure and a heart attack.

Barbara O'Neil- Ellen O'Hara

"The interesting thing about Barbara O'Neil was that she was only twenty-eight when she played Scarlett O'Hara's mother—only three years older than Vivien Leigh!" said GWTW collector Dr. Chris Sullivan.

Selznick, wanting to keep with Margaret Mitchell's description of Ellen O'Hara chose O'Neil as she was just about to turn twenty-nine. In the book, Ellen married at age fifteen and gave birth to Scarlett the next year.

Barbara O'Neil died at seventy of asthma and tuberculosis after taking an ocean swim near her home in Connecticut.

Oscar Polk- Pork

Oscar Polk, who played Gerald O'Hara's valet Pork, was in a number of Broadway plays in the 1930s and played Gabriel in the 1937 production *The Green Pastures*.

During the pre-production and production stages of *Gone With The Wind*, there were black publications that made it known they had their eye on Selznick International Pictures and how they treated the blacks both on-screen and off. Russell Birdwell the Selznick publicist, had the idea to contact the "black press" in attempts to have them get behind *Gone With The Wind*. He persuaded some of the black actors to do positive articles on it. According to Leonard J. Leff's article in Atlantic Online, Oscar Polk was one of those who helped Birdwell with his publicity campaign.

"As a race we should be proud that we have risen so far above the status of our enslaved ancestors," Polk said in a letter to the Chicago Defender, a weekly black magazine. "(We) should be glad to portray ourselves as we once were because in no other way can we so strikingly demonstrate how far we have come in so few years."

Oscar Polk was a very dedicated actor. It has been said he rehearsed out loud on the set in front of a mirror. Even on days when he had only one line, he wanted that one line to be perfect.

Marcella Rabwin- Unsung Hero

David O. Selznick dictated many of his famous "Memos," to his executive assistant Marcella Rabwin, but most of the letter writing was left to other staff members she hired. If the memo was important or secretive, she would handle it herself, and her son credits her with saving some jobs by not sending selected memos when he asked.

"She knew David so well she knew when he meant it, and when it might be a good thing to sit on the memo rather than send it," said Paul Rabwin. "He would be angry with someone and write a long memo to them, and then later my mother would say 'I'm not really going to send this, am I?'"

Selznick would think nothing of calling his executive assistant in the middle of the night. He often called her at two or three o'clock in the morning.

"That can take a toll on a person," said Rabwin. "And on the weekends he would often summon her to his house at a moment's notice. He lived in a mansion in Beverly Hills above Sunset Boulevard."

After the production of *Gone With The Wind*, Marcella realized that if she were to have a family life she would not be able to work for such a demanding man.

"One morning when she came to work, she told him, 'I have to leave by 8:00 because I have a big engagement this evening'. David said to her, 'I have some appointments so let's get the work done and then you may leave'."

The time rolled on and Marcella was getting more and more upset because she had asked off at a specific time and her boss did not take into consideration that it was a big event for her.

"She kept saying, 'I need to leave', and he never seemed to listen," said Paul Rabwin. "Finally she said, 'I am leaving, Mr. Selznick'. He protested and she said, 'No, you don't understand—I'm leaving'. And she left and never went back.

"That was the way she finally quit her job with him. She had a life to live and he didn't appreciate it. He wasn't mean, he was just demanding."

George Reeves- Stuart Tarleton

George Reeves played Stuart Tarleton, one half of the red-headed Tarleton brothers. As noted, the rolling credits at the beginning of *Gone With The Wind* mistakenly listed Reeves as Brent Tarleton though he indeed played Stuart.

"He was a great friend of mine," said Fred Crane who played his brother.

After *Gone With The Wind*, Reeves had much success playing Superman, but came to a strange death. He died in 1959 of what appeared to be a self-inflicted gunshot wound to the head, and controversy still surrounds his death. It was listed as a suicide, but many questions remain unanswered as Reeves was allegedly having an affair with the wife of a movie executive. Fred Crane was one who did not believe it was a suicide.

On the set of *Gone With The Wind,* Reeves and Crane were known for their youthful spirit. Though they both went on to bigger achievements in their respective careers, they shared the Tarleton twins' fun-loving attitudes.

As a coincidence, Reeves was originally from the same small town in mid-America as Greg Giese, who played infant Beau and infant Bonnie Blue.

"George Reeves lived in Belleville, Illinois, when he was a child, just as I did," said Giese, who after living in California most of his life, has moved back to Belleville.

Leona Roberts- Mrs. Meade

The actress that played Mrs. Caroline Meade, Leona Roberts was born in 1881 and also raised in Illinois. Besides *Gone With The Wind* she was in other movies including *Chicago Defender*, *Of Mice and Men*, and *Bringing Up Baby.*

Her character Mrs. Meade spent much of the movie in widow's black as she and her husband, Dr. Meade lost their son in the Battle of Gettysburg. She added some comedy after Rhett Butler's elaborate cover-up story about them all being over at Belle Watling's house. She asked her husband if he was really there and what was it like. She wanted to know all about the girls and the chandeliers, curtains, and mirrors. He answered with a terse, "Good heavens, Mrs. Meade! Remember yourself!"

Leona Roberts was married briefly to actor Billy Bevan who appeared in the comedies of Mack Sennett during the silent movie years.

Ann Rutherford- Carreen O'Hara

Ann Rutherford was already a successful actress when she took on the role of Scarlett's sister, Carreen O'Hara, in *Gone With The Wind*. She started on radio and was signed by Republic Studios when she was seventeen. She worked with actors like John Wayne and Gene Autry at Republic, and then moved to MGM where she appeared as Polly Benedict with Mickey Rooney in the *Andy Hardy* series.

She was working for MGM at the time she did *Gone With The Wind*, and has appeared in more than seventy movies, including *Pride and Prejudice* and *The Secret Life of Walter Mitty*. She appeared on television, in four Perry Mason episodes, and in the Newhart Show as Newhart's mother-in-law.

Ann Rutherford has always remained a very active person. Often asked to appear at events celebrating *Gone With The Wind,* she is very gracious to the fans when she does. Though she has had roles much bigger than Carreen O'Hara, she enjoys being at the events.

"Ann fell several years ago and damaged her leg and hip but she still gets around very well," said Mickey Kuhn, who played Melanie and Ashley Wilkes' son, Beau "She lives in Beverly Hills and does appearances on behalf of *Gone With The Wind*."

"Ann is wonderful, so full of life," said Novella Perrin, a *Gone With The Wind* collector from Missouri who has met her at various events. "She is just overall fun!"

Perrin met first met Ann Rutherford at the unveiling of one of her costumes from the movie for an exhibit at the Road To Tara Museum in Jonesboro.

"She has been to many of our GWTW events," she said. "When she enters the room, the whole place lights up."

Fans are excited to meet the still beautiful Ann Rutherford whose enthusiastic personality never disappoints.

Rutherford would recall when she'd first asked Louis B. Mayer if she could play the part of Carreen and he answered that it was a "nothing part." But, as indicated, she did not care about the size of the part. She loved the movie so much she wanted to be involved no matter what.

David O. Selznick

David O. Selznick's father, the flamboyant, Lewis J. Selznick, had been a famed silent picture director and major rival of Hollywood movie mogul Louis B. Mayer.

Selznick ended up going bankrupt and it has been said that his son David wanted to make the family name great again. *With Gone With The Wind*, he did what he set out to do and he did it in front of his father's old arch enemy: Mayer, who had actually become his father-in-law.

Selznick had added the "O" to his name later in life, thinking a middle name would make him seem more powerful, like Louis B. Mayer. It has been written that the "O" stood for nothing but his executive assistant said once he picked a good strong initial then he came up with a name.

"He decided his middle name would be Oliver," said Marcella, David's executive assistant.

Though his father hated Mayer, Selznick was hired by MGM in 1924 where he started in an entry-level studio position. He became friends with Irving Thalberg, who at the time was the head of production. Selznick moved to Paramount and then to RKO. Once Irving Thalberg became ill, Louis B. Mayer convinced Selznick to return to MGM. Thalberg ended up being, later on, was one of the first to invest in David Selznick's company.

Much to the horror of Mayer, David O. Selznick fell in love with Mayer's daughter, Irene. It was one thing for Louis B. Mayer to have Selznick as an asset to his company, but he did not want his daughter marrying a Selznick. Irene was intent on marrying him, so her father gave in.

David Selznick wanted more respect than he would get at MGM after marrying the "boss's daughter," so he struck out on his own, starting Selznick International Pictures in 1933 with financier John Hay (Jock) Whitney. Selznick's brother Myron also put money into the company. It has been said that both Myron and David Selznick sought to resurrect the name of Selznick in their father's honor after he died.

Selznick was known for his many memos and Marcella Rabwin was the woman who either wrote them or hired the secretaries who did—depending on the importance or secrecy of the memo. Her son credits her with saving some jobs by not sending selected memos when he asked.

The obsessive memo writing actually started when Selznick was sixteen. His father told David that people remember what they read better than what they hear—especially if they are told specifics. He said that most people take fifteen minutes to say what could be said in three. Selznick's memos went to unbelievable lengths. He would send memos to his own executive assistant Marcella Rabwin who was sitting in the next room. He would even send memos to his wife.

Ten years later, the week after Margaret Mitchell died, Selznick did something that seemed so out of character, but then maybe it was completely in character. The man who was too busy to stop and notice anything was also the man who was obsessed with details.

"David Selznick sent a gift to the emergency room nurse who tried to help Margaret Mitchell when she was rushed into Memorial Grady Hospital after being hit by a car," said Faye Bell, owner of Gone With The Wind Memories in Plant City, Florida and friend of the nurse. "He sent her a beautiful double orchid corsage."

Wilma Fowler still had the corsage sixty years later. According to reports there are several other nurses who went home with orchids that day, also.

That was in 1949 and Selznick had just married his second wife, actress Jennifer Jones. Selznick devoted himself to Jones' career, directing her many films. He died of a heart attack in 1965, but his only daughter with Jennifer Jones would suffer mental illness and come to an early death on May 11, 1976, one day after what would have been Selznick's 74th birthday.

Unfortunately Selznick did not profit from *Gone With The Wind*, and actually lost money on it. By the time it was over he had just enough money to invest in his next movie, *Rebecca,* and it was lucky he did because he then won Best Picture two years in a row. Selznick had given away most of his profits after the first year to MGM in the deal to get Clark Gable.

"Who knew it would be this successful?" said Ann Rutherford, "Up to that time there was no movie that had lasted that long."

Chapter Fifteen
That's A Wrap!

Once the actors were finished, Selznick had the job of trying to get the movie down to a decent length. This was before the days of mini-series, and the producer had at least a six hour film on his hands.

The cutting room was the scene of many heated discussions. David Selznick and his Chief Film Cutter Hal Kern worked until the end.

Marcella recalled working late at night when they edited *Gone With The Wind,* scooping up reels of film they cut and throwing it all in the trash bin. "If only I knew to save those outtakes!" she moaned.

"Those two worked for months trying to decide what would be in the movie," said Marcella Rabwin. "They worked twenty hours a day and Selznick lived on Benzedrine. It kept him awake, kept him alive, and almost ruined his marriage. His wife, Irene, used to keep two cooks: one to prepare dinner at the time it was to be served with the children; and if he didn't get there then, someone else would be in the kitchen to prepare his dinner in the middle of the night."

Selznick and Irene lived with their sons in a beautiful home on Summit Drive. Irene enjoyed decorating it in English chintzes and antiques. The home had a projection room, a game room, tennis courts, and a swimming pool. During the production and post-production of *Gone With The Wind*, he very rarely saw anything but the kitchen and bedroom as he left early and arrived home late.

Not until the final day of shooting did they have the entire script finished. The production wrapped at the end of June 1939. It had taken seven months to shoot. They did not shoot the scenes in order but when it came to the last scene in the movie, Selznick wanted it to be memorable.

In the book, Margaret Mitchell wrote Gable's famous line as 'My dear, I don't give a damn'. Selznick wanted it to really pop. He wanted it to be a memorable line. It came to him, and he added a single word: 'Frankly'.

Once it was shot, Selznick wanted him to do it again with another ending because of the Hays Code. Gable had known there was a good chance they would take "damn" out. In the end they filmed an alternate ending with Gable saying, "Frankly, my dear, I just don't care." Imagine how different it would have turned out with that simple change

So the movie was finally finished filming. Now the daunting task was to take the film, which was extremely long, and cut it down to size. That job was left to Selznick and Kern. Selznick had announced to the world that the movie would debut in December, and though the film was shot, they were nowhere near ready. They had to cut it down, plus the music was not finished and the credits were not done.

Max Steiner was known as a genius in the music world. An Austrian-born musician, and one of the first to integrate music for a movie with on-screen actions, creating a musical score for the entire movie, he had done the music for *King Kong* in 1933. He became one of Hollywood's most sought-after composers.

For the musical score, an orchestra of fifty musicians was set up. There were three females and forty-seven males. In those days it was a rarity to have women in the orchestra pit. One of those women was Lilane Covington who lives in Greenwood, South Carolina. She played the oboe. At the time this book was written, Lilane was living in a retirement community playing the piano for the residents on occasion. Reportedy one of her favorites to play is *Tara's Theme* from *Gone With The Wind*.

"Since the article about her work as principal oboist with Hollywood orchestras in the 30's, 40's, and 50's appeared in the local newspaper (and its online site) she's received a good deal of attention," said her stepson, Philip Covington. "She's a wonderful conversationalist and I never tire of hearing her talk about those days."

Lilane Covington started in the orchestra for Warner Brothers when she was very young and she played her oboe for the musical scores in more than a hundred films, short subjects, and cartoons. Of all the talented composers she worked with, Max Steiner, who she called "Maxie" was her favorite. She remembered he would play the parts he created for the various instruments on his piano first, and she said he could make anything sound like an orchestra.

Steiner could not complete the musical score until the movie was closer to the final edits, so Selznick had to concentrate on the editing phase.

"At one time they worked for 48 hours straight and we wore out four secretaries," according to Marcella Rabwin. "It was worse than the Battle of Jonesboro. They were fighting and arguing. Should we cut this, should we keep that? It was a 'piecemeal' thing. Selznick made the ultimate decisions but his cutter (Kern) was an enormous help to him."

Once the shorter version was ready, the censors had to look over the film again. Joseph Breen was the Director of the Production Code Administration, also called the Hays Code. Breen was not a popular person with the movie studios because he had the power to change scripts and scenes, which did not sit well with directors, writers, and producers.

Breen read Sidney Howard's original script in October of 1937 but much had changed since then, including complete rewrites. Some of the organization's concerns with the early script were: there should be no suggestion of 'rape' or the suggestions of struggles due to rape, Rhett should not be characterized as an 'immoral' or an 'adulteress' man, Belle Watling's establishment should not be characterized as a 'bawdy house' or 'house of assignation'. They had gone through the script the first time and made a list of comments. Selznick knew they would be watching him on those points. The initial comments asked if Belle's house could be a drinking establishment or gambling place. They also said Belle should not be characterized as a 'prostitute' but rather a 'loose character' operating a drinking saloon or gambling hall.

There was so much involved in living up to the Hay's Code because Selznick felt many of the suggestions changed the meaning of Margaret Mitchell's book. Mitchell had covered some touchy subjects in her book, and Breen and his people felt it was their duty to be the moral authority for the country. Though they gave suggestions, it was understood that they meant what they said.

They were against dialog involving the 'pain and suffering of childbirth'. When Scarlett was at the jail offering her body to Rhett in exchange for money, the Hays Commission thought it would be better to say she was offering herself in marriage to him.

Breen's group scoured the entire movie one more time to be sure Selznick went along with the suggestions given to them at the beginning of the film. Times were sure different back then. Rhett's line of "I still want you more than any woman on this earth" had to be changed to "I still care for you more than any woman on this earth," changing the meaning—even if just a bit. That was just what filmmakers in 1939 had to face.

When the film got down to four and a half hours Selznick told Rabwin to have Louis B. Mayer come right over to see that version. Marcella, Mayer, and Selznick sat in the projection room.

"I knew we had a hit," said Rabwin, "Because he only went to the bathroom once! Louis B. Mayer had seen all the great films Selznick had done and all the other great films and he told us this was the greatest picture he had ever seen."

This was a personal satisfaction to Selznick as he had spared no expense and had gone above and beyond on this film, partly to prove to his father-in-law that he could do it. He was jubilant that the film was finished. The next step was the titles and credits, and eventually they would do some sneak previews

As those involved in the film worked to get it done, Margaret Mitchell and John Marsh were back in Atlanta packing their things to move into a new apartment. Both of them were in ill health as they packed. There were boxes and boxes of papers as well as their collection of *Gone With The Wind* in foreign printings. In early autumn of 1939, they moved a few blocks away to an apartment on Piedmont. It was a little bigger than the cramped place they had shared but still not a house.

One good thing about it was that it was close to the Piedmont Driving Club, one of their favorite restaurants. Mitchell did not like to drive and had always been afraid of cars so she was happy they could walk down the street to the Driving Club and a theater was also nearby.

As the Marshes were getting settled in their new place, Hal Kern was working day and night with David O. Selznick trying to finish the film.

In Marcella Rabwin's opinion, one of Kern's great contributions to the film was the 'movie title' in the opening. He went to a title company and tried photographing various types of lettering.

According to Rabwin, he said, "I want something that looks as if it were really being blown by the wind." The title company man sat down with him and they looked at all sorts of lettering.

"Finally he found the one with the 'Curly Q" lettering," Marcella Rabwin explained. "He tried to make the alphabet look like it was moving. It's not an easy trick. They finally got the idea of having it come from one corner and then go across the screen, but that wasn't it yet. Finally Hal Kern got the idea— 'motion'—and it was perfect!"

Once the title was made and the film was cut down to three hours and forty-five minutes, it needed to be screened before a live audience. The problem was the film had gotten so much publicity that America was literally waiting for it. There would be no way to do it in secret.

"David decided to show it to just a few people," said Marcella. "We went to a theater there in California. There were just a few of us, Mr. Selznick, his wife, his brother, the cutter (Hal Kern), the director (Victor Fleming), and my dear husband (Dr. Marcus Rabwin). I had the big job of walking up to the manager of the theater and said, 'We have a preview for you, and would like very much to make an announcement that there will be a preview; that it will be a very long picture, and that anyone who wants to leave can leave now'.

"The screening was so top-secret that we announced that only one phone call was allowed and there would be time for a bathroom break but besides that the doors would not be opened during the preview. They locked the doors.

"They turned the lights down and the screaming began with the 'G'" said Rabwin. "The minute the letter 'G' came on the film, before the 'O' got there you never heard such bedlam in your life! People literally jumped up and down. They were hysterical in the aisles. I have never seen such a reaction to a preview in all my life. It was wild, exciting, thrilling. They settled down as the names started coming up there."

When the movie was over, the original hysteria began all over again. People began hugging, cheering. They could not believe that they were the first people to view the much awaited *Gone With The Wind*.

Back then, when movies showed previews, they would pass out 'preview cards' and usually about five percent of the audience would respond. They would use comments like, 'I liked it but I thought so and so was no good'.

For the *Gone With The Wind* preview, every member of the audience filled out a card and most of them put 'It was the greatest film I've ever seen'.

"Seven academy awards tell the beginning of the end of the story of *Gone With The Wind*," said Marcella Rabwin. "Only Clark Gable did not win the Best Actor award; it was sentimentally given to the much admired British actor, Robert Donat, for his role as *Mr. Chips*. He was then dying of emphysema. It was a cruel rejection of Gable's finest role. David O. Selznick, however received the grandest honor of the Academy Awards—the Thalberg Award for Best Producer. His kind of genius no longer exists."

David Selznick felt his family name had been vindicated. His father had been rivals with Louis B. Mayer and now, years later he had achieved something so great he gained Mayer's respect.

"He may not have made a lot of money out of it," Marcella Rabwin acknowledged. "But he did have the most enormous satisfaction. One day they said it was 'Selznick's Folly' and the next day it was considered the masterpiece of all time. David Selznick is a man the world will never forget."

"Who would have known the movie would still be as popular today?" said Ann Rutherford. "When we made *Gone With The Wind* we had all adored the book. We would have done anything to be in it. It never occurred to us it would last this long. Movies ran a while and that was it. This has been amazing."

When the movie came out it was the topic on the lips of people all over the United States. The people in Atlanta were thrilled at the idea of having the World Premiere right there in their hometown; everyone except Margaret Mitchell. She loved her town, but she knew the premiere would bring more unwanted publicity on her.

Chapter Sixteen
Atlanta, Dec. 1939
The World Premiere of *Gone With The Wind*

From the mind of David Selznick came a brilliant public relations idea—have the "World Premiere" in the author's hometown of Atlanta, Georgia.

He could not have chosen a better location. Actually, it chose him. In publicity attempts Selznick had mentioned the idea, but then when he started backing down on it he found out how much it meant to the people of Atlanta. They all pitched in—put up signs, made costumes, created commemorative events, decorated the entire town, called off school and declared a holiday to take off work. It was all very exciting with the prospect of movie stars coming in. Balls and parties were arranged to welcome the stars, and Margaret Mitchell was invited to everything. The locals were proud of Mitchell and many even knew her personally.

Phone calls and telegrams were sent back and forth between Marcella Rabwin and those in Atlanta. The stars would be arriving in several groups and it all had to be planned out. Rabwin really wanted to attend the festivities herself, but, as she would observe, later, "Someone had to mind the store."

Ann Rutherford, though already an accomplished actress, was still a teenager living with her mother at the time of the movie. On Wednesday, December 13th, she was the first to arrive, and there was a big picture of her in the Atlanta newspaper.

"I took the train with my mother from Los Angeles," she remembered, seventy years later. "We went to Lexington, Kentucky, where my mother had grown up. We got to see some of my relatives, and then we continued on to Atlanta."

The daughter was surely impressed. The mayor met them at the train, and *Gone With The Wind* seemed the biggest thing that had ever happened to Atlanta.

"I think *Gone With The Wind* is what put Atlanta on the map," said Ann, a sentiment still shared by many—all these years later, and for those who attended the premiere festivities, it was one of the thrills of their life.

Mayor William Hartsfield, a friend of Margaret Mitchell, hosted the three-day celebration, declaring the holiday and supporting the many teas, luncheons, and celebrations honoring the premiere.

Atlantans, of course, knew Margaret Mitchell. Her family was well respected and she had been a debutante, and who hadn't heard of the book and movie? Mitchell had also written for the local newspaper, and her father and brother were prominent lawyers in the city. The choice was perfect for the premiere. Since the story took place partly in Atlanta, it was a natural backdrop for the big celebration, with the entire city involved in the Premiere. Businesses put fake "fronts" on their buildings, turning the town into a veritable Hollywood set. The Georgian Terrace Hotel, Atlanta's most prestigious, was chosen to house the stars.

Every day for weeks before and after the premiere, the local newspapers carried articles about the latest excitement. The day of the parade the Atlanta Board of Education voted to shut down the schools at one p.m. so the children could get downtown to see it. A call went out to the Boy Scouts for help. Scout executive Joe Ballenger issued a plea in the newspapers asking for one thousand boys to participate in complete uniform. He requested they each bring a ten-foot rope, adding that those who participated would be excused from school.

The city was clearly transformed to the days of *Gone With The Wind*—antebellum mansions with white columns, costumed women in hoop skirts, men in Confederate uniforms and extra magnolias.

Selznick, known for being a control freak, had his hands on every aspect of the premiere down to the weight of paper used for the programs.

In one of his memos he wrote, "Be very careful of the paper you select for the program ... sometimes their crackling makes it difficult to hear the dialogue."

He was picky about the crackling paper yet he could not have foreseen the real problems that would surface. The climate in Atlanta offered a problem of a different kind. Collectors have several different versions of the program as it went through last minute changes. The original one approved by Selznick contained the five main characters: Scarlett, Rhett, Ashley, Melanie, and Mammy; but the powers that be in Atlanta at the time said they could not have Hattie McDaniel (Mammy) on the cover. It was too late to get a new picture, so there was much scrambling around to get a different version.

"There was a blank-back that was hastily put together to use in Atlanta after the one planned with Hattie McDaniel was not used," said GWTW collector Novella Perrin, Ph.D. "It was decided not to use the so-called 'Mammy back' programs in the South."

Out of the program-back changes, there came several versions.

"They are different because of the backs," explained Perrin. "The Mammy-backs that had been printed were used in the North and West, and then India Wilkes' (Alicia Rhett) picture replaced Mammy and these were the programs that were used most often."

Many people know of the three different programs, but it does not stop there.

"Actually there are at least six types of programs," she said. "Some of the programs have Suellen in a cream and green dress and on some the same dress is cream and purple. Also, there are programs with the Tarleton twins' names wrong (they had been listed wrong in the movie credits) and others where they have been corrected.

"There are also programs where the information on one page is different in the final paragraph, and finally there are differences on the back in how the publishers list their name and address. Sometimes it is abbreviated and sometimes it is spelled out."

Though the problems with the programs were a major headache for the producer, it provides more fun for *Gone With The Wind* collectors. The Atlanta premiere produced more than just the programs for future

GWTW collectors. There are chairs from the theater, movie posters, and whatever they could get their hands on.

On the day of the parade some of the stars arrived. At the Atlanta airport Vivien Leigh came in with her fiancé Laurence Olivier, as of course did Olivia de Havilland, David O. Selznick and others. Clark Gable was to arrive the next day.

There were last-minute worries galore as Selznick tried to pull together the loose ends. He had not wanted Olivier to travel with Vivien Leigh since the two were not married yet, but Leigh would not go without him. They came up with a plan saying he was there to promote his next movie, *Rebecca*; a great idea since it was a Selznick movie, too.

There were also problems with Clark Gable. For a time it appeared as though he would not be coming. The week before the premiere, plans would change after they were set. Clark Gable had originally been against attending. As the biggest star of the day, he did not need or want to do it. Then he decided to be a team player and show up. But when called and asked to go a day earlier so that he could attend another function, he felt that MGM was "using" him. Thus to sort of 'get back at them' for using him, he withdrew Carole from coming on the trip

Clark changed his mind again and decided to bring her, but ironically, almost comically, at the last minute he learned that Victor Fleming pulled out. According to some, Fleming, feeling insulted by David O. Selznick, had cancelled his trip when his buddy Clark Gable originally backed out, but then as earlier noted Douglas Fairbanks, Sr. had the heart attack and Fleming's attention turned to him. The memos were flying that week, along with plenty of hustling behind the scenes, but things finally worked out and Clark and Carole Lombard arrived on an MGM private plane.

David Selznick had planned to bring Hattie McDaniel (Mammy) and Butterfly McQueen (Prissy) and was furious when he found out they would not be welcome. He had to be grateful to the city for welcoming the cast for the premiere, yet he was extremely indignant at the slight to McQueen and, especially Hattie McDaniel whom he believed had delivered "one of the greatest supporting performances of all time."

Realizing that problem ahead of time, McDaniel and McQueen both sent their regrets so as not to put anyone in an awkward situation.

Among the many festivities celebrating the film and welcoming the movie stars was the Junior League Ball which took place Thursday, December 14th. Though the actors attended, including Clark Gable and his wife Carole Lombard, Margaret Mitchell turned down the invitation. Various reasons were given, leading many to speculate even years later that it had to do with a long-standing feud Mitchell reportedly had with the organization. Evidently the Junior League had not extended an invitation to her to join when she was in her younger, debutante days, and it had been said she held a grudge against them.

During what should have been the biggest week of her life, Margaret Mitchell seemed to be in hiding. According to the Finis Farr book, based in part on writings from her brother Stephens Mitchell, Margaret was suffering one of the many injuries that seemed to plague her at major times in her life. He mentioned a pending abdominal surgery, and mentioned that when she attended a luncheon put on by the Atlanta Women's Press Club, doctors had "strapped her in bandages to support the back she had wrenched in a fall the previous day."

The Junior League took over the Atlanta Municipal Auditorium and covered it with Confederate colors and flags. In the center above the marquis, one huge American flag hung. Guests wore period clothing, with many of the city's blue-bloods wearing authentic family heirlooms from the Civil War.

The entire auditorium was transformed into a scene like the Confederate Bazaar scene in the movie. The stage looked like a plantation mansion complete with white columns

An interesting side note is that the Ebenezer Baptist Church choir sang spirituals and the Reverend Dr. Martin Luther King, Jr. was one of the children who entertained.

Everybody who was 'anybody' attended, with the newspapers carrying lists of the dignitaries and celebrities. Among those besides the stars themselves and the local government officials were Captain Eddie Rickenbacker, people with last names the order of Vanderbilt and Rockefeller, Mr. and Mrs. William Paley (of CBS), and Governors from several states including Georgia, South Carolina, Alabama, Florida, and Tennessee.

Life Magazine ran an article which mentioned a contest the Junior League had conducted: "Happiest girl in Atlanta was pretty brunette Margaret Palmer, whose figure conformed more closely than any other Junior Leaguer's to the measurements of Vivien Leigh."

The Junior League had run a contest to find the perfect Scarlett from within their own group. Lucky Margaret Palmer, voted "Atlanta's Scarlett," got to wear the green sprigged dress from the movie and to lead the Grand March at the *Gone With The Wind* Ball.

As the celebrities paraded in for the event, Clark Gable honored Mayor Hartsfield by escorting his daughter, and in turn, the mayor had Gable's wife, Carole Lombard, on his arm.

Baseball announcer Ernie Harwell was working the Sports Desk at the *Atlanta Constitution,* and the editor asked him to help out with a project involving *Life Magazine.*

The magazine, which was very popular at the time, was planning on covering the premiere and they needed a little assistance in the area, so they contacted newspaper editor Ralph McGill.

"*Life Magazine* was going to do a big cover story on the premiere," said Harwell. "They had this famous photographer, George Karger coming in to do the photo shoot. He was supposed to be one of the best theatrical photographers in the world, but he didn't know Carole Lombard from Shirley Temple; so Ralph asked me and George Tisinger to help out."

The big magazine cover picture was to feature Clark Gable with the happy Junior Leaguer Margaret Palmer the day after the ball, and was going to be taken at the city landmark, the Cyclorama.

Life Magazine bringing in George Karger rather than using one of the many competent local photographers, rubbed the local photographers the wrong way, so when they heard about it, they decided to take matters into their own hands.

"This was going to be a big exclusive for *Life Magazine* and they spent a fortune getting George Karger in to take the picture," said Harwell. "Well somebody had tipped off the other papers because suddenly in burst some photographers and they all took the picture and put it on the front page of the local newspapers the next morning. There went *Life*

Magazines' exclusive cover picture. They used the picture on the inside with the article."

From the start of the festivities the actors and others were asking when they could meet Margaret Mitchell. She had issued a statement saying she hoped to attend "one or two small affairs." The author of the book which had caused all the great fanfare was noticeably absent at most of the events.

Mitchell felt comfortable attending a gathering in the lounge of the Piedmont Driving Club, which was planned by friends of hers. The guest list was small, and the Piedmont Driving Club (really a high society gathering place) was very near the Marsh's home. She had only to get dressed and walk a small distance and she was there. It was at this party that she met Clark Gable, who had made it no secret that he was looking forward to meeting her. After the cast and crew were paraded around, along with governors from five states, politicians, and 'anyone who was anyone'—the climax of the week was the showing on December 15, 1939, of *Gone With The Wind* at the Loew's Grand Theater on Peachtree Street.

The theater held only about two thousand people but thousands more lined the streets hoping to catch a look at some of the famous people. It was a huge and memorable time for people from Georgia. President Jimmy Carter, who as President of the United States had been all over the world and around every famous person that the job afforded him, later commented that the premiere was the "biggest event to happen in the South in my lifetime."

Identical twins Ruby and Ruth Crawford, who have since become well-known around Atlanta, traveled about 40 miles to attend the parade.

"I stood at Five Points, the financial area of the city with my sister," remembered Ruby. "We waited for hours to get a good view. We were so excited to see Clark Gable, Vivien Leigh, Ann Rutherford and the others."

The Crawford twins who went on to become lawyers—and in doing so became friends with Stephens Mitchell—braved the cold for the parade.

"I remember we had on our fur coats," she said. "But we didn't care how cold it was, just the thought of seeing Clark Gable! And then we did!"

Ruby and her sister moved to Atlanta several years later and became popular figures in the community. They lived near Mayor Hartsfield eventually becoming good friends with him, being members of the bar, and volunteering at the Jimmy Carter Center. Like everybody else, they had read *Gone With The Wind* and were eager to see the movie.

"I think it is the greatest film I've ever seen," Said Ruby.

As a young girl, Elizabeth (Lib) McDowell Walker of Monroe, Georgia—forty-five minutes from Atlanta, went to the premiere and remembers the excitement that surrounded the introduction of the movie

"I was at the premiere—outside the Loews Grand Theater in Atlanta," said Walker, who was a fourth cousin of Doc Holliday and hence shared some genealogy with Margaret Mitchell. "My friend's mother invited me and another friend of ours. We were in the throng watching the arrival of Margaret Mitchell and the stars—Clark Gable, Carole Lombard, Vivien Leigh…. It was very exciting."

She saw the large spotlights and the beacons which bounced into the night sky proclaiming that Hollywood was there in all its glory. Peachtree Street, closed to traffic, was now packed with people.

Nowadays, Lib Walker usually reads large-print books, but after reminiscing about that night she got out her old small print version of *Gone With The Wind*, re-living the nostalgia with every page.

"My youngest son and his wife bought a newspaper photo of the crowd made from about the spot where we were standing. They had it framed and gave it to me as a Christmas gift. It now hangs on my living room wall, bringing back fond memories."

As it turned out, Lib Walker had a connection to the production.

"Ed Almand owned the funeral home in town (Monroe, Georgia) and his grandson George Leonard would visit every summer and bring some of his buddies. One of George's friends, an accomplished piano player by the name of Eugene Kurtz, would come to my house with the group and he would 'tear up' our beautiful piano while the rest of us danced in the living room and hallway. Eugene's father, Wilbur Kurtz, was the historian involved with the making of *Gone With The Wind*."

"I knew Wilbur Kurtz," said Herb Bridges, who at one time owned what was thought to be the world's largest collection of *Gone With The Wind* Memorabilia. "Mr. Kurtz had some great memories of Margaret Mitchell. One thing he remembered, she was a chain smoker. He said, 'she'd come to my office and sit on this little stool and click her heels on the foot rest of the barstool and smoke just one after the other'."

Bridges, who lived in a small town near Atlanta, got to know both Susan Myrick and Wilbur Kurtz.

"Mr. Kurtz told me Margaret had a great sense of humor and she liked to tell jokes," he recalled. "He said she told some really risqué jokes!"

As noted, Myrick sent information back to Mitchell during the film's shooting in Hollywood.

"Susan Myrick was a dear lady," said Bridges. "She had wonderful pictures of that time. While she was in Hollywood she always had a camera around her neck. I'd love to see where those pictures ended up."

"Susan Myrick kept a diary the whole time," said Ernie Harwell, whose brother Richard was good friends with Margaret Mitchell and wrote several books about her. "Susan documented her time with the movie and my brother got to see it for a book."

Richard Harwell was the editor of *White Columns in Hollywood* that contained many of Myrick's memories and observations.

Ernie Harwell also went to school with Wilbur Kurtz's son.

"Wilbur was out in Hollywood most of the time the movie was being shot," said Harwell.

At the premiere Wilbur Kurtz sat in the Loew's Theater, proudly watching the finished product.

Margaret Mitchell had a seat of honor next to Jock Whitney, the financial backer of Selznick International who had pushed so hard to do the movie. Mayor Hartsfield served as master of ceremonies. It was said that Clark Gable, exhausted from all the festivities, nodded off during the show.

Gone With The Wind as a book had been such an overwhelming success and the excitement that led up to the finished movie put such a buzz in the theater that the patrons were on the edge of their seats with anticipation. They were not disappointed.

According to *Life Magazine*, "At the announcement of War (1861), the audience rose to its feet with Rebel yells (Yee-aay-ee or wah-hoo-ee or yaaa-yeee). The Band played Dixie, and Atlanta relived American history."

Atlanta loved the movie. Selznick was so happy with the performance and reception from the people of Atlanta he had tears in his eyes. After the wild applause died down at the end of the movie, the mayor called for silence and on the arm of Clark Gable, the author was escorted to the front along with the other movie stars. The theater erupted in more applause, and this time it was for their hometown writer, Margaret Mitchell. She thanked everyone and it was a happy moment for all of Atlanta.

Afterwards, members of the cast were invited to the Marsh residence.

"It was not the little apartment you hear about," said Ann Rutherford, one of those who went. "It was more like a little bungalow. We all got to enjoy a lovely early morning breakfast. There were eggs, and they had the Virginia Ham and the beaten biscuits and all the classic food. She was the dearest, quietest little lady."

She may have appeared quiet to the guests, but she had a mission. She wanted to speak to the producer, Rutherford recalled.

"Margaret said, 'I must find David (Selznick) and apologize to him, so I can tell him how right he was about Rhett'. And I said, 'Well, he was right about everything', she said 'Yes, he was. As it turns out he was right about everything but… Clark Gable really wasn't my choice for Rhett Butler'."

Ann Rutherford couldn't believe her ears, Gable had seemed like the perfect choice.

"I said 'Well for Heaven's sake, whom did you choose?' She said, 'I was sure it was going to be Basil Rathbone!' Well I'd only thought of him as playing a detective, which he did, with the earflaps and the cigar. She said 'I was describing what I see in Basil Rathbone' which was just a shock because Clark Gable fulfilled everyone's thought, that was the first casting that anybody could come up with."

Gone With The Wind collector Tim Lee owns some writings from

Mitchell's friend, Lillian Ashley Whitner give insight into the author's feelings on who should play Rhett. Whitner had recorded her memories of Mitchell and this one was written on the back of a newspaper advertisement for a department store.

"On the Davidson's ad," said Tim Lee, "Lillian writes, 'Peggy had eye trouble when the book came out and had to stay in a darkened room—I went to see her and mentioned that Clark Gable would be great as Rhett Butler. She hit the roof—said he was too 'Negroid'—her choice was Basil Rathbone'."

Basil Rathbone was best known for playing Sherlock Holmes in the 1930s and 1940s. Margaret Mitchell might have seen him in 1925 when he played in *The Masked Bride* or in 1930 as detective Philo Vance in *The Bishop Murder Case,* but most of his fame came in the 1930s when he played dramatic villains. Rathbone's first two Sherlock Holmes films, *The Adventures of Sherlock Holmes* and The *Hound of the Baskerville,* came out in 1939, the same year as *Gone With The Wind.*

"The night of their breakfast, Margaret Mitchell was missing for a while as was Clark Gable," said Rutherford. "Finally with a shout of glee, David found them—they were curled up in the bathroom! That was the only place they could have any privacy. They locked the door and kept people out. She wanted to chat with Clark Gable and tell him how wonderful she thought he was."

Because she had skipped most of the events, Margaret Mitchell had not had the chance to chat with the stars from the movie—who brought her characters to life on the big screen. It was a time for her and John Marsh to meet them and thank them for the wonderful job they did, and the stars were happy to be able to have an intimate gathering with the elusive author.

As far as Margaret Mitchell was concerned, once the Atlanta Premiere festivities were over she could go back to her normal life. It had been a whirlwind being Margaret Mitchell, the author of *Gone With The Wind* for the last few days, and it would be nice to get back to being Peggy Marsh—but of course that would never happen.

Chapter Seventeen
The Aftermath

Once *Gone With The Wind* hit the theaters, Margaret Mitchell's already chaotic life got even more crazy. People everywhere tried to get the author to make appearances, answer fan mail, or do media interviews. She just wanted to remain a private citizen.

"I used to talk to her at Jacobs Drugstore, at the counter," said Ruby Crawford, an Atlanta resident. "My sister and I worked at the First National Bank and we would go to the drugstore on our lunch breaks. Margaret Mitchell would come in and sit by us and we'd talk to her. She was a very attractive lady."

Ruby and her twin sister Ruth started working at the bank in 1943 and that is when they started seeing her at the lunch counter.

"She dressed very neatly," Ruby remembered. "She was just delightful, very friendly. She would usually come in there by herself and just sit down and talk to us."

Gone With The Wind is one of the most watched movies of all time. It tops the list in many movie categories and makes at least the top-ten in most. The image of Scarlett O'Hara and her father, Gerald O'Hara, standing together with the father's arm around the daughter gazing up at Tara with the sunset in the distance is known by many. The musical score, by Max Steiner, featured the unforgettable Tara's Theme that will always be associated with *Gone With The Wind*.

The costumes and the vivid colorful scenery, the Technicolor, and the unforgettable performances of the actors have caused people all over the world to love the movie. What fun it would be to wear big floppy hats and hooped skirts and attend lavish barbecues and dance with lots of young men.

This romantic notion of the South is what draws so many people to all things *Gone With The Wind*. The *Road To Tara Museum* in Jonesboro, Clayton County is a popular spot for vacationers and tourists to the Atlanta, Georgia area. The museum is filled with memorabilia from the collection of Herb Bridges. The costumes from the movie are a big attraction, and there is a lovely "dollhouse" type of miniature Tara on display.

In 2009, plans were underway in the city of Morrow, Georgia, to build a development called Tara; a cooperative effort between the City of Morrow and Tara Traditions, LLC established by Dr. Donald L. Stokes in 2007. The new Tara is being planned to look like the movie façade.

"The blueprints were made to spec on the movie version of Tara," said Dr. Donald Stokes, who added he hoped Tara would become a popular site for weddings, events and daily tours.

Many people throughout the world today have *Gone With The Wind* collections. Patrisha Henson is one who enjoys attending various GWTW events throughout the country.

"Unlike most 'Windies' I can not tell you the first time I read *Gone With the Wind* or saw the film, but I can tell you when I started my collection," said Henson. "It started in 1994 when I was flipping through a T.V. Guide and saw an advertisement for a miniature sculpture of Tara. I had to have it." She sent away for it, and her collection was started.

"When it arrived in the mail, you would have thought it was Christmas! I fell in love with it. I was hooked. I dug out my copy of the novel and started reading it again, bought the movie from a video store for 25.00 and was on the hunt."

At first she did not own a computer and because she was from a small town it was hard to acquire items, but once she got her computer and went on the internet her collection really took shape.

"One day I came across a link that led me to information about the Clark Gable Foundation (in Cadiz, Ohio) and the fact that they had just had a *Gone With the Wind* event. I could not believe it—there were others out there like me... as if I was some sort of Alien or something."

She contacted the director of the Foundation and got the information so she could attend an event where she met many of the stars.

"I thought it could not get any better than this –I met others who share my interest and love for all things 'GWTW' *and* I discovered that this was not a rare thing, these people gather as much as possible to honor the memory of Margaret, GWTW and the surviving cast members. They call themselves 'Windies'. I didn't realize it at the time but I was already a 'Windie'."

It should be pointed out that not all collectors or *Gone With The Wind* lovers call themselves Windies—but many of them do!

"Since that first event in Cadiz, Ohio at the Clark Gable Foundation I have met the best friends of my life and have no doubt that they will remain the best friends anyone could ever hope to meet," said Henson.

Dr. Chris Sullivan was one of the collectors Ann Rutherford became friends with.

"He was determined he would collect anything and everything that had to do with *Gone With The Wind*," said Rutherford. "He has a big collection, a very nice collection. I went to Scarlett On The Square with Bob Osborne in 2006 for a special celebration for Margaret Mitchell's birthday, and then again in 2008. It's a historic red brick building that has been turned into a museum."

Scarlett on the Square has been host to several *Gone With The Wind* events including Fourth of July parades featuring some of the stars from the movie. The museum is full of items collected by Sullivan—everything from the Bengaline gown Scarlett wore on her honeymoon to personal correspondence from the stars.

Not all *Gone With The Wind* ventures are in the Atlanta area. When Bobbie Hardy and her husband moved from Houston, Texas to Jefferson, Texas they decided to build a "reproduction" house, and since she had a *Gone With The Wind* memorabilia collection they had their new home built to look like Tara. They had an old building on the land converted into a museum where she stored her collection. "We got to thinking, 'We're building this big house, we might as well build a bed and Breakfast'. When we started to decorate it, I decided we would just decorate each room with a theme from *Gone With The Wind*," Bobby Hardy recalled.

One room is Scarlett's Bedroom, and other rooms were inspired by Mammy, Aunt Pittypat and other characters from the book and movie. Mammy's room is done in red, for the red petticoat Rhett Butler bought her. Every detail is there, including the phone number.

Bobby Hardy explained. "I wanted to use 1936, the year the book came out, and 1939, the year the movie came out, so I called the phone company as soon as I got the idea and we reserved the numbers. We paid for them for two years before the house was completed. The phone number to the bed and breakfast is (903) 665-1939."

In 2003, they had a *Gone With The Wind* event and Cammie King, the actress who played Bonnie Blue Butler, attended. "She was there and everyone just loved meeting her," said Bobbie Hardy. "She was so patient and just signed autographs for everyone. We also had Herb Bridges, who once had the largest *Gone With The Wind* Collection in the world."

Hardy has a pretty good collection herself, including copies of *Gone With The Wind* in at least thirty-five different languages.

"People have come from all over the world to stay at the bed and breakfast and see the museum," said Hardy. "It is so interesting for someone from Japan to see the Japanese copy of *Gone With The Wind* there."

Hardy says her museum is "really a hobby out of control." Her husband passed away several years ago and she has found comfort in the collection and the enjoyment she gets from it and the visitors who come. Her collection has opened many doors for her, and she has friends all over the country who are also interested in *Gone With The Wind*.

"I'm so glad I have this collection," she said. "It helps me stay busy."

Through her collection she has attended various events held throughout the country such as the 50th Anniversary Celebration in Atlanta where Marcella Rabwin was a guest speaker.

Another person who has enjoyed collecting *Gone With The Wind* memorabilia and has decorated in the *Gone With The Wind* motif is store owner Faye Bell. She was operating a secretarial/word processing business in Plant City, Florida, when she bought two Queen Anne chairs for the lobby, and decided to decorate the wall with several *Gone With The Wind* pictures she had bought from a collector.

"I was just going to decorate that one area and then I started buying things here and there to decorate the office," she said. "I went to the big celebration in Atlanta for the Re-Premiere for the 50th Anniversary of the movie and pretty soon I was hooked. People would peek in the window of my office after hearing about it from someone. They may not have known my name but they'd say, 'She's that gal with the *Gone With The Wind* decorations'."

In 1996 she started her website (www.gwtwmemories.com) and soon she dropped her secretarial business for the more interesting and lucrative *Gone With The Wind* business.

"It's been amazing," she said. "I have shipped items to forty-five countries!"

The most recent was to Zulu, South Africa.

Each year Plant City plays host to The Strawberry Festival, a country fair-type event and Faye Bell sets up a *Gone With The Wind* table. One day she got a big surprise when two executives from the Anheuser-Busch-owned Cypress Gardens, in nearby Lakeland, Florida, asked if she would like to set up a shop there. For five years she operated a shop in the Magnolia Mansion inside Cypress Gardens, and moved out only after new ownership came in and changed the focus of the park.

Faye Bell's collection grew until soon she, too, had one of the largest *Gone With The Wind* collections on display. In August, 2005, one of her customers asked if he could purchase her collection and he bought the entire lot.

"I remember it was the day after Hurricane Katrina," said Bell. "I had over 2,000 pieces of vintage items. I asked if they planned to put them on display but he said they bought it for their private enjoyment."

Bell, like Bobbie Hardy, has hosted *Gone With The Wind* events.

"I've had several three-day events," she said. "We've had actors from the movie, *Gone with the Wind* games; we've shown bloopers from the movie. We just have a ball at the events."

She still has her store and her website, and she enjoys taking time out to play golf with friends like Patrick Curtis and Mickey Kuhn, both actors who played Beau Wilkes at various stages in the movie.

When talking about *Gone With The Wind*, Herb Bridges is the one everyone turns to as being the foremost authority on it.

"I was from Sharpsburg, Georgia, an area just south of Atlanta," said Bridges. "There came a time in the 1960s when Atlanta started building large hotels to attract the convention business. People began coming to Atlanta in great numbers and they had this romantic picture of *Gone*

With The Wind in mind. They were asking questions and I found a niche, using my interest in *Gone With The Wind* for lecturing and speaking at conventions."

His collection grew and grew and soon he had a topic to speak about people were interested in. Bridges had 'first editions' of the books and copies of *Gone With The Wind* in every language in which it was printed.

Bridges enjoys offering his expertise to assist The Margaret Mitchell House and the Road To Tara Museum. He sold the bulk of his collection through Christie's Auction House, turning his hobby into a profit, but remains active in writing about and *promoting Gone With The Wind.*

The Margaret Mitchell House, which opened in 1997, is listed on the National Register of Historic Places by the National Trust for Historic Preservation in Washington, D.C. Margaret Mitchell and John Marsh lived in a small apartment in the back of a larger house when she was writing her book. Tourists come from around the world to see the place where the famous author lived. Herb Brooks has some of his items on display there.

Bridges, a sought-after expert on *Gone With The Wind,* speaks at conventions and meetings.

"Herb Bridges is a wonderful man," said Ann Rutherford. She has donated items to Herb because she knows he will put them on display for many to enjoy. Just as Star Trek has its "Trekkies," *Gone With The Wind* has its "Windies." Anyone wanting to find out more about these activities need go no further than the internet to search. There are blogs, groups, and even websites dedicated entirely to the book and movie. Each year there is a celebration in the Atlanta area to commemorate Margaret Mitchell's birthday.

There are many collectors and outlets who sell to the collectors. *Gone With The Wind* collectors enjoy meeting each other and buying or trading items back and forth. John Wiley, Jr. of Richmond, Virginia publisher of the *The Scarlett Letter* www.thescarlettletter.com, has produced several events billed as *Gone With The Wind* Forums.

"We had one in Richmond in 1991, just after *Scarlett,* the sequel, came out and two forums in Atlanta (1993 and 1996)," said Wiley.

"Each event featured celebrities or experts on *Gone With The Wind*. We've had Marcella Rabwin, Carlton Jackson, who wrote a biography of Hattie McDaniel, and even Margaret Mitchell's nephews came to two of them."

Eugene Mitchell, one of the sons of Mitchell's brother Stephens, passed away in 2007, and Mitchell's other nephew Joseph, who is retired, was living in Atlanta at the time this was written.

"Stephens Mitchell's sons were quiet," according to Wiley. "When they talked, you could tell they had a great love and respect for their aunt. They were teenagers when she (Margaret) died and then a year later their own mother died."

Now Wiley has a huge collection, including what he believes to be the only complete collection of all American editions of Margaret Mitchell's novel.

"My first purchase was the mass market paperback edition which I bought at a school book fair for $1.25 as a kid," said Wiley, whose hobby has enabled him to meet many people.

"I got to know Richard Harwell through my collecting," he said. Harwell, a Civil War historian, compiled a book of Margaret Mitchell's letters and became a friend of Mitchell's.

"Richard claimed to have had the first book Margaret Mitchell ever autographed," said Wiley. "He was a book reviewer working at Emory University at the time. In fact, *Gone With The Wind* was one of the first books he reviewed. She was speaking at a library just before the book came out and he had the advance copy the publisher had sent him."

"That story is true," said Ernie Harwell, Richard's brother. "That was when they met and they had such similar interests, the history of the South being one, they just became friends."

Richard Harwell started a *Gone With The Wind* memorabilia collection after he got that first autographed book. He acquired quite a few things, and some say he had the second largest collection in the world—second to Herb Bridges at the time. After Harwell's death, his family sold it.

According to Wiley, Mitchell and Richard Harwell became good friends and she wrote him letters when he was in the Navy. Her friendship with Harwell may have been what led her to back the Navy so strongly when she donated money toward the SS Atlanta.

"She was to have supper with him the night she was killed," Wiley said, recalling a story that Richard Harwell had told him.

"That was the dinner that never took place," Ernie Harwell reminded. "Maybe if she had gone to dinner with my brother things would have turned out differently for her."

When John Wiley, Jr. thinks of the fictional Tara of *Gone With The Wind,* he can picture several items he owns from the Hollywood set, but one item he treasures from a real-life home is a plate owned by Margaret Mitchell. Among items in his collection –10,000, but who's counting— is a piece of her personal china.

According to Wiley, "Margaret Mitchell's china was the Queen Rose pattern made by Rosenthal. She had a wide range of close friends and enjoyed being with them, wanting to live as normal a life as possible. She lived in an apartment and kept her phone number listed in the phone book until 1949, the year she died."

When one says someone has 'the largest collection in the world', it is relative because in the world of collecting, people buy and sell all the time and their collection sizes change. Dr. Novella Perrin, who lives in the mid-west, has a large collection and she enjoys traveling to the various *Gone With The Wind* venues to meet up with her other collector friends. While some collectors just keep their items in boxes, and others in one room, there are those like Hardy, Bell, Sullivan, and Bridges who display their items for others to see in museum-like settings.

Perrin prefers keeping hers to herself—and her many friends who enjoy looking at it. She likes to catalog her items, and this has created a hobby for her. She owns one of the chairs from the Premiere at Loews in Atlanta and several costumes worn in the move, but she really enjoys organizing the drawers and drawers of pictures and letters she has collected over the years.

There is one thing about *Gone With The Wind* collectors that is universal. They all strive for that coveted autograph of the author who was not known for signing a lot of books.

Margaret Mitchell, known for enjoying the spotlight and being the center of attention with the men when she was young, enjoyed much quieter outings as an adult. She had many women friends she liked to have lunch with, laugh and gossip with. She was also a member of the Atlanta Woman's Club.

"Back then you had to be from Atlanta, (to be in the Woman's Club) and I had only moved there so I was not a member, but I saw her there frequently," said Billie Sawyer, who was involved with the Woman's Club through the Girl Scouts.

The Club is still at its historical original spot, though a fire caused it to go under some renovation in the 1990s. Built in 1906 as an upscale mansion for the Wimbish family of Atlanta, it had tall fireplaces, gothic columns, crystal chandeliers, and polished hardwood floors.

"They held monthly meetings there," said Billie Sawyer. "Margaret was a member and I would see her when I went. She fit in like everybody else."

But she was not like everybody else. Her successful book and movie had thrust her into the spotlight, a position she did not enjoy. Margaret Mitchell had written only one book, but the fame from that book provided her with so much stress and so many headaches that she never got around to writing another one.

In today's world she might have sought a counselor and gone into therapy. At times she seemed to suffer from depression and it worsened with every demand she felt imposed on her by the general public. Many times people would try to capitalize on the popularity of *Gone With The Wind,* and if it were not done through the proper channels the Mitchell family put a stop to it. Stephens Mitchell was known for the many lawsuits he filed against people who did not seek their permission.

According to Fayetteville historian John Lynch, one time the people of Fayetteville decided to put on a play to raise money for a library. They planned to put on a musical based on *Gone With The Wind,* and felt entitled to do that because many events in the book happened to their own residents. They used relatives of the real people in the play.

"The people of Fayetteville put on a play called 'A Romance of the '60s'," said Lynch. "Real people's relatives were in it. When Margaret Mitchell heard about it, she drove to Fayetteville to see what it was all about.

"She was sitting on a stool in Beadles Drug Store drinking a Coke. Mrs. Beadles didn't know her but she knew there was a lot of hoopla going on about the play and she asked the woman at the counter, 'Did you read *Gone With The Wind*?'"

Margaret Mitchell looked at her. She suddenly realized the woman did not know who she was. "'Quite frankly, I wrote it', she said," according to Lynch. "Mrs. Beadles got so excited she called everybody in town to come down to her drugstore and see Margaret. They got to talking to her and she helped the town fund their library."

That was typical of Margaret Mitchell. She would rather do something for a small group of people, than do something in public and get credit for it. She was a person who liked people and she liked talking. Though she suffered many illnesses, she always made time, even when she was sick, to write back to the many people who wrote her. That was one of the reasons she felt so much pressure after the book came out.

It was important to her that she answer all the mail she received, and she wrote an enormous amount of letters both to people who wrote her and to people who did not.

Author Herb Bridges knew Mitchell's secretary Margaret Baugh.

"Margaret Mitchell wrote so many letters," he said. "In her earlier days she hand wrote them but there came a time when she hired a secretary to help her type. Margaret Baugh was actually brought in by John Marsh, who hired several typists to help finish up the manuscript; and then she stayed on to assist Mitchell in the letter writing."

The letters Baugh typed were typed with carbon paper, and that is one reason so many of them exist today. All of the letter writing took a toll on Mitchell. She worried over all of the publicity the book got once it was published and she wrote to everyone who made mention of it in print, whether she knew them or not.

Margaret Mitchell did not like to cook. She had employees who did the cooking for her, but she enjoyed going out to dinner with John or with her friends. One of her favorite restaurants in Atlanta was Mary Mac's Tea Room. She was a regular there.

"I used to see her in there with her husband," said Billie Sawyer, who has been going to Mary Mac's since the first owner Mary McKenzie opened it in the 1940s and eventually sold it to Margaret Mitchell's cousin, Margaret Lupo.

"Mary Mac's is a very attractive restaurant with very good food," said Billie Sawyer, whose sister had lived across the street when it first opened. In those days, if a woman was going to open a restaurant, she would call it a "Tea Room" and though years have gone by, the current owner, John Ferrell, continues with the tradition of the name.

"There are lots of pictures on the wall of all the famous people who have eaten there," said Billie Sawyer. "I've seen just about every governor we've had in the State of Georgia. They'd come over from the capitol and eat there."

According to Billie, when Mary Mac's first opened there were about ten tables. There was Jacob's Pharmacy, a drugstore on the corner, and next to it was Mary Mac's and then another store. Over the years the restaurant expanded but the tradition that Mitchell enjoyed, has remained. They use all fresh ingredients and bake the breads on the premises and the owners know the customers and talk to them.

They even have a welcoming "Ambassador." Jo Carter makes sure that the customers receive personal treatment and get to experience the Southern dining traditions. "Try the cracklin' cornbread," she encourages. Margaret Mitchell would dip the cracklin' cornbread in her soup. A frequent visitor, she sometimes dined with her relatives such as cousin Margaret Lupo. Perhaps that was why Lupo bought the restaurant.

"When I first met Margaret Lupo, I didn't even realize she had bought Mary Mac's," said Billie Sawyer. "She was as nice as could be and would talk to all of the customers. Margaret Mitchell would go in there at various times. People left her alone. They respected her privacy and the integrity of the restaurant, so they just smiled and said hello as they would do with anyone, and she would smile and say hello back."

Margaret and John had gotten in a car accident, and then Margaret had one herself so she was afraid of driving. She did drive, but drove very slowly. That is why she and John preferred going places they could walk to. Mary Mac's was a little over a mile from their apartment on Piedmont near the South Prado.

"When the Marshes dined, they would be as any other married

couple," Sawyer said. "Sitting and chatting and enjoying the meal. They always dressed as if they were coming from work. He would always have a suit and be wearing a tie and she always had a dress or skirt on."

The people around Atlanta knew Margaret Mitchell when they saw her.

"She carried herself well and appeared to be a Southern Lady," Billie Sawyer said. "She was not overly beautiful, but was attractive, and carried herself well."

When she described Margaret Mitchell in that manner, she did not realize the first line of the book: "Scarlett O'Hara was not beautiful, but men seldom realized it when caught by her charm..." In describing Margaret Mitchell, she was describing Scarlett O'Hara.

Mitchell was comfortable in this part of town and she also frequented Jacob's Pharmacy next door often. Interestingly, Jacob's Pharmacy is where the roots of Coca-Cola were formed.

Dr. John Stith Pemberton of Atlanta, came up with a headache cure in the late 1800's, which he sold in Jacob's Pharmacy as Pemberton's French Winde Coca." It was advertised as a nerve tonic, stimulant and headache remedy. When prohibition came he had to figure out what to do with his invention so he dropped the wine and sweetened it with sugar.

According to Coke's website: "On May 8, 1886, Dr. John Stith Pemberton, a local pharmacist, produced the syrup for Coca-Cola®, and carried a jug of the new product down the street to Jacobs' Pharmacy, where it was sampled, pronounced "excellent" and placed on sale for 5 cents a glass as a soda fountain drink."

It was still a nickel when Mitchell sat at the soda fountain.

Another favorite place to enjoy dinner and drinks was the previously mentioned Piedmont Driving Club. Perhaps the Club was one of the reasons the Marshes chose the location of their last apartment. It was just a short walk from their apartment.

The club's own description on their website is: "Since 1887, the Piedmont Driving Club has enjoyed a reputation as one of the most prestigious private clubs in the South."

Mitchell had been going to the Club since she was a young girl.

It had been the scene of many fun times. During the big Premiere in December, 1939, The Atlanta Women's Press Club hosted a luncheon tea party in her honor there.

Even though she preferred to eat out, she did enjoy entertaining friends. Ever since she was young, Margaret Mitchell would have friends over, and the Marshes continued that tradition. She often bought cakes baked by Helen Barksdale Harwell, the mother of Richard and Ernie Harwell.

"Our father had multiple sclerosis when he was in his 30s and our mother became the breadwinner for the household," said Ernie Harwell. "Margaret would have parties with her old debutante friends and my mother would make sandwiches and cakes for them."

She continued ordering the food for special occasions after she was married. Helen Barksdale Harwell would deliver the food and Bessie, the Marsh's maid, would arrange it all on beautiful silver trays or china plates.

All was not fun and games for Mitchell like it should have been after producing such a successful book. The late 1930s and the entire 1940s were filled with either her own illnesses or the illnesses of her father (who died in 1944), of her husband John, and even her beloved employee, Bessie.

"Margaret Mitchell seemed to always have some kind of illness," said Herb Brooks, who came to know her brother Stephens very well. "She always needed some sort of medical attention."

"Her whole family was accident prone," said Bridges.

He cited an incident that happened to her brother as an amazing happening.

"One day Mr. Mitchell (Stephens) was walking down the sidewalk on a street in Atlanta," he said. "A crate fell off of a truck and hit him and broke his shoulder right there on the sidewalk. What are the chances of a crate falling off a truck and just happening to hit you?"

In 1940 Margaret Mitchell checked herself into St. Joseph's Hospital, the favorite hospital she always used—the one where her cousin Sister Melanie worked. She had one of her many surgeries and, shortly after that, John Marsh went to the same hospital with a high fever and they were in the hospital together. Marsh had a mysterious illness; and after returning to work for a short time, he took a leave of absence to take Margaret on a trip to Arizona. He went back to work but continued ailing.

Margaret was sick off and on and Marsh tended to her, all the while growing sicker himself. When she was ill she would go to bed for weeks on end, with John taking care of her. Margaret had been born in 1900, so in 1940 she was only 40 years old, such a young age to be bedridden so much. Even thought they were in such bad shape, they would continue walking to their destinations, trudging slowly together.

John Marsh had a heart attack in 1945, and Margaret was forced to give up her own injuries and illnesses in favor of trying to nurse him back to health. For the next year Marsh rarely got out of bed. With the sedentary life they were living they both gained weight and continued seeking medical treatment for their various ailments.

According to her letters, shortly after the movie came out in 1939 and for the next ten years, which proved to be the rest of her life, she was either sick or nursing someone who was. The woman who set the world on fire with the most-popular-book-turned-movie ever seemed to be watching her life slipping away with the wind.

Illness and accidents were just a part of life for Margaret and John Marsh. Sometimes it seemed she lived her life wondering when the next catastrophe would happen. She suffered from nightmares of impending doom. Premonitions or dreams of the future were common in her life. According to the Finis Farr book (page 26), Margaret Mitchell's great-grandmother, Eleanor (Ellen) Fitzgerald (the wife of Philip Fitzgerald) had a recurring dream that British troops would storm her house. This ended up coming true, but they were Yankees—which was even worse.

In *Gone With The Wind*, Scarlett O'Hara had a recurring dream which she told Rhett Butler about. She was running through the fog. She talked about the nightmare (page 856) that featured her being cold, tired, and hungry running through the mist—looking for something but she did not know what.

At the end of the book she realized that what she was looking for—that warm, safe place that was always hidden in the mist was not Ashley—it was, of course, Rhett.

And in real life, Margaret Mitchell had dreamed she would be killed in an automobile accident. She was known for driving very slowly because of the car accidents and she feared another. She even told people of this dream… and just as Ellen Fitzgerald's nightmare came true, Margaret Mitchell was killed in that car accident, run down by a speeding car on the street very near where she lived.

On August 16th, 1949, Davison's Department Store was having a sale. They had fall skirts for $3.99. There was a special on new fall suits for $8.98. The Nuremberg Trials in Germany had recently ended. Minimum wage was 40 cents an hour and gasoline was 26 cents a gallon.

Outside Grady Memorial Hospital, the four ambulances sat with their gas tanks full. There was the one Cadillac that the drivers did not use because the gears jerked; the two Fords, smaller and boxier than the other two; and the red Chevrolet. A few steps away from where they were parked, the crowds were getting larger.

Just ten years after the exciting gala premiere of *Gone With The Wind*, the author was dead, and at such a young age. Several of the principals of the movie had already died, including writer Sidney Howard, Leslie Howard (Ashley) and Laura Hope Crewes (Aunt Pittypat). Also to die in 1949 were directors Victor Fleming and Sam Wood, as well as Howard Hickman (John Wilkes), Harry Davenport (Dr. Meade) and Oscar Polk (Pork). Strangely enough, Polk was hit by a taxi driver as he tried to cross the street.

Berrien Upshaw, Mitchell's first husband also died in 1949. He had committed suicide just seven months earlier. They had really only lived together for several months, but the impact they may have had on each other's lives was significant.

His own half-sister said he does not deserve more than a few lines in a book and certainly not a full chapter. Still, just as Margaret Mitchell had sent flowers to the grave of Clifford Henry on the anniversary of his death every year, she also kept in touch with Berrien Upshaw's parents to see how he was doing.

Upshaw and Mitchell had both lost their mothers the same year in the flu epidemic and both longed for companionship and lived their lives on the edge when they were together. Strange they both died the same year before either had reached the age of fifty.

Five days after she was hit by the car, Margaret Mitchell breathed her last breath. Flags in Georgia were flown at half-staff. There was a graveside service at the Oakland Cemetery in Atlanta performed by an Episcopalian minister. Collectors have printed invitations which were sent out for the funeral. She was buried next to her parents in the same cemetery where golfing great Bobby Jones is buried.

Mitchell seemed to have known she would die young. Just a year earlier she had made a will, and here she was dead from a car accident at the age of 48— almost the same age her mother had been when she died.

A week after Margaret Mitchell was buried, a florist arrived at Grady Memorial Hospital. He delivered flower arrangements for the nurses' station and individual orchid corsages for the nurses who cared for Margaret. Wilma Fower, who spent the first night with her got a double orchid corsage. The card was signed, *David O. Selznick.*

A few nights later, Wilma Fowler was working the eleven to seven (overnight) shift, with just about three weeks until her graduation. She was looking forward to that magical day when she would receive her white nurse's cap. One of the girls at the nurses' station called her over and a woman introduced herself as Margaret Baugh, the secretary to Margaret Mitchell and John Marsh. She had something in her hand and handed it to Wilma.

"She gave her a half-empty bottle of Heaven Scent perfume," said Faye Bell owner of GWTW Memories website and store, who knows Fowler. "She said it was the last thing Margaret Mitchell had touched before they left for the movie that night, and John Marsh wanted her to have it."

Chapter Eighteen
Postscript

There were two amazing women trailblazers born about the same time whose stories are amazingly similar. Both were thin, almost boyish at times and seemed to be urged on by men they had married, with whom their sexual attractions had been ambiguous. Both of these women turned out to be powerful role models for their gender and accomplished something that would be remembered far beyond their young deaths—both before age fifty.

Amelia Earhart, the famous aviator was born in 1897, just three years before Margaret Mitchell. Both were born in their grandparent's homes, and raised with one sibling. To Margaret's pony riding and daring horseback riding accidents, Amelia Earhart rode her sled off the sloping roof of the barn.

The writing bug had bitten Margaret Mitchell at a young age and she wrote stories and made up plays which were performed for the neighbor kids. Earhart knew she wanted to fly after that first time she slid off the roof in that sled. "It's just like flying!" she said.

Both women had fathers who were lawyers, were raised with servants and spent much time with their grandmothers and relatives. They both loved to read and had read the classics at a young age. As a teenager, Amelia Earhart trained to be a nurse with the Red Cross, and Mitchell did work with the war efforts and the Red Cross. Earhart, who was living in Massachusetts at the time, enrolled in Smith College, the same school Mitchell attended for one year, but at the last minute she changed her mind and went to Columbia University to take courses in medicine. Mitchell said in print that she had originally wanted to be a doctor. Just like Mitchell, Earhart only stayed in college for one year and then returned home due to a family situation.

Earhart took her first plane ride in Dec. 1920. During that year Peggy Mitchell was flying high as a carefree flapper.

Both women wore their hair cropped short and at times looked like a boy. Margaret Mitchell was called "Jimmy" for a time when she was young because she would wear boys' pants, preferring that look to the more feminine attire her father and grandmother encouraged. Earhart wore male clothing and even looked a little like Charles Lindbergh, which earned her the nickname of "Lady Lindy." They both wore pants in a time when it was frowned upon.

On Sept. 2, 1922, Margaret Mitchell began her adult life by marrying Berrien Upshaw. A month later, Amelia Earhart bought her first plane. Both women seemed to live tormented lives, each striving to live on their own terms, with the outside world interfering. In the end, they succeeded in doing what they wanted to do even though at times they were bucking the trends of the time. Although reaching the pinnacle of their careers, neither woman seemed to achieve happiness.

Even their love lives were similar. Amelia Earhart was engaged to marry one man yet later married another. Out of convenience, it seemed, she married G.P. Putnam, the man who had been her best friend and stood by her. Putnam, a publisher, encouraged her flying career. Through any controversy that arose, he was by her side all the way. To the outside world Earhart presented a strong-willed woman persona, but it was in private to G.P that she could confide her weaknesses.

Margaret Mitchell, who had been engaged to a man who was killed in World War I, and divorced her first husband had ended up marrying her trusted friend, John Marsh, who also shared in her career. It was Marsh who encouraged Mitchell to write the book, and during all of the turmoil she went through after the book became so famous, Marsh supported her unfailingly. Though Margaret Mitchell was the famous author who was sought after for the limelight, Marsh loved her as his Peggy and would do anything for her.

Both women kept their maiden names publicly, even though it was not the custom at the time, and they had no children. A fire in the family home destroyed many of Amelia Earhart's papers and mementos, and after her death, many of Margaret Mitchell's personal things were also destroyed in a fire.

Earhart was the first woman to fly solo across the Atlantic Ocean and she won the Distinguished Flying Cross, the first woman to do so. To

Earhart's Distinguished Flying Cross, Mitchell won the coveted Pulitzer Prize.

In 1935, Harold Latham of Macmillan first laid eyes on Margaret Mitchell's manuscript for *Gone With The Wind* and that same year Amelia Earhart became the first person to make a solo flight from Honolulu, Hawaii, to Oakland, California. A year later, June 30, 1936, Margaret Mitchell's book *Gone With The Wind* was published.

1937 was a major year in the lives of these two incredible women. Margaret Mitchell was on top of the world as the sales of her book were skyrocketing and she won the Pulitzer, as well as an award from the American Bookseller's Association. Similarly, Amelia Earhart's fame was at its height as she set out to make a historic flight around the world—a flight from which she would never return. Though she was one of the world's most famous women at the time, her death was sensational and tragic—and broadcast around the world.

Margaret Mitchell had also become one of the world's most recognized women and the tragic circumstances surrounding her death, after being hit by a drunk driver, made headlines around the world.

When Amelia Earhart plane disappeared, the world waited for details every day to see if she would be rescued. After Margaret Mitchell was hit by the car she lingered on in the hospital for five days. Each day the Atlanta newspapers and national news radio broadcasts reported updates of her condition until the author died at the young age of forty-eight.

These two women became role models for so many young girls who could look to them and say, 'If she could do that, maybe I can achieve my goals'. Their life stories were both about survival but in the end, they were not able to do that; and they died way too young.

Both women had led vibrant lives yet came to such violent crashes at the end; one by a drunk driver, and one presumably in a plane crash. Margaret Mitchell was on her way to the theater; Amelia Earhart was on her way to setting yet another record. One moment they were smiling, and the next, their lives were cut short.

These strong women offer inspiration and motivation through their life stories. Amelia Earhart's story provides 'wings' of hope to those wondering if they should take a chance. Ever since she was a child, she wanted to fly and she did what she had to do to get sponsors for her flights, never giving up when the task seemed impossible.

Margaret Mitchell's life, her ancestors' lives, and the great work it all provided gave us one of the most motivational themes ever. If a person is ever feeling down or defeated, they need only look at her life and the classic she wove together, *Gone With The Wind*. Our lives are like a book, being written, with notes and changes made along the way to becoming a masterpiece. The great thing about life is that nothing is ever definite; there is always the possibility of a sequel and updated editions.

Margaret Mitchell's theme for *Gone With The Wind* was survival. Scarlett O'Hara achieved her goals though less than honorable means, but the message of 'survival' and never giving up is worthwhile for everyone.

Those who lived through the Civil War had to find ways to survive, just as those facing any war throughout history. Margaret Mitchell's relatives displayed great courage just as did every other U.S. citizen at the time, whether on the North side or the South.

Once Mitchell's book came out and she felt she was under siege from the public, she did everything in her power to survive what she thought was a terrible ordeal. One of her survival tactics was to hire good lawyers; to be sure they would always be working for her. Her brother Stephens basically spent his entire life, after she wrote the book, doing the business of *Gone With The Wind*. The company formed by Stephens Mitchell and his partners continued protecting Margaret Mitchell after her death and they still continue after Stephens' death.

In 2005, a man named Phillip Battles inherited a cabinet from his father, and in one of the drawers he discovered some papers pertaining to the book and movie. It was unclear if they had belonged to Mitchell or the law firm, but when he realized what a find he had he tried to sell it. The lawyers from the estate of Stephens Mitchell jumped in. They reached an agreement, but the outcome was never disclosed.

Margaret Mitchell said she wrote about people who had gumption and about those who did not. She had gumption throughout her young life, but it seemed that once her book became famous she was overwhelmed. Perhaps the way she survived each day was to take her own advice. Throughout the book, when presented with a major challenge, Scarlett stepped back. 'If I think of it now, I'll go crazy', she would say to herself and put the bad things in a box for later, gathering up her strength to do the things she had to do at that moment.

If you are ever presented with a problem, a situation that seems out of control, or you feel desperate like there is no way out, there is always hope. There is never no hope. Just remember Scarlett's advice from the last line of Margaret Mitchell's one and only book and save your problem until tomorrow, because, "after all, tomorrow is another day."

The End

Famous Lexington madam, Belle Brezing,
the possible inspiration for Belle Watling.
(Photo courtesy: Collection 2003AV1, Item 1, Belle Brezing Collection,
University of Kentucky Libraries, Jason Flahardy, archivist)

Margaret Mitchell's great-aunt Mary Fitzgerald (also known as Mamie).
(Photo courtesy Marie Nygren)

Margaret Mitchell's great-aunt
Sarah Jane Fitzgerald (also known as Sis or Sadie).
(Photo courtesy Marie Nygren)

John Henry "Doc" Holliday's life may have played a small part in
Gone With The Wind.
(Photo courtesy of Colorado Historical Society,
copyright CHS, Doc Holliday Mazzulla Collection, Box 4, FF 325)

Margaret Mitchell's grandmother, Annie Fitzgerald Stephens
(Courtesy Kenan Collection, Atlanta History Center, Photo VIS 140.106)

Margaret Mitchell's great-grandfather, Philip Fitzgerald
(Courtesy Kenan Collection, Atlanta History Center, Photo VIS 140.104)

Sister Melanie/Mattie Holliday, Philip Fitzgerald was her uncle.
Her mother married a Holliday, making her Doc Holliday's cousin
and also related to Margaret Mitchell.
(Courtesy Kenan Collection, Atlanta History Center, Photo VIS 140.115)

Margaret Mitchell's great-grandmother, Ellen (Eleanor) Fitzgerald.
This is a page from the scrapbook which lists the Fitzgerald daughters.
(Photo courtesy Marie Nygren)

Katie Fitzgerald, great-aunt of Margaret Mitchell,
and sister of Annie Fitzgerald.
(Photo courtesy Marie Nygren)

Lucille Stephens Kennon and her sister Isabell,
relatives of Margaret Mitchell.
They were raised by Mitchell's elderly aunts who lived at Rural Home.
(Photo courtesy Marie Nygren)

*Cover of Mitchell family
scrapbook.
(Photo courtesy of Marie Nygren)*

*Lucille Stephens Kennon, who
kept the scrapbook.
Her grandfather was Philip
Fitzgerald, Margaret Mitchell's
great-grandfather.
(Photo courtesy Marie Nygren)*

*Mary Mac's Tea Room, once owned by Margaret Lupo,
grand-daughter of Lucille Stephens Kennon who kept the scrapbook.
Margaret Lupo was Margaret Mitchell's cousin and they both shared
the same great-grandparents: Ellen and Philip Fitzgerald.*

Judy Barrett, Mickey Kuhn, Ann Rutherford, Patrick Curtis,
Greg Giese, Evelyn Keyes, and Rand Brooks.
(Photo courtesy Greg Giese)

Celebrating Clark Gable with his son, John Clark Gable
at the Golden Boot Awards.
From left, Mickey Kuhn, Patrick Curtis, Ann Rutherford,
Gable's son John, Phyllis Callow, and Fred Crane.
(Photo courtesy Patrick Curtis)

The day the U.S. Post Office dedicated the Hattie McDaniel stamp.
Ann Rutherford at the microphone, from her right, Fred Crane,
Patrick Curtis, Cammie King, and Mickey Kuhn.
(Photo courtesy of Cammie King.)

Greg Giese and Olivia de Havilland.

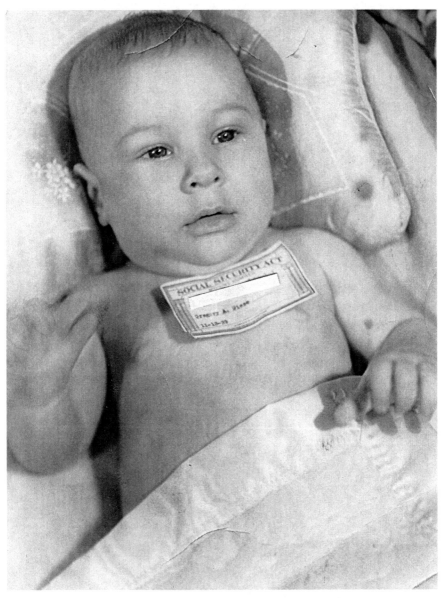

Greg Giese, with his Social Security Card.
He was the youngest person ever to receive Social Security Card at that time.
(Photo courtesy Greg Giese)

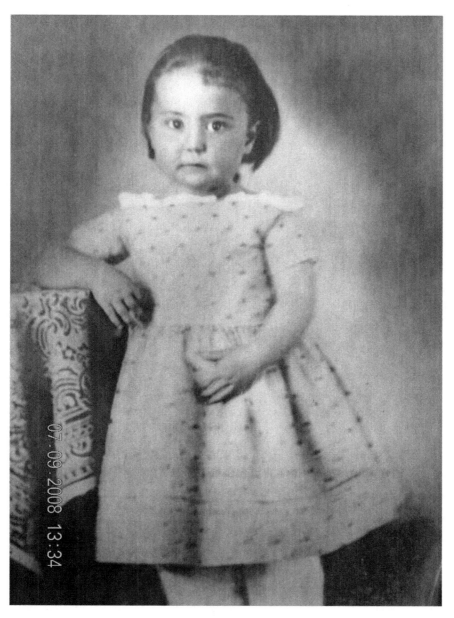

Crawford girl.
The Crawfords were friends of Mitchell's relatives the Fitzgeralds
and may have inspired the Wilkes family in Gone With the Wind.
(Courtesy of Gene Talmadge)

The Harper twins, neighbors of the Fitzgeralds.
Horse owners, the Harpers are said to be a possible inspiration
for the red-headed Tarleton family.
(Photo Courtesy Debbie Whittemore,
descendent of the Harpers—whole family knew Margaret Mitchell.)

Herb Bridges, author, collector, Gone With The Wind expert.

*Holliday-Dorsey-Fife Museum, a home owned by members of
Doc Holliday's family which once housed Annie Fitzgerald
when she was attending the Fayetteville Academy for Girls.*

Cover picture by Rena Hoyt-Hasse (copyright 2008, all rights reserved)
Picture shows Margaret Mitchell as a young flapper being surrounded
by five boyfriends one time she was in the hospital.
The picture above her head shows her possibly thinking of Scarlett O'Hara
at the Wilkes Barbecue surrounded by many men.

Lib Walker, who is a fourth cousin to Doc Holliday proudly displaying a picture she has from the night of the movie Premiere in Atlanta. (Photo courtesy Elizabeth McDowell Walker.)

*This sawmill was originally owned by
Margaret Mitchell's great-uncle, William Stephens.
Relatives are not sure if it is the one that Annie Fitzgerald
later owned as he was her brother-in-law.
(Photo courtesy of Marie Nygren)*

Marcella Rabwin in the original green sprigged dress
Vivien Leigh wore in Gone With The Wind.
(Photo courtesy Rabwin Family)

David O. Selznick's executive assistant Marcella Rabwin
gave speeches and made appearances on Gone With The Wind
(Photo courtesy Marcella Rabwin Family)

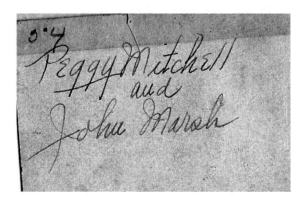

Name card that Margaret Mitchell made for the front door
of the apartment known as "The Dump"
shortly after she and John Marsh were married.
(Picture courtesy Tim Lee, Atlanta, GA)

Clark Gable, Cammie King and Mickey Kuhn.
(Photo courtesy Mickey Kuhn)

*Alicia Rhett (sitting left), Laura Hope Crewes, Leslie Howard (holding
Mickey Kuhn) as Vivien Leigh and Clark Gable look on.
(Photo courtesy Mickey Kuhn)*

Director, Victor Fleming had a way with kids.
Here he is trying to cheer Mickey Kuhn up after he performed a crying
scene. (Photo courtesy of Mickey Kuhn)

Nancy Egerton holds her family's original copy of Gone With The Wind.
Her half-brother Berrien Upshaw was Mitchell's first husband.
(Photo courtesy Nancy Egerton)

Mitchell cousin Marie Nygren with her grandmother Kennon's scrapbook and a newspaper article about Annie Fitzgerald being the model for Scarlett. (Photo courtesy Marie Nygren)

Betty Talmadge, who bought the Tara Hollywood façade and the Fitzgerald family's Rural Home and moved them to her property known as the Crawford-Talmadge estate, visits with former Texas Governor, Ann Richards. (Photo courtesy of Gene Talmadge)

Margaret Mitchell's great-grandfather Philip Fitzgerald,
like Gerald O'Hara had fought in the Indian Wars
as inscribed on Fitzgerald's grave in the Fayetteville Cemetery.

*Marcella Rabwin and her husband Dr. Marcus Rabwin at an
antebellum costume party with their friends Lucille Ball and Desi Arnaz.
(Photo courtesy of the Rabwin Family)*

Rhett Turnipseed.
Could his great-grandfather have provided inspiration
for the "star-crossed lovers" storyline of Rhett and Scarlett?
(Photo courtesy Rob Rains)

*"Rural Home as I knew it" wrote Lucille Stephens Kennon
on this picture in her scrapbook.
Note the caption "Original house in* Gone With The Wind.*"
(Photo courtesy Marie Nygren)*

It has been said that a young girl shot a Yankee on these steps in the original Thomas Crawford house, now owned by the Talmadge family. (Photo courtesy Gene Talmadge)

Crawford boy.
The Crawfords were good friends with the Fitzgeralds,
just as the Wilkes were friends with the O'Hara's.
(Photo courtesy Gene Talmadge)

Crawford-Talmadge house.
The Crawfords may have provided the inspiration for the Wilkes family.
(Photo courtesy Gene Talmadge)

The Hollywood façade of Tara has been stored in a garage
on the Talmadge estate. (Photo courtesy Gene Talmadge)

Vivien Leigh, Clark Gable, Margaret Mitchell, David O. Selznick, and Olivia de Havilland during festivities of the Atlanta Premiere in 1939. (Photo Courtesy Kenan Collection, Atlanta History Center)

Clark Gable.
(Photo courtesy Patrick Curtis)

Fred Crane, Cammie King, Patrick Curtis, and Butterfly McQueen, 1988. (Photo courtesy of Patrick Curtis)

Olivia de Havilland with Patrick Curtis
(Melanie and Beau Wilkes)
(Photo courtesy of Patrick Curtis)

Bonus Material
Book Club Section, Interviews, and Extras

Book Discussion Questions

1. Compare Margaret Mitchell's great-grandfather Philip Fitzgerald with the fictional Gerald O'Hara, father of Scarlett O'Hara.

2.. In what ways do Melanie and Ashley represent the Old South? Contrast this with Rhett and Scarlett.

3. Discuss the male-female, husband-wife role of the Antebellum South using Ellen and Gerald as the example, and then Ashley and Melanie.

4.. Compare and contrast Margaret Mitchell's husbands Berrien Upshaw and John Marsh, and talk about the traits that each of them have for Rhett Butler and Ashley Wilkes.

5. Throughout the process of producing the movie, Selznick tried to include author Margaret Mitchell as much as possible, but she clearly did not want to be involved. She did answer him about some things, but when it came to certain characters, her lack of wanting to discuss them drew a wedge between author and producer. If you were Margaret Mitchell and had written the successful *Gone With The Wind*, would you have been involved with the movie and what would be your reasoning?

6. How do the words 'honor' and 'honorable' fit into the book?

7. Discuss how the treatment of the black race differed in the movie and book. Do you think it should have been done any differently than it was in either the book or film? How do you think the movie would be different if it had been written today?

8. Talk about how "mothers" played a role, both in Margaret Mitchell's real life and others who were real people as well as in the story.

9. Talk about power, money and greed and the roles they all play in the book and movie.

10. Discuss the negatives and positives of what Scarlett did to save Tara throughout the book.

To help get your discussions going...

1. Philip Fitzgerald, like Gerald O'Hara came from Ireland and had a love for the land. They both had sons who had died and ended up raising daughters. They both liked to ride horses and jump fences as well as play poker. Both men died in horse accidents.

2. Melanie and Ashley start the movie full of life and they both slowly die, just as the Old South did. Ashley seems to lose his way. At the end of the story, Rhett Butler tells Scarlett Melanie never had any strength, she had heart. The South did not have the strength that the North had as far as military, but they had heart. Rhett Butler and Scarlett represented the "New South" most of the time.

3. Ellen O'Hara seemed to run the O'Hara household. She was strong and did what she felt she had to. When she found out the Overseer had been having relations with Emmy Slattery and was her baby's father, she told her husband to fire him; and he did. When Ashley told Scarlett he did not want to work at the saw mill in Atlanta, Melanie told him he should do it and he listened to his wife.

4. When comparing Rhett Butler and Ashley Wilkes to the author's real-life husbands Berrien Upshaw and John Marsh, one thing is clear, there are bits and pieces of Upshaw in Butler, and Wilkes has some of Marsh's qualities. For example, Rhett Butler has the daring, 'bad boy' image that Berrien Upshaw had and both men had shady ways of making a living. (Upshaw was a bootlegger, Butler a blockade runner.) At times, though, Rhett Butler took on some of the tender qualities that John Marsh had, and like Marsh was always there for Margaret Mitchell, so Rhett Butler showed his unceasing devotion to Scarlett. She gave John Marsh's blonde hair, love of books, and devotion to his wife to Ashley Wilkes.

5. Margaret Mitchell had an aunt who was threatening to sue her and she had other relatives who knew that there was at least one diary or scrapbook out there with many of the same stories that she put in her novel. Mitchell might have gone to them and shared the experience and it may have helped bring them to her side. Most authors in her situation would have wanted some say in the movie

to protect (as Paul Rabwin said) "the franchise."

6. Honor—this is what kept Ashley from growing as a character. He always did the honorable thing. He married Melanie (because 'Wilkes always marry their cousins') went to war when he was supposed to, even though he did not think the South could win; he helped Scarlett with the sawmill when Melanie told her he should.

7. Many blacks do not like the way the blacks were portrayed in the movie and do not want to pass the portrayal on to their children. They don't want the next generation to see 'Mammy' and Pork used as comedic characters in the book and movie. David O. Selznick worked very hard to make the movie in a way that would be respectful towards the blacks yet accurately portray history. He brought in the pre-cursors to the NAACP to look at it and work with his staff to ensure fair treatment. Still, history has been recorded in many ways, and it is a difficult subject to accurately portray because there were two sides to the story. Margaret Mitchell wrote about the side she knew about.

8. Margaret Mitchell's mother died when she was a teenager. She was not able to get there in time before she died. Though she may not have had a close relationship with her in life, she glamorized her relationship after she died. Her first husband, Berrien Upshaw's mother also died during the same time period as Mitchell's.

   Scarlett O'Hara's mother died right before the teenager was able to get back to Tara. When Scarlett got there her father had lost his mind, unable to cope with his grief. According to writings by Margaret Mitchell's brother, Stephens, their father also took his wife's death so hard that he was not able to face reality for a time.

9. Power, money and greed were recurring themes both in Margaret Mitchell's life and in the characters she created. In real life, Annie Fitzgerald, Mitchell's grandmother was so obsessed with power and money that she lost her husband over it. In the novel, it caused Scarlett O'Hara to steal her sister's fiancé and marry Frank Kennedy. Power is shown in many characters, and the opposite applies for some who have no interest or use for such things.

There were times that the love of money, and power turned out to be good things as they gave strength to those who wanted it. Scarlett O'Hara may have never made it had she not had that poignant scene in the radish field where she said, "With God as my witness, I'll never go hungry again!" She decided right then and there she would do everything in her power to get their money back and that was a recurring theme throughout the book.

10. Scarlett vowed to do whatever it took and in the process she hurt a lot of people. On the other hand, there were so many people who may have died of starvation and though her actions were unscrupulous, she was able to get food for her family and save Tara so they would have a place to live.

A Conversation With Sally Tippett Rains
How did you get the idea to do this book?

I was told about a chapter in the book, *A Dance With Deception*, by Charles Colson, the story of a couple named Rhett Turnipseed and Emelyn Louise Hannon, and according to this story Margaret Mitchell had used this couple when she came up with her idea for Scarlett and Rhett. After reading it, I realized the story being told was about what would have happened after Scarlett left Rhett. According to the story, this couple was very star-crossed. What if it were true? What if she did get the idea for the 'star-crossed lovers' from this couple? It really piqued my curiosity.

I contacted Colson through his Prison Ministries and found out that he got the information for that chapter from an article which appeared in the *Washington Times*. When I checked the internet and found that many ministers around the world had used this story in their sermons after reading Colson's book. I decided to research that story and as I did, I stumbled onto more people and pretty soon I was writing a book. The funny thing was about a year into my research, the book *Rhett Butler's People* came out and almost the exact same story was told again in the Washington Times. It was written by the managing editor at the time so one would assume he'd gotten it somewhere.

How did you find Rhett Turnipseed's great-grandson?

Genealogy! My sister-in-law, Sharon Bedgood, is a whiz with Ancestry. com and she, along with another researcher helped me immensely with my genealogical research. We got to a certain point and then just started looking in the phone book.

How did you locate Mark Rabwin and Paul Rabwin, sons of Marcella Rabwin the Executive Assistant to *Gone With The Wind* Producer David O. Selznick?

I have some advantages that Margaret Mitchell did not have, specifically the computer and the internet! I wondered if Marcella had any sons or daughters so I "Googled" the word "Rabwin." An entry came up for a high school reunion at Beverly Hills High School. It said, "For more information contact Mark Rabwin." I e-mailed him and sure enough it was her son. Mark was eager to talk about his mother, and he referred me to his brother Paul, a Hollywood Producer.

They could not have been nicer, sharing many stories about their mother with me. Because their mother worked with Selznick and their father was doctor to the stars they grew up around a lot of famous people. There were stories of having Danny Kaye entertain at a childhood birthday party and growing up around so many interesting and famous people. I enjoyed our phone conversations so much I could have talked to them both all day. They were both so kind and took time out of their busy schedules to explain things I didn't know.

Were you a fan of Gone With The Wind before you started your book?

Yes, I had read the book once and seen the movie several times when I started the project. In the past several years I have watched it many more times and read it three more times. I'm probably not very much fun to watch it with because I've watched it so much I can quote much of it.

As a child I loved the hooped skirts and the fun everyone was having at the barbecue. I remember the lovely colors standing out in my mind and the beginning was so spectacular. We could only see it on special times because it was before the days of videos and DVDs. I watched it with my family. I pictured my sisters and I wearing fancy dresses and hats to go with them. I think the enormity of the Civil War was lost on me. As an adult I can see why some people find the movie offensive. That was a terrible time in our nation's history –which thank goodness is history. It happened so many years ago. But the vivid descriptions Margaret Mitchell used to tell her story, and the great acting and timelessness of the movie still make it one of the most amazing books and movies ever made. It truly is a classic.

What was your purpose in writing the book?

As I said, it all started out with the initial curiosity about Rhett Turnipseed and Emelyn Hannon, but when I actually found a guy named Rhett Turnipseed whose grandfather had ties to Clayton, County Georgia I could not stop myself. As a fan *of Gone With The Wind* I had read that Margaret Mitchell denied she based her characters on real people. But as I went along, I realized she wasn't lying, she was merely answering the question as she was asked. She may not have based Scarlett on her grandmother, but it sure seems like she put parts of her grandmother in the character. I gained a great respect for Margaret Mitchell as I worked on this project. Once I got into my research I had so much fun finding out about Mitchell and her family and looking at the family scrapbook. It was amazing to compare the real-life happenings to the book and movie. I guess I wrote it for all the people like me who enjoy things like this.

What was the most amazing thing you found out in your research?

The most exciting was when I traveled to Georgia to meet Marie Nygren, whose mother was Margaret Mitchell's cousin and friend. Marie said she had the crucifix that hung in Philip Fitzgerald's (Margaret Mitchell's great-grandfather's) house. According to Fitzgerald Family lore, General Sherman took one look at the cross and instructed his men not to destroy the home; his wife was Catholic and it reminded him of her.

Marie was a little late to our meeting because she could not find the cross. She did find a few things which she threw in a bag which she handed me and said I was welcome to look through. As I went through the pile of things haphazardly thrown into a grocery bag my eyes spotted a scrapbook. I opened it and there they were: The two elderly aunts, Aunt Mamie and Aunt Sis, who I had read so much about. They weren't old, they were young ladies in the pictures which were from the 1800s. These were the aunts that Margaret had visited so many times and from whom she had learned so much about the Civil War. Then I saw a picture of Rural Home, the home in which Philip Fitzgerald had lived and raised Margaret Mitchell's grandmother, Annie Fitzgerald Stephens.

This scrapbook has been in a box all these years and no one has seen it. I could not believe my eyes!

But the most amazing thing was the handwritten note from Marie's grandmother— a first cousin to Margaret Mitchell—that not only mentioned *Gone With The Wind* but said many of the stories were based on family happenings; and she went on to tell about them. She said she wanted the story told! I was shaking when I saw all of this. It was like someone was telling me, 'It's OK to tell this story'.

What were your overall thoughts on writing this book?

It was three of the most pleasurable years of my recent life. I was so fortunate to meet Herb Bridges, who at one time owned one of the largest (or maybe THE largest) *Gone With The Wind* collections in the world. Herb introduced me to many people who helped me along the way. Dr. Christopher Sullivan also offered valuable assistance and helped me get in touch with some of the actors. The actors were very nice to me and spent quite a bit of time talking about their memories of *Gone With The Wind* with me. It was all a big thrill.

Can you imagine being given a big movie star like Ann Rutherford's home phone number and calling it and she answers the phone? There was no going through an agent or manager. I called her and she answered. Though she is kind enough to make appearances on behalf of *Gone With The Wind*, Ann was a big star in Hollywood, and the role of Carreen O'Hara (Scarlett's sister) was one of her smallest roles, although maybe the most memorable. She remembered fondly that Louis B. Mayer did not even want her to do the movie at the time and told her it was a "nothing part." After she cried, he let her do it; and as she likes to say, "that 'nothing part' has turned my 'golden years' into platinum!"

At first Ann asked me what were my qualifications for writing the book? After all, she was using movie lingo and I was asking her to explain it, so she knew I was not an expert on the movies. I thought about it and realized. My qualification for writing this book is I have a natural curiosity, I love to do research, and I am a writer! This is my 11th book. That's what I do.

She, after all was no expert on the Civil War, however she did a beautiful job of playing the daughter of a plantation owner. Why? Because she is an actress, and a very talented one at that. Every time we watch the movie, we get to see the wonderful acting, fantastic costumes and the vivid Technicolor pictures. Margaret Mitchell was the writer who gave us the gift of *Gone With The Wind* and aren't we all so lucky that those actors and actresses led by David O. Selznick gave us a second gift: the movie.

Here we are all these years later and we're still talking about *Gone With The Wind*.

Conversations With Some Of The Actors

The movie *Gone With The Wind* celebrated its 70th Anniversary in 2009 so if an actor was a baby in the movie he or she would be at least seventy years old. Unfortunately many of the stars have passed away, but some of those who remain make appearances on behalf of the movie. They share their stories and fans once again feel young as they remember the first time they read the book or saw the movie.

It is interesting to hear the stories of *Gone With The Wind* from those who were children or teenagers at the time because there is a whole different perspective than what has been previously written. Emphasis has always been on Vivien Leigh and Clark Gable, but there were many other interesting things going on with the other actors.

When this book was started, Alicia Rhett (born February 1, 1915)— who played India Wilkes— was the oldest living actress from *Gone With The Wind* and Fred Crane was the oldest living male, but he passed away in August of 2008. Olivia de Havilland (born July 1, 1916) was the only one remaining from Selznick's top five characters (Scarlett, Rhett, Melanie, Ashley, and Mammy.) Olivia lived many years in Paris. Those who knew her personally described her as a lovely, vibrant woman still enjoying her life. She loves music, and had live music at her 90th birthday party in Paris. In recent years she has been spending more time in Los Angeles.

Fred Crane's last public appearance, just a month before his death, was at the Marietta Gone With The Wind Museum Scarlett On The Square in Marietta, Georgia. My son Mike and I got to meet Fred and spend time talking to him. He talked about his fond memories *of Gone With The Wind*. It was there he met George Reeves, who went on to play *Superman*, on television, and the two hit it off as the Tarleton brothers and friends in real-life. Fred was an inexperienced actor at the time, as was George. Director George Cukor spent time working with the two spirited young men. George Reeves was the best man at Fred Crane's first wedding. Fred talked with enthusiasm about a book he and his wife Terry Lynn were working on, joking just having five wives gave him enough to put in a book! He also talked about his days in radio. He taught voice lessons and was an announcer for many years for KFAC, a widely respected classical music station in Los Angeles.

Alicia Rhett does not do the public appearances and tout *Gone With The Wind*. Instead, she lives a quiet life as an artist in South Carolina. I know someone who went up to her house and actually got her autograph but that is as close as I got to her, though efforts were made in her hometown of Charleston.

One of the most popular actors who at the time this book came out was still making the *Gone With The Wind* events is Ann Rutherford. When she found out David Selznick wanted her to do *Gone With The Wind* she was so excited, but her studio boss, Louis B. Mayor almost kept her from doing it. Once he finally agreed, she was thrilled because she had read the book and loved it. When she saw the expensive costumes and the extent to which Walter Plunkett the costume designer went she could not believe it.

"I had done Westerns, and for those we just put on our hoops and then the muslin petticoat and the dress and that was it," she said. "Here they were endowing us with one petticoat after another, each with real lace on it and ribbons run through it and little bows. I knew they were expensive. When David Selznick came in to see how they looked on me I said 'Mr. Selznick you've spent too much money on these characters' clothes. In the book it says they don't let Carreen stay up to go to the ball...' [Selznick said] young lady, your father is one of the most important plantation owners of the South, and this is the way Mrs. O'Hara dressed her daughters, so you better rethink about that!"

Ann really liked David Selznick and one of the reasons was that he was so thorough about everything.

Cammie King (Scarlett and Rhett's daughter Bonnie Blue Butler), remembers how much she liked her costumes. As a child she loved prancing around the studio in her little outfits, including a muff which had a real, live kitten in it.

She wrote *Bonnie Blue Butler, a Gone With The Wind Memoir.* which contains memories of *Gone With The Wind* and about how glad she was she got to live a 'normal' life. Cammie did not become a child actor; that was her only role besides being in the 1942 Disney animated film, Bambi. She was the voice of young 'Faline' the deer.

Though several actors would play Beau Wilkes, the son of Melanie and Ashley Wilkes, Mickey Kuhn had the distinction of being the one who said the lines and got the on-screen credit. The others were babies and he was seven years old. During the times Melanie (Olivia de Havilland) was well, Beau was a baby. At the end of the movie the character had grown to seven years old, but Melanie was dying, so she was in the bedroom and he was out in the hall with Ashley. Years later he again met Olivia and told her that he played Beau and they had their pictures taken together.

"I was seven years old at the time I got the part," said Mickey. "Beau was the son of Ashley and Melanie, there were four of us in the show, the infant, the baby, the toddler and me. I had the speaking lines. It was fun."

He may have thought it was fun seventy years later but being a little kid at the time he told his mother he didn't want to try out. In the end he was glad he did the movie and afterwards something happen to him that he never forgot.

"At the end of the movie when we were getting ready to go home, my mother and I were summoned by Mr. Selznick to his office. Well, my mother panicked, she turned as white as a sheet, because to get called into the producer's office!—I started shaking because I knew my career was over at age seven! So we went there and Marcella Rabwin, let us in. "This gentlemen got up from his seat and struck the classic pose, and Mr. Selznick said, "Do you know Joseph Cotten?' to my mother. My mother just about passed out again over that! Joseph Cotten was an idol in those days. Mr. Selznick congratulated me and said I did a good job in the movie. He said, 'To show how much I appreciated your work, I want to give you a gift. It was a 16 millimeter projector and movie camera and he said 'this is so you can pursue your movie career'. I could not believe it."

Mickey Kuhn continued acting and was a child actor appearing in more than thirty movies in the 1930s and '40s. He won the Golden Boot Award in 2005 honoring the Kids of the West, but he always felt the highlight of his career was getting to work with Vivien Leigh in the two movies for which she won her Academy Awards.

Patrick Curtis played Beau as a baby.

"I come from an entertainment background. It was something we did. I worked right after that as baby Nicky on *Thin Man*; I was Nick and Nora Charles son. I don't think I worked for quite a while after that. It was not my parents' intention for me to go into acting.

Patrick, who was once married to Raquel Welch, and worked as production assistant on *Leave It To Beaver*, was always interested in Westerns. His dad worked at Republic Studios and on Saturdays all the Western stars would come to his house to play cards. He produces The Golden Boot Awards and produced a DVD Western called *Meanwhile Back At The Ranch* featuring clips of many of the old cowboys.

One of the biggest surprises the author got while writing this book was finding out that Greg Giese, who played infant Beau (and infant Bonnie), lived right across the river from her. He had spent most of his adult life in California and up until the editing process of this book he had not been located. By a stroke of luck she was given his phone number and when they realized how close they were, they met for lunch.

"I work at Fairmont Race Track," said Giese. Fairmont offers Thoroughbred and Harness racing in Collinsville, Illinois. "I also enjoy hanging out with my golfing buddies."

Fans continue to come out whenever there is a *Gone With The Wind* event and it is a big thrill for them to meet the actors. The movie is still selling like crazy and the book has gone into another printing. Each new anniversary of *Gone With The Wind* brings the opportunity for the fans to celebrate the masterpiece it really is.

Author Recommendations

Did This Book Rekindle Your Interest In
Gone With The Wind?
Then re-read it and watch the movie.

The Author Recommends These Books You May Not Know About (others are listed in the bibliography):

Barnes, Tom. *Doc Holliday's Road To Tombstone*: Xlibris Press, 2005

Bridges, Herb and Boodman, Terry C. *Gone With The Wind, The Definitive Illustrated History of the Book, The Movie And The Legend.* New York, Fireside by Simon and Schuster, 1989

Rabwin, Marcella: *Yes, Mr. Selznick, Recollections of Hollywood's Golden*

Era, Pittsburgh, PA, Dorrance Publishing, 1999.

O'Connell, David. *The Irish Roots of Margaret Mitchell's Gone With The Wind:* Decatur, GA, Claves and Petry, Ltd., 1996.

Coker, Clent. *Barnsley Gardens at Woodlands, The Illustrious Dream.* Atlanta, The Julia Publishing Company, 2000.

And just out…King, Cammie. **Bonnie Blue Butler, A Gone With The Wind Memoir, 2009.**

Fun Newsletter About *Gone With The Wind*

The Scarlett Letter (www.thescarlettletter.com)

Be Sure To Visit…

The Road To Tara Museum, Jonesboro, GA- Features part of the collection of Herb Bridges.

Mary Mac's Tearoom, Atlanta, GA- One of Margaret Mitchell's favorites

The Margaret Mitchell House, Atlanta, GA

The Marietta Gone With The Wind Museum, Scarlett On The Square, Marietta, GA- Features the collection of Dr. Christopher Sullivan

Gone With The Wind Memories, Plant City, FL

Scarlett O'Hardy's Bed and Breakfast, Jefferson, TX

The Inn at Serenbe, B&B, Palmetto, GA

The Holliday-Dorsey-Fife Museum, Fayetteville, GA

Coming Soon- Tara Home, Morrow, GA
Cadiz, OH Birthplace of Clark Gable

To order prints of the picture on the title page of this book: www.WriteAsRains.NET

And be watching for the television documentary based on *The Making Of A Mastepiece*.

New from Creative Book Publishers International….

INSTANT REPLAY—
the day that changed sports forever—Written by its inventor, Tony Verna. On December 7, 1963, TV and sports history was made with the first 'instant replay'.

THE GLENN MILLER CONSPIRACY The Never-Before-Told True Story of His Life—and Death, by Award-Winning Author Hunton Downs, Lt. Col. US Army, —Ret., a former Government Agent, it reveals The Never-Before-Told Story of Glenn Miller's Secret Life as a Spy for the Allies in World War II.

WOMEN: DECODE THE LAW OF ATTRACTION–*The Definitive Coaching Book For Women, "How To Deal With Your Negative 'Inner Voice' and Attract What You Really Want,"* written by Orly Katz, MBA, a leading international expert in Women's Coaching and holder of the highly sought-after accredited coaching diploma from the ICF (International Coaching Federation) and graduate of the prestigious *College of Executive Coaching* and the *Life Coaching Institute. FREE WORKBOOK INCLUDED.*

THE MAKING OF "THE LORDS OF FLATBUSH" — **the fascinating, humorous and revealing behind-the-scenes story of the classic film that launched the careers of Sylvester Stallone and Henry Winkler**–by the film's writer and director Stephen Verona, telling the amazing, fascinating and funny saga of this cult-classic, low-cost independent film that launched the careers of *Sylvester Stallone and Henry Winkler* (the "Fonz") and became (based on cost to return) one of the highest financial-returning films of all time.

AWA MARU–**Titanic of Japan**-The True Story of the ill-fated ship carrying more than 2,000 Japanese women and children who had been given safe passage back to Japan by the Allies in World War II, but who died when the ship was accidentally torpedoed by an American Submarine. AVAILABLE NOW!

GET THE JOB YOU WANT (The Interview Scriptbook—What To Say and How To Say It)—The definitive book on how the get your first job-or ANY job-authored by [Lawrence C. Bassett, CMC, one of the country's leading management consultants.

10 Academy Awards
for
Gone With The Wind
(8 regular, 2 honorary)

1. Best Picture— Selznick International Pictures (David O. Selznick Producer)
2. Best Director— Victor Fleming
3. Best Actress— Vivien Leigh
4. Best Writing, Screenplay— Sidney Howard
5. Best Supporting Actress— Hattie McDaniel
6. Best Cinematography, Color—Ernest Haller and Ray Rennahan
7. Best Film Editing— Hal Kern
8. Best Art Direction— Lyle Wheeler, James Newcom
9. Honorary Award— William Cameron Menzies (Outstanding Use of Color)
10. Irving Thalberg Award— David O. Selznick

Plus Five Additional Nominations:

Best Actor—Clark Gable

Best Supporting Actress— Olivia de Havilland (lost to Hattie McDaniel)

Best Special Effects— Fred Albin, Jack Cosgrove, Arthur Johns

Best Music, Original Score— Max Steiner (lost to Herbert Stothart, Wizard of Oz)

Best Sound Recording— Thomas T. Moulton (Samuel Goldwyn Studio Sound Dept.)

Bibliography

Books:

Allen, Patrick ed., *Margaret Mitchell, Reporter*: Athens, Ga.: Hill Street Press, 2000

Barnes, Tom. *Doc Holliday's Road To Tombstone*: Xlibris Press, 2005

Bridges, Herb and Boodman, Terry C.: *Gone With The Wind, Screenplay*, Simon & Schuster, 1989

Bridges, Herb: *Frankly My Dear, Gone With The Wind Memorabilia*, Mercer University Press, Macon, GA 1995

Bridges, Herb and Pratt, William. *Scarlett Fever, The Ultimate Pictorial Treasury of Gone With The Wind*. New York, Collier Books, 1977.

Bridges, Herb and Boodman, Terry C. *Gone With The Wind, The Definitive Illustrated History of the Book, The Movie And The Legend*. New York, Fireside by Simon and Schuster, 1989

Coker, Clent. *Barnsley Gardens at Woodlands, The Illustrious Dream*. Atlanta, The Julia Publishing Company, 2000.

Craig, Donald. *Rhett Butler's People*: New York, St. Martin's Press, 2007.

Duncan, Rev. Watson A. *Twentieth Century Sketches Of the South Carolina Conference, ME Church, South*. Columbia, SC, The State Company, 1914

Edwards, Anne. *The Road To Tara, The Life of Margaret Mitchell*: New Haven, New York, Ticknor and Fields, 1983.

Edwards, Anne. *Vivien Leigh, A Biography.* New York, Simon and Schuster, 1977.

Eiland, William. *Nashville's Mother Church, The History of the Ryman Auditorium*: Opryland, USA, 1992.

Eskridge, Jane. ed., *Before Scarlett: Girlhood Writings of Margaret Mitchell*: Athens, GA, Hill Street Press, 2000.

Farr, Finis. *Margaret Mitchell of Atlanta, the Author of "Gone With the Wind"*: New York, William Morrow, 1965.

Freer, Debra. *Lost Laysen, Margaret Mitchell, Author of Gone With The Wind*: New York, Scribner, 1996.

Harris, Warren G. *A Biography of Clark Gable*: New York, Harmony Books, 2002.

Harwell, Richard Barksdale. *Gone With The Wind as Book and Film*: Columbia University of South Carolina Press, 1983.

Harwell, Richard. *Margaret Mitchell's Gone With The Wind Letters, 19361–949*: New York, Macmillan, 1976.

Harwell, Richard. *White Columns in Hollywood, Reports From the GWTW Sets by Susan Myrick*: Macon, GA, Mercer University Press, 1982.

Jackson, Carlton. *Hattie: the Life of Hattie McDaniel*, Madison Books, 1990

McCullough, David. *Mornings on Horseback: The Story of an Extraordinary Family, a Vanished Way of Life and the unique Child Who Became Theodore Roosevelt.* New York, Simon & Schuster.1982.

Mitchell, Margaret. *Gone With The Wind*: New York, Macmillan Company, 1936.

Moore, Joseph Henry Hightower. *The History of Clayton County, Georgia*, ed. Alice Copeland Kilgore, Edith Hanes Smith, and Frances Partridge Tuck. W. H. Wolfe Associates, Roswell, GA, 1983

Morella, Joe and Epstein, Edward Z. *Paulette, The Adventurous Life of Paulette Goddard.* New York, St. Martin's Press, 1985.

O'Connell, David. *The Irish Roots of Margaret Mitchell's Gone With The*

Wind: Decatur, GA, Claves and Petry, Ltd., 1996.

Peacock, Jane Bonner. *Margaret Mitchell: A Dynamo Going To Waste, Letters to Allen Edee.* Atlanta, Peachtree Publishers, Ltd., 1985

Phillips, Gene: *George Cukor:* Chicago, Loyola University Press, 1982.

Pyron, Darden Asbury. *Southern Daughter:* Oxford Press, Oxford, OH, 1991

Rabwin, Marcella: *Yes, Mr. Selznick, Recollections of Hollywood's Golden Era,* Pittsburgh, PA, Dorrance Publishing, 1999.

Roberts, Gary L. *Doc Holliday, The Life and Legend.* New York, John Wiley & Sons, Inc., 2006

Sragow, Michael. *Victor Fleming: An American Movie Master,* Pantheon, 2008

Spano, Sara. *I Could've Written Gone With The Wind, But Cousin Margaret Beat Me To It.* McNaughton & Gunn, 1990.

Spignesi, Stephen J. *The Official Gone With The Wind Companion,* New York, Plume by Penguin Group. 1993.

Tanner, Karen Holliday. *Doc Holliday: A Family Portrait.* Oklahoma City, Oklahoma University Press, 2002

Taylor, Helen. *Scarlett's Women, Gone With The Wind And Its Female Fans:* Rutgers University Press, NJ, 1989.

Thompson, E.I. Buddy. *Madam Belle Brezing,* Buggy Whip Press, Kentucky, 1983.

Tornabene, Lyn. *Long Live The King, A Biography of Clark Gable:* NY, NY, Pocket Books, 1976.

Vanderbilt, Cornelius Jr., *Queen of the Golden Age: The Fabulous Grace Wilson Vanderbilt.* New York: McGraw Hill Book Company, Inc., 1956.

Vertrees, Alan David: *Selznick's Vision: Gone With The Wind And Hollywood Filmmaking:* Austin, TX, University of Texas Press, 1997.

Walker, Marianne. *Margaret Mitchell and John Marsh: The Love Story*

Behind Gone With The Wind. Atlanta, Peachtree Publishing, 1993.

Watts, Jill. *Hattie McDaniel, Black Ambition, White Hollywood*: New York, Amistad, an imprint of Harper Collins Publishers, 2005.

Magazines or Newspapers

Dixon, Crawford. "The Inside Love Story of Jennifer Jones." Screen and Television Guide, April 1949.

Flahardy, Jason. "Belle Brezing, A Short Biography of Lexington's Most Famous Lady." Audio/Visual Archives, University of Kentucky.

Life Magazine. "Gone With The Wind: Atlanta Premiere Stirs South To Tears and Cheers." Life Magazine 12/25/1939 p.9.

Karson, Robin. "A Garden Designer From Hollywood's Golden Age." Garden Design Magazine, Summer, 1989.

Observer, Athens. "Death of "Ashley Wilkes" (Leslie Howard)." Athens Observer, Athens, GA, June 8, 1995.

Perkerson, Medora Field. Article in Atlanta Journal, Dec. 18, 1949.

Time Magazine. "Gone With the Wind: After 3 Years of Hullabaloo, It Emerges a Great Picture"

Newsweek, 12/25/1939 pg. 262–9;

Wylly Folk St. John article in Dec. 18, 1949 Atlanta Journal Magazine.

Nichols, Katherine. Article in Honolulu Star Bulletin, May 4, 2008.

Radio:

WSB Radio- Medora Field Perkerson-Margaret Mitchell Interview. Portions re-printed with permission from WSB.

Internet Websites and articles:

Archives of Dawson County, by Roadside Georgia, www.roadsidegeorgia.com;

Margaret Mitchell House and Museum, www.gwtw.org/margaretmitchell. html;

New Georgia Encyclopedia, http://www.georgiaencyclopedia.org/nge/Article.jsp?id=h-2566;

Prohibition of Alcohol in the 1920's www.geocities.com/Athens/troy/4399/;

The Civil War and Reconstruction, http://americanhistory.si.edu/presidency/timeline/pres_era/3_656.html;

Atlanta-Fulton Public Library System, Margaret Mitchell and the Atlanta Public Library by Katharine Suttell and Celeste Tibbetts, www.afplweb.com/margaret_mitchell_and_the_public_library.html;

Windsor House Apartments (Crescent Apartments), http://apps.atlantaga.gov/citydir/URBAN/windsor.htm;

The Circuit Riders and the Spread of Early Methodism, Forgotten Word Ministries, http://www.forgottenword.org/circuitriders.html, http://freepages.genealogy.rootsweb.com/~hillsofsalem/bchhis.html;

Rev. Samuel Porter Jones, Etowah Historical Society, http://www.evhsonline.org/people/jones.html

Sequoia Cemetery: Lost But Not Forgotten, By Will Chavez, Cherokee Phoenix And Indian Advocate; http://www.yvwiiusdinvnohii.net/Cherokee/News2003/Jul2003/CPIA%20SequoyahCemetery.htm;

Sequoia High School Website, http://www.sequoyah.k12.ok.us/SHShistory.html;

Into the Wind: Rhett Butler and the Law of War at Sea, University of Texas at Austin Law Library–E-Texts, http://tarlton.law.utexas.edu/lpop/etext/jmlc/jones31.htm;

The Experience Of A Slave In South Carolina by John Andrew Jackson, London: Passmore & Alabaster, Wilson St. Finsbury, 1862, http://docsouth.unc.edu/fpn/jackson/menu.html;

Essay: My Life in the South: Electronic Edition. Stroyer, Jacob, 18491–908, http://docsouth.unc.edu/neh/stroyer85/stroyer85.html;

Civil War Reconstruction, The Travails of Reconstruction, The Goodings Describe Reconstruction in South Carolina, http://memory.loc.gov/learn/features/timeline/civilwar/recon/goodings.html;

The "Real Rhett Butler" Revealed © 1997 by Narwhal Press Inc., http://www.shipwrecks.com/George Trenholm.htm; New Georgia Encyclopedia website www.Newgeorgiaencyclopedia.org, www.genealogymagazine.com; www.mygeorgiagenealogy.com (about Clayton County history).

Gone With The Wind—Finding the Real Margaret Mitchell By Mike McLeod—www.rvfreewheelin.com/gwtw.htm.

Geneology of "Doc" Holliday on Rootsweb.com http://www.rootsweb.com/~kypoc/hollidays/holliday_doc.htm.

www.USMM.org ©1998—2006 U.S. Maritime Service Veterans. You may quote material on this web page as long as you cite American Merchant Marine at War, www.usmm.org, as the source.

Special thanks to these museums:

Road to Tara Museum, Jonesboro, GA; Marietta Gone With the Wind Museum, Scarlett on the Square, Marietta, GA; Holliday-Dorsey-Fife Museum, Fayetteville, GA; Margaret Mitchell House, Atlanta, GA; Clark Gable Foundation, Cadiz, OH.

Some of the people interviewed or consulted for the book:

1. Tom Barnes, Author, historian, PBS Documentary on Georgia's History

2. Michael Barry, Sigma NU, University of Georgia Chapter

3. Faye Bell, GWTW collector and owner of Gone With The Wind Memories Store

4. Anna Blair, *Gone With The Wind* collector

5. Beth Boord , Assistant Dean of Development and Alumni Relations, Vanderbilt Divinity School. Helped with Turnipseed records and questions

6. Ann Boutwell, docent, Margaret Mitchell House

7. Herb Bridges, GWTW author, expert, speaker, and collector

8. Mickey Carroll, Actor, Munchkin in *The Wizard of Oz*, was directed by Victor Fleming

9. Steve Case, State Library of NC in Raleigh, NC

10. Clent Coker, Barnsley Gardens Historian

11. Lilane Covington, played oboe for Max Steiner and performed in the orchestra for Gone With The Wind

12. Phillip Covington, stepson of Lilane Covington who played oboe for Max Steiner and performed in the orchestra for *Gone With The Wind.*

13. Fred Crane, played Brent Tarleton in GWTW

14. Terry Lynn Crane, Fred Crane's wife

15. Patrick Curtis, played Baby Beau in GWTW

16. Abb Dickson, descendent of Dickson family who lived near Fitzgeralds

17. Sarah Dollacker, Communications Manager for Margaret Mitchell House and Museum

18. Patrick Duncan, Clayton County Convention Bureau

19. Nancy Egerton, Berrien Upshaw's half-sister. Upshaw was Mitchell's first husband

20. John Ferrell, owner of Mary Mac's Tearoom one of Margaret Mitchell's favorites

21. Sharon Freed—Oakwood Cemetery where Margaret Mitchell's first husband, Berrien Upshaw is buried

22. Jason Flahardy, AV Archives, University of Kentucky Libraries, research on Belle Brezing-Belle Watling connection

23. Wilma Fowler, the nurse who took care of Margaret Mitchell the night she was hit by the car

24. Julia George, her grandfather Art Felix was a stuntman and friend of Yakima Canutt, the stunt double for Clark Gable in GWTW who also played the Renegade Soldier

25. Alice Hardy, lives in Berrien Upshaw's former house and was a former neighbor who knew the family

26. Bobbie Hardy, GWTW collector and owner Scarlett O'Hardy's Bed and Breakfast

27. Ernie Harwell, Margaret Mitchell's paperboy, his brother Richard Harwell was Margaret's friend and wrote several books about her. Ernie Harwell is a journalist who worked at the Atlanta Constitution and went on to the Baseball Hall of Fame, Broadcasters wing

28. Michael Heimos, Hollywood actor

29. Patrisha Henson, *Gone With The Wind* Collector

30. Karen Holliday Tanner, author, cousin of John Henry 'Doc' Holliday

31. Carlton Jackson, author, Hattie: the Life of Hattie Mc Daniel, University Distinguished Professor (Emeritus), Western Kentucky University

32. Brenda Jenkins, Clayton County research

33. Cammie King Conlon, actress who played Bonnie Blue Butler

34. Mickey Kuhn. Played Beau Wilkes in GWTW

35. Susan Lindsley, niece of Susan Myrick, who was a friend of Mitchell's

36. Janet Lee, from U of GA records department

37. Tim Lee, GWTW Collector

38. John W. Lynch, Holliday-Dorsey-Fife Museum, Museum Manager

39. Kathleen Marcaccio (GWTW Answer Lady)

40. Ric McGee, Executive Director—Ashland Terrace Retirement Home, Lexington, Kentucky— help with Belle Brezing research

41. Ethel McQueary, Lexington, Kentucky, memories of Belle Brezing

42. Katherine Nichols, Honolulu Star Bulletin

43. John Edward Niles, son of famed folk singer John Jacob Niles who knew Belle Brezing, the possible model for Belle Watling

44. Tom Niles, son of John Jacob Niles who knew Belle Brezing

45. Marie Nygren, second cousin once removed to Margaret Mitchell. Daughter of Margaret Lupo, who once owned Mary Macs Tearoom, Margaret Lupo and Margaret Mitchell were cousins

46. David O'Connell, Ph.D., author of *The Irish Roots of Margaret Mitchell*

47. Ron Pen, John Jacob Niles Center for American Music. Author of book on Niles

48. Novella Perrin, Ph.D.—*Gone With The Wind* collector

49. Paul Rabwin, Hollywood producer; son of Marcella Rabwin, executive assistant to David O. Selznick

50. Mark Rabwin, son of Marcella Rabwin, executive assistant to David O. Selznick

51. Robert Rosterman, worked for MGM distribution in Chicago, GWTW enthusiast

52. Dee Rowan, employee, Talmadge estate

53. Billie Sawyer. Billie was referred to me by John Ferrell who owns Mary Macs. She is 90 and is a frequent customer who knew Margaret Mitchell

54. Rennie Sloan, *Gone With The Wind* collector

55. Jeff Smith, Ph.D., History Professor, Lindenwood University, Civil War expert

56. Mary Lucy Spano, former daughter-in-law of Sara Spano, Margaret Mitchell's cousin who wrote the book: *I Could've Written Gone With The Wind, But Cousin Margaret Beat Me To It.*

57. Michael Sragow, author of *Victor Fleming: An American Movie Master*

58. Dr. Don Stokes, "Tara" Development

59. Dr. Christopher Sullivan, *Gone With The Wind* Collector

60. Connie Sutherland, Marietta *Gone With The Wind* Museum, Scarlett on the Square

61. Sophia Thomas, Jonesboro resident

62. Gene Talmadge, son and grandson of two GA governors

63. The Rev. Melvin Tinker, Vicar of St John Newland Church in England

64. Denise Tucker, *Gone With The Wind (But Not Forgotten)* Blog

65. Rhett Turnipseed, research on his ancestor, Rhett Turnipseed I who according to The Washington Times and Charles Colson's book *A Dance With Deception*, may have been part of the inspiration for Margaret Mitchell's star-crossed lovers

66. Saundra Voter, helped Sara Spano type her book, friend of Margaret Mitchell's cousin

67. Ann Walker, in Doc Holliday's family tree

68. Elizabeth (Lib) Walker, a fourth cousin of Doc Holliday's who attended the GWTW Premiere

69. Marianne Walker- author of *Margaret Mitchell and John Marsh The Love Story Behind Gone With The Wind*

70. Robert Warren, *Gone With The Wind* collector, Margaret Mitchell House volunteer

71. Charles Whittemore- Assistant Athletic Director for the University of Georgia, research on Mitchell's first husband, Berrien Upshaw

72. Debbie Whittemore, relative of friend of Margaret Mitchell's family. (Harper descendent)

73. John Wiley, Jr. Editor of The Scarlett Letter, Newsletter for GWTW fans and collectors

74. James Kemper Millard, CTA, President/ CEO of the Lexington History Museum

Others who were consulted:

Wesley Chenault, Kenan Research Center, Atlanta History Center, Atlanta, GA

Betsy Rix, Kenan Research Center, Atlanta History Center, Atlanta, GA

Jason Flahardy, Special Collections, University of Kentucky, Lexington, KY

Connie Sutherland, Marietta Gone With The Wind Museum

Sharon Bedgood, genealogy researcher

Voncille Bush, genealogy researcher

Carolyn Cary, Fayette County official historian for over 25 years

Steve Case, State Library of NC in Raleigh, NC

Gianina Ferraiuolo, Nashville Public Library, research department

Keith Hernandez, Civil War enthusiast

Rena Hoyt Hasse, artist

Gloria Jones, Turnipseed story

Pat Knox, location research, Mississippi

Cesar Milan, legal

Rob Rains, editorial consulting

Carolyn Roth, legal

Patricia Sleade, proofreading

Margie and Jack Tippett, consulting, proofreading

Jan Wenk, genealogy consultant

And…Chris Arehndt, Kathy Bosch, Debra Bryant, Jo Carter, Robert Crow, Keith Dodel, Sean Dodel, Marian Farmer, Alice Webb Caviness Hardy, Barbara Hathaway, Kristi Hesse, and the Marietta Country Club, Dr. Debra Peppers, Joanie Protzel, Joel Reese, Rennie Sloan, Therese Syberg, Sophia Thomas, Annie Ruffin Webb, Corinne Weiss, Barb Touchette Wills, Christina Wolf

Who's Who—Real Or Fictional?

Real—From Margaret Mitchell's Life or Other	Fictional Characters Created By Margaret Mitchell
Philip and Eleanor (Ellen) Fitzgerald	Gerald and Ellen O'Hara
Their daughters-Annie, Agnes, Mary, Sarah Isabelle, Adelle, Catherine (Katie) (Son died in infancy)	O'Hara daughters- Katie Scarlett, Suellen and Carreen (Son died in infancy)
Mary and Sarah - Margaret Mitchell's great aunts (They ended up raising several of their siblings' children)	Aunt Pittypat-Melanie's aunt who raised her
Annie Fitzgerald Stephens' children, Maybelle, Eugenia, Edith, Eleanor, Anna, and and one son, John.	Scarlett's children- Eugenia Victoria (Bonnie), Ella Lorena (not in movie), Wade (not in the movie).
Catherine's daughter- Lucille with the scrapbook Maybelle is a first cousin to Lucille. Margaret Mitchell is a second cousin to Lucille's daughter Margaret Lupo (Margaret Lupo's daughter, Marie Nygren is the fourth generation down from Philip & Eleanor Fitzgerald the great-great grandparents)	
Margaret Mitchell to Marie Nygren -second cousins (once removed) Lucille to Margaret Mitchell -first cousins (once removed)	
Sister Melanie (Philip Fitzgerald's niece, Mattie Holliday)	Melanie Hamilton (Cousin of the Wilkes Family)
John Henry "Doc" Holliday – Sister Melanie's cousin and close friend, some say love interest	Melanie married her cousin Ashley Wilkes

Other Real People Who May Have Contributed

Real	Fictional Characters
Belle Brezing, the famous madam from Lexington, KY	Belle Watling
Lon and Al Harper, red headed twins from Clayton County	Brent and Stuart Tarleton, red headed twins
Crawfords- friends of the Fitzgeralds	Wilkes daughters the same age as Fitzgeralds
Harper Family, friends of the Fitzgeralds	Tarleton Family, friend of the O'Haras
Possible Star-Crossed Lover Connection: Rhett Turnipseed Emelyn Louise Hannon	Possible inspiration Rhett Butler / Scarlett O'Hara
Margaret Mitchell's Husbands: Berrien Upshaw	Some saw some of his characteristics in Rhett
John Marsh	Some saw some of his characteristics in Ashley
Locations- Rural Home, Fitzgerald plantation	Tara, O'Hara plantation
Young girl shot Yankee on the stairs (Crawford)	In *Gone With The Wind* it happened at the O'Hara's
Made dresses from curtains (Crawford)	In *Gone With The Wind* it at Tara

Fitzgerald-Stephens-Mitchell Family Tree

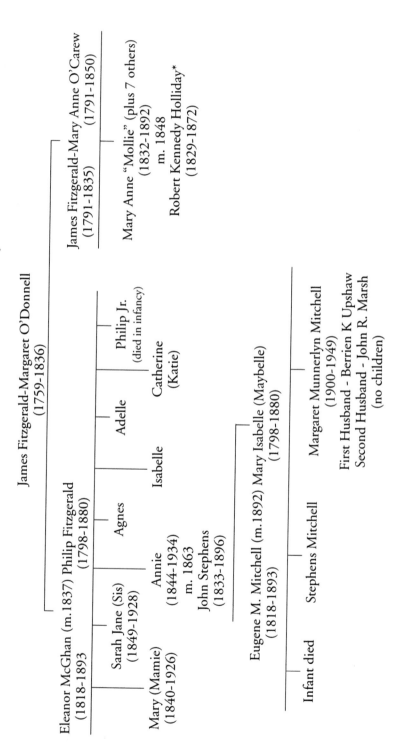

Doc Holliday Family Connection to Fitzgerald Family

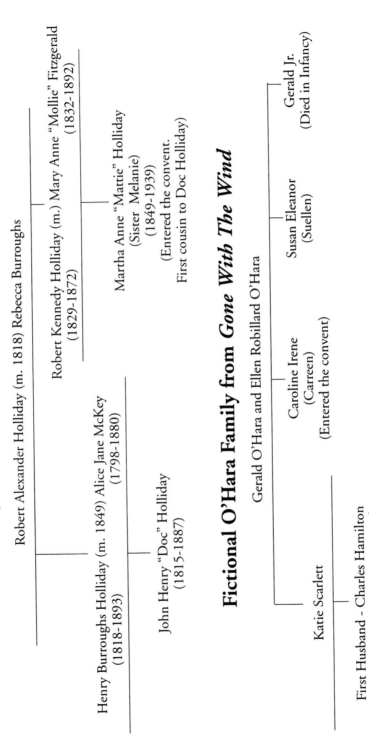

Robert Alexander Holliday (m. 1818) Rebecca Burroughs

Robert Kennedy Holliday (m.) Mary Anne "Mollie" Fitzgerald
(1829-1872) (1832-1892)

Martha Anne "Mattie" Holliday
(Sister Melanie)
(1849-1939)
(Entered the convent.
First cousin to Doc Holliday)

Henry Burroughs Holliday (m. 1849) Alice Jane McKey
(1818-1893) (1798-1880)

John Henry "Doc" Holliday
(1815-1887)

Fictional O'Hara Family from *Gone With The Wind*

Gerald O'Hara and Ellen Robillard O'Hara

Gerald Jr.
(Died in Infancy)

Susan Eleanor
(Suellen)

Caroline Irene
(Carreen)
(Entered the convent)

Katie Scarlett

First Husband - Charles Hamilton
Second Husband - Frank Kennedy
Third Husband - Rhett Butler

INDEX

H

Melanie Hamilton 11, 118
Pittypat Hamilton 115
Emelyn Louise Hannon 42, 43, 50
Alice Hardy 60
Bobbie Hardy 281, 282, 283
Harper family 117, 118, 120, 126
Ernie Harwell 7, 79, 163, 165, 273,
    276, 285, 286, 291
Richard Harwell 6, 156, 158, 165, 187,
    207, 276, 285, 286
Hays Code 178, 263, 264
Michael Heimos 180
Clifford Henry 25, 27, 71, 76, 293
Doc Holliday 124, 136, 138, 139, 140,
    143, 144, 146, 147, 187, 188
Mattie Holliday 136, 138, 139, 147,
    188
Melanie Holliday 144, 147
Holliday family 98, 136, 143
Leslie Howard 183, 196, 207, 208, 211,
    246, 247, 248, 293
Sidney Howard 186, 187, 194, 204,
    213, 214, 264, 293

I

Thomas Ince 167, 178, 200, 248
Influenza epidemic 26, 59, 60

J

Battle of Jonesboro 34, 40, 108, 123,
    124, 125, 126, 128, 129, 264
Bessie Berry Jordan 6, 10, 221
Victor Jory 213, 235, 248

K

Frank Kennedy 13, 29, 86, 88, 115,
    128, 132, 134, 135, 213, 255

Lucille Stephens Kennon 17, 21, 35, 36,
    40, 55, 99, 101, 110, 112, 114,
    131, 147, 159, 162
Evelyn Keyes 170, 211, 233, 248, 249
Cammie King 81, 193, 203, 209, 210,
    211, 229, 231, 239, 252, 282
Mickey Kuhn 182, 210, 211, 212, 229,
    230, 233, 239, 242, 243, 252,
    259, 283
Wilbur Kurtz 129, 174, 176, 186, 190,
    191, 216, 223, 224, 275, 276

L

Harold Latham 82, 152, 297
Robert E. Lee 113
Tim Lee 81, 277
Vivien Leigh 5, 51, 171, 181, 182, 183,
    185, 195, 197, 203, 204, 205,
    207, 208, 210, 211, 216, 217,
    230, 231, 244, 249, 250, 251,
    254, 256, 270, 271, 272, 274,
    275
Carole Lombard 175, 183, 184, 185,
    208, 212, 245, 246, 271, 273,
    275
Margaret Lupo 29, 35, 40, 289
John Lynch 100, 111, 116, 126, 130,
    138, 139, 140, 144, 145, 150,
    155, 172, 287

M

Macmillan Company 152, 153, 162
Macon Telegraph newspaper 176
Mammy 11, 13, 15, 26, 102, 112, 119,
    126, 132, 142, 146, 209, 217,
    218, 220, 221, 222, 223, 252,
    270, 281
Kathleen Marcaccio 164

Breinigsville, PA USA
10 December 2009
229021BV00004B/31/P